Once Upon a Time
(She Said)

Jane Yolen

Edited by Priscilla Olson

The NESFA Press
Post Office Box 809
Framingham, MA 01701
2005

FIRST EDITION
August, 2005

International Standard Book Number:
1-886778-61-2

First Appearances

(note: if no editor is mentioned, the book is by Jane Yolen or was edited by her.)

"Allerleirauh" - *The Armless Maiden and Other Tales for Childhood's Survivors,* ed. Terri Windling, Tor, 1995.

"America's Cinderella" - (excerpt) *Children's Literature in Education,* 1977.

"The Barbarian and the Queen: Thirteen Views" - *Starlight 3,* ed. Patrick Nielsen Hayden, Tor, 2001.

"Beans" - first publication.

"Beauty and the Beast: An Anniversary" - *The Faery Flag,* Orchard Books, 1989.

"Become a Warrior" - *Warrior Princesses,* ed. Elizabeth Ann Scarborough, Martin H. Greenberg, DAW, 1998.

"The Bird of Time" - Thomas Y. Crowell, 1971.

"Black Dog Times" - Jabberwocky, 2005.

"The Boy Who Drew Unicorns" - *The Unicorn Treasury,* ed. Bruce Coville, Doubleday, 1988.

"The Brothers Grimm and Sister Jane" - *The Reception of Grimm's Fairy Tales,* ed. Donald Haase, Wayne State University Press, Detroit, 1993 (also contains "Toads" - Isaac Asimov's SF, June, 1989.)

"Crows" - first publication.

"Dawn-Strider" - *The Girl Who Cried Flowers and Other Stories,* Thomas Y. Crowell, 1974.

"Deirdre" - *Storyteller,* NESFA Press, 1992.

Dream Weaver - William Collins, 1979.

    "The Boy Who Sang for Death" - *Dream Weaver* , 1979.

    "Brother Hart" - The Magazine of F&SF, v55 #5, Nov. 1978.

    "The Cat Bride" - *Dream Weaver* , 1979.

    "Man of Rock, Man of Stone" - *Dream Weaver,* 1979.

    "The Pot Child" - The Magazine of F&SF, v56 #2,Feb. 1979.

    "Princess Heart O'Stone" - *Dream Weaver* , 1979.

    "The Tree's Wife" - The Magazine of F&SF, v54 #6,June, 1978.

"The Elf King's Daughter" - *Once Upon a Midnight,* ed. Thomas E. Fuller, Michael N. Langford, James A. Riley, Unnameable Press, 1995.

"Evian Steel" - *Imaginary Lands,* ed. Robin McKinley, Orbit, 1985.

"The Face in the Cloth" - The Magazine of F&SF, v68 #2, Feb. 1985.

"The Faery Flag" - *The Faery Flag,* Orchard Books, 1989.

"Fantasy Novels: Truth in Disguise?: the Footnotes" - The Medusa, v1 #1, 1992.

"Fat is Not a Fairy Tale" - *Such a Pretty Face,* ed. Lee Martindale, Meisha Merlin, 2000.

"The Fisherman's Wife" - *Mermaids!*, ed. Jack Dann, Gardner Dozois, Ace Fantasy Books, 1986.

"Flight" - *Olympus*, ed. Martin H. Greenberg, Bruce D. Arthurs, DAW, 1998.

"The Foxwife" - *Moonsinger's Friends*, Bluejay Books, 1986.

"Frog Prince" - The Magazine of F&SF, v73 #4, Oct. 1987.

"The Girl Who Cried Flowers" - *The Girl Who Cried Flowers and Other Stories*, Thomas Y. Crowell, 1974.

"The Golden Balls" - *Tales of Wonder*, Schocken, 1983.

"The Golden Stair" - *The Faery Flag*, Orchard Books, 1989.

"Great Selkie" - *Orphans of the Night*, ed. Josepha Sherman, Walker&Co., 1995.

"Green Plague" - *Ribbeting Tales*, ed. Nancy Springer, Philomel, 2000.

"The Gwynfahr" - *Tales of Wonder*, Schocken, 1983.

"Happy Dens or a Day in the Old Wolves' Home" - *Elsewhere 3*, ed. Terri Windling, Mark Alan Arnold, Ace, 1984.

"The Honey-Stick Boy" - *The Moon Ribbon and Other Tales*, Curtis Brown Ltd., 1976.

"The Hundredth Dove" - The Magazine of F&SF, v52 #4, Apr. 1977.

"Impedimenta" - Peregrine, v 20/21 20th Anniversary Double Issue, Amherst Writers & Artists Press, 2004.

"Inscription" - *The Ultimate Witch*, ed. Bryan Preiss, John Betancourt, DAW, 1993.

"Into the Wood" - Isaac Asimov's SF Magazine, v9 #2, Feb. 1985.

"Johanna" - *Shape Shifters*, Seabury Press, 1978.

"The King's Dragon" - *Spaceships & Spells*, ed. by Jane Yolen, Martin H. Greenberg, Charles G. Waugh, Harper & Row, 1987.

"Knives" - *Snow White, Blood Red*, ed. Ellen Datlow, Terri Windling, AvoNova/Morrow, 1993.

"The Lad Who Stared Everyone Down" - *The Girl Who Cried Flowers and Other Stories*, Thomas Y. Crowell, 1974.

"The Lady and the Merman" - The Magazine of F&SF, v51 #3, Sep 1976.

"The Maiden Made of Fire" - The Magazine of F&SF, v53 #6, July 1977.

"Märchen" - Merveilles, University of Colorado, May 1994.

"The Mirror Speaks" - *The Armless Maiden and Other Tales for Childhood's Survivors*, ed. Terri Windling, Tor, 1995.

"The Moon Ribbon" - *The Moon Ribbon and Other Tales*, Curtis Brown Ltd., 1976.

"The Moon Child - *The Moon Ribbon and Other Tales*, Curtis Brown Ltd., 1976.

"Mother Goose's Maladies" - first publication.

"My Father Died Seven Times" - first publication.

"Oh, God, Here Come the Elves" - *Storyteller*, NESFA Press, 1992.

"Once Upon a Time, She Said" - National Storytelling Journal, Spring, 1987.

"Orkney Lament" - *Xanadu 2*, Tor, 1994.

"Prince Charming Comes" - *Tales of Wonder*, Schocken, 1983.

"The Promise" - *The Hundredth Dove and Other Tales*, Thomas Y. Crowell, 1977.

"Remembering Books" - Calendar, Children's Book Council Features, v47 #1, Spring-Summer 1994.
"Ridinghood" - StarLine, 2004.
"The Ring at Yarrow" - *Xanadu,* Tor, 1993.
"The River Maid" - The Magazine of F&SF, v60 #1, Jan. 1981.
"Rosechild" - *The Moon Ribbon and Other Tales,* Curtis Brown Ltd., 1976.
"Sans Soleil" - *The Moon Ribbon and Other Tales,* Curtis Brown Ltd., 1976.
"The Seventh Mandarin" - Seabury, 1970.
"Silent Bianca" - *The Girl Who Cried Flowers and Other Stories,* Thomas Y. Crowell, 1974.
"The Singer of Seeds" - *The Faery Flag,* Orchard Books, 1989.
"Snow in Summer" - *Black Heart, Ivory Bones,* ed. Ellen Datlow, Terri Windling, Avon, 2000.
"Somewhen" - *The Moon Ribbon and Other Tales,* Curtis Brown Ltd., 1976.
"Song of the Cailleach Bheur" - *The Green Man,* ed. Ellen Datlow, Terri Windling, SFBC, Viking, 2002.
"The Sow, the Mare, and the Cow" - *Tales of Wonder,* Schocken, 1983.
"The Story Between" - *Storyteller,* NESFA Press, 1992.
"The Storyteller" - National Storytelling Journal, Winter 1984.
"Swan/Princess" - *Xanadu 3,* Tor, 1995.
"The Tale of the Seventeenth Eunuch" - *Aladdin, Master of the Lamp,* ed. Mike Resnick, Martin H. Greenberg, DAW, 1992.
"Ten Things You May Not Know About Me" - Mudlark, online poetry journal, poster #23, 2000.
"The Tower Bird" - *Ariel, the Book of Fantasy: v4,* ed. Thomas Durwood, Ariel Books/Ballantine, 1978.
"When Raven Sang" - Peregrine, Amherst Writers & Artists Press, 1994.
"The White Seal Maid" - Parabola, Myth and Quest for Meaning, 1977.
"Will" - Magazine of Speculative Poetry, Spring 1992.
"The Wind Cap" - *The Hundredth Dove and Other Tales,* Thomas Y. Crowell, 1977.
"Winter's King" - *After the King,* ed. Martin H. Greenberg, Tor, 1992.
"The Woman Who Loved a Bear" - *Tales from the Great Turtle,* ed. Piers Anthony, Richard Gilliam, Tor, 1994.
"Women's Stories" - *Sisters in Fantasy 2,* ed. Susan Shwartz, Martin H. Greenberg, ROC, 1996.
"Words of Power" - *Visions,* ed. Donald R. Gallo, Delacorte Books, 1987.

Contents

Once Upon a Time
(She Said)

JANE YOLEN: AN INTRODUCTION

Although I'd known of Jane Yolen for many years, I didn't actually meet her until we were both trying to hide at a convention. She introduced herself first and conspiratorially, we found a quiet spot to get acquainted. I liked her very much, indeed. She's forthright, genial and non-judgemental, with a keen sense of humor. She's also married and had children so we already had things in common besides being women writing s-f.

Then I did a book called "A Diversity of Dragons" with my friend, Richard Woods. He handled the usual dragon literature while I plumbed the s-f and fantasy ones. This search led me inevitably to Jane Yolen's dragons—who were taught to fight and much money was made and lost on the creatures. It was a very good yarn and, by the time I reached it in the 232 novels I read, one of the more outstanding. So we had another common cause.

Then I received a letter from her in 1990, asking if I would consider writing for two anthologies she was doing for young adults for Delacorte...one was about what life would be like fifty years from now, and the second was to be set in the Arthurian legend: could I consider either or both.

Well, I said yes immediately on the anthology to be called *2041,* but havered about Arthur since the legend has been milked dry. Then I thought of a line in Rosemary Sutcliffe's excellent Arthurian novel, *Sword at Sunset,* and realized that I could contribute to both, and sent her an acceptance.

"The Quiet One" for *2041* is about a girl in a high tech world wanting to ride a horse. She can actually learn how, of course, on a mechanized facsimile of a horse. But, as any rider can tell you, a live horse is a much different proposition than the kind of fun hall bucking bull often found in western saloons. She wants, above all else, to ride a real live horse.

(Horsebackriding has always had a strong and strange fascination for young girls. Ask me. I was one and have had several outstanding mounts.)

For the Arthurian story, my starting point was the fact that, when King Arthur was trying to organize a rapid response to Saxon invasions of the East Coast of Britain, he needed horses big enough and strong to enough to carry armed men long distances to counter invasion. So he went to the horse fair at Septimania, at the base of the Pyrenees in Spain to buy the big, black Libyan mares. They are big Arabs: 16 and 17 hands high and well able to carry heavy loads for long distances.

I've never worked so hard on perfecting a short story. Jane sent it back five or six times before she was satisfied...grammatically and dramatically. The effort was well worth my patience, though at times I wondered how she could spot so many errors or places for improvement in such a short yarn. She reminded me that stories for young adults *had* to be perfect...especially if we wanted to help our readers appreciate and under-stand well-written stories.

I got to know my young hero, Galwyn, almost as well as I know my own sons. And how much I could have wished for my boys to have had a role model like Artos, Comes Britannorum. But Galwyn liked being alive, if only in a story book, and he nagged at me (characters sometimes do this to a susceptible writer) until I told the entire story about him and his unusual part in helping the charismatic Artos defeat the Saxon invaders. Jane worked me through many details, asking me to explain more about farriery...horse-shoeing. I don't know if I got any young man interested in the profession but it was fun to figure out how it all started.

There's an adage—"no hoof, no horse". And Arthur, using horses bred to desert travel and sand, would have had to find a way to keep the feet of his cavalry in good condition over rock and pebble country in their rapid response jaunts. So, for the purposes of the book, I decided farriery began in Arthur's time. Historical fact supports that theory. But I learned a great deal from Jane about how, and how *not* to write for young adults: tips that still keep coming to mind as I work on adult novels and improving my own work. Thanks, Jane.

I know you'll enjoy these yarns no matter what age you are: we all still like fairy tales and appreciate craftsmanship as well as imagination. Read on now and enjoy the yarns: you're in the hands of a fine story-teller.

PS: oddly enough, Jane and I both have sons who are following in their mothers' footsteps: Todd J. McCaffrey has now published three books, furthering the Pern adventure and Adam Stemple is debuting with his excellent Singer of Souls. We're both very proud of our sons.

Anne McCaffrey
Dragonhold-Underhill, Wicklow, Ireland

ONCE UPON A TIME, SHE SAID

"Once upon a time," she said,
and the world began anew:
a vee of geese flew by,
plums roasting in their breasts;
a vacant-eyed princess
sat upon a hillock of glass;
a hut strolled through a tangled wood,
the nails on its chickenfeet
blackened and hard as coal;
a horse's head proclaimed advice
from the impost of an arch;
one maiden spoke in toads,
another in pearls,
and a third with the nightingale's voice.
If you ask me,
I would have to say
all the world's magic
comes directly from the mouth.

SANS SOLEIL

There was once a prince called Sans Soleil, which is to say Sunless. It had been prophesied at his birth that he would grow so handsome his beauty would outshine the sun. That he might not be killed by the jealous star, he had to be kept in the dark, for it was said that he would die if ever a shaft of sunlight fell upon his brow.

So the very night he was born, his father, the king, had him carried away to a castle that was carved out of rock. And in that candlelit cave-castle, the young prince grew and flourished without ever seeing the sun.

Now by the time Sans Soleil was twenty years old, the story of his strange beauty and of the evil prediction had been told at every hearth and hall in the kingdom. And every maiden of marrying age had heard his tragic tale.

But one in particular, Viga, the daughter of a duke, did not believe what she heard.

"Surely," she said, tossing her raven-black hair from her face, "surely the king has hidden his son from the light because he is too monstrous to behold."

Her father shook his head.

"Nay," he replied. "I have been to this cave-castle and have seen this prince. He is handsomer than the sun."

But still Viga did not believe what her father told her. "The sun cannot harm anyone," she said. "There is no sense in what you say." And she took herself to the king dressed in her finest gown of silver and gold.

"Sire," she said, "at court you have been taken in by lies. The sun is not harmful. It nourishes. It causes all things to grow. It will not kill the prince."

The king was touched by the girl's sincerity. He was moved by her beauty. He was awed by her strength of purpose, for it is no little thing to contradict a king. Still, he shook his head and said, "It was prophesied at his birth that he would die if ever a shaft of sunlight struck his brow."

"Old wives and young babes believe such tales. They should not frighten you, Sire. They do not frighten me," Viga replied.

"They do not frighten you because you are not the one who would die," said the king, and at these words all the courtiers smiled and nodded their heads and murmured to one another. "Still, I will give the matter more thought."

Viga gave a low curtsey. And as she rose, she said quietly, so that only the king could hear it, "It does seem strange that *sun* and *son* do sound the same." Then she smiled brightly and departed.

The king was true to his word and gave the matter more thought. And what he concluded was this: that his son and Viga should be wed. For he liked her courage and admired her beauty, and thought she would make his son a most suitable wife. So the king and the duke set the wedding date for a week from the following night.

When the night was deep and no spot of sun still lit the kingdom, a carriage with drawn curtains arrived at Viga's door. Out stepped the handsomest man she had ever seen. He was dressed all in red and gold, like the sun.

They were wed by candlelight, and their golden rings were carved with images of the sun. There was feasting and dancing till three. Then the two talked and kissed far into the night as befits a couple who are but newly wed.

But at the crowing of the village cocks announcing that the sun would soon rise, Sans Soleil stood up.

"I must go. I cannot allow the sun to shine upon me."

"Do not leave me," Viga said. "Now that we are wed, I cannot bear to have you away from my sight. Do not be afraid of the sun. It will not harm you. Stay here with me."

"No, I am safe only in my cave. You are my wife, come and live in my cave-castle with me."

"Live in a cave?" said Viga. "Never."

So the prince tore himself from her grasp and ran out into the waiting golden carriage. With a crack of the whip, the horses were away before the sun could gain the sky.

However, Viga was a woman of strong will. So determined was she to prove to Sans Soleil that she was right and he would not be killed by the sun, she devised a plan. That very day she sent her maidservants to buy up all the cockerels in the kingdom. Then she had her footmen bind the birds and throw them down into the duke's deepest dungeons, where it would always be dark as night.

But there was one rooster the servants could not buy, the pet of the potter's boy. The child cried so much at the thought of losing his bird, his father would not part with it.

"What is one cockerel out of so many?" the servants asked themselves. And so they neglected to tell their mistress of the last bird.

That evening again Sans Soleil's carriage came to Viga's door. As before the prince was dressed all in red and gold, like the sun, and the feathers on his cap stood out like golden rays. In his hand he carried a sunburst, a ruby brooch with beams like a star.

"This is my only sun," he said to Viga. "Now it is yours."

And they forgave one another for the harsh words of the morn. They touched and kissed as married couples do, far into the night.

At the coming of the dawn, far off in the village, the cockerel belonging to the potter's child began to crow.

"Is that a cockerel I hear?" asked Sans Soleil, sitting up.

"There is no cockerel," replied Viga sleepily, for she thought indeed there was none.

But again the rooster crowed out, and, hearing no answering call from his brothers, he sang out louder than before.

"I am sure I hear the warning of the sun's approach," said Sans Soleil.

"It is nothing but a servant's snore," Viga replied.

"Stay quiet. Stay asleep. Stay with me."

But on the third crow, Sans Soleil leaped up.

"I must go," he said.

"I cannot allow the sun to shine upon me."

"Do not put your faith in such old wives' tales," cried Viga. "The sun cannot hurt you. Put your faith in me."

But it was too late. The prince was gone, running down into his golden carriage and away to his cave-castle before the sun could start up in the sky.

However, Viga was a woman of strong will and passion. She was determined not to lose her lover for a single day because of such a foolish tale. She was convinced that if the prince but forgot the sun, he would learn that it could do him no harm. So she decided to have the last rooster put in her father's dungeon.

But she did not trust her servants anymore. With her cloak wrapped about her and covering her face with a sleeve, Viga slipped out into the streets. By the potter's hut she saw the bird strutting and preening its feathers in the sun. Quickly she looked around, but there was no one in sight. She reached down, snatched up the cockerel, and hid it under her cloak. In the night of her garment the bird made no sound.

She was back in her own home before the potter's child could set up his wail. The cockerel she put with its brothers in the dark. Then she waited impatiently for the sun to set that she might see her lover again.

That evening, so great was his haste, Sans Soleil himself drove the golden carriage to the door. He leaped to the ground and in a graceful bound ran to the waiting girl.

They ate and touched and sang and danced and talked until the night was through. But there were no cockerels to crow and warn them of the dawn.

Suddenly the prince glanced out of the window.

"It is becoming light," he cried.

"I must leave. You know that I cannot allow the sun to shine on me."

"Love me. Trust me. Stay with me," said Viga, smoothing his hair with her strong hands.

But Sans Soleil glanced out of the window again.

"Is that the sun? Tell me, for I have never seen it shine."

Viga smoothed his neck with her fingers. "Forget your foolish fears. The sun nourishes. It does not kill. Stay with me here and greet the dawn."

The prince was moved by her plea and by his love for her. But just as he was about to stay, fear, like an old habit, conquered him. He jumped up and blinked at the light. "I must go to my cave. Only there will I be safe," he cried. And before she could stop him, he tore from her grasp and sped out into the dawn.

Viga ran after him. "Do not be afraid," she called. Her long black hair streamed out behind her like the rays of a black star. "It is but a tale. A tale for children. *You* are the sun."

But the prince did not hear her. As he ran out into the courtyard, the sun rose in full brilliance over the wall. Sans Soleil had never seen anything so glorious before. He stood and stared at the burning star. The sunlight struck him full in the face. And with a single cry of pain or anger or regret, he fell down dead.

Viga saw him fall. She cried out, "Oh, Sans Soleil, it was true. Who would have believed it? Now it is I who am sunless, for you were my sun."

She threw herself upon his still form, her breast against his, her cool white brow on the ashes of his, and wept.

The next year, in the courtyard where Sans Soleil had fallen, a single sunflower grew. But unlike others of its kind, it bloomed all year round and always turned its face away from the sun.

Viga had a belvedere built around it. There she spent her days, tending the flower, watering it, and turning its soil.

When visitors arrived at her father's house, she would tell them the story of her love for Sans Soleil. And the story always ended with this caution: "Sometimes," Viga would say, "what we believe is stronger than what is true."

THE TALE OF THE SEVENTEENTH EUNUCH

It is true that I am the seventeenth eunuch of the Lady Badroulboudour, and the last of the bed guardians chosen to serve her. Some of us were born so, some were created so by other men, and a few are self-made—or self-unmade. But none of the eunuchs had so odd a borning as I.

When I came to the Lady Badroulboudour, her husband The Aladdin was already some years dead. Their illustrious sons were the rulers of kingdoms, court viziers, and members of the advisory. Their daughters were wives to neighboring princes and caliphs and emirs. Exiled to her own apartments—for the new sultan, her eldest son, knew how mothers can interfere in the running of kingdoms—she had nothing better to do than practice such small magicks as her husband had instructed her in, read trashy tales of houris and kings, and care for her many cats. She had white cats with fur like the tops of waves, brown cats the color of the dunes at dusk, gray cats as dark as storms. And one brawling black cat just newly acquired.

The eunuchs cared for the rest. They tried to pleasure her—for do not think that eunuchs are devoid of sexual passion. It is just that we cannot father a child. And—truth be known—we take far less pleasures ourselves in our duties.

But the Lady Badroulboudour had no interest other than in her memories. Her husband The Aladdin had been a manly man, his black hair and beard long and luxuriant, his voice resonant and low. He had been gallant and frequent and manly in his loving—as attested to by their numerous progeny. The Lady Badroulboudour made many loud exclamations to that effect.

Why, then, did her son, the sultan, allow her so many eunuchs? Perhaps because he believed the stories fostered by the harem that no man can perform save he has all his parts. Or perhaps because he firmly believed that if his mother were satisfied in all ways, she would leave the running of the kingdom to him.

Now it was on the tenth day of the third month of Lady Badroulboudour's fiftieth year that she came upon the lamp that The Aladdin owed all his wealth and power to. She had been looking for it in desultory fashion ever since he died, as she was only partially convinced there was any such thing. No one but she had even believed the old stories of the lamp anyway, except her crazy mother-in-law, who was dead now as well.

The discovery of the lamp happened in this fashion. The eunuchs in their high-pitched voices had fallen to quarrel over some inconsequential and Lady Badroulboudour had banished them to the outer rooms. Then, wanting to feed the cats, she noticed that she was short one dish, for the black cat was but newly arrived, a present from her son, the sultan. She wanted to comfort the new black cat with sweetmeats and a dish of cream, that being her way.

So she went from inner room to inner room, then outer room to outer room, looking for a suitable container, rejecting rouge pots and flower vases and a basin containing rose petals in water. And at last, way down the hall, she looked into a storeroom that had been closed for years. There, in a comer, as if thrown by an angry or disinterested hand, was an unprepossessing copper lamp with a small wick and a handle with a chink out of the right side. It was the chink she dimly recalled, having handled it only once, when abducted by the Afrik magician long ago.

She pounced on it with a cry not unlike that of one of the brown cats, which brought the new black cat running into the room to twine around her legs. She picked up cat in one hand, lamp in the other, and made her way back to her rooms.

"Lady, your pleasure?" asked the fifth eunuch, a pudgy, hairless, whey-faced man much given to candies and flatulence.

She dismissed him and the others with a wave of her hand. And when they were all gone, exiled to the outer rooms, she settled herself down on her great bed with her pillows and white cats at her head and feet.

"Could it be?" she mused to herself. The black cat and two brown ones echoed her. "Could it be?" She remembered The Aladdin's hints about magic. Then she added, "If I could have a wish, surely I would ask for my dear Aladdin back."

At his name, all the cats but the black one jumped down to the floor and made themselves scarce for often the mere mention of the name caused Lady Badroulboudour to weep and wail and throw pots and bowls. Only the black cat did not run away. He was, you must remember, new to the palace. And not yet moving quite so fast as the rest.

"But," Lady Badroulboudour reminded herself, "I must attend to my dress." For it is true that since the death of The Aladdin she had lived in great neglect of her person, except for the occasional state dinner. So she took a long and luxuriant bath with soft oils and many powders after, filling the apartments with a heady aroma, not unlike that of nepeta, mintlike and pungent. The cats all rolled about and frisked with pleasure.

Then she put on a gown of silk the color of the sea—green and blue and black. Around her waist she placed a girdle of diamonds set in gold. She set about her neck the six-strand necklace of pearls. On her wrists she put bracelets of diamonds and rubies. Her eyes she outlined with kohl and she put rouge on her mouth and cheeks. She was a woman in her prime.

Then, taking the lamp in hand, she sat back down on her bed, leaning against the black cat. The cat did not complain, but purred both deep and low.

"If there is a genie," Lady Badroulboudour said aloud,""I shall set it free." And she turned the lamp this way and that, looking for a magical key. For though The Aladdin—and the Afrik magician—had both spoken of the lamp, neither of them in the telling had thought to mention how it worked.

She pulled at the wick. She tried to light it. She stuck her finger inside the spout. She blew across both top and bottom. At last, in frustration, she tried to shine the lamp as if by doing so she might find some written instructions on the side.

No sooner had she stroked it, than a strange bituminous smoke began to ascend from the spout, coalescing into a shape that was as rounded and hairless and large as a eunuch, only wafting about four feet above the bedclothes.

"Oh, I have had enough of you half-men!" she cried, sitting up.

"I am no man, lady," said the genie.

"I did not really believe it," said Lady Badroulboudour.

"I am ready to obey thee as thy slave," the genie answered.

"So it is true," Lady Badroulboudour replied.

And they would have gone on and on like this at cross-purposes and not actually corresponding, if the black cat had not been made so playful by the scent of nepeta that the feline took a swipe at the smoke where it was connected to the spout, all but severing the genie's legs from the lamp.

At that Lady Badroulboudour gathered up the cat to her bosom, where it was distracted by the six strands of pearls

"Then, slave, restore to me my husband, The Aladdin."

The genie managed to look nonplussed, not an easy trick for a man of smoke. Then he laughed. "If you have me bring him back, lady, he would be nought but winding cloth and bones. Is that your desire? For you must mind what you ask for, mistress."

"Give him back to me as he was, not as he is."

The genie laughed again. "That I cannot. I can only bring you what is, not what is no longer."

"I want Aladdin!" She pouted for a moment, looking just like the princess whom The Aladdin had loved so long ago.

"Alas, that cannot be," said the genie. Somewhere a door shut or opened and the breeze it let in made him sway gently over the bed.

"Then what good is your magic?" Lady Badroulboudour cried, and she threw the lamp, genie and all, across the room where they fetched up against the north wall with a clatter and a bang. Before the lamp actually hit, the genie managed to disappear back down the spout, though there was a small, pitiful cry from inside the lamp when it landed.

Lady Badroulboudour did not come out of her room the entire day, nor did she pick up the lamp. She lay on her bed, angry and speechless, until the sixth eunuch, who was given to honeycakes and moist eyes, threatened to call her son the sultan. And the ninth eunuch, who was given to candied dates and belching, threatened to call her son the vizier. When the sixteenth eunuch, who was given to buttered toast and tears, bent over to pick up the lamp, Lady Badroulboudour sat up in the bed and screeched so loudly that all of the bed guardians left the room at once, the last slamming the door behind him.

Then Lady Badroulboudour rose from her bed and looked at herself in the mirror. She drew more kohl around her eyes and pinched her cheeks until they were red. She took off the dress the color of the sea, took another long bath, then put on a dress the color of sand—brown and white and gray. She rearranged the diamond girdle, the necklace of pearls, and the bracelets. She put red jewels in her ears. She was a woman in her prime.

Then she picked up the lamp and stroked its side with a feather touch.

This time a strange ocherous smoke ascended from the spout, coalescing into a shape that was as rounded and hairless and *twice* as large as any eunuch. The genie wafted about three feet above the lamp.

"So," Lady Badroulboudour said.

"What one wish wouldst thou have?" asked the genie.

"Can you bring back my husband any better than your brother can?" she asked.

"No more than he, mistress," said the genie. "Save in winding cloth and bones. Oh—and a bit of wormy matter as well. I have taken the opportunity to check."

"That is all?" Lady Badroulboudour asked.

"That is all," said the genie. "But..." he wavered a bit, right hand raised. "I could bring you a substitute. One who is like and yet not like your former master, The Aladdin."

"And by this you mean...?" asked Lady Badroulboudour.

"I can bring you a dark-bearded man from the streets of your city, or a deep-throated man from the gateposts of a neighboring town, or a well-muscled man from the taverns of another kingdom, or from the Antipodes for that matter."

"Where they walk upon their hands and eat the dust of the road?" shouted Lady Badroulboudour. "Never!" And this time she threw the lamp, genie and all, against the south wall with a clatter and a bang. The genie managed to disappear—all but his left foot—back through the spout before the lamp actually hit the wall. But there was a rather loud pitiful cry from inside the lamp and a bit of strange muck ran down the lamp's side.

This time Lady Badroulboudour did not come out of her room for a week, nor did she pick up the lamp. She lay on her bed, angry and speechless—and hungry—though the eunuchs fed all the cats. All but the black cat, who refused to eat till she did. The eighth eunuch, who was given to tippling and weeping late at night, threatened to call her daughters. And the second eunuch, who had no faults at all, save he stared with popped eyes and so always managed to look startled, threatened to call her father's maiden aunt, and she, dear lady, was well into her nineties and had a voice like an angry camel. Still nothing worked until the thirteenth eunuch bent over to pick up the lamp. At that, Lady Badroulboudour screeched so loudly that they all left, slamming the door behind them.

Then Lady Badroulboudour rose from her bed, scattering cats white and brown and gray, and looked at herself in her mirror. She drew yet another circle of kohl around her eyes, but left her cheeks white. She took off the dress the color of sand, took a long bath with many new oils, and put on a dress the color of fire—yellow and orange and red. She rearranged the diamond girdle, the necklace of pearls, the bracelets, and the red jewels in her ears. She placed a chain of gold on her left ankle. She was a woman in her prime.

Then she picked up the lamp, thoughtfully rubbing it on both sides and vigorously down the middle.

This time a strange opalescent smoke ascended from the spout, coalescing into a shape that was rounded and hairless and three times larger than any eunuch. It wafted fully five feet above the lamp.

"No tricks," said Lady Badroulboudour.

"What one wish wouldst thou have?" asked the genie.

"I assume you cannot bring me back Aladdin whole either?"

The genie shook his head, though whether from dismay or from a passing breeze it was hard to say. "We cannot bring back what is no longer, mistress."

"And you have only men from the street or the taverns or the Antipodes to offer me?"

"My brothers of the lamp are good and they are kind," said the genie. "But I understand your reluctance, O princess, daughter of the mighty sultan, wife of the late great Aladdin, to take a lesser man."

Lady Badroulboudour nodded.

"And my brothers of the lamp are young, both in their time in this copper prison and their magic," said the genie. "I, on the other hand, can offer an exchange."

"An exchange?" Lady Badroulboudour asked. "Do you mean a trade? A swap? A bargain? Like camel merchants at a bazaar?"

"I can make you a man out of a camel, mistress."

"To spit in my face?"

"Or a bird..."

"To peep and preen?"

"Or a dog..."

"To water my bedposts?"

"Or..."

Just then the black cat stretched and arched its back.

"He must have luxurious black hair and beard and a deep, soothing voice," said Lady Badroulboudour, as the black cat purred under her hand.

"If those are the characteristics of the animal," the genie said. He held up his opalescent hand. "This one wish, my mistress, and no other."

She gathered the black cat up from the bed, and held it out to the genie. "This cat, then."

"I ask again, my mistress, to be absolutely certain. And you must mind how you ask. What wouldst thou have?"

A smile played about Lady Badroulboudour's mouth. Two dimples which had not been seen since the death of her husband suddenly appeared in her cheeks. "I wish, genie, that this cat, this black cat that I hold in my arms..." and the cat purred loudly in a low, deep tremolo. "That this cat were exchanged into a man."

The genie nodded and moved his great hands above the cat. The cat stretched, yowled once, stretched again, and shook itself free of Lady Badroulboudour's hands. As it touched the floor, its back legs lengthened and she could hear the creaking and groaning and unknotting of its bones.

Closing her eyes contentedly and only listening to the sounds of her bargain being made, Lady Badroulboudour waited a moment or two longer than necessary. When she opened her eyes again, a handsome, dark-bearded man was kneeling before her, naked and unashamed.

"My lady," he said, his voice low and with a kind of deep, dark burr in it.

Lady Badroulboudour looked at that face, at the green eyes staring up at her, at the curl of his dark beard. She looked down at his well-muscled shoulders and chest. She looked further down...

"Genie..." she said, her voice suddenly stony.

"I told you to mind what it was you asked for," said the genie. And he was gone back into the spout.

Lady Badroulboudour suddenly remembered what she should have remembered before. All the cats in her apartments—male and female—were neutered, some as kittens and some rather later on.

"My lady," the low, purring voice came again. She looked down into his handsome dark-bearded face.

"Well, two out of three ain't bad," she said, affecting the language of the camel market. Then she lifted me up to clasp me in her arms.

I took her eagerly, for the memory of my recent maleness was still upon me, she smelled deliciously of nepeta, and she was, after all, a lady still in her prime.

RIDINGHOOD

Writers wear their craft
like a ridinghood, proudly,
saying: See—I am an artist;
What do I care
for money? Except
to live on. And on. And on.
I publish that my soul
not perish.
Ask my agent,
that resident wolf.
Ten percent teeth,
five percent howl.
She goes to bed with editors,
rises up again
with a muzzle full of fleas.
One day I shall have to kill her.
It is an old story.

Happy Dens
or A Day in the Old Wolves' Home

Nurse Lamb stood in front of the big white house with the black shutters. She shivered. She was a brand-new nurse and this was her very first job.

From inside the house came loud and angry growls. Nurse Lamb looked at the name carved over the door: HAPPY DENS. But it didn't sound like a happy place, she thought, as she listened to the howls from inside.

Shuddering, she knocked on the door.

The only answer was another howl.

Lifting the latch, Nurse Lamb went in.

No sooner had she stepped across the doorstep than a bowl sped by her head. It splattered against the wall. Nurse Lamb ducked, but she was too late. Her fresh white uniform was spotted and dotted with whatever had been in the bowl.

"Mush!" shouted an old wolf, shaking his cane at her. "Great howls and thorny paws. I can't stand another day of it. The end of life is nothing but a big bowl of mush."

Nurse Lamb gave a frightened little bleat and turned to go back out the door, but a great big wolf with two black ears and one black paw barred her way. "Mush for breakfast, mush for dinner, and more mush in between," he growled. "That's all they serve us here at Happy Dens, Home for Aging Wolves."

The wolf with the cane added, "When we were young and full of teeth it was never like this." He howled.

Nurse Lamb gave another bleat and ran into the next room. To her surprise it was a kitchen. A large, comfortable-looking pig wearing a white hat was leaning over the stove and stirring an enormous pot. Since the wolves had not followed her in, Nurse Lamb sat down on a kitchen stool and began to cry.

The cook put her spoon down, wiped her trotters with a stained towel, and patted Nurse Lamb on the head, right behind the ears.

"There, there, lambkin," said the cook. "Don't start a new job in tears. We say that in the barnyard all the time."

Nurse Lamb looked up and snuffled. "I...I don't think I'm right for this place. I feel as if I have been thrown to the wolves."

The cook nodded wisely. "And, in a manner of speaking, you have been. But these poor old dears are all bark and no bite. Toothless, don't you know. All they can manage is mush."

"But no one told me this was an old *wolves'* home," complained Nurse Lamb. "They just said 'How would you like to work at Happy Dens?' And it sounded like the nicest place in the world."

"And so it is. And so it is," said the cook. "It just takes getting used to."

Nurse Lamb wiped her nose and looked around. "But how could some-one like *you* work here? I mean..." She dropped her voice to a whisper. "I heard all about it at school. The three little pigs and all. Did you know them?"

The cook sniffed. "And a bad lot they were, too. As we say in the barn-yard, 'There's more than one side to every sty.' "

"But I was told that the big bad wolf tried to eat the three little pigs. And he huffed and he puffed and..." Nurse Lamb looked confused.

Cook just smiled and began to stir the pot again, lifting up a spoonful to taste.

"And then there was that poor little child in the woods with the red riding hood," said Nurse Lamb. "Bringing the basket of goodies to her sick grandmother."

Cook shook her head and added pepper to the pot. "In the barnyard we say, 'Don't take slop from a kid in a cloak.' " She ladled out a bowlful of mush.

Nurse Lamb stood up. She walked up to the cook and put her hooves on her hips. "But what about that boy Peter? The one who caught the wolf by the tail after he ate the duck. And the hunters came and—"

"Bad press," said a voice from the doorway. It was the wolf with the two black ears. "Much of what you know about wolves is bad press."

Nurse Lamb turned and looked at him. "I don't even know what bad press means," she said.

"It means that only one side of the story has been told. There is another way of telling those very same tales. From the wolf's point of view." He grinned at her. "My name is Wolfgang, and if you will bring a bowl of that thoroughly awful stuff to the table"—he pointed to the pot—"I will tell you *my* side of a familiar tale."

Sheepishly, Nurse Lamb picked up the bowl and followed the wolf into the living room. She put the bowl on the table in front of Wolfgang and sat down. There were half a dozen wolves sitting there.

Nurse Lamb smiled at them timidly.

They smiled back. The cook was right. Only Wolfgang had any teeth. Three, to be exact.

WOLFGANG'S TALE

Once upon a time (began the black-eared wolf) there was a thoroughly nice young wolf. He had two black ears and one black paw. He was a poet and a dreamer.

This thoroughly nice wolf loved to lie about in the woods staring at the lacy curlings of fiddlehead ferns and smelling the wild roses.

He was a vegetarian—except for lizards and an occasional snake, which don't count. He loved carrot cake and was partial to peanut-butter pie.

One day as he lay by the side of a babbling brook, writing a poem that began

> *Twinkle, twinkle, lambkin's eye,*
> *How I wish you were close by...*

he heard the sound of a child weeping. He knew it was a human child because only they cry with that snuffling gasp. So the thoroughly nice wolf leaped to his feet and ran over, his hind end waggling, eager to help.

The child looked up from her crying. She was quite young and dressed in a long red riding hood, a lacy dress, white stockings, and black patent-leather Mary Jane shoes. Hardly what you would call your usual hiking-in-the-woods outfit.

"Oh, hello, wolfie," she said. In those days, of course, humans often talked to wolves. "I am quite lost."

The thoroughly nice wolf sat down by her side and held her hand. "There, there," he said. "Tell me where you live."

The child grabbed her hand back. "If I knew that, you silly growler, I wouldn't be lost, would I?"

The thoroughly nice wolf bit back his own sharp answer and asked her in rhyme:

Where are you going
My pretty young maid?
Answer me this
And I'll make you a trade.
The path through the forest
Is dark and it's long,
So I will go with you
And sing you a song.

The little girl was charmed. "I'm going to my grandmother's house," she said. "With this." She held up a basket that was covered with a red-checked cloth. The wolf could smell carrot cake. He grinned.

"Oh, poet, what big teeth you have," said the child.

"The better to eat carrot cake with," said the thoroughly nice wolf.

"My granny hates carrot cake," said the child. "In fact, she hates anything but mush."

"What bad taste," said the wolf. "I made up a poem about that once:

If I found someone
Who liked to eat mush,
I'd sit them in front of it,
Then give a..."

"Push!" shouted the child.

"Why, you're a poet, too," said the wolf.

"I'm really more of a storyteller," said the child, blushing prettily. "But I do love carrot cake."

"All poets do," said the wolf. "So you must be a poet as well."

"Well, my granny is no poet. Every week when I bring the carrot cake over, she dumps it into her mush and mushes it all up together and then makes me eat it with her. She says that I have to learn that life ends with a bowl of mush."

"Great howls!" said the wolf, shuddering. "What a terribly wicked thing to say and do."

"I guess so," said the child.

"Then we must save this wonderful carrot cake from your grandmother," the wolf said, scratching his head below his ears.

The child clapped her hands. "I know," she said. "Let's pretend."

"Pretend?" asked the wolf.

"Let's pretend that you are Granny and I am bringing the cake to *you*. Here, you wear my red riding hood and we'll pretend it's Granny's night-cap and nightgown."

The wolf took her little cape and slung it over his head. He grinned again. He was a poet and he loved pretending.

The child skipped up to him and knocked upon an imaginary door. The wolf opened it. "Come in. Come in."

"Oh, no," said the child. "My grandmother never gets out of bed."

"Never?" asked the wolf.

"Never," said the child.

"All right," said the thoroughly nice wolf, shaking his head. He lay down on the cool green grass, clasped his paws over his stomach, and made a very loud pretend snore.

The child walked over to his feet and knocked again.

"Who is it?" called out the wolf in a high, weak, scratchy voice.

"It is your granddaughter, Little Red Riding Hood," the child said, giggling.

"Come in, come in. Just lift the latch. I'm in bed with aches and pains and a bad case of the rheumaticks," said the wolf in the high, funny voice.

The child walked in through the pretend door. "I have brought you a basket of goodies," said the child, putting the basket by the wolf's side. She placed her hands on her hips. "But you know, Grandmother, you look very different today."

"How so?" asked the wolf, opening both his yellow eyes wide.

"Well, Grandmother, what big eyes you have," said the child.

The wolf closed his eyes and opened them again quickly. "The better to see you with, my dear," he said.

"Oh, you silly wolf. She never calls me *dear*. She calls me *Sweetface*. Or *Punkins*. Or her *Airy Fairy Dee*."

"How awful," said the wolf.

"I know," said the child. "But that's what she calls me."

"Well, I can't," said the wolf, turning over on his side. "I'm a poet, after all, and no self-respecting poet could possibly use those words. If I have to call you that, there's no more pretending."

"I guess you can call me *dear*," said the child in a very small voice. "But I didn't know that poets were so particular."

"About *words* we are," said the wolf.

"And you have an awfully big nose," said the child.

The wolf put his paw over his nose. "Now that is uncalled-for," he said. "My nose isn't all that big—for a wolf."

"It's part of the game," said the child.

"Oh, yes, the game. I had forgotten. The better to smell the basket of goodies, my dear," said the wolf.

"And Grandmother, what big teeth you have."

The thoroughly nice wolf sat up. "The better to eat carrot cake with," he said.

At that, the game was over. They shared the carrot cake evenly and licked their fingers, which was not very polite but certainly the best thing to do on a picnic in the woods. And the wolf sang an ode to carrot cake which he made up on the spot:

> Carrot cake, o carrot cake
> The best thing a baker ever could make,
> Mushy or munchy
> Gushy or crunchy
> Eat it by a woodland lake.

"We are really by a stream," said the child.

"That is what is known as poetic license," said the wolf. "Calling a stream a lake."

"Maybe you can use your license to drive me home."

The wolf nodded. "I will if you tell me your name. I know it's not *really* Little Red Riding Hood."

The child stood up and brushed crumbs off her dress. "It's Elisabet Grimm," she said.

"Of the Grimm family on Forest Lane?" asked the wolf.

"Of course," she answered.

"Everyone knows where that is. I'll take you home right now," said the wolf. He stretched himself from tip to tail. "But what will you tell your mother about her cake?" He took her by the hand.

"Oh, I'm a storyteller," said the child. "I'll think of something."

And she did.

"She did indeed," said Nurse Lamb thoughtfully. She cleared away the now empty bowls and took them back to the kitchen. When she returned, she was carrying a tray full of steaming mugs of coffee.

"I told you I had bad press," said Wolfgang.

"I should say you had," Nurse Lamb replied, passing out the mugs.

"Me, too," said the wolf with the cane.

"You, too, what?" asked Nurse Lamb.

"I had bad press, too, though my story is somewhat different. By the by, my name is Oliver," said the wolf. "Would you like to hear my tale?"

Nurse Lamb sat down. "Oh, please, yes."

OLIVER WOLF'S TALE

Once upon a time there was a very clever young wolf. He had an especially broad, bushy tail and a white star under his chin.

In his playpen he had built tall buildings of blocks and straw.

In the schoolyard he had built forts of mud and sticks.

And once, after a trip with his father to the bricklayer's, he had made a tower of bricks.

Oh, how that clever young wolf loved to build things.

"When I grow up," he said to his mother and father not once but many times, "I want to be an architect."

"That's nice, dear," they would answer, though they wondered about it. After all, no one in their family had ever been anything more than a wolf.

When the clever little wolf was old enough, his father sent him out into the world with a pack of tools and letters from his teachers.

"*This* is a very clever young wolf," read one letter.

"Quite the cleverest I have ever met," said another.

So the clever young wolf set out looking for work.

In a short while he came to a crossroads and who should be there but three punk pigs building themselves houses and making quite a mess of it.

The first little pig was trying to build a house of straw.

"Really," said the clever wolf, "I tried that in the playpen. It won't work. A breath of air will knock it over."

"Well, if you're so clever," said the pig, pushing his sunglasses back up his snout, "why don't you try and blow it down."

The wolf set his pack by the side of the road, rolled up his shirt-sleeves, and huffed and puffed. The house of straw collapsed in a twinkling.

"See," said the clever wolf.

The little pig got a funny look on his face and ran one of his trotters up under his collar.

The wolf turned to the second little pig who had just hammered a nail into the house he was trying to build. It was a makeshift affair of sticks and twigs.

"Yours is not much better, I'm afraid," said the clever wolf.

"Oh, yeah?" replied the pig. "Clever is as clever does." He thumbed his snout at the wolf. "Let's see you blow *this* house down, dog-breath."

The wolf sucked in a big gulp of air. Then he huffed and puffed a bit harder than before. The sticks tumbled down in a heap of dry kindling, just as he knew they would.

The second little pig picked up one of the larger pieces and turned it nervously in his trotters.

"Nyah, nyah nyah, nyah nyah!" said the third little pig, stretching his suspenders and letting them snap back with a loud twang. "Who do you think's afraid of you, little wolf? Try your muzzle on this pile of bricks, hair-face."

"That won't be necessary," said the clever wolf. "Every good builder knows bricks are excellent for houses."

The third little pig sniffed and snapped his suspenders once again.

"However," said the wolf, pointing at the roof, "since you have asked my opinion, I think you missed the point about chimneys. They are supposed to go straight up, not sideways."

"Well, if you're so clever..." began the first little pig.

"And have such strong breath..." added the second little pig.

"And are such a know-it-all and tell-it-ever..." put in the third little pig.

"Why don't you go up there and fix it yourself!" all three said together.

"Well, thank you," said the clever wolf, realizing he had just been given his very first job. "I'll get to it at once." Finding a ladder resting against the side of the brick house, he hoisted his pack of tools onto his back and climbed up onto the roof.

He set the bricks properly, lining them up with his plumb line. He mixed the mortar with care. He was exacting in his measurements and careful in his calculations. The sun was beginning to set before he was done.

"There," he said at last. "That should do it." He expected, at the very least, a thank-you from the pigs. But instead all he got was a loud laugh from the third little pig, a snout-thumbing from the second, and a nasty wink from the first.

The clever wolf shrugged his shoulders. After all, pigs will be pigs and he couldn't expect them to be wolves. But when he went to climb down he found they had removed the ladder.

"Clever your way out of this one, fuzz-ball," shouted the third little pig. Then they ran inside the house, turned up the stereo, and phoned their friends for a party.

The only way down was the chimney. But the wolf had to wait until the bricks and mortar had set as hard as stone. That took half the night. When at last the chimney was ready, the wolf slowly made his way down the inside, his pack on his back.

The pigs and their friends heard him coming. And between one record and the next, they shoved a pot of boiling mush into the hearth. They laughed themselves silly when the wolf fell in.

"That's how things end, fur-tail," the pigs shouted. "With a bowl of mush."

Dripping and unhappy, the wolf ran out the door. He vowed never to associate with pigs again. And to this day—with the exception of the cook—he never has. And being a well-brought-up wolf, as well as clever, he has never told his side of the story until today.

"Well, the pigs sure talked about it," said Nurse Lamb, shaking her head. "The way *they* have told it, it is quite a different story."

"Nobody listens to pigs," said Oliver Wolf. He looked quickly at the kitchen door.

"I'm not so sure," said a wolf who had a patch over his eye. "I'm not so sure."

"So you're not so sure," said Oliver. "Bet you think you're pretty clever, Lone Wolf."

"No," said Lone Wolf. "I never said I was clever. *You* are the clever little wolf."

Wolfgang laughed. "So clever he was outwitted by a pack of punk pigs." The other wolves laughed.

"You didn't do so well with one human child," answered Oliver.

"Now, now, now," said the cook, poking her head in through the door. "As we say in the barnyard, 'Words are like wood, a handy weapon.' "

"No weapons. No fighting," said Nurse Lamb, standing up and shaking her hoof at the wolves. "We are supposed to be telling stories, not getting into fights."

Lone Wolf stared at her. "I never in my life ran from a fight. Not if it was for a good cause."

Nurse Lamb got up her courage and put her hand on his shoulder. "I believe you," she said. "Why not tell me about some of the good causes you fought for?"

Lone Wolf twitched his ears. "All right," he said at last. "I'm not boasting, you understand. Just setting the record straight."

Nurse Lamb looked over at the kitchen door. The old sow winked at her and went back to work.

LONE WOLF'S TALE

Once upon a time there was a kind, tender, and compassionate young wolf. He had a black patch over one eye and another black patch at the tip of his tail. He loved to help the under-dog, the under-wolf, the under-lamb, and even the under-pig.

His basement was full of the signs of his good fights. Signs like LOVE A TREE and HAVE YOU KISSED A FLOWER TODAY? and PIGS ARE PEOPLE, TOO! and HONK IF YOU LOVE A WEASEL.

One day he was in the basement running off petitions on his mimeo machine when he heard a terrible noise.

KA-BLAAAAAAAM KA-BLOOOOOOOIE.

It was the sound a gun makes in the forest.

Checking his calendar, the kind and tender wolf saw with horror that it was opening day of duck-hunting season. Quickly he put on his red hat and red vest. Then he grabbed up the signs he had made for that occasion: SOME DUCKS CAN'T DUCK and EAT CORN NOT CORN-EATERS and DUCKS HAVE MOTHERS, TOO. Then he ran out of his door and down the path as fast as he could go.

KA-BLAAAAAAAM KA-BLOOOOOOOIE.

The kind and tender wolf knew just where to go. Deep in the forest was a wonderful pond where the ducks liked to stop on their way north. The food was good, the reeds comfortable, the prices reasonable, and the linens changed daily.

When the kind and tender wolf got to the pond, all he could see was one small and very frightened mallard in the middle of the pond and thirteen hunters around the edge.

"Stop!" he shouted as the hunters raised their guns.

This did not stop them.

The kind and tender wolf tried again, shouting anything he could think of. "We shall overcome," he called. "No smoking. No nukes. Stay off the grass."

Nothing worked. The hunters sighted their guns. The wolf knew it was time to act.

He put one of the signs in the water and sat on it. He picked up another sign as a paddle. Using his tail as a rudder, he pushed off into the pond and rowed toward the duck.

"I will save you," he cried. "We are brothers. Quack."

The mallard looked confused. Then it turned and swam toward the wolf. When it reached him, it climbed onto the sign and quacked back.

"Saved," said the kind and tender wolf triumphantly, neglecting to notice that their combined weight was making the cardboard sign sink. But when the water was up to his chin, the wolf suddenly remembered he could not swim.

"Save yourself, friend," he called out, splashing great waves and swallowing them.

The mallard was kind and tender, too. It pushed the drowning wolf to shore and then, hidden by a patch of reeds, gave the well-meaning wolf beak-to-muzzle resuscitation. Then the bird flew off behind the cover of trees. The hunters never saw it go.

But they found the wolf, his fur all soggy.

"Look!" said one who had his name, *Peter,* stenciled on the pocket of his coat. "There are feathers on this wolf's jaws and in his whiskers. He has eaten *our* duck."

And so the hunters grabbed up the kind and tender wolf by his tail and slung him on top of the remaining sign. They marched him once around the town and threw him into jail for a week, where they gave him nothing to eat but mush.

"Now, wolf," shouted the hunter Peter when they finally let him out of jail, "don't you come back here again or it will be mush for you from now 'til the end of your life."

The kind and tender wolf, nursing his hurt tail and his aching teeth, left town. The next day the newspaper ran a story that read: PETER & THE WOLF FIGHT. PETER RUNS FOR MAYOR. VOWS TO KEEP WOLF FROM DOOR. And to this day no one believes the kind and tender wolf's side of the tale.

"I believe it," said Nurse Lamb looking at Lone Wolf with tears in her eyes. "In fact, I believe all of you." She stood up and collected the empty mugs.

"Hurray!" said the cook, peeking in the doorway. "Maybe this is one young nurse we'll keep."

"Keep?" Nurse Lamb suddenly looked around, all her fear coming back. Lone Wolf was cleaning his nails. Three old wolves had dozed off. Wolfgang was gazing at the ceiling. But Oliver grinned at her and licked his chops. "What do you mean, keep?"

"Do you want *our* side of the story?" asked Oliver, still grinning. "Or the nurses'?"

Nurse Lamb gulped.

Oliver winked.

Then Nurse Lamb knew they were teasing her. "Oh, you big bad wolf," she said and patted him on the head. She walked back into the kitchen.

"You know," she said to the cook. "I think I'm going to like it here. I think I can help make it a real *happy* HAPPY DEN. I'll get them to write down their stories. And maybe we'll make a book of them. Life doesn't *have* to end with a bowl of mush."

Stirring the pot, the cook nodded and smiled.

"In fact," said Nurse Lamb loudly, "why don't we try chicken soup for lunch?"

From the dining room came a great big cheer.

WILL

The past will not lie buried.
Little bones and teeth
harrowed from grave's soil,
tell different tales.
My father's bank box told me,
in a paper signed by his own hand,
the name quite clearly: *William.*
All the years he denied it,
that name, that place of birth,
that compound near Kiev,
and I so eager for the variants
with which he lived his life.
In the middle of my listening,
death,
that old interrupter,
with the unkindness of all coroners,
revealed his third name to me.
Not William, not Will, but Wolf.
Wolf.
And so at last I know the story,
my old wolf, white against the Russian snows,
the cracking of his bones,
the stretching sinews,
the coarse hair growing boldly
on the belly, below the eye.
Why grandfather, my children cry,
what great teeth you have,
before he devours them
as he devoured me,
all of me, bones and blood,
all of my life.

42

The Sow, the Mare, and the Cow

Not so very long ago, a sow, a mare, and a cow were friends. They lived together on a farm in a green and pleasant land.

One day the sow said to her friends, "I am tired of man and his fences. I want to see the world."

She grunted this so loudly that all the other animals on the farm heard her and turned their backs. But her friends did not.

"I agree," said the mare.

"And I," said the cow.

So that very night, the cow and the mare leaped over the fence; the sow crawled under. Then the three companions went one hoof after another down the road to see the world.

But the world was full of men and fences all down the road.

The sow shook her head. "I am going into the woods," she said.

"I agree," said the mare.

"And I," said the cow.

So they pushed through branch after branch, and bramble after briar, till the way grew dark and tangled. At last they found a small clearing where no fence had ever been built and no man had ever dwelt. They settled there for the night.

The sow and the mare took turns standing guard, but the cow fell right to sleep.

The mare began to nod.

Then the sow.

Soon all three were asleep, and no one was left to guard the others in the small clearing in the dark wood.

Suddenly a low growling filled the forest.

The sow and the mare woke up with a start. The cow lowed in alarm and hid her eyes with her hooves.

The growling got louder.

The cow jumped up.

Back to back, the three friends spent the rest of the night awake and trembling.

In the morning the sow said, "I think we should build a barn. Then we will be safe from the growlers in the night."

"I agree," said the mare.

"And I," said the cow.

So the mare gathered twigs and boughs for walls. The sow rooted leaves and moss for the roof. And the cow showed them where everything should be placed.

Branch by branch, bramble after briar, they built a fine barn.

That night the three friends went inside their barn. The sow and mare took turns standing guard, but the cow fell right to sleep.

The mare began to nod.

Then the sow.

Soon all three were asleep, and no one was left to guard the others in the fine barn in the small clearing in the darkwood.

Suddenly a high howling filled the forest.

The sow and the mare woke up with a start. The cow lowed in alarm and tried to hide in a corner.

The howling got higher and closer.

The sow ran to guard the door. The mare ran to guard the window. The cow turned her face to the wall. The three friends spent the rest of the night awake and trembling.

In the morning, the sow said, "I think we should build a high fence around our fine barn to keep away the growlers and the howlers in the night."

"I agree," said the mare.

"And I," said the cow.

So the mare gathered logs and stumps. The sow pushed boulders and stones. And the cow showed them where everything should be placed.

Then stick by stone, and bramble after briar, they built themselves a high fence. The three friends went inside their fine barn which was inside their high fence, to spend the night.

The sow and the mare took turns standing guard, but the cow fell right to sleep.

The mare began to nod.

Then the sow.

Soon all three were asleep, and no one was left to guard the others in the fine barn inside the high fence in the small clearing in the dark wood.

Suddenly there was a scratching at the door and a scrabbling on the roof.

The sow and mare awoke with a start. The cow lowed in alarm and fell to her knees. They waited for someone or something to enter. But nothing did.

Still the three friends spent the rest of the night awake and trembling.

In the morning the three friends were tired and pale and a little uncertain. They looked at one another and at the fine barn inside the high fence in the small clearing in the dark wood.

Then the cow spoke. "I have a sudden great longing for man and his fences."

But the mare did not say, "I agree."

And the sow did not say," "And I."

They were suddenly both much too busy digging ditches, fixing fences, mending roofs, and laying a path to their door.

So the cow put one hoof after another all the way back to the farm in the middle of the green and pleasant land. There she lived a long and happy life within man's fences.

But the sow and the mare opened the door that very night and met the growlers and the howlers, the scratchers and the scrabblers who were just the forest folk who had come to make them welcome. And they too lived long and happy lives within fences of their own making. And if you can tell which one of the three was the happiest, you are a better judge of animals than I.

THE BROTHERS GRIMM
AND SISTER JANE

My first taste of fairy tales was in the collected color fairy books of Andrew Lang. Bowdlerized and tarted up as they were, the stories in those books still mesmerized me. Though I was a New York City child, I rode across the steppes of Russia, swam in the cold Scandinavian rivers, ran down African forest paths, hunted in the haunted Celtic woods with the heroes of the stories I read. I became in turn the girl on the back of a great white bear riding east of the sun and west of the moon, the Hoodie-crow's lovely wife, the farmer's woman stolen away by the fairies.

Like an addict, I went from the Lang samplers to the stronger stuff. The local librarians got used to me pulling out dusty collections from the shelves: the Afanas'ev Russian stories, Asbjørnsen and Moe's Norwegian tales, Yeats's Irish fairy lore, the *Thousand and One Nights*. (It was years before I learned it was the expurgated version.) And—of course—the Brothers Grimm.

By the time I was ten, a tomboy by day and a reader by night under the covers, I had devoured whole cultures. To the outsider, I must have seemed omnivorous in my reading, catholic in my taste. But there were three stories in the Grimm collection that were my favorites. Though I could not have known it at the time, they were *life myths* to me. As it says in one of the early Gnostic gospels, *The Gospel According to Thomas:* "Whoever drinks from my mouth shall become as I am and I myself will become he, and the hidden things shall be revealed to him." If *that* is not a fairy-tale transformative curse—or blessing—I have misspent my youth! In loving these three particular stories, I became them. They were my meat and I theirs, a literary eucharist.

The three were: "Faithful John" (No.6), "Brother and Sister" (No. 11), and "The Three Little Men in the Woods" (No. 13).

It is an odd trio I adopted. They are certainly not the most popular stories in the Grimm canon. Disney has not touched them. Nor are they found in picture-book format for the youngest readers. One must search them out within the body of the Grimm tales, a task for the true child bibliophile. Yet though these were not the popular and often reprinted stories, each spoke to me in a way that knifed clear to the soul. Like Yeats's description of the class of people who loved the folk tales, the peasants who "have steeped everything in the heart; to whom everything was a symbol" (xii), I was a breather-in of stories. Those three tales, though I did not understand it at the time, were to be accurate forecasters of my adult concerns.

The first of the trio, "Faithful John," is the story of a servant to the king who promises the dying monarch that he will be equally faithful to the prince "even if it should cost me my life" (43). And of course, as such stories go, John is forced to be as good as his word. He accompanies his young master on his bridal trip and overhears three ravens prophesying what dire things await the bridal pair. Furthermore, the ravens state that anyone foolish enough to explain it to the king would immediately be turned to stone. Naturally, Faithful John saves the royal couple three times and, when ordered to explain his actions, does so and becomes stone. Only when the king and queen willingly sacrifice their own children and use the innocents' blood to return the stone to life does the tale end happily. Happily for the children, too, for they are magically restored as well.

The story is full of magic, sacrifice, and reward, all the wonderful accoutrements of a fairy tale. It is satisfyingly rounded, wasting little time between the opening, in which the dying king accepts Faithful John's pledge, to the conclusion in which "They dwelt together in much happiness until their death" (51). An economical tale between two dyings, a critic might carp. But oh, as a child, how I loved that tale.

The faithful servant—tale type 516—was well known for centuries before the Grimms' particular version was recorded, traveling from India both orally and in the eleventh-century *Ocean of Story* collection. Some scholars point out a connection as well with the French romance *Amis and Amiloun,* which contains both the stone and the disenchantment by means of innocent children's blood. (For a fuller discussion of this see Stith Thompson's *The Folktale* 111-12.) But all that mattered to me as a child was the driving force behind that story: that faithfulness, even unto a quasi-death, would be rewarded in the end.

By the time I was an adult, only vaguely remembering the outlines of the story, I had become a peace marcher, a stander-on-line for causes. I was—in essence—a Faithful John, willing to go to jail or even to be turned to stone as the possible consequence of my actions. My stories, too, had more than a casual reference to the old tale. *Dove Isabeau* is a picture-book fairy tale about a prince who is turned to stone because of his willingness to save his own true love. He does what must be done—knowing full well that stone is his doom, that he will, quite literally, become his own monument. He is saved in the very end by a drop of blood from an innocent girl. *Friend,* a biography of my hero, that great stander-up-to-power George Fox, the first Quaker, was another offshoot of the "Faithful John" story. And "The Hundredth Dove" is a fairy tale about a faithful servant to his king who even wears the motto "Servo"—*I serve*—over his breast until he is forced to serve his king in an ignoble and terrible fashion. That was a story fueled by the Watergate hearings, but its antecedent is, unquestionably, Grimm story No. 6.

The second tale that imprinted itself on my consciousness was "Brother and Sister," an odd tale in the Grimm collection because it has always seemed unfinished to me, or strangely conglomerate, as if two stories had been badly or inappropriately stitched together.

A brother and sister who are abused by their stepmother "go forth together into the wide world" (67) and become lost in a forest whose very brooks have been bewitched by their sorcerous foe. Dying of thirst, they go from one stream to another, not daring to drink, for the first two announce, "Who drinks of me will be a tiger" and "Who drinks of me will be a wolf" (68). (Does this sound remarkably like the *Gospel According to Thomas* quotation with which I began this essay?) At last, the brother cannot stand it any longer and drinks from a stream that promises he will become a deer. His sister ties her golden garter around his neck and leads him even further into the woods where they discover an empty cottage. There they live until a king comes upon them, falls in love with the girl, and brings them both back to the palace. Of course the wicked stepmother substitutes her own ugly daughter for the queen at the moment of childbirth, and the story finishes with the rightful queen restored, the false queen torn to pieces by wild beasts in the very woods her mother had enchanted, and the witch burnt at the stake. The deer—at last—is turned back into a man.

It was the relationship between the brother and sister that first compelled me. As an older sister to an adored younger brother, I considered myself a twin to the heroine of the tale. As she is not named in the story, I named her—Jane.

Tale type 450, called after the story "Little Brother, Little Sister," it is the prototype story of family loyalty that has been found in many different cultures. Family loyalty was prized in our house.

*

When I became a writer, I used the tale very consciously in my own story "Brother Hart," though that particular tale is more a romance than a fairy story, with a bittersweet ending. It is a story of jealousy and possessiveness, created at the height of feminist rage and the ongoing discussions about a woman's place in a loving relationship. Not just a recasting of an old, familiar story, it is a tale that could only have been written in the mid-twentieth century. I also used the transformation motif in a variety of other stories, all harkening back to "Brother and Sister." "The Promise," in which a boy transformed into a fish by a sorcerer is saved by his own true love; "The Cat Bride," in which a cat becomes a human girl in order to be married; "The White Seal Maid," in which a seal becomes a woman and bears seven sons to a fisherman to revive her dying tribe; and the transfigured brother and sister in the "Wild Goose and Gander" section of my fairy-tale novel *The Magic Three of Solatia* are just a few of them.

The third—and in some ways the oddest—of my life stories was the relatively unknown "The Three Little Men in the Woods." It begins with a widow and widower marrying and the stepmother offering preferment to her own ugly daughter. The beautiful stepdaughter is sent out into the woods in the middle of winter in a paper frock to gather strawberries, a traditional "impossible task." Since she is as good as she is beautiful, she treats the three little men she meets in the woods politely and shares her meagre dinner—a piece of hard bread—with them, thus winning their approval. They wish that she grow more beautiful every day, that whenever she speaks gold should fall from her lips, and that she marry a king. When she returns home with strawberries found miraculously in the snow, speaking a fortune at every utterance, the stepmother packs her own daughter off for the same trip. Of course she is swathed in furs and carries along a bread-and-butter cake which she neglects to share with the little men, whom she snubs. Naturally she is cursed: that she grow uglier every day, that toads spring from her mouth, and that she die a miserable death. As the adventure proceeds, both the blessings and the curses come true.

Similar to the more popular Grimms' "Frau Holle" or "Mother Holle" (No. 24), the tale at its core contains the well-known motif "Kind and unkind" daughter (Q2). Other Grimm stories also revolve around Q2: "Bearskin" (No. 101) and "The Water of Life" (No. 97; unkind sons in this case). But it was the idea of the gold pouring out of the good girl's mouth, the toads from the bad's, that riveted me. It was—though I did not know it at the time—a metaphor for the life I was to choose.

I was to use that toad image in *Sleeping Ugly*, a parody of several fairy tales, in which the nasty Princess Miserella is cursed, for a moment, to speak in toads until the homely but goodhearted Plain Jane asks for a reprieve. I also used the image in the following poem, part of a series of fairy-tale poems I wrote in the mid and late 1980s:

Toads

Sure, I called her *stupid cow*
and *witch*,
but only under my breath.
And I took an extra long lunch
last Friday,
and quit right at five
every day this week,
slapping my desk top down
with a noise
like the snap of gum
She could've fired me right then.
Or docked my check,
Or put a pink slip
in my envelope
with that happy face
she draws on all her notes.
But not her.
Witch!
This morning
at the coffee shop,
when I went to order
a Danish and a decaf to go,
instead of words,
this great gray toad
the size of a bran muffin
dropped out between my lips
onto the formica.
It looked up at me,
its dark eyes sorrowful,
its back marked
with Revlon's Lady Love
the shape of my kiss.
Tell me,
do you think
I should apologize?
Do you think I should let
the shop steward know?

I also used the idea of something unnatural coming from a girl's mouth in
the story "Silent Bianca." Bianca speaks in slivers of ice, and anyone who
wants to know what she is saying has to gather the slivers and warm them

by the hearthfire until the slivers melt and the room is filled with the sounds of Bianca's voice.

Every author hopes that the words pouring from the pen—or typewriter, word processor, or number 2 pencil, all mouth substitutes—are golden, indeed. Golden means the words are precious, important, powerful. Golden means that the author can make a good living. Golden suggests permanence and worth. However, I—and most writers I know—suspect that when we open our mouths we usually spit out toads, as big as bran muffins, onto the plates of our eager readers. For that nightmare—for that metaphor—we have the Brothers Grimm to thank.

Works Cited

Grimm, Brothers. *The Complete Grimm's Fairy Tales*. Trans. Margaret Hunt. Rev. James Stern. 1944. New York: Pantheon Books, 1972.

Thompson, Stith. *The Folktale*. 1946. Berkeley: University of California Press, 1977.

Yeats, William Butler. *Irish Fairy and Folk Tales*. New York: Random, n.d.

Yolen, Jane. "Brother Hart." *Dream Weaver* 10–20.

———. "The Cat Bride." *Dream Weaver* 43–47.

———. *Dove Isabeau*. San Diego: Harcourt, 1989.

———. *Dream Weaver*, New York: Philomel Books, 1989.

———. *Friend: The Story of George Fox and the Quakers*. New York: Seabury Press, 1972.

———. *The Hundredth Dove and Other Tales*. New York: Crowell, 1977.

———. "The Hundredth Dove." *The Hundredth Dove* 1–9.

———. *The Magic Three of Solatia*. New York: Crowell, 1974.

———. "The Promise." *The Hundredth Dove* 39–50.

———. "Silent Bianca." *The Girl Who Cried Flowers and Other Tales*. New York: Crowell, 1974. 45–55.

———. *Sleeping Ugly*. New York: Coward, 1981.

———. "Toads." *Isaac Asimov's Science Fiction Magazine*, June 1989: 145.

———. "The White Seal Maid." *The Hundredth Dove* 29–37.

THE HUNDREDTH DOVE

There once lived in the forest of old England a fowler named Hugh who supplied all the game birds for the high king's table.

The larger birds he hunted with a bow, and it was said of him that he never shot but that a bird fell, and sometimes two. But for the smaller birds that flocked like gray clouds over the forest, he used only a silken net he wove himself. This net was soft and fine and did not injure the birds though it held them fast. Then Hugh the fowler could pick and choose the plumpest of the doves for the high king's table and set the others free.

One day in early summer, Hugh was summoned to court and brought into the throne room.

Hugh bowed low, for it was not often that he was called into the king's own presence. And indeed he felt uncomfortable in the palace, as though caught in a stone cage.

"Rise, fowler, and listen," said the king. "In one week's time I am to be married." Then, turning with a smile to the woman who sat by him, the king held out her hand to the fowler.

The fowler stared up at her. She was neat as a bird, slim and fair, with black eyes. There was a quiet in her, but a restlessness too. He had never seen anyone so beautiful.

Hugh took the tiny hand offered him and put his lips to it, but he only dared to kiss the gold ring that glittered on her finger.

The king looked carefully at the fowler and saw how he trembled. It made the king smile.

"See, my lady, how your beauty turns the head of even my fowler. And he is a man who lives as solitary as a monk in his wooded cell."

The lady smiled and said nothing, but she drew her hand away from Hugh.

The king then turned again to the fowler. "In honor of my bride, the Lady Columba, whose name means dove and whose beauty is celebrated in all the world, I wish to serve one hundred of the birds at our wedding feast."

Lady Columba gasped and held up her hand. "Please do not serve them, sire."

But the king said to the fowler, "I have spoken. Do not fail me, fowler."

"As you command," said Hugh, and he bowed again. He touched his hand to his tunic, where his motto, *Servo* ("I serve"), was sewn over the heart.

Then the fowler went immediately back to the cottage deep in the forest where he lived.

There he took out the silken net and spread it upon the floor. Slowly he searched the net for snags and snarls and weakened threads. These he rewove with great care, sitting straightbacked at his wooden loom.

After a night and a day he was done. The net was as strong as his own stout heart. He laid the net down on the hearth and slept a dreamless sleep.

Before dawn Hugh set out into the forest clearing which only he knew. The trails he followed were narrower than deer runs, for the fowler needed no paths to show him the way. He knew every tree, every stone in the forest as a lover knows the form of his beloved. And he served the forest easily as well as he served the high king.

The clearing was full of life, yet so silently did the fowler move, neither bird nor insect remarked his coming. He crouched at the edge, his brown and green clothes a part of the wood. Then he waited.

A long patience was his strength, and he waited the whole of the day, neither moving nor sleeping. At dusk the doves came, settling over the clearing like a gray mist. And when they were down and greedily feeding, Hugh leaped up and swung the net over the nearest ones in a single swift motion.

He counted twenty-one doves in his net, all but one gray-blue and meaty. The last was a dove that was slim, elegant, and white as milk. Yet even as Hugh watched, the white dove slipped through the silken strands that bound it and flew away into the darkening air.

Since Hugh was not the kind of hunter to curse his bad luck, but rather one to praise his good, he gathered up the twenty and went home. He placed the doves in a large wooden cage whose bars he had carved out of white oak.

Then he looked at his net. There was not a single break in it, no way for the white dove to have escaped. Hugh thought long and hard about this, but at last he lay down to the cooing of the captured birds and slept.

In the morning the fowler was up at dawn. Again he crept to the forest clearing and waited, quieter than anystone, for the doves. And again he threw his net at duskand caught twenty fat gray doves and the single white one.

But as before, the white dove slipped through his net as easily as air.

The fowler carried the gray doves home and caged them with the rest. But his mind was filled with the sight of the white bird, slim and fair. He was determined to capture it.

For five days and nights it was the same except for this one thing: on the fifth night there were only nineteen gray doves in his net. He was short of the hundred by one. Yet he had taken all of the birds in the flock but the white dove.

Hugh looked into the hearth fire but he felt no warmth. He placed his hand upon the motto above his heart. "I swear by the king whom I serve and by the lady who will be his queen that I will capture that bird," he said. "I will bring the hundred doves to them. I shall not fail."

So the sixth day, well before dawn, the fowler arose. He checked the net one final time and saw it was tight. Then he was away to the clearing.

All that day Hugh sat at the clearing's edge, still as a stone. The meadow was full of life. Songbirds sang that had never sung before. Strange flowers grew and blossomed and died at his feet yet he never looked at them. Animals that had once been and were no longer came out of the forest shadows and passed him by: the hippocampus, the gryphon, and the silken swift unicorn. But he never moved. It was for the white dove he waited, and at last she came.

In the quickening dark she floated down, featherlight and luminous at the clearing's edge. Slowly she moved, eating and cooing and calling for her missing flock. She came in the end to where Hugh sat and began to feed at his feet.

He moved his hands once and the net was over her, then his hands were over her, too. The dove twisted and pecked but he held her close, palms upon wings, fingers on neck.

When the white dove saw she could not move, she turned her bright black eyes on the fowler and spoke to him in a cooing woman's voice.

"Master fowler, set me free,
Gold and silver I'll give thee."

"Neither gold nor silver tempt me," said Hugh. "Servo" is my motto. I serve my master. And my master is the king."

Then the white dove spoke again:

> *"Master fowler, set me free,*
> *Fame and fortune follow thee."*

But the fowler shook his head and held on tight. "After the king, I serve the forest," he said. "Fame and fortune are not masters here." He rose with the white dove in his hands and made ready to return to his house.

Then the bird shook itself all over and spoke for a third time. Its voice was low and beguiling:

> *"Master fowler, free this dove,*
> *The queen will be your own true love."*

For the first time, then, though night was almost on them, the fowler noticed the golden ring that glittered and shone on the dove's foot. As if in a vision, he saw the Lady Columba again, slim and neat and fair. He heard her voice and felt her hand in his.

He began to tremble and his heart began to pulse madly. He felt a burning in his chest and limbs. Then he looked down at the dove and it seemed to be smiling at him, its black eyes glittering.

"*Servo,*" he cried out, his voice shaking. "*Servo.*" He closed his eyes and twisted the dove's neck. Then he touched the motto on his tunic. He could feel the word *Servo* impress itself coldly on his fingertips. One quick rip and the motto was torn from his breast. He flung it to the meadow floor, put the limp dove in his pouch, and went through the forest to his home. The next day the fowler brought the hundred doves—the ninety-nine live ones and the one dead—to the king's kitchen. But there never was a wedding.

The fowler gave up hunting and lived on berries and fruit the rest of his life. Every day he made his way to the clearing to throw out grain for the birds. Around his neck, from a chain, a gold ring glittered. And occasionally he would touch the spot on his tunic, above his heart, which was shredded and torn.

But though songbirds and sparrows ate his grain, and swallows came at his calling, he never saw another dove.

THE PROMISE

There were once fond and loving friends who were delivered of children on the same day and hour. They rejoiced in their good fortune and named the boy Kay and the girl Kaya, promising each other that the two children would never be parted. Indeed, they spoke often of that promise to the boy and girl. And the children, a laughing, talkative pair, took up the promise as their own and gave it freely one to the other.

But the fond friends died within days of one another, when the children were thirteen years old. The promise was not kept. Kay and Kaya were sent off to a distant city to live with their relatives, the boy to stay with an old uncle who was a sorcerer and the girl to a convent whose abbess was her aunt.

When they arrived at the city and stood hand in hand by the carriage, the old uncle looked them over and frowned. He pulled thoughtfully at the graying ends of his mustache, then dismissed the boy with a shrug. But the girl Kaya took his heart. He swore silently by the dark gods he worshipped that he would marry her when she came of age.

This decision the sorcerer did not speak at once, for he was used to a life built upon secrets which he rubbed to himself in the silence of his room 'til they festered like sores. Yet by the time he had delivered Kaya to the convent's care, he tumbled his secret into the air, for the girl's garrulous open nature had worked upon him and forced it out.

"I shall marry this girl, Sister," he said to the old abbess. "When she is sixteen I shall come for her."

Kaya shrank back from each syllable and her bright little face darkened. She began to tremble. "It is Kay I am to marry," she said. "It was promised."

The sorcerer did not seem to hear. He spoke directly to the abbess. "Treat the girl well. I shall come for her. I swear it."

The abbess did not reply, for she was vowed to silence. But she held the trembling girl to her all the while the sorcerer was near. And when he had departed, dragging Kay after him, the abbess brought the girl into the convent and shut the gates after them with a mighty clang as if the noise alone could drive out demons.

The nuns went their silent ways, but Kaya wept. She had not their assurances. She alone among them had not been promised heaven. She played and read and sat wrapped in her own misery by the convent pool. Under the willow, with its green rosary of buds, where only the whisper of the water and tree disturbed the convent silence, Kaya grew into a woman. She could speak but she did not, except to the tree and the abbess' pool, for they alone returned her answers.

Now, though he had ignored it, the sorcerer had heard Kaya's cry. It shook his dark pride. And when he returned with Kay to their rooms, his heart was already hardened toward the boy, Kaya's promised one. Whereas he might have been a tolerant master, he was now a cruel one; whereas he might have pitied the boy's loneliness, now he felt no pity at all.

Kay bore it bravely for a long while—indeed he had no reason to do otherwise. He expected nothing from the old man and so he was not disappointed when nothing was his lot.

But at night, when the sorcerer was asleep, hands resting like withered leaves on his breast, the boy would lift the curtain of the single window in his room and look out at the glittering stars. He would lean on his elbows and breathe half-remembered prayers whose words fell away from him with every passing day. As each word slipped away from memory, he substituted the one name he could recall: Kaya.

One night, when Kay was thus occupied, the old sorcerer awoke. The sounds of the boy's prayers were small daggers in his heart, for innocent prayer is the enemy of sorcery. He lifted himself from his bed and came silently to the boy's room.

There, elbows on the windowsill, Kay stuttered at the stars:

> *"And though I walk through...*
> *The shadowed valley....*
> *...I will not fear for...*
> *...Oh, Kaya, Kaya...be with me."*

"Kaya will never be with you," cried the old man, striking the boy with his hand.

As Kay cringed from the unexpected blow, the sorcerer moved his hand in a circle. "You *will* fear," he spat out. "And you will not pray. Indeed you will not say another word more." And he cast a spell on the boy.

Kay would have cried out then, more in anger than in fear, but he could not. His tongue cleaved to the roof of his mouth. His lips could not part. The sorcerer's magic had sealed them. He was as dumb as a beast.

"Go to bed," said the sorcerer, and turned in bleak triumph back to his own sleep.

But wordless, Kay was the enemy that, with words, he would never have been. He determined to resist the old man. Yet he was too young and too weak to fight the sorcerer outright. His resistance was a sly one. He began to undo the old man's long, tortuous spells. He dropped beakers in which potions were kept. He swept dust onto the pentagram on the floor. He ripped holes like mouse bites from the pages of the sorcerer's great books. And with each small act of resistance, Kay began to remember more words from his prayers until at last he could recall them all and repeat them in his head, though the words could not pass his mouth.

One evening, in the dead part of winter, Kay was ripping a snippet from *The Book of Night*. He used his nails, which had grown long and sharp in the sorcerer's service. Carefully he carved out a section in imitation of a mouse bite.

Suddenly the sorcerer swooped down on him as if from a great height.

"It is *you*. It has been you all this time, breaking my spells and undoing my enchantments. Well, I will make an enchantment you cannot break," the old man screamed.

The boy did not dare look at the sorcerer straight on, yet he did not dare look away. He clouded his eyes over in order not to see the old man clearly.

"All your defiances are for nothing," said the sorcerer. "You are lost—and your Kaya is lost to you forever."

At Kaya's name, the boy leaped at the sorcerer's eyes and would have found them with his nails if the old man had not quickly spat out a spell:

"Beast to fish
In virgin well,
A kiss alone
Can break the spell."

At the words, Kay felt his bones shrinking, contracting, growing smaller and lighter. His arms clung to his sides. His feet grew together. The air in his lungs was hot and seared his throat. He tried to breathe and could not. He gasped and gasped, and at each gasp the sorcerer laughed at him.

"You will leap upon no one again," the old man said. "Your only leaping shall be done in a pool." He threw Kay, who was now a silver carp, into a bucket of dirty water. Then, leaning over the bucket, where the fish swam around in maddened circles, the old man laughed again. "I shall show you your Kaya. You shall see her daily, and she you, but she will not be pleased with your appearance. A fish is the one pet the nuns are allowed. You shall be as chaste as they, and I shall have your Kaya."

The sorcerer lifted the bucket and put it by his bed, where he slept the rest of the night in dreamless sleep. In the morning he delivered the bucket with the silver carp to the convent with the admonition that none but Kaya should tend it.

The nun who took the fish in its bucket said nothing in thanks. Instead she went straight to the pool where Kaya sat wrapped in her own silences, her fingers idling in the water. The nun tapped the girl on the shoulder and Kaya looked up, her oval face framed by a halo of black hair.

Without further ceremony, the nun dumped the water-smooth silver fish into the pool. It circled once and came in under Kaya's fingers.

The girl was so frightened by this, she pulled her hand from the water and stared. At that, the fish gave a bubbling sigh and dove to the bottom of the pool. It did not come up again.

Kaya stood up and went inside.

But the next morning she was by the pool again. Sadness, like an old habit, claimed her. And when she put her fingers in the pool, drawing wavery pictures in the water, the great fish surfaced and circled them. And as he swam, the sunlight was caught in his scales and made iridescent patterns on the steep pool sides.

"What a strange and beautiful fish," said Kaya, trying out her words in the convent silence.""I wish you were mine, for I have no one at all."

At that, the carp circled under the green fingers of the willow tree and back again to the girl as if offering itself. And though she could not bear to feel its cold, scaly skin, Kaya fed the fish from her own fingers, dropping the crumbs of hard bread moments before the fish's mouth could touch her hands.

Less than a week later the old sorcerer came to the convent, and ordered Kaya brought to him. He stood, gnarled and frowning, in his black coat as the girl came to the door.

"It has been determined," he said, though he did not say by whom, "that tomorrow we shall be wed."

Kaya, who had not spoken to another human being since arriving at the convent, moved away from his words. She could find only one of her own in return.

"Kay," she said .

At the name, the sorcerer smiled, showing gray teeth beneath his mustache. "Kay cannot marry you."

"But we were promised to each other! Is he dead?"

The sorcerer's magic impelled him to the truth, but a strange truth, warped to his own purpose. "Not dead. But deeply changed, child. Changed beyond recognition. He does not want you as he is."

"He does not want me?"

"No."

Kaya began to weep and her old words tumbled between them. "I do not care. I want Kay. It was promised. It must be so."

The sorcerer was angry, but he could do no magic here, at the convent door. There was no way to stop the girl's tongue save in his own house in his own time.

"If Kay will not have me, no man will have me," said Kaya. "I shall become one of the nuns."

"You have been promised to me instead. I am to take Kay's place," said the old man, neglecting to mention that he himself was the one who had made the promise.

Kaya stopped crying. All her life she had been told about the power of promises. A promise given must be kept. She could not dismiss it lightly.

The sorcerer knew this. He saw his words working a subtle magic on Kaya's face. Seeing her consideration, he took it as acceptance. "The gift I sent, the carp. It should be nicely fatted by now. We shall have it today for our wedding feast."

Kaya looked clearly at the sorcerer for the first time. He stood before her playing idly with the iron button of his cloak. The threat behind his gentle tone was revealed by his casual cruelty to her fish. Suddenly she knew his promise for a lie. Still, she saw no way to escape him. So, to gain a little more time to think of a solution, she gave a lie in return.

"Tomorrow," she said.

"Tomorrow," said the old man, and left with a quick step.

Kaya waited until night, well past the hour of compline when the nuns spoke their last prayers in the candlelit chapel. Then, knowing the sisters were all asleep, Kaya rose and wrapped her cloak around her thin nightdress. She went out into the garden and stood by the abbess' pool.

"Fish," she called softly, "fish, come up."

The carp swam lazily to the surface. He never slept, but he lay for hours on the cool bottom of the pool. Although he was sleepless, he was not without dreams.

"*He* would marry me," said Kaya in a whisper."*He* would serve you for the wedding feast." And though she did not name the sorcerer in that holy place, the fish knew and shuddered.

"Do not fear, little friend," said the girl. "He shall have neither of us. I will drown you in the air and myself in the pool. This I promise. And we shall be together in Paradise."

She took off her cloak and laid it carefully under the tree, shivering slightly in the cool night air. Then she closed her eyes and reached for the fish that she had never dared touch before. It swam into her hands and lay there silently in her fingers. She pulled it out of the pool, and it neither gasped for air nor moved but shimmered silently in the moonlight.

"Ah, fish," said Kaya. "Would that I were your mate deep down in the abbess' pool." And she stroked the fish's damp head and, on a sudden notion, kissed it. "Farewell."

As she bent to put the fish on the cloak, it suddenly began to struggle and turn in her hands. She held it more firmly, but it kept struggling, and as it moved, it began to grow and change. Its scales sloughed off like little silver halos. Its tail cleaved in two. Its neck stretched and lengthened and on its head silken hair began to grow. It pulled free of her at last, a naked man.

Kaya leaped back and gave a little cry, and at her voice the sisters stirred in their cells and rose up by twos and threes. Kaya heard them coming to the convent garden, their steps sounding unnaturally loud in the stillness of the night.

Quickly Kaya bent down and picked up her cloak from beneath the tree and wrapped it around the man.

"Who are you?" she whispered, for his face was deep in the shadows.

But just as the nuns came to the garden, he turned his head and the moonlight fully lit his face.

"Kay!" she cried, and ran to his arms.

He smiled and embraced her but he said nothing in return. Though he was a man again, he still had no tongue to tell it.

A priest was summoned, and upon hearing their tale, married them at once by the pool with the old abbess nodding her agreement. So their promise was kept, and once they were joined in that holy place, the sorcerer and his magic could not come between them.

Kay never regained his speech. But Kaya, who had grown used to the wordless ways of the convent, was content. And the silence they shared throughout their long and loving life together was as variously shaded as speech.

MOTHER GOOSE'S MALADIES
OR: AREN'T YOU GLAD YOU ASKED?

1. The Knee
So pleased the goose can fly me about,
since with the titanium shaft
I have had since December last,
airports are a bother.
The women with wands need easier magic,
Their hands are rough and familiar.
But I sure could use a faster goose.
No—don't offer,
I have heard it all before.

2. The Back
Goose feather beds help,
but who can spend a life sleeping?
Only beauties, I suppose.
For me, sitting, standing are an imposition,
signing books an agony.
My mother always said
one must suffer for beauty,
but look what it got me.
Suffering for art comes with the territory,
ask any artist with arthritic fingers,
stooped backs, eyes that once
could see the wind
without the help of science

3. The Colon
If we hadn't be born with miles
of intestines, kinked, pocketed,
ready for an explosion;
that snake in the belly;
that oxbow tangle;
it would have taken a fairy tale writer
to invent them.
Or a poet.
Nothing rhymes with diverticulitis,
but pain.
You don't get it?
Wait a few years and you will.

4. Reflux
Old enough, famous enough
to buy the best chocolates,
the dryest wines
the finest champagnes,
yet I live on gruel.
God's little joke
But the goose relaxes.
Pates are no good for reflux, either.

5. Memory
I have forgotten names,
nouns,
how many kittens and
how many mittens,
where Jack met Jill,
Humpty's patronymic,
what Spratt and his Mrs eat,
how many blackbirds
get baked in a pie,
or mice run down
the cruel pendulum.
I have forgotten
all the cell phone numbers
of the children in the shoe.

I can no longer remember
the exact color
of a New England spring sky,
what to call the sun
passing its shadow across the moon,
the succession of colors in the rainbow,
and my grandchildren's birthdays.
But I remember some things.
I remember friendships.
I remember old loves.

6. The Old Gander
Speaking of old loves,
he's doing fine, thanks,
wandering all over creation,
wafting his wings together,
listening to bird song,
as if he understood it,
following little white balls
across a great expanse of green,
just for the walk.
The sauce is just for the gander.
Ma goose prefers to write.

Envoi:
What are maladies after all
but the body's old melodies
sung to a slower beat.
In the winter of my living,
I make my own heat,
dance my own dance,
fly high, holding my hat to my head.
And I can still carry a tune.

The White Seal Maid

On the north sea shore there was a fisherman named Merdock who lived all alone. He had neither wife nor child, nor wanted one. At least that was what he told the other men with whom he fished the haaf banks.

But truth was, Merdock was a lonely man, at ease only with the wind and waves. And each evening, when he left his companions, calling out "Fair wind!"—the sailor's leave—he knew they were going back to a warm hearth and a full bed while he went home to none. Secretly he longed for the same comfort.

One day it came to Merdock as if in a dream that be should leave off fishing that day and go down to the sea ledge and hunt the seal. He had never done such a thing before, thinking it close to murder, for the seal had human eyes and cried with a baby's voice.

Yet though he had never done such a thing, there was such a longing within him that Merdock could not say no to it. And that longing was like a high, sweet singing, a calling. He could not rid his mind of it. So he went.

Down by a gray rock he sat, a long sharpened stick by his side. He kept his eyes fixed out on the sea, where the white birds sat on the waves like foam.

He waited through sunrise and sunset and through the long, cold night, the singing in his head. Then, when the wind went down a bit, he saw a white seal far out in the sea, coming toward him, the moon riding on its shoulder.

Merdock could scarcely breathe as he watched the seal, so shining and white was its head. It swam swiftly to the sea ledge, and then with one quick push it was on land.

Merdock rose then in silence, the stick in his hand. He would have thrown it, too. But the white seal gave a sudden shudder and its skin sloughed off. It was a maiden cast in moonlight, with the tide about her feet.

She stepped high out of her skin, and her hair fell sleek and white about her shoulders and hid her breasts.

Merdock fell to his knees behind the rock and would have hidden his eyes, but her cold white beauty was too much for him. He could only stare. And if he made a noise then, she took no notice but turned her face to the sea and opened her arms up to the moon. Then she began to sway and call.

At first Merdock could not hear the words. Then he realized it was the very song he had heard in his head all that day:

> Come to the ledge,
> Come down to the ledge
> Where the water laps the shore.
>
> Come to the strand,
> Seals to the sand,
> The watery time is o'er.

When the song was done, she began it again. It was as if the whole beach, the whole cove, the whole world were nothing but that one song.

And as she sang, the water began to fill up with seals. Black seals and gray seals and seals of every kind. They swam to the shore at her call and sloughed off their skins. They were as young as the white seal maid, but none so beautiful in Merdock's eyes. They swayed and turned at her singing, and joined their voices to hers. Faster and faster the seal maidens danced, in circles of twos and threes and fours. Only the white seal maid danced alone, in the center, surrounded by the castoff skins of her twirling sisters.

The moon remained high almost all the night, but at last it went down. At its setting, the seal maids stopped their singing, put on their skins again, one by one, went back into the sea again, one by one, and swam away. But the white seal maid did not go. She waited on the shore until the last of them was out of sight.

Then she turned to the watching man, as if she had always known he was there, hidden behind the gray rock. There was something strange, a kind of pleading, in her eyes.

Merdock read that pleading and thought he understood it. He ran over to where she stood, grabbed up her sealskin, and held it high overhead.

"Now you be mine," he said.

And she had to go with him, that was the way of it. For she was a selchie, one of the seal folk. And the old tales said it: The selchie maid without her skin was no more than a lass.

They were wed within the week, Merdock and the white seal maid, because he wanted it. So she nodded her head at the priest's bidding, though she said not a word.

And Merdock had no complaint of her, his "Sel" as he called her. No complaint except this: she would not go down to the sea. She would not go down by the shore where he had found her or down to the sand to see him in his boat, though often enough she would stare from the cottage door out past the cove's end where the inlet poured out into the great wide sea.

"Will you not walk down by the water's edge with me, Sel?" Merdock would ask each morning.""Or will you not come down to greet me when I return?"

She had never answered him, neither "Yea" nor "Nay." Indeed, if he had not heard her singing that night on the ledge, he would have thought her mute. But she was a good wife, for all that, and did what he required. If she did not smile, she did not weep. She seemed, to Merdock, strangely content.

So Merdock hung the white sealskin up over the door where Sel could see it. He kept it there in case she should want to leave him, to don the skin and go. He could have hidden it or burned it, but he did not. He hoped the sight of it, so near and easy, would keep her with him; would tell her, as he could not, how much he loved her. For he found he did love her, his seal wife. It was that simple. He loved her and did not want her to go, but he would not keep her past her willing it, so he hung the skin up over the door.

And then their sons were born. One a year, born at the ebbing of the tide. And Sel sang to them, one by one, long, longing wordless songs that carried the sound of the sea. But to Merdock she said nothing.

Seven sons they were, strong and silent, one born each year. They were born to the sea, born to swim, born to let the tide lap them head and shoulder. And though they had the dark eyes of the seal, and though they had the seal's longing for the sea, they were men and had men's names; James, John, Michael, George, William, Rob, and Tom. They helped their father fish the cove and bring home his catch from the sea.

It was seven years and seven years and seven years again that the seal wife lived with him. The oldest of their sons was just coming to his twenty-first birthday, the youngest barely a man. It was on a gray day, the wind scarcely rising, that the boys all refused to go with Merdock when he called. They gave no reason but "Nay.""

"Wife," Merdock called, his voice heavy and gray as the sky. "Wife, whose sons are these? How have you raised them that they say 'Nay' to their father when he calls?" It was ever his custom to talk to Sel as if she returned his words.

To his surprise, Sel turned to him and said. "Go. My sons be staying with me this day." It was the voice of the singer on the beach, musical and low. And the shock was so great that he went at once and did not look back.

He set his boat on the sea, the great boat that usually took several men to row it. He set it out himself and got it out into the cove, put the nets over, and never once heard when his sons called out to him as he went, "Father, fair wind!"

But after a bit the shock wore thin and he began to think about it. He became angry then, at his sons and at his wife, who had long plagued him with her silence. He pulled in the nets and pulled on the oars and started toward home. "I, too, can say 'Nay' to this sea," he said out loud as he rode the swells in.

The beach was cold and empty. Even the gulls were mute.

"I do not like this," Merdock said. "It smells of a storm."

He beached the boat and walked home. The sky gathered in around him. At the cottage he hesitated but a moment, then pulled savagely on the door. He waited for the warmth to greet him. But the house was as empty and cold as the beach.

Merdock went into the house and stared at the hearth, black and silent. Then, fear riding in his heart, he turned slowly and looked over the door.

The sealskin was gone.

"Sel!" he cried then as he ran from the house, and he named his sons in a great anguished cry as be ran. Down to. the sea-ledge he went, calling their names like a prayer: "James, John, Michael, George, William, Rob, Tom!"

But they were gone.

The rocks were gray, as gray as the sky. At the water's edge was a pile of clothes that lay like discarded skins. Merdock stared out far across the cove and saw a seal herd swimming. Yet not a herd. A white seal and seven strong pups.

"Sel!" he cried again. "James, John, Michael, George, William, Rob, Tom!"

For a moment, the white seal turned her head, then she looked again to the open sea and barked out seven times. The wind carried the faint sounds back to the shore. Merdock heard, as if in a dream, the seven seal names she called. They seemed harsh and jangling to his ear.

Then the whole herd dove. When they came up again they were but eight dots strung along the horizon, lingering for a moment, then disappearing into the blue edge of sea.

Merdock recited the seven seal names to himself. And in that recitation was a song, a litany to the god of the seals. The names were no longer harsh, but right. And he remembered clearly again the moonlit night when the seals had danced upon the sand. Maidens all. Not a man or boy with them. And the white seal turning and choosing him, giving herself to him that he might give the seal people life.

His anger and sadness left him then, He turned once more to look at the sea and pictured his seven strong sons on their way.

He shouted their seal names to the wind. Then he added, under his breath, as if trying out a new tongue, "Fair wind, my sons. Fair wind."

SILENT BIANCA

Once far to the North, where the world is lighted only by the softly flickering snow, a strange and beautiful child was born.

Her face was like crystal with the features etched in. And she was called Bianca, a name that means "white," for her face was pale as snow and her hair was white as a moonbeam.

As Bianca grew to be a young woman, she never spoke as others speak. Instead her words were formed soundlessly into tiny slivers of ice. And if a person wanted to know what she was saying, he had to pluck her sentences out of the air before they fell to the ground or were blown away by the chilling wind. Then each separate word had to be warmed by the hearthfire until at last the room was filled with the delicate sounds of Bianca's voice. They were strange sounds and as fragile as glass.

At first many people came to see the maiden and to catch her words. For it was said that she was not only beautiful but wise as well.

But the paths to her hut were few. For the frost cut cruelly at every step. And it took so long to talk with Bianca that after a while, no one came to visit her at all.

Now it happened that the king of the vast country where Bianca lived was seeking a wife who was both beautiful and wise. But when he asked his council how to find such a bride, the councilors scratched their heads and stroked their beards and managed to look full of questions and answers at the same time.

"Can you do such a thing?" asked one. "Can you not do such a thing?" asked another. "How is it possible?" asked a third. And they spent a full day looking up to the ceiling and down to the floor and answering each question with another.

At last the king said, "Enough of this useless noise. I will find a way and I will find a woman. And the one who will be my bride will be filled with silence and still speak more wisdom than any of you."

At that the councilors left off talking and began to laugh. For it was well known that wisdom was to be found in things said, not in silence. And it was also known that no one—not even the king—was as wise as the members of the king's council.

But the king sent his most trusted servant, a gentle old painter named Piers, to the corners of the kingdom. Piers was to talk with all the maidens of noble birth. Then he was to bring back portraits of the most beautiful of these from which the king might choose a bride.

Piers traveled many days and weeks. He wearied himself in the great halls and draughty palaces listening to the chattering, nattering maidens who wanted to marry the king. At last, his saddlebags filled with their portraits and his mind packed with their prattle, he started for home.

On his way home from the cold lands, Piers became lost in a fierce snowstorm. He was forced to seek shelter in a nearby hut. It was the hut where Bianca made her home. Piers meant to stay but a single day. But one day whitened into a second and then a third. It was soon a week that the old man had remained there, talking to Bianca and warming her few words by the fire. He never told her who he was or what his mission. If she guessed, she never said. Indeed, in *not* saying lay much of her wisdom.

At last the storm subsided and Piers returned to the king's castle. In his saddlebags he carried large portraits of the most beautiful noble maidens in the kingdom. But the old man carried on a chain around his neck a miniature portrait of Bianca. She had become like a daughter to him. The thought of her was like a calm, cool breeze in the warmer lands where he lived.

When the day came for the king to make his choice, all of the king's council assembled in the Great Hall. Piers drew the large portraits from his saddlebags one by one and recalled what the maidens had spoken. The king and his council looked at the pictures and heard the words. And one by one they shook their heads.

As Piers bent to put the final portrait back into his pack, the chain with the miniature slipped out of his doublet. The king reached over and touched it. Then he held it up to the light and looked at the picture.

"Who is this?" he asked. "And why is this portrait smaller and set apart from the rest?"

Piers answered, "It is a maiden known as Bianca. She lives in the cold lands far to the North. She speaks in slivers that cut through lies." And he told them about the storm and how he had met the beautiful silent girl and discovered her great wisdom.

"This is the one I shall marry," said the king.

"It would be most improper," said the councilors together. "She is not noble-born."

"How does one judge nobility?" asked the king. "How does one measure it?"

The councilors scratched their heads and looked puzzled.""Can you do such a thing?" asked one. "Can you not do such a thing?" said another. "How is it possible?" asked a third. And they continued this way for some time.

At last the king silenced them with his hand. "Enough of this noise. I will make a measure. I will test the wisdom of this Silent Bianca," he said. And under his breath, he added, "And I will test *your* wisdom as well."

Then the king sent his council, with Piers to guide them, off to the cold lands to bring Bianca back to the throne.

Piers and the councilors traveled twenty days and nights until the stars fell like snow behind them and at last they came to the chilly land where Bianca made her home. There they packed up Bianca and her few belongings and immediately started back to the king.

But when they reached the road that ran around the castle, strange to say, they found their way blocked by soldiers. Campfires blossomed like flowers on the plain. At every turning and every straightaway stood a guard. It seemed there was no place where they could pass.

"This is very odd," said Piers. "There have never been soldiers here before. Could some unknown enemy have captured the castle while we were away?"

The councilors tried to question the guards, but none would answer. Not even a single question. Unused to silence, the councilors fell to puzzling among themselves. Some said one thing and some said another. They talked until the sun burned out behind them, but they could figure out no way to get beyond the guards and so bring Bianca to the king.

The air grew cold. The dark drew close. The councilors, weary with wondering, slept.

Only Bianca, who had said nothing all this time, remained awake. When she was certain that all the councilors were asleep, and even Piers was snoring gently, Bianca arose. Slowly she walked along the road that circled around the castle. Now and then she opened her mouth as if to scream or speak or sigh. But of course no sounds came out of her mouth at all. Then she would close it again, kneeling humbly when challenged by a silent guard's upraised spear. For the guards still spoke not a word but remained closemouthed at their posts.

And so from path to path, from guard to guard, from campfire to camp-fire, Bianca walked.

Just at dawn, she returned to the place where the councilors and Piers slept leaning on one another's shoulders like sticks stacked up ready for a fire.

As the sun flamed into the sky, a sudden strange babble was heard. At first it was like a single woman crying, calling, sobbing. Then, as the sun grew hotter and the morning cookfires were lit, it was as though a thousand women called to their men, wailing and sighing at each campfire and at every turning. It was the slivers of Bianca's voice which she had so carefully placed during her long night's walk; the slivers warmed and melted by the rising sun and the burning coals.

But the guards did not know this. And they looked around one way and another. Yet the only woman near them was Bianca, sitting silently, smiling, surrounded by Piers and the puzzled councilors.

And then, from somewhere beyond the guards, a chorus of women cried out. It was a cry like a single clear voice. "Come home, come home," called the women. "Leave off your soldiering. You need no arms but ours. Leave off your soldiering. No arms...no arms but ours."

The guards hesitantly at first, by ones and twos, and then joyfully by twenties and hundreds, threw down their weapons. Then they raced back home to their wives and sweethearts. For they were not really an unknown enemy at all but townsmen hired by the king to try the wisdom of the councilors and of Bianca.

When the councilors realized what Bianca had done, they brought her swiftly to the king. Instead of scratching their heads and looking puzzled, they spoke right out and said, "She is most certainly wise and more than fit for a king to marry."

The king, when he heard how Bianca had fooled the guards, laughed and laughed for he thought it a grand joke. And when he stopped laughing and considered the meaning of her words, he agreed she was indeed even wiser than old Piers had said.

So the king and Bianca were married.

And if the king had any problems thereafter, and his council could give him only questions instead of answers, he might be found at the royal hearthstone. There he could be seen warming his hands. But he was doing something more besides: He would be listening to the words that came from the fire and from the wise and loving heart of Silent Bianca, his queen.

THE RING AT YARROW

You take the pail,
I the jug,
and we will to Yarrow
where the fairies dance
all in a ring
by the burnside.

We will offer them the drink,
whiter than milk,
redder than blood,
sucked from the nipple
closest to the heart.

We will dance all night,
our shoen worn through,
the little bones sticking
through the sole
like thorns on a rose.

Their stained glass wings
beating above us,
they will hold our necks
in their icy hands;
they will pump us
like small koo.

Our mouths pricked with kisses,
sharper than serpent's bite,
sharper than gnats' teeth,
sharper than the venomed dart
of a southern tribe.

You take the pail,
I the jug,
And we will to Yarrow
this night and the next
and all the nights
till the moon burns down
behind our backs
and we leave our burnished bones as warning.

DREAM WEAVER

BROTHER HART
MAN OF ROCK, MAN OF STONE
THE TREE'S WIFE
THE CAT BRIDE
THE BOY WHO SANG FOR DEATH
PRINCESS HEART O'STONE
THE POT CHILD

"A penny, a penny, kind sir," cried the Dream Weaver as she sat at the bottom steps of the Great Temple. Her busy fingers worked the small hand loom. *"Just a penny for a woven dream."*

The King of Beggars passed her by. He had no time for dream weaving. It was too gossamer, too fragile. He believed in only one dream, that which would fill his belly. He would not part with his penny for any other. Gathering his rags around him, a movement he considered his answer, he went on.

The old Dream Weaver continued her wail. It was a chant, an obeisance she made to every passer-by. She did not see the King of Beggars' gesture for she was blind. Her sightless eyes stared only into the future, and she wove by the feel of the strands.

New footsteps came to the Dream Weaver's ear. Her hand went out.

"A penny, a penny, young miss." She knew by the sound there was a girl approaching, for the step was light and dancing.

"Oh, yes, buy me a dream," the girl said, calling over her shoulder to the boy who followed.

The Weaver did not speak again. She knew better than to wheedle. The girl was already caught in her desire. The young so loved to dream. The Weaver knew the penny would come.

"I do not know if I should," said the boy. His voice was hesitant, yet pleased to be asked.

"Of course you should," said the girl. Then her voice dropped, and she moved close to him. "Please."

His hand went immediately to his pocket and drew out the coin.

Hearing the movement, the Dream Weaver cupped her right hand. "A dream for a beautiful young woman," she said in a flattering voice, though to her all the young were beautiful.

"How do you know?" It was the girl in surprise.

"She is beautiful," said the boy. "There is no one as beautiful in the whole world. She has my heart." His words were genuine, but the girl shrugged away his assurances.

The Weaver had already taken threads from her basket and strung the warp while the boy was speaking. And this was the dream that she wove across the strands.

Brother Hart

Deep in a wood, so dark and tangled few men dared enter it, there was a small clearing. And in that clearing lived a girl and her brother Hart.

By day, in his deer shape, Brother Hart would go out and forage on green grass and budlings while his sister remained at home.

But whenever dusk began, the girl Hinda would go to the edge of the clearing and call out in a high, sweet voice:

> Dear heart, Brother Hart,
> Come at my behest.
> We shall dine on berry wine
> And you shall have your rest.

Then, in his deer heart, her brother would know the day's enchantment was at an end and run swiftly home. There, at the lintel over the cottage door, he would rub between his antlers until the hide on his forehead broke bloodlessly apart. He would rub and rub further still until the brown hide skinned back along both sides and he stepped out a naked man.

His sister would take the hide and shake it out and brush and comb it until it shone like polished wood. Then she hung the hide up by the antlers beside the door, with the legs dangling down. It would hang there until the morning when Brother Hart donned it once again and raced off to the lowland meadows to graze.

What spell or sorcerer had brought them there, deep in the wood, neither could recall. Their faces mirrored one another, and their lives were twinned. Their memories, like the sorcerer, had vanished. The woods, the meadow, the clearing, the deer hide, the cottage door, were all they knew.

Now one day in late spring, Brother Hart had gone as usual to the lowland meadows, leaving Hinda at home. She had washed and scrubbed the little cottage until it was neat and clean. She had put new straw in their bedding. But as she stood by the window brushing out her long dark hair, an unfamiliar sound greeted her ears: a loud, harsh calling, neither bird nor jackal nor good gray wolf.

Again and again the call came. So Hinda went to the door, for she feared nothing in the wood. And who should come winded to the cottage but Brother Hart. He had no words to tell her in his deer form, but blood beaded his head like a crown. It was the first time she had ever seen him bleed. He pushed past her and collapsed, shivering, on their bed.

Hinda ran over to him and would have bathed him with her tears, but the jangling noise called out again, close and insistent. She ran to the window to see.

There was a man outside in the clearing. At least she thought it was a man. Yet he did not look like Brother Hart, who was the only man she knew.

He was large where Brother Hart was slim. He was fair where Brother Hart was dark. He was hairy where Brother Hart was smooth. And he was dressed in animal skins that hung from his shoulders to his feet. About the man leaped fawning wolves, some spotted like jackals, some tan and some white. He pushed them from him with a rough sweep of his hand.

"I seek a deer," he called when he glimpsed Hinda's face, a pale moon, at the window.

But when Hinda came out of the door, closing it behind her to hide what lay inside, the man did not speak again. Instead he took off his fur hat and laid it upon his heart, kneeling down before her.

"Who are you?" asked Hinda. "What are you? And why do you seek the deer?" Her voice was gentle but firm.

The man neither spoke nor rose but stared at her face.

"Who are you?" Hinda asked again. "Say what it is you are."

As if she had broken a spell, the man spoke at last. "I am but a man," he said. "A man who has traveled far and who has seen much, but never a beauty such as yours."

"If it *is* beauty, and beauty is what you prize, you shall not see it again," said Hinda. "For a man who hunts the deer can be no friend of mine."

The man rose then, and Hinda marveled at the height of him, for he was as tall as the cottage door and his hands were grained like wood.

"Then I shall hunt the deer no more," he said, "if you will give me leave to hunt that which is now all at once dearer to me."

"And what is that?"

"You, dear heart," he said, reaching for her. Startled, Hinda moved away from him, but remembering her brother inside the cottage, found voice to say, "Tomorrow." She reached behind her and steadied herself on the door handle. She thought she heard the heavy breathing of Brother Hart through the walls. "Come tomorrow."

"I shall surely come." He bowed, turned, and then was gone, walking swiftly, a man's stride, through the woods. His animals were at his heels.

Hinda's eyes followed him down the path until she counted even the shadows of trees as his own. When she was certain he was gone, she opened the cottage door and went in. The cottage was suddenly close and dark, filled with the musk of deer.

Brother Hart lay on their straw bed. When he looked up at her, Hinda could not bear the twin wounds of his eyes. She turned away and said, "You may go out now. It is safe. He will not hunt you again."

The deer rose heavily to his feet, nuzzled open the door, and sprang away to the meadows.

But he was home again at dark.

When he stepped out of his skin and entered the cottage, he did not greet his sister with his usual embrace. Instead he said, "You did not call me to the clearing. You did not say my name. Only when I was tired and the sun had almost gone, did I know it was time to come home."

Hinda could not answer. She could not even look at him. For even more than his words, his nakedness suddenly shamed her. She put their food on the table and they ate their meal in silence. Then they lay down together and slept without dreams like the wild creatures of the wood.

When the sun called Brother Hart to his deerskin once again, Hinda opened the door. Silently she ushered him outside, silently watched him change, and sent him off on his silent way to the meadows without word of farewell. Her thoughts were on the hunter, the man of the wolves. She never doubted he would come.

And come he did, neither silently nor slowly, but with loud purposeful steps. He stood for a moment at the clearing's edge, looking at Hinda, measuring her with his eyes. Then he smiled and crossed to her.

He stayed all the day with her and taught her wonders she had never known. He told her tales of kingdoms she had never seen. He sang songs she had never heard before, singing them softly into her ears. He spoke again and again of his love for her, but he touched no more than her hand.

"You are as innocent as any creature in the woods," he said over and over in amazement.

So passed the day.

Suddenly it was dusk, and Hinda looked up with a start. "You must go now," she said.

"Nay, I must stay."

"No, no, you must go," Hinda said again. "I cannot have you here at night. If you love me, go." Then she added softly, her dark eyes on his, "But come again in the morning."

Her sudden fear puzzled him, but it also touched him, so he stood and smoothed down the skins of his coat. "I will go. But I will return."

He whistled his animals to him, and left the clearing as swiftly as he had come.

Hinda would have called after him then, called after and made him stay, but she did not even know his name. So she went instead to the clearing's edge and cried:

> Dear heart, Brother Hart,
> Come at my bidding.
> We shall dine on berry wine
> And dance at my wedding.

And hearing her voice, Brother Hart raced home.

He stopped at the clearing's edge, raised his head, and sniffed. The smell of man hung on the air, heavy and threatening. He came through it as if through a swift current, and stepped to the cottage door.

Rubbing his head more savagely than ever on the lintel, as if to rip off his thoughts with his hide, Brother Hart removed his skin.

"The hunter was here," he said as he crossed the threshold of the door.

"He does not seek you," Hinda replied.

"You will not see him again. You will tell him to go."

"I see him for your sake," said Hinda. "If he sees me, he does not see you. If he hunts me, he does not hunt you. I do it for you, brother dear."

Satisfied, Brother Hart sat down to eat. But Hinda was not hungry. She served her brother and watched as he ate his fill.

"You should sleep," she said when he was done. "Sleep, and I will rub your head and sing to you."

"I *am* tired," he answered. "My head aches where yesterday he struck me. My heart aches still with the fear. I tremble all over. You are right. I should sleep."

So he lay down on the bed and Hinda sat by him. She rubbed cinquefoil on his head to soothe it and sang him many songs, and soon Brother Hart was asleep.

When the moon lit the clearing, the hunter returned. He could not wait until the morning. Hinda's fear had made him afraid, though he had never known fear before. He dared not leave her alone in the forest. But he moved quietly as a beast in the dark. He left his dogs behind.

The cottage in the clearing was still except for a breath of song, wordless and longing, that floated on the air. It was Hinda's voice, and when the hunter heard it, he smiled for she was singing a tune he had taught her.

He moved out into the clearing, more boldly now. Then suddenly he stopped. He saw a strange shape hanging by the cottage door. It was a deerskin, a fine buck's hide, hung by the antlers and the legs dangling down.

Caution, an old habit, claimed him. He circled the clearing, never once making a sound. He approached the cottage from the side, and Hinda's singing led him on. When he reached the window, he peered in.

Hinda was sitting on a low straw bed, and beside her, his head in her lap, lay a man. The man was slim and naked and dark. His hair was long and straight and came to his shoulders. The hunter could not see his face, but he lay in sleep like a man who was no stranger to the bed.

The hunter controlled the shaking of his hands, but he could not control his heart. He allowed himself one moment of fierce anger. With his knife he thrust a long gash on the left side of the deerskin that hung by the door. Then he was gone.

In the cottage Brother Hart cried out in his sleep, a swift sharp cry. His hand went to his side and suddenly, under his heart, a thin red line like a knife's slash appeared. It bled for a moment. Hinda caught his hand up in hers and at the sight of the blood she grew pale. It was the second time she had seen Brother Hart bleed.

She got up without disturbing him and went to the cupboard where she found a white linen towel. She washed the wound with water. The cut was long, but it was not deep. Some scratch he had got in the woods perhaps. She knew it would heal before morning. So she lay down beside him and fitted her body to the curve of his back. Brother Hart stirred slightly but did not waken. Then Hinda, too, fell asleep.

In the morning Brother Hart rose, but his movements were slow. "I wish I could stay," he said to his sister. "I wish this enchantment were at an end."

But the rising sun summoned him outside. He donned the deerskin and leaped away.

Hinda stood at the door and raised her hand to shade her eyes. The last she saw of him was the flash of white tail as he sped off into the woods.

She did not go back into the cottage to clean. She stood waiting for the hunter to come. Her eyes and ears strained for the signs of his approach. There were none.

She waited through the whole of the long morning, until the sun was high overhead. Not until then did she go indoors, where she threw herself down on the straw bedding and wept.

At dusk the sun began to fade and the cottage darkened. Hinda got up. She went to the clearing's edge and called:

> Dear heart, Brother Hart,
> Come at my crying.
> We shall dine on berry wine
> And...

But she got no further. A loud sound in the woods stayed her. It was too heavy for a deer. And when the hunter stepped out of the woods on the very path that Brother Hart usually took, Hinda gave a gasp, part delight, part fear.

"You have come," she said, and her voice trembled.

The hunter searched her face with his eyes but could not find what he was seeking. He walked past her to the cottage door. Hinda followed behind him, uncertain.

"I have come," he said. His back was to her. "I wish to God I had not."

"What do you mean?"

"I sought the deer today," he said.

Hinda's hand went to her mouth.

"I sought the deer today. And what I seek, I find." He did not turn. "We ran him long, my dogs and I. When he was at bay, he fought hard. I gave the beast's liver and heart to my dogs. But this I saved for you."

He held up his hands then, and a deerskin unrolled from it. With a swift, savage movement, he tacked it to the door with his knife. The hooves did not quite touch the ground.

Hinda could see two slashes in the hide, one on each side, under the heart. The slash on the left was an old wound, crusted but clean. The slash on the right was new, and from it blood still dripped.

She leaned forward and touched the wound with her hand, tears in her eyes. "Oh, my dear Brother Hart," she cried. "It was because of me you died. Now your enchantment *is* at an end."

The hunter whirled around to face her then. "He was your brother?" he asked.

She nodded. "He was my heart." Looking straight at him, she added, "We were one at birth. What was his is mine by right." Her chin was up, and her head held high. She reached past the hunter and pulled the knife from the door with an ease that surprised him. Gently she took down the skin. She shook it out once, and smoothed the nap with her hand. Then, as if putting on a cloak, she wrapped the skin around her shoulders and pulled the head over her own.

As the hunter watched, she began to change. It was as if he saw a rippled reflection in a pool coming slowly into focus: slim brown legs, brown haunch, brown body and head. The horns shriveled and fell to the ground. Only her eyes remained the same.

The doe looked at the hunter for a moment more. A single tear started in her eye, but before it had time to fall, she turned, sprang away into the fading light, and was gone.

The dream was finished. The Weaver's hand stopped.

"I would have kept them both," said the girl. "No need to lose one man for another."

"You will never lose me," the boy said quickly, with such yearning in his voice that the Dream Weaver knew he would never have this girl.

"Never," said the girl. "It was a foolish dream. Not even worth the penny."

"I thought it moving," said the boy in a whisper to the Dream Weaver as the girl moved off. "I felt the slash under my heart." His voice broke on the last word. Then he turned and followed the girl.

The Dream Weaver listened to them go, the girl's steps always a bit faster, always anticipating the boy's.

She ripped the skein from the loom and finished it off, putting the fabric in a bag by her side. She sent out a sigh into the air. "People never want to keep their dreams," she said to herself, patting the bag. "I wonder why?"

She heard a carriage come around the corner, the horses blowing gustily through their noses. A heavy carriage by the sound, and rich, for there were four horses. The carriage stopped near the Dream Weaver's place. Her hand went up at once, and her cry began again: "A penny, a penny, a penny for a dream."

An old couple stepped out of the landau. They were richly dressed in the brightest of colors, as if reds and golds could deny their years. Though the woman put her hand on the man's arm to be steadied, there was no warmth for either of them in the touch. And when they talked, as they did for a moment in sharp angry bursts, they did not look into one another's eyes but always stared an inch or two away, concentrating on the collarbone, on a lock of hair, on the lines etched in the forehead.

They would have passed by the Dream Weaver, but the old woman stumbled. The Dream Weaver heard the faulty step and put her raised hand up to help.

In a swift, practiced movement, the man reached into his pocket and paid off the Dream Weaver, as if she were a beggar in the street.

"Please, sir," said the Dream Weaver, for the touch of his hand told her that he was a man; the size of the coin, his peerage. "Please, sir, for the coin, let me weave you a dream."

"We have no time for such mystic nonsense," the man began. Impatiently he looked up at the Great Temple and shook his head.

"It takes but a moment in the weaving, a moment in the telling, but it is beyond time for it will last forever," said the Dream Weaver.

The old man glanced at the sky, judging the time once more, and clicked his tongue. "Forever?" he said, and hesitated.

"A moment," said the Dream Weaver, counting his hesitation as consent. Her fingers scuttled over the warp, and this was the dream that she wove.

Man of Rock, Man of Stone

There was once a quarrier named Craig, who worked stone down in a pit. Stone before him and stone behind, he labored each day from dark to dark. He was a tall man and broad, a mountain working a mountain. The years of his pit work were printed in dust upon his face and grained in the backs of his hands.

He worked alone and spoke not even to himself, except to curse the sun when it shone full upon him or when it did not. And the habit of silence and curses was as engrained in him as the dust.

At home he was like the rocks of his quarry: silent, unmoving, stolid before anyone who would weather him. He was a man of stone.

He had married a woman who was soft where he was hard, and moved by every tenderness he had forgotten. She never gave up trying to water him with her tears as if he were a plant capable of growth. But he was not. He was a man of stone.

Only in the quarry, under the hot eye of the sun, did he take on a semblance of life. There, his hammer above him, he would suck in a breath of dust, then ram the hammer down, expelling dust from his lungs. He took great pride in the sweat that ran down the solid line of his back and stained his clothes, proof of the life within him.

But when the sun went down, life ended for him. He would pack his hammer and chisels into a grayed and cracked satchel and go home.

"Wife," he would call at the door as if he had forgotten her name or thought it too soft for his lips, "I'd eat."

His wife had a name, as soft and pliant as the memory of her youth that still hovered about her lips: Cybele. But if she thought of herself at all now, it was as Wife. The rest was gone.

She had been given to the quarrier by her father, one stone gifting another. She was to keep Craig's house, to feed him, and to warm his bed, no more. Her tears at the time had moved neither of them. That was the way of it. And if late at night, lying by the unmoving mound of her husband, she dreamed of green meadows and a child touched by the wind, it was a fancy spun into an unheeding night. There were no meadows, no green, no child.

Her life was bounded by her husband and her house. There was a hardscrabble garden she tended with little success. Only occasionally would brown plants push through the slate, their roots digging shallow graves in the pumice. And Cybele clung, like tender moss, to the outer edge of the man of stone.

All she had ever wanted was a child, but she had dared ask only twice before his silence and his anger overwhelmed her wish.

The first time she asked was the night they were married. Her hand had been transferred from father to husband before the cold eye of the celibate priest. Craig's hand was hard in hers, the knuckles on it rose like hills of flint. She had put her mouth on those hills to quicken them. She looked up at him, her eyes brimming over. "Will we make a child tonight?" she had wondered aloud, a bridal wish.

"No child," he growled. "I'll have no child." It was a statement, not a guess.

Months later, when she knew him and had only started to fade into hopelessness, she had tried again.

"With a child between us," she began.

But he gnawed at the words. "No child."

So the years were all that they shared between them; and sorrow was all she bore.

There might never have been a third time if a false spring had not brought a gentle wind to their house. Cybele startled a brown bird off its nest. There were two small graying eggs. The bird did not return, and so finally, fearfully, she brought the eggs inside and tried to hatch them near the fire. But the eggs turned cold before the day's end. She cracked the eggs open and found the unborn chicks inside, their dead bodies only partially formed. Blind membraned eyes seemed to stare up at her. She buried them under a stone in the garden, afraid she might otherwise have to feed them to Craig.

But she dreamed of the birds in her sleep and cried out: "The children."

It woke Craig, and he in turn woke her.

They sat up in the bed, staring at one another in the half-light of dawn. "Children?" he asked. "What children?"

"It was a dream," she replied.

"I said there would be no children," Craig said, his voice rising to a shout.

She shrugged and turned from him. "A stone cannot make a child."

"You scorn the stone? The stone that gives me a living? The stone that gives us a life?"

Her back to him, she lay down again and said, "I do not scorn the stone that is your work, but *you* who are stone instead of man. And a man of stone cannot make a child."

"You think I am incapable of making a child? I *shall* make one," he said, leaping out of the bed. "But not with you. No, I shall make a child of stone." He dressed himself in silence, picked up his tools, and went from the house.

The silence after his leaving struck Cybele like a blow. She had never heard so many words from him at one time. She had never spoken so many in return. She feared her words had damaged him beyond healing, had shattered something inside him that would not come right again. She dressed in the darkness of the house and went outside into the dawn.

She had never been to the quarry before. Indeed she was not even sure of the way. Craig had made it clear that the quarry was his and the house hers. But she followed a path she had often seen him take and came within minutes to the place where he worked.

The quarry was lit by both the setting moon and the rising sun. No shadows yet marked its face. It stood waiting for the touch of Craig's hammer, waiting to submit to each blow.

Craig had set to work at once. His first angry strokes had been so quick, they seemed random, unplanned, a cleaving of rock and rock. But as his anger drained from him and his body took up the rhythm of his work again, a rough shape began to emerge from the quarry wall.

He had thought to make a child of stone, but the hammer had chosen differently. In all his life he had never really looked at a child, so the form that came from the stone was as tall as a man and as broad.

Once the form was wrested from the rock, Craig took out his finer chisels. Using his own body as a model, he shaped each nail, each muscle, each hair in the rock. Only the face he left blank.

The sun traveled overhead. His wife watched silently, unheeded, by a tree at the quarry's edge.

Craig worked without stopping, shaping the rock to his will. He breathed heavily, and the rock dust swirled about him, rising and falling with each breath.

The sun struck its zenith and went down. Craig wiped the sweat from his eyes, felt the sweat running down his arms and legs, collecting in his body's cracks, and pooling in his hair.

Before him the man of rock stood faceless but otherwise complete. Only one cord of rock attached the figure to the quarry's side.

Craig stood tall, the hammer in his hand. He drew in a deep breath and threw out his chest. His lungs ached with the effort. He felt a wild exaltation. With a cry, he brought the hammer full force on the fragile link between rock and rock.

"*Aiee,*" he called, "my son!"

The faceless man of rock shuddered with the releasing blow. It seemed as if the figure itself might shatter.

Craig shook his head free of the sweat which clouded his eyes. Drops spattered the rock form. It stumbled forward, caught itself, stood upright, then turned its blank face towards Craig. It raised its arms in supplication.

The movement frightened Craig. He was not prepared for it. He raised the hammer once again, this time to shatter the man of rock.

"Oh, no," cried Cybele from the quarry's edge. "He is your son."

Craig turned at the sound, and the man of rock readied out and wrested the hammer from his grasp. With a silent shout it brought the hammer down.

Craig fell, face into the earth, and lay like a pile of jumbled stones.

The man of rock stood still for a moment. Then he turned his head toward the sky, blindly seeking light. The risen moon cast shadowly features on his face. Raising his fingers to his head, the man of rock engraved those shadows onto the blank: eyes, nose, a firm slash of mouth. Then he bent over and picked up the rest of Craig's tools. When he straightened again, he looked over at the piles of stones, crumpled and unmoving, on the quarry floor.

"*Aieee,* my father," he whispered into the silence. In his new eyes were the beginnings of tears.

He turned and saw Cybele, standing on the path.

"Mother?" he asked. She said nothing, but smiled, and that smile drew him surely into her waiting arms.

As the woman listened to the dream, her hand smoothed the sides of her dress with long strokes. At dream's end, she looked up at her husband and tried to reach his eyes with hers. A smile trembled uncertainly on her lips.

He looked for a moment down at her: then his eyes slid away from hers. "You can't mean you believe such childish tales? There is no man, no woman, no rock, no stone. There is no truth in it. It was a waste of time, and time is the only truth in this world that one can be sure of. Come, we are late." He held out his arm.

Hand upon arm, they walked up the steps toward the Great Temple and left the dream behind.

Hearing them go, the Dream Weaver shook her head. She finished off the dream and put it in the bag. The morning sun was warm on her face. She folded her hands before her and almost slept.

"I want a dream!" The voice was a man's, harsh and insistent. She had heard it many times before, but in her half-sleep his remembered footsteps had merged with the sounds of the day. "I have your money, old woman. Give me a good one."

"Just a penny," said the Dream Weaver, rousing herself.

"It is a five-penny piece," said the man. "For that I expect something special."

The Weaver sighed. The man came nearly every week with the same request. Five pennies for a one-penny dream. Yet he was never happy with the result. She pulled new threads from her basket and began.

In a village that sat well back in a quiet valley, there lived an old woman and the last of her seven sons. The others had gone to join the army as they came of age, and the only one left at home was a lad named Karl.

Even if he had not been her last, his mother would have loved him best for he had a sweet disposition and a sweeter voice. It was because of that voice, pure and clear, that caroled like spring birds, that she had called him Karel. But his brothers, fearing the song name would unman him, had changed it to Karl. So Karl he had remained.

"No," said the man harshly. "I do not like it. I can see already it is not the dream for me. I am no singer, no minstrel. I am a man of consequence."

"But you must wait until it is done," said the Dream Weaver. "Dreams are not finished until the very end. They change. They flow. They have undercurrents. Perhaps it is not a story about singing at all. How can you know?"

"I know enough," said the man. "I do not want to hear more."

The Dream Weaver felt the wool snarl under her fingers. She sighed.

"I would have given five pennies for a good dream," said the man. "But that is only the smallest part of a dream, and not a good dream at that." He threw a small coin at the Dream Weaver's feet.

"It is enough," said the old woman, finding the penny with her fingers. And then, to the man's back as his footsteps hurried away from her, she added, "Enough for me. But what is enough for you?" She finished off the fragment with knowing fingers and put it with the others in her pack.

She stretched then, carefully, but did not arise. It was a good place that she had, by the steps. People passed it all the time. She did not want someone else to take it.

Raising her face to the sun, she would have fallen into that half sleep which age so easily granted her, when a sound down the walkway stopped her. She put her hand out again and took up her call: "A penny, a penny, a penny for a dream."

A young woman, tall and slim, dressed in black, came slowly toward the steps. She held a child by the hand. As they neared the Dream Weaver, the old woman called out again, "A penny for a dream."

The child, also in black, strained at his mother's hand. At the Dream Weaver's call, he turned in surprise to look up at his mother. "You said all the dreams were dead. How can they be if this granny can make a new one? And just for a penny."

"Child," his mother began painfully. Her hand moved her black veil aside, and she looked at the Dream Weaver with swollen eyes. Dropping the veil again, she repeated, "Child."

"But I have a penny, Mother. Here." The child's hand dug into his pocket and emerged with a sticky coin. "Please."

The veiled head looked down, shook slowly once, twice; but still the woman took the coin. Handing it to he Dream Weaver cautiously, she said, "Weave us a dream, granny, for the boy and me. But I pray that it is a gentle one, full of loving."

The Dream Weaver took the coin, making it disappear in her robes. Then she settled herself to the task. Her hands flew over the loom, and she plucked the strings as if she were a musician, her fingers gentle yet strong. And this was the dream that she wove.

The Tree's Wife

There was once a young woman named Drusilla who had been widowed longer than she was wed. She had been married at fifteen to a rich old man who beat her. She had flowered despite his ill treatment, and it was he who died, within the year, leaving her all alone in the great house.

Once the old man was dead, his young widow was courted by many, for she was now quite wealthy. The young men came together, and all claimed that she needed a husband to help her.

But Drusilla would have none of them. "When I was poor," she said, "not one of you courted me. When I was ill treated, not one of you stood by me. I never asked for more than a gentle word, yet I never received one. So now that you ask, I will have none of you."

She turned her back on them, then stopped. She looked around at the grove of birch trees by her house. "Why, I would sooner wed this tree," she said, touching a sturdy birch that stood to one side, "A tree would know when to bend and when to stand. I would sooner wed this tree than marry another man."

At that very moment, a passing wind caused the top branches of the birch to sway.

The rejected suitors laughed at Drusilla. "See," they jeered, "the tree has accepted your offer."

And so she was known from that day as the Tree's Wife.

To keep the jest from hurting, Drusilla entered into it with a will. If someone came to the house, she would put her arms around the birch, caressing its bark and stroking its limbs.

"I have all I need or want with my tree," she would say. And her laugh was a silent one back at the stares. She knew that nothing confounds jokers as much as madness, so she made herself seem very mad for them.

But madness also makes folk uneasy; they fear contagion. And soon Drusilla found herself quite alone. Since it was not of her choosing, the aloneness began to gnaw at her. It was true that what she really wanted was just a kind word, but soon she was so lonely almost any word would have done.

So it happened one night, when the moon hung in the sky like a ripe yellow apple, that a wind blew fiercely from the north. It made the trees bow and bend and knock their branches against Drusilla's house. Hearing them knock, she looked out of the windows and saw the trees dancing wildly in the wind.

They seemed to beckon and call, and she was suddenly caught up in their rhythm. She swayed with them, but it was not enough. She longed for the touch of the wind on her skin, so she ran outside, leaving the door ajar. She raised her hands above her head and danced with the trees.

In the darkness, surrounded by the shadow of its brothers, one tree seemed to shine. It was her tree, the one she had chosen. It was touched with a phosphorescent glow, and the vein of each leaf was a streak of pale fire.

Drusilla danced over to the tree and held her hands toward it. "Oh, if only you *were* a man, or I a tree," she said out loud. "If you were a man tall and straight and gentle and strong then—yes—then I would be happy."

The wind died as suddenly as it had begun, and the trees stood still. Drusilla dropped her hands, feeling foolish and shamed, but a movement in the white birch stayed her. As she watched, it seemed to her that first two legs, then a body, then a head and arms emerged from the bark; a shadowy image pulling itself painfully free of the trunk. The image shimmered for a moment, trembled, and then became clear. Before her stood a man.

He was tall and slim, with skin as white as the bark of the birch and hair as black as the birch bark patches. His legs were strong yet supple, and his feet were knotty and tapered like roots. His hands were thin and veined with green, and the second and third fingers grew together, slotted like a leaf. He smiled at her and held out his arms, an echo of her earlier plea, and his arms swayed up and down as if touched by a passing breeze.

Drusilla stood without movement, without breath. Then he nodded his head, and she went into his arms. When his mouth came down on hers, she smelled the damp woody odor of his breath.

They lay together all night below his tree, cradled in its roots. But when the sun began its climb against the farthest hills, the man pulled himself reluctantly from Drusilla's arms and disappeared back into the tree.

Call as she might, Drusilla could not bring him out again, but one of the tree branches reached down and stroked her arm in a lover's farewell.

She spent the next days under the tree, reading and weaving and playing her lute. And the tree itself seemed to listen and respond. The branches touched and turned the pages of her book. The whole tree moved to the beauty of her songs.

Yet it was not until the next full moon that the man could pull himself from the tree and sleep away the dark in her arms.

Still Drusilla was content. For as she grew in her love for the man of the tree, her love for all nature grew, a quiet pullulation. She felt kin to every flower and leaf. She heard the silent speech of the green world and, under the bark, the beating of each heart.

One day, when she ventured into the village, Drusilla's neighbors observed that she was growing more beautiful in her madness. The boldest of them, an old woman, asked, "If you have no man, how is it you bloom?"

Drusilla turned to look at the old woman and smiled. It was a slow smile. "I am the tree's wife," she said, "in truth. And he is man enough for me." It was all the answer she would return.

But in the seventh month since the night of the apple moon, Drusilla knew she carried a child, the tree's child, below her heart. And when she told the tree of it, its branches bent around her and touched her hair. And when she told the man of it, he smiled and held her gently.

Drusilla wondered what the child would be that rooted in her. She wondered if it would burgeon into a human child or emerge some great wooden beast. Perhaps it would be both, with arms and legs as strong as the birch and leaves for hair. She feared her heart would burst with questions. But on the next full moon, the tree man held her and whispered in her ear such soft, caressing sounds, she grew calm. And at last she knew that however the child grew, she would love it. And with that knowledge she was once again content.

Soon it was evident, even to the townsfolk, that she blossomed with child. They looked for the father among themselves—for where else *could* they look—but no one admitted to the deed. And Drusilla herself would name no one but the tree to the midwife, priest, or mayor.

And so, where at first the villagers had jested at her and joked with her and felt themselves plagued by her madness, now they turned wicked and cruel. They could accept a widow's madness but not a mother unwed.

The young men, the late suitors, pressed on by the town elders, came to Drusilla one night. In the darkness, they would have pulled her from her house and beaten her. But Drusilla heard them come and climbed through the window and fled to the top of the birch.

The wind raged so that night that the branches of the tree flailed like whips, and not one of the young men dared come close enough to climb the tree and take Drusilla down. All they could do was try and wound her with their words. They shouted up at her where she sat near the top of the birch, cradled in its branches. But she did not hear their shouts. She was lulled instead by the great rustling voices of the grove.

In the morning the young men were gone. They did not return.

And Drusilla did not go back into the town. As the days passed, she was fed by the forest and the field. Fruits and berries and sweet sap found their way to her doorstep. Each morning she had enough for the day. She did not ask where it all came from, but still she knew.

At last it was time for the child to be born. On this night of a full moon, Drusilla's pains began. Holding her sides with slender fingers, she went out to the base of the birch, sat down, and leaned her back against the tree, straining to let the child out. As she pushed, the birch man pulled himself silently from the tree, knelt by her, and breathed encouragements into her face. He stroked her hair and whispered her name to the wind.

She did not smile up at him but said at last, "Go." Her breath was ragged and her voice on the edge of despair. "I beg you. Get the midwife. This does not go well."

The tree man held her close, but he did not rise.

"Go," she begged. "Tell her my name. It is time."

He took her face in his hands and stared long into it with his woods-green eyes. He pursed his lips as if to speak, then stood up and was gone.

He went down the path towards the town, though each step away from the tree drew his strength from him. Patches of skin peeled off as he moved, and the sores beneath were dark and viscous. His limbs grew more brittle with each step, and he moved haltingly. By the time he reached the midwife's house, he looked an aged and broken thing. He knocked upon the door, yet he was so weak, it was only a light tapping, a scraping, the scratching of a branch across a window pane.

As if she had been waiting for his call, the midwife came at once. She opened the door and stared at what stood before her. Tall and thin and naked and white, with black patches of scabrous skin and hair as dark as rotting leaves, the tree man held up his grotesque, slotted hand. The gash of his mouth was hollow and tongueless, a sap-filled wound. He made no sound, but the midwife screamed and screamed, and screaming still, slammed the door.

She did not see him fall.

In the morning the townsfolk came to Drusilla's great house. They came armed with clubs and cudgels and forks. The old midwife was in the rear, calling the way.

Beneath a dead white tree they found Drusilla, pale and barely moving, a child cradled in her arms. At the townsfolk's coming, the child opened its eyes. They were the color of winter pine.

"Poor thing," said the midwife, stepping in front of the men. "I knew no good would come of this." She bent to take the child from Drusilla's arms but leaped up again with a cry. For the child had uncurled one tiny fist, and its hand was veined with green and the second and third fingers grew together, slotted like a leaf.

At the midwife's cry, the birches in the grove began to move and sway, though there was not a breath of breeze. And before any weapon could be raised, the nearest birch stretched its branches far out and lifted the child and Drusilla up, up towards the top of the tree.

As the townsfolk watched, Drusilla disappeared. The child seemed to linger for a moment longer, its unclothed body gleaming in the sun. Then slowly the child faded, like melting snow on pine needles, like the last white star of morning, into the heart of the tree.

There was a soughing as of wind through branches, a tremble of leaves, and one sharp cry of an unsuckled child. Then the trees in the grove were still.

"Thank you," said the widow softly. She patted the Dream Weaver's shoulder. Then she spoke to her child, "Come. We will go to your father's people. They will take us in, I know that now." She held out her hand.

The child took her hand, and as they began walking, he asked, "Did you like it? Was it a good dream? I thought it was sad. Was it sad?"

But his mother did not answer him, and soon the child's voice, like their footsteps, faded away.

The Dream Weaver took the dream from the loom. "They, too, left without the dream. Such a small bit of weaving, yet they had no room for it. But it was not a sad dream. Not really. It had much loving in it. She should have taken it for the child—if not for herself." And still mumbling, the Dream Weaver snipped the threads and finished off the weaving, stretching it a bit to make it more pliant. Then she put it, with the others, in her bag.

"Dream Weaver," came a chorus of voices. The Dream Weaver sorted out three. Three children. Girls, she thought.

The boldest of the three, the middle child, stepped closer. All three were tawny-haired, though the oldest had curls with an orange tinge to them. "Dream Weaver, we have only one penny to spend. One for the three of us. Can you weave us one dream? To share?"

"Share a dream?" The old woman laughed. "It is the best way. Of course you can share. Are you..." she hesitated, then guessed, "sisters?"

"How can she tell?" whispered the youngest.

"Hush," cautioned the middle child. "Manners!"

The oldest ignored them. On the edge of womanhood, she was aware of urges in herself she could not yet name. She gathered her skirts and her courage, and squatted down by the weaver. "Could you," she began tentatively, "could you put true love in it?"

The Dream Weaver smiled. She had heard such requests many times over. But she would never have convinced the girl of that. Better to let the child think she was the only one with such a dream.

"Oh, true love!" said the middle child. "That's all you ever think about— now. You used to be fun."

The youngest girl lisped. "A cat, please, granny. Please let there be a cat in it."

"A cat! True love! I only want it to be fun. For the penny we should have a good laugh," the middle child said.

The Dream Weaver smiled again as she pulled the threads from her basket. "Well, we shall see, little ones. A cat and true love and a laugh. I have had stranger demands. But one never knows about a dream until it is done. Still, I will try. And since it is your dream, you each must try as well."

"Try?" the three exclaimed as one. And the youngest added, "How shall we try, granny?"

"Hold hands, and I shall weave. And as I weave, you must believe."

"Oh, we will," said the youngest breathlessly. The other two laughed at her, but they held hands. The warp was strung. The weaver began.

The Cat Bride

There was once a noddy old woman who had only two things in the world that she loved—her son and a marmalade cat. She loved them both the same, which seemed strange to her neighbors but not to her son, Tom.

"I bring home food, and the cat keeps it safe. Why should we not share equally in her affections?" he asked sensibly. Then he added, "Though I am not the best provider in the land, the cat is surely the best mouser. *Ergo,* it follows."

But of course it did not follow for the neighbors. To them such sense was nonsense. However, as it was none of their business, the old woman ignored their mischievous tongues and loved boy and cat the same.

One day the old woman caught a chill, grew sicker, and likened to die. She called Tom and the cat to her bed. The village elders came, too, for they went to deathbeds as cats to mackerel; the smell, it was said, drew them in.

"Promise me, Tom," said the old woman in a voice as soft as down.

"Anything, Mother," said Tom as he sat by her bed and held on to her hand.

"Promise me you will marry the marmalade cat, for that way she will remain in our family forever. You are a good boy, Tom, but she is the best mouser in the land."

At her words, the elders cried out to one another in horror.

"Never," cried one.

"Unheard of," cried the second.

"It is against the law," declared the third.

"What law?" asked the old woman, looking over at them. "Where is it written that a boy cannot marry a cat?"

The elders looked at one another. They twisted their mouths around, but no answer came out, for she was right.

"I promise, Mother," said Tom, "for I love the marmalade cat as much as you do. I will keep her safe and in our family forever."

As soon as Tom had finished speaking, the cat jumped onto the bed and, as if to seal its part of the bargain, licked the old woman's face, first one cheek and then the other, with its rough-ribbed tongue. Then it bit her softly on the nose and jumped down.

At the cat's touch, the elders left the room in disgust. But the old woman sat up in bed. Color sprang into her faded cheeks, and she let out a high sweet laugh.

Tom's heart sang out a silent hallelujah. He rose to shut the door. When he turned back again, there was an orange-haired girl with green eyes standing where the cat had been, but the cat was nowhere in sight.

"Who are you, and where is the cat?" asked Tom.

"Why, I *am* the cat," said the girl. "But if we are to be wed, it is best that I wear human clothes."

"I liked you well enough before," said Tom, looking at the floor.

"Well, you will like her well enough after," said his mother sensibly. She got out of bed, toddled to the door, and called out to the village elders who were already more than halfway down the road.

Smelling a miracle, the elders turned back. And though they did not like it all the way through, they agreed to marry Tom and the girl at once. "For," said one to the others, "a girl with orange hair and green eyes and the manners of a cat should not be left to wander the village on her own."

Several days went by before the elders returned for a visit.

"We are glad to see you are still well," the first said to the old woman as she sat and nodded by the fire.

"Some miracles are but a moment long," said the second. He tried not to stare at Tom's new wife who lay dozing on the hearth, her skirts tucked up around her long slim legs.

But the third leaned closer to the old woman and whispered in her ear. "I have been wanting to ask—how is she as a bride?"

"Cat or girl, I love her still with all my heart," said the old woman. "And she is the perfect girl for Tom. She is neat and clean. She is quick on her feet. She has a warm and loving heart."

"Well," said the third elder, twisting his mouth around the word, "I suppose *that* is good."

"Well," said the old woman, smiling up at him, "if that were all, it would be good enough. But there is even better."

"Better?" asked the elder.

"Better," said the old woman with a mischievous grin. "She is neat and clean and quick on her feet and has a warm and loving heart. And," she paused, "she is still the best mouser in the land."

The three girls laughed their thanks and walked away, laughing. They left the dream behind.

The Weaver began to remove the dream when angry steps caused her to pause.

"You again," she said.

"It might not be a minstrel's dream. You said that. So, for the coin I gave you already, finish the dream."

"I cannot finish that one," said the Dream Weaver. "The fragment is already packed away."

"Do not try to wheedle another penny from me," the man shouted. He moved as if to turn away.

The Dream Weaver shook her head. "I want no more from you," she said, "though I would not turn down another penny."

"Here," he said, and threw a coin at her feet.

The Dream Weaver found it and tucked it away, then added, "I will pick threads that are close to the first ones. But they might not be a match. Will you stay through this time and listen to your dream?"

The man grunted his answer and watched as the old woman finished off the girls' dream and rummaged in her thread basket. She pulled out several.

"How can you be sure those are near the color of the last when you cannot see?" asked the man.

The Dream Weaver was silent as she finished sorting the threads.

"Well?"

"By the feel, man. Just as I can tell, from your voice, the look of your face, though I have no eyes."

"And what is that look?" he asked.

"My answer would not flatter you!" she said. "So hush, for the dream is beginning." She threaded the warp and began.

The Boy Who Sang for Death

In a village that lay like a smudge on the cheek of a quiet valley, there lived an old woman and the last of her seven sons. The oldest six had joined the army as they came of age, and her husband was long in his grave. The only one left at home was a lad named Karl.

Even if he had not been her last, his mother would have loved him best for he had a sweet disposition and a sweeter voice. It was because of that voice, pure and clear, that caroled like spring birds, that she had called him Karel. But his father and brothers, fearing the song name would unman him, had changed it to Karl. So Karl he had remained.

Karl was a sturdy boy, a farm boy in face and hands. But his voice set him apart from the rest. Untutored and untrained, Karl's voice could call home sheep from the pasture, birds from the trees. In the village, it was even said that the sound of Karl's voice made graybeards dance, the lame to walk, and milk spring from a maiden's breast. Yet Karl used his voice for no such magic, but to please his mother and gentle his flock.

One day when Karl was out singing to the sheep and goats to bring them safely in from the field, his voice broke; like a piece of cloth caught on a nail, it tore. Fearing something wrong at home, he hurried the beasts. They scattered before him, and he came to the house to find that his mother had died.

"Between one breath and the next, she was gone," said the priest.

Gently Karl folded her hands on her breast and, although she was beyond the sound of his song, he whispered something in her ear and turned to leave.

"Where are you going?" called out the priest, his words heavy with concern.

"I am going to find Death and bring my mother back," cried Karl, his jagged voice now dulled with grief. He turned at the door and faced the priest who knelt by his mother's bed. "Surely Death will accept an exchange. What is one old tired woman to Death who has known so many?"

"And will you recognize Death, my son, when you meet him?"

"That I do not know," said Karl.

The priest nodded and rose heavily from his knees. "Then listen well, my son. Death is an aging but still handsome prince. His eyes are dark and empty for he has seen much suffering in the world. If you find such a one, he is Death."

"I will know him," said Karl.

"And what can you give Death in exchange that he has not already had many times over?" asked the priest.

Karl touched his pockets and sighed. "I have nothing here to give," he said. "But I hope that he may listen to my songs. They tell me in the village that there is a gift of magic in my voice. Any gift I have I would surely give to get my mother back. I will sing for Death, and perhaps that great prince will take time to listen."

"Death does not take time," said the old priest, raising his hand to bless the boy, "for time is Death's own greatest possession."

"I can but try," said Karl, tears in his eyes. He knelt a moment for the blessing, stood up and went out the door. He did not look back.

Karl walked for many days and came at last to a city that lay like a blemish on three hills. He listened quietly but well, as only a singer can, and when he heard weeping, he followed the sound and found a funeral procession bearing the coffin of a child. The procession turned into a graveyard where stones leaned upon stones like cards in a neglected deck.

"Has Death been here already?" asked Karl of a weeping woman.

"Death has been here many times," she answered. "But today she has taken my child."

"*She?*" said Karl. "But surely Death is a man."

"Death is a woman," she answered him at once. "Her hair is long and thick and dark, like the roots of trees. Her body is huge and brown, but she is barren. The only way she can bear a child is to bear it away."

Karl felt her anger and sorrow then, for they matched his own, so he joined the line of mourners to the grave. And when the child's tiny box had been laid in the ground, he sang it down with the others. But his voice lifted above theirs, a small bird soaring with ease over larger ones. The townsfolk stopped singing in amazement and listened to him.

Karl sang not of death but of his village in the valley, of the seasons that sometime stumble one into another, and of the small pleasures of the hearth. He sang tune after tune the whole of that day, and just at nightfall he stopped. They threw dirt on the baby's coffin and brought Karl to their home.

"Your songs eased my little one's passage," said the woman. "Stay with us this night. We owe you that."

"I wish that I had been here before," said Karl. "I might have saved your baby with a song."

"I fear Death would not be cheated so easily of her chosen child," said the woman. She set the table but did not eat.

Karl left in the morning. And as he walked, he thought about Death, how it was a hollow-eyed prince to the priest but a jealous mother to the woman. If Death could change shapes with such ease, how would he know Death when they finally met? He walked and walked, his mind in a puzzle, until he came at last to a plain that lay like a great open wound between mountains.

The plain was filled with an army of fighting men. There were men with bows and men with swords and men with wooden staves. Some men fought on horseback, and some fought from their knees. Karl could not tell one band of men from another, could not match friend with friend, foe with foe, for their clothes were colored by dirt and by blood and every man looked the same. And the screams and shouts and the crying of horns were a horrible symphony in Karl's ears.

Yet there was one figure Karl *could* distinguish. A woman, quite young, dressed in a long white gown. Her dark braids were caught up in ribbons of white and looped like a crown on her head. She threaded her way through the ranks of men like a shuttle through a loom, and there seemed to be a pattern in her going. She paused now and then to put a hand to the head or the breast of one man and then another. Each man she touched stopped fighting and, with an expression of surprise, left his body and followed the girl, so that soon there was a great wavering line of gray men trailing behind her.

Then Karl knew that he had found Death.

He ran down the mountainside and around the flank of the great plain, for he wanted to come upon Death face to face. He called out as he ran, hoping to slow her progress, "Wait, oh, wait, my Lady Death; please wait for me."

Lady Death heard his call above the battle noise, and she looked up from her work. A weariness sat between her eyes, but she did not stop. She continued her way from man to man, a hand to the brow or over the heart. And at her touch, each man left his life to follow the young girl named Death.

When Karl saw that she would not stop at his calling, he stepped into her path. But she walked through him as if through air and went on her way, threading the line of dead gray men behind her.

So Karl began to sing. It was all he knew to do.

He sang not of death but of growing and bearing, for they were things she knew nothing of. He sang of small birds on the apple spray and bees with their honeyed burden. He sang of the first green blades piercing the warmed earth. He sang of winter fields where moles and mice sleep quietly under the snow. Each tune swelled into the next.

And Lady Death stopped to listen.

As she stopped, the ribbon of soldiers that was woven behind her stopped, too, and from their dead eyes tears fell with each memory. The battlefield was still, frozen by the songs. And the only sound and the only movement and the only breath was Karl's voice.

When he had finished at last, a tiny brown bird flew out of a dead tree, took up the last melody, and went on.

"I have made you stop, Lady Death," cried Karl. "And you have listened to my tunes. Will you now pay for that pleasure?"

Lady Death smiled, a slow, weary smile, and Karl wondered that someone so young should have to carry such a burden. And his pity hovered between them in the quiet air.

"I will pay, Karel," she said.

He did not wonder that she knew his true name, for Lady Death would, in the end, know every human's name.

"Then I ask for my mother in exchange," said Karl.

Lady Death looked at him softly then. She took up his pity and gave it back. "That I cannot do. Who follows me once, follows forever. But is it not payment enough to know that you have stayed my hand for this hour? No man has ever done that before."

"But you promised to pay," said Karl. His voice held both anger and disappointment, a man and a child's voice in one.

"And what I promise," she said, looking at him from under darkened lids, "I do."

The Dream Weaver's voice stopped for a moment.

"Is that all?" asked the man. "That's no ending. What of the coins I gave you?"

"Hush," the Dream Weaver said to him. "This is strange. This has never happened before. There is not one ending but two. I feel that here," and she held up her hands.

"Then tell them to me. Both. I paid," he said.

The Dream Weaver nodded. "This is the first way the dream ends," she said, and wove.

Lady Death put her hand in front of her, as if reaching into a cupboard, and a gray form that was strangely transparent took shape under her fingers. It became a harp, with smoke-colored strings the color of Lady Death's eyes.

"A useless gift," said Karl. "I cannot play."

But Lady Death reached over and set the harp in his hand, careful not to touch him with her own.

And as the harp molded itself under his fingers, Karl felt music surge through his bones. He put his thumb and forefinger on the strings and began to play.

At the first note, the battle began anew. Men fought, men bled, men suffered, men fell. But Karl passed through the armies untouched, playing a sweet tune that rose upward, in bursts, as the lark and its song spring toward the sun. He walked through the armies, through the battle, through the plain, playing his harp, and he never looked back again.

The Dream Weaver hesitated but a moment.
And the other ending," the man commanded.
But she had already begun.

"And what I promise," Death said, looking at him from under darkened lids, "I do."

She turned and pointed to the field, and Karl's eyes followed her fingers.

"There in that field are six men whose heads and hearts I will not touch this day. Look carefully, Karel."

He looked. "They are my brothers," he said.

"Them, I will spare." And Lady Death turned and stared into Karl's face with her smoky eyes. "But I would have you sing for me again each night in the small hours when I rest, for I have never had such comfort before. Will you come?" She held out her hand.

Karl hesitated a moment, remembering his farm, remembering the fields, the valleys, the warm spring rains. Then he looked again at Lady Death, whose smile seemed a little less weary. He nodded and reached for her hand, and it was small and soft and cool in his. He raised her hand once to his lips, then set it, palm open, over his heart. He never felt the cold.

Then, hand in hand, Karl and Lady Death walked through the battlefield. Their passing made not even the slightest breeze on the cheeks of the wounded, nor an extra breath for the dying. Only the dead who traveled behind saw them pass under the shadows of the farthest hills. But long after they had gone, the little bird sang Karl's last song over and over and over again into the darkening air.

"I liked the other ending best," said the man. "It was the better bargain."

"Bargain?" The Dream Weaver's mouth soured with the word.

"A bargain, old one," he said. "The boy bought a salable talent with his song. He got better than he gave and that is always a bargain. I like that." The man chuckled to himself and went away, his footsteps tapping lightly on the street.

"A bargain was it?" the Weaver mumbled to herself, finishing off the tale and its two separate endings. "A bargain!" she said again, shaking her head. She thought for a moment of taking the first ending apart, saving the threads for another time. She knew the man would not be back for it, and it had not pleased her, that ending. Still, she could not bear to unravel her work, so she put it with the others in her bag.

The Dream Weaver fingered the coins in her pouch. Five already, no, six, and the sun was on its downward swing. It had been a good day. She could begin her slow dark trip home.

"There she is, the Dream Weaver," came a voice. "Stop her. Oh, stop!"

The Dream Weaver, half standing, heard the voice and running steps as one. She turned and waited. Another coin to put in the pouch, to hold against the rains or the long, cold winter days.

"You are not through, Dream Weaver?" It was a young voice, a girl just become a woman. She sounded only slightly worried, stuttering a bit from the run.

"No, child, not if you want a dream."

"We want a dream. Together, Dream Weaver." It was almost a man's voice, just out of boyhood but already gone through its change. "We made our pledges to one another today. We will be married by year's end. We have saved a coin to celebrate our fortune and we have decided together on a dream. Give us a good one."

The old woman smiled. "I have already spun one true love dream today. I do not know if there is another in these old fingers. " She held them up before her eyes as if she could see them. She was proud of them, her clever fingers. She knew that they were strong and supple despite their gnarled appearance.

"Oh, we do not need a true love dream," came the girl's quick response. "We have that ourselves, you see. Our parents would have married us to others— for gold. But we persuaded them to let us wed. It took a long time, too long. But..." She stopped as if to let the boy finish for her, but he was silent, simply staring at her while she spoke.

"Well, give me the coin then, and we shall see what the threads have to say," said the Dream Weaver. "They never lie. But sometimes the dream is not easy to read."

The young man handed her the coin, and she slipped it into the pouch. She heard not even a rustle of impatience. They simply waited for her to begin, confident in their own living dreams.

The Dream Weaver picked out the threads with more flourish than was necessary. She would give them their penny's worth.

"Watch as I thread the warp," commanded the Dream Weaver, knowing they might need prompting to look at her rather than at one another.

At her command, they turned to watch. And this was the dream that she wove.

Princess Heart O'Stone

In the days when woods still circled the world and heroes could talk with beasts, there lived a princess whom everyone pitied.

She was the most beautiful girl imaginable. Her hair was the color of red leaves in the fall, burnished with orange and gold. Her eyes were the green of moss on stone, and her skin the color of fresh cream. She was slim and fair, and her voice was low. But she had a heart of stone.

When she was born, the midwife had grasped her firmly and slapped her lightly to bring out the first cry. But the first cry was the midwife's instead.

"Look!" the woman gasped, pointing to the child's breast. And there, cold and unmoving under the fragile shield of skin, was the outline of a heart. "She has a heart of stone."

Then the child made a sound that was neither laugh nor cry and opened her eyes, but the stone in her breast did not move at all.

The king put his right palm on the child's body, nearly covering it. He shook his head.

The queen turned her face against the pillow, but she could not weep until she heard the king weep. Then they wept as one.

The midwife was paid twice over in gold to stop her tongue, but it was too late. Her cry had already been heard. It went round the castle before the child had been wrapped.

"The princess has a heart of stone."

"The princess has a heart of stone."

The child grew up, hearing the whispers. And knowing her heart was made of stone and could feel neither sorrow nor joy, she felt nothing. She accepted the friendship of birds and beasts who asked neither smiles nor tears of her but only the comfort of her hand. But she stayed aloof from the companionship of people. And that is why she was called Princess Heart O'Stone—and was pitied.

Her parents would have done anything for her, but what could they do? They called in physicians who examined her. They thumped her bones and pulled at her skin and looked at her ears and eyes. They gave advice and said what was already known. "She is perfectly fit, except—except that her heart is made of stone."

The king and queen called in poets and painters and singers of songs. They told of love never plighted, of wars never won, of mothers whose children all died.

The princess did not cry.

"If we can not move her, nothing can," they said and left.

The royal couple called in clowns. And the courtyards of the kingdom filled with jongleurs and jesters, jugglers and jokers, who fell over one another in their efforts to fill the princess with delight. But as she had never cried, so she never laughed.

"What a heartless creature," said the clowns. And they went away.

At last the king and queen gave up hope for a cure. Indeed they had lived through so many false promises and so much useless advice that they declared no one was ever again to speak of changing the princess's condition. To do so was to invite a beheading.

Now in that same kingdom lived a simple woodcutter whose name was Donnal.

As fair as the princess was, Donnal was fairer. He had an angel's face set round with golden curls. He was tall and straight, and his heart was tender. If he had a fault, it was this: he was proud of his strong back and perfect limbs and liked to admire his image in the forest pools.

Now one day, deep in the woods where he worked, Donnal heard a faint cry. As he knew the songs of birds, he ran to the sound and there he found a sparrow hawk caught in a net. Donnal took out his knife and cut the bird free. It flew straight to a low branch and called its thanks to the lad:

> Heart O'Stone
> is all alone.

"Well, that is strange thanks, indeed," thought Donnal. But the call stayed with him all that day. And as he thought about it, his tender heart cried out with pity. Though he lived in the woods by himself, *he* was not alone. He had all the birds and beasts and his own fair reflection for company. He could enjoy them and laugh or cry at will. But the princess, fair and stonehearted, was truly all alone.

Still it did not occur to Donnal to go to her. He was a woodcutter, after all. How could he presume to help her when physicians and poets and clowns could not?

The very next day, when Donnal was again hard at work, he heard a second cry. It was deeper than the voice of the bird. Donnal ran to it and found a small vixen caught in a trap. He bent down and opened the trap and the little fox ran free. She cowered for a moment under a bush and, in thanks, barked:

> Carry her heart,
> Never part.

"Well," said Donnal, "that is certainly true enough. If you carry someone's heart, and she yours, then you *will* never part. But if you mean Princess Heart O'Stone, why that would be a very heavy burden indeed."

He saluted the fox, and they both sped away. Donnal went home thinking about the fox's words. But finally he laughed at himself, for when does a poor woodcutter get to carry a princess' heart?

The next day Donnal was outside, stacking wood into piles, when he heard a third cry for help, low and angry. It was not a plea but a demand. This time he found a bear in a pit.

Donnal puzzled for a moment, wondering if he should try to bring the bear up, when he noticed that it wore a collar with gold markings.

"That is no ordinary bear," said Donnal aloud. At the sound of his voice, the bear stood up and began twirling ever so slowly around and around in the pit.

Donnal lay down on his stomach, to look at the bear more closely. It was the king's dancing bear, no doubt of it, though what it was doing so far from the castle, Donnal did not know.

"Just a minute, friend," he called. Then he leaped up and ran back home for his ax. He felled a nearby tree and with a chain dragged it to the pit, shoved it in partway, and the bear climbed out.

"And do you have thanks for me, too?" asked Donnal. He gave a small laugh then, for the bear stood on its hind legs and bowed. Then it ambled off without a word.

However, when the bear reached the edge of the clearing, it turned and looked back over it shoulder and growled:

Heart of stone crack,
Ride on your back.

Donnal thought about this. All three—the hawk, the fox, and the bear—had called out their thanks. Yet none of it had to do with Donnal and his rescuing. It all had to do with the princess. He remembered the stories about Princess Heart O'Stone, how she spent her time with birds and beasts and none at all with humans. He wondered if all the animals were her special friends. And then he called out to the bear. "Wait, wait for me," and ran after it, waving his hand.

The bear waited at the forest edge, and when Donnal caught up, it allowed the woodcutter to ride on its shoulders. They rode swifter than the winter wind and passed by the guards at the castle gate between one blink and the next. And when they came to the throne room, the bear pushed open the enormous door with its snout.

"What is this?" shouted the king to his flatterers and friends, and when none of them could answer, he asked the question of the bear.

At its master's voice, the bear bowed low, and Donnal slid over its head to the floor.

"I think I know how to help your daughter, Princess Heart O'Stone," said Donnal when he had picked himself up. "I may be only a poor woodcutter, but I can tell you what has been told me. It is here in my head."

"Then you shall part with it now," said the king in an angry yet controlled voice.

"The knowledge?" asked Donnal.

"No, woodcutter, your head," said the king. "For I have sworn to kill anyone who refers to the princess's problem. "

"Wait," cried Donnal. "First listen and then take my head if you must. What I say will change your mind."

"I can change my mind no more than my poor daughter can change her heart," said the king.

The guards advanced on the woodcutter, their swords held high.

"It was the animals who told me," said Donnal.

"Wait," came a voice. And at that command, all motion in the throne room ceased for the voice belonged to Princess Heart O'Stone herself and never before had she taken any interest in court proceedings.

She walked over to her father and stood by the throne. Her voice was low, but it could be heard throughout the room. "A handsome, brave lad riding in on a bear. If I *could* laugh, I would find that funny. Yet you want to behead him. If I *could* cry, I would find that sad. But as I can do neither, at least I can listen. For I have found that people talk a lot and say nothing while animals talk infrequently and say much. A boy who has conversed with beasts is sure to say something interesting."

At her voice, Donnal looked up. And seeing her beauty, he looked down. He came over and knelt before her and spoke to the floor. It was all he could dare.

"Heart O'Stone is all alone," he whispered, for he knew at once it was true.

The princess reached down and held his chin in her hand, forcing him to look up at her. As Donnal looked into her eyes, he saw in those twin green pools his own fair reflection. And as he stared further, it seemed to him that in those pools was the faintest of ripples.

"I am," she said, "*all* alone. I thought no one had remarked it."

Then Donnal stood up and held both her hands in his.

At this, the king jumped up himself and would have cleaved Donnal's head from his shoulders with his own sword had not the queen put out a hand to stop him.

But Donnal did not notice. He saw only the princess. "I have remarked it," he said. "And it fairly breaks my heart to see you all alone. But you need not ever be alone again, for I am here."

"You?" said the princess.

And then Donnal added, *"Carry her heart, never part."*

The princess shook her head. "Would you dare carry such a burden?"

"If it were *your* heart, though truly made of stone, I would carry it gladly," said Donnal. "And that would be a light task indeed for a back as straight and strong as mine. "

Then the princess moved right up next to Donnal, and he spoke only to her. No one in the throne room but the princess heard his final words. *"Heart of stone crack, ride on my back,"* he said.

And as Donnal spoke, a great cracking sound was heard. as if the world itself were breaking in two. At that. the princess sighed. Tears ran down her cheeks and over her smiling mouth, but she never heeded them. She turned to her parents and cried out, "Mother, Father. I can laugh. I can cry. I can love."

She turned to Donnal, "And I will marry whom I will." She put her little hands on each side of his broad ones and brought them together as if in prayer.

"Marry him?" said the queen. "But he is a woodcutter. And besides, he is ill formed."

The courtiers all looked, and it was true. How could they have not seen it before. Donnal's face was beautiful still, but his proud straight back was now crooked. A hump, like a great stone, grew between his shoulders.

"She shall marry this man and no other," said the king, for while the others had been watching the princess all the time, he alone had kept his eyes on Donnal. He knew what it was that rested on the boy's shoulders. "He is a man of courage and compassion," said the king, "who knows the difference between advice and action. He shall carry the burdens of the kingdom on that crooked back with ease, of this I am sure."

So the two were married at once and ruled after the king died. The princess was known for her laughter and her tears, which she was quick to give to any who asked. King Donnal Crookback never minded his hump, for the only mirrors he sought were the princess's eyes. And when they told him that he was straight and true, he knew they did not lie. And it was said, by all the people in the kingdom, that as loved as Queen Heart O'Stone was, King Donnal was more beloved still, for he had not one heart, but two: the one he carried hidden away in his breast, but the other he carried high between his shoulders, where it could be seen and touched by even the least of his people.

"That's how I feel," said the girl when the dream was done. *"That I am carrying your heart, and it is no heavy burden."*

But the boy directed his words to the Dream Weaver. *"The story was fine. Just meant for us."*

"Story?" the old woman said as she finished off the piece and held it out to him. *"That was not just a story—but a woven dream. Here, take it. For your new life. Keep it safe."*

The boy pushed her hand away gently. "We do not need to take that with us, Dream Weaver. We have it safe—here." He touched his hand to his chest.

The girl, realizing the Dream Weaver could not see his gesture, added, "Here in our hearts."

As if to make up for his tactlessness, and because he had a gentle nature, the boy said, "Help us celebrate our good fortune, Dream Weaver." He dug into his pocket. "Here, I have one more coin. It is part of the marriage portion. We would have you weave yourself a tale."

The girl nodded, delighted with his words. "Yes, yes, please."

"Myself?" The old woman looked amazed. "All these years I have been on street corners, weaving dreams for a penny. Yet no one has ever suggested such a thing before. Weave for myself?"

"Were you never tempted to do one anyway?" It was the girl.

"Tempted?" The Dream Weaver put her head to one side, considering the question. "If I had been sighted, I might have been tempted. But the eye and the ear are different listeners. So there was no need to weave a dream for myself. Besides..." and she gave a short laugh. "Besides, it would have brought no coin."

They laughed with her. The boy took the Dream Weaver's hand and placed the coin gently in it, closing her fingers around the penny. "Here is the coin, then, for your own dream."

The Dream Weaver smiled a great smile that split her brown face in unequal halves. "You two watch closely for me, then. Be my eyes for the weaving. I shall hear the tale on my own."

And this was the tale that she wove.

The Pot Child

There was once an ill-humored potter who lived all alone and made his way by shaping clay into cups and bowls and urns. His pots were colored with the tones of the earth, and on their sides he painted all creatures excepting man.

"For there was never a human I liked well enough to share my house and my life with," said the bitter old man.

But one day, when the potter was known throughout the land for his sharp tongue as well as his pots, and so old that even death might have come as a friend, he sat down and on the side of a large bisque urn he drew a child.

The child was without flaw in the outline, and so the potter colored in its form with earth glazes: rutile for the body and cobalt blue for the eyes. And to the potter's practiced eye, the figure on the pot was perfect.

So he put the pot into the kiln, closed up the door with bricks, and set the flame.

Slowly the fires burned. And within the kiln the glazes matured and turned their proper tones.

It was a full day and a night before the firing was done. And a full day and a night before the kiln had cooled. And it was a full day and a night before the old Potter dared unbrick the kiln door. For the pot child was his masterpiece, of this he was sure.

At last, though, he could put it off no longer. He took down the kiln door, reached in, and removed the urn.

Slowly he felt along the pot's side. It was smooth and still warm. He set the pot on the ground and walked around it, nodding his head as he went.

The child on the pot was so lifelike, it seemed to follow him with its lapis eyes. Its skin was a pearly yellow-white, and each hair on its head like beaten gold.

So the old potter squatted down before the urn examining the figure closely, checking it for cracks and flaws, but there were none. He drew in his breath at the child's beauty and thought to himself, "*There* is one I might like well enough." And when he expelled his breath again, he blew directly on the image's lips.

At that, the pot child sighed and stepped off the urn.

Well, this so startled the old man that he fell back into the dust.

After a while, though, the potter saw that the pot child was waiting for him to speak. So he stood up and in a brusque tone said, "Well, then, come here. Let me look at you."

The child ran over to him and, ignoring his tone, put its arms around his waist, and whispered "Father" in a high sweet voice.

This so startled the old man that he was speechless for the first time in his life. And as he could not find the words to tell the child to go, it stayed. Yet after a day, when he had found the words, the potter knew he could not utter them for the child's perfect face and figure had enchanted him.

When the potter worked or ate or slept, the child was by his side, speaking when spoken to but otherwise still. It was a pot child, after all, and not a real child. It did not join him in his work but was content to watch. When other people came to the old man's shop, the child stepped back onto the urn and did not move. Only the potter knew it was alive.

One day several famous people came to the potter's shop. He showed them all around, grudgingly, touching one pot and then another. He answered their questions in a voice that was crusty and hard. But they knew his reputation and did not answer back.

At last they came to the urn.

The old man stood before it and sighed. It was such an uncharacteristic sound that the people looked at him strangely. But the potter did not notice. He simply stood for a moment more, then said, "This is the Pot Child. It is my masterpiece. I shall never make another one so fine."

He moved away, and one woman said after him, "It *is* good." But turning to her companions, she added in a low voice, "But it is *too* perfect for me."

A man with her agreed. "It lacks something," he whispered back.

The woman thought a moment. "It has no heart," she said. "That is what is wrong."

"It has no soul," he amended.

They nodded at each other and turned away from the urn. The woman picked out several small bowls, and, paying for them, she and the others went away.

No sooner were the people out of sight than the pot child stepped down from the urn.

"Father," the pot child asked, "what is a heart?"

"A vastly overrated part of the body," said the old man gruffly. He turned to work the clay on his wheel.

"Then," thought the pot child, "I am better off with out one." It watched as the clay grew first tall and then wide between the potter's knowing palms. It hesitated asking another question, but at last could bear it no longer.

"And what is a soul, Father?" asked the pot child. "Why did you not draw one on me when you made me on the urn?"

The potter looked up in surprise. "Draw one? No one can draw a soul."

The child's disappointment was so profound, the potter added, "A man's body is like a pot, which does not disclose what is inside. Only when the pot is poured do we see its contents. Only when a man acts do we know what kind of soul he has."

The pot child seemed happy with that explanation, and the potter went back to his work. But over the next few weeks the child continually got in his way. When the potter worked the clay, the pot child tried to bring him water to keep the clay moist. But it spilled the water and the potter pushed the child away.

When the potter carried the unfired pots to the kiln, the pot child tried to carry some, too. But it dropped the pots, and many were shattered. The potter started to cry out in anger, bit his tongue, and was still.

When the potter went to fire the kiln, the pot child tried to light the flame. Instead, it blew out the fire.

At last the potter cried, "You heartless thing. Leave me to do my work. It is all I have. How am I to keep body and soul together when I am so plagued by you?"

At these words, the pot child sat down in the dirt, covered its face, and wept. Its tiny body heaved so with its sobs that the potter feared it would break in two. His crusty old heart softened, and he went over to the pot child and said, "There, child. I did not mean to shout so. What is it that ails you?"

The pot child looked up. "Oh, my Father, I know I have no heart. But that is a vastly overrated part of the body. Still, I was trying to show how I was growing a soul."

The old man looked startled for a minute, but then, recalling their conversation of many weeks before, he said, "My poor pot child, no one can *grow* a soul. It is there from birth." He touched the child lightly on the head.

The potter had meant to console the child, but at that the child cried even harder than before. Drops sprang from its eyes and ran down its cheeks like blue glaze. "Then I shall never have a soul," the pot child cried. "For I was not born but made."

Seeing how the child suffered, the old man took a deep breath. And when he let it out again, he said, "Child, as I made you, now I will make you a promise. When I die, you shall have *my* soul for then I shall no longer need it."

"Oh, then I will be truly happy," said the pot child, slipping its little hand gratefully into the old man's. It did not see the look of pain that crossed the old man's face. But when it looked up at him and smiled, the old man could not help but smile back.

That very night, under the watchful eyes of the pot child, the potter wrote out his will. It was a simple paper, but it took a long time to compose for words did not come easily to the old man. Yet as he wrote, he felt surprisingly lightened. And the pot child smiled at him all the while. At last, after many scratchings out, it was done. The potter read the paper aloud to the pot child.

"It is good," said the pot child. "You do not suppose I will have long to wait for my soul?"

The old man laughed. "Not long, child."

And then the old man slept, tired after the late night's labor. But he had been so busy writing, he had forgotten to bank his fire, and in the darkest part of the night, the flames went out.

In the morning the shop was ice cold, and so was the old man. He did not waken, and without him, the pot child could not move from its shelf.

Later in the day, when the first customers arrived, they found the old man. And beneath his cold fingers lay a piece of paper that said:

> When I am dead, place my body in my kiln and light the flames. And when I am nothing but ashes, let those ashes be placed inside the Pot Child. For I would be one, body and soul, with the earth I have worked.

So it was done as the potter wished. And when the kiln was opened up, the people of the town placed the ashes in the ice-cold urn.

At the touch of the hot ashes, the pot cracked: once across the breast of the child and two small fissures under its eyes.

"What a shame," said the people to one another on seeing that. "We should have waited until the ashes cooled."

Yet the pot was still so beautiful, and the old potter so well known, that the urn was placed at once in a museum. Many people came to gaze on it.

One of those was the woman who had seen the pot that day so long ago at the shop.

"Why, look," she said to her companions. "It is the pot the old man called his masterpiece. It *is* good. But I like it even better now with those small cracks."

"Yes," said one of her companions, "It was too perfect before."

"Now the pot child has real character," said the woman. "It has...heart."

"Yes," added the same companion, "it has soul."

And they spoke so loudly that all the people around hem heard. The story of their conversation was printed and repeated throughout the land, and everyone who went by the pot stopped and murmured, as if part of a ritual, "Look at that pot child. It has such heart. It has such soul."

"Ah," sighed the Dream Weaver when the tale was done. It was a great relief to her to have it over, both the weaving and the telling. She dropped her hands to her sides and thought about the artist of the tale and how he alone really knew when his great work was done, and how he had put his own heart and soul into it. For what was art, she thought, but the heart and soul made visible.

"I thank you, my young friends," she said to the boy and girl as they waited, hand upon hand, until she was through. "And now I can go home and sleep."

She finished the piece of weaving and held it up to them. "Will you take this one with you?" she asked.

"But it was your dream," said the boy hesitantly.

The girl was more honest still. "There is nothing on it, Dream Weaver. On that—or on the other."

"Nothing? What do you mean—nothing?" Her voice trembled.

"A jumble of threads," said the girl. "Tightly woven, true, but with no picture or pattern."

"No picture? Nothing visible? Was there never a picture?" asked the old woman, her voice low.

"While you told the tale," said the boy, "there were pictures aplenty in my head and in my heart."

"And on the cloth?"

"I do not really know," admitted the girl. "For your voice spun the tale so well, I scarcely knew anything more."

"Ah," said the Dream Weaver. She was silent for a moment and then said, more to herself than to the two, "So that is why no one takes their dreams."

"We will take your weaving if it would please you," said the boy.

The Dream Weaver put away her loom and threads. "It does not matter," she said. "I see that now. Memory is the daughter of the ear and the eye. I know you will take the dream with you, in your memory, and it will last long past the weaving."

They helped her strap the baskets to her back. "Long past," they assured her. Then they watched as the Dream Weaver threaded her way down the crooked streets to her home.

FROG PRINCE

It is so hard these days
to find a proper prince.
The world is dappled
with pretenders,
as spotty with them
as an adolescent's skin.
I have three daughters;
I have three wedding portions
waiting, waiting
for the marriage offer.
A kingdom
is but a small return
for fifteen years
of tending
these hothouse plants.
Can one read the heart?
Can one judge the mind?
Can one guess the future
from a handshake by a well,
from a dinner conversation,
from a single night in bed?
Yet my first wants to marry
a drummer in a rock band,
my second a man who works with cars.
What next, I ask you?
A grocer's lad?
       A stable boy?
   An enchanted frog?

Green Plague

It was only a small village high up in the mountains, but the tourists loved it. The water was clean, the air fresh, and the native population wore quaint costumes, not unlike the ones their great-great-grandparents had worn, only made more comfortable with zippers and Velcro fastenings.

The village's fortunes were based on the legend of a piper and a plague of rats some five centuries earlier, and they had carefully cultivated it for the tourist trade.

Not that anyone believed the legend. As the mayor said, "A lie, but our own."

And a very profitable lie it was. There were dioramas of the alleged incident in the town hall. Schoolchildren, in their adorable costumes, sang songs about the rats in the amphitheater for visitors, in German, Spanish, Italian, French, English, and Japanese. Trips to the town's cheese factories were the highlight of every tour, with twiddly oompapa music piped into the factory elevators. In fact, all of the brochures about holidays in the little town were decorated with pictures of rats, though they bore little resemblance to the rodents of old, but were as cuddly as the plush toy mice that were sold in the village gift shop, along with plastic piccolos that could flute half an octave at best.

Very profitable indeed.

Still the townsfolk were more than a little surprised when they awoke one morning, less than a month till high season, to another kind of plague.

"Frogs!" thundered the village mayor to the hastily convened council. His fleshy jowls trembled with the word. He held one of the offending green invaders by a leg and waved it above his head.

"They're everywhere," complained a thin-faced man who was the mayor's chief rival. He shuddered with distaste.

"In the bathtub," said one councilor.

"And the buttery," said another.

"Under the beds," said a third.

"And doing the breaststroke in the toilet bowl," thundered the mayor. He was popular for saying things plainly and because of it had been elected seven years in a row, a village record. "These frogs will ruin business. And we have just been named Attraction of the Year by the National Board of Tourism." They all knew that this was an important citation. It meant that booklets about the village would be in every guide and information shop in the country free of charge. It meant they could expect an increase in visitors of almost 300 percent in the upcoming year. "We must do something to rid ourselves of this green invasion," the mayor concluded.

The council wrestled for about an hour with the problem while green peepers, leopard frogs, and bullfrogs hopped about their feet.

At last the mayor thundered, "This is a plague of biblical proportions!"

"In proportion to what?" asked the thin man.

That started them on one of their epic arguments. No one expected to get out of council chambers until noon.

But just then a very large and hairy frog climbed onto the council table. Its eyes bulged in a horrible manner, as if any minute they were going to fall right out of its head.

"*Trichobatrachus robustus,*" the thin man said, shuddering again as he did so, "from West Africa. I, at least, have been doing my homework."

The big frog stared right at the mayor, who, in a sudden panic, hastily adjourned the meeting until the early afternoon.

Gratefully, the councilors all fled the room, leaving the frogs in charge.

In the center of the village, the full extent of the green plague could now be seen. What had been a trickle of family Ranidae at breakfast had, by lunch, become a tidal wave.

Put simply: There were frogs everywhere.

Some were small green blobs and some were enormous ten-inch-round boulders. They seemed to stretch from the foot of Grossmutter to the foot of Harlingberg, the two mountains that made up the sides of the village's valley.

The children were the only ones who were enjoying the spectacle. They had abandoned their own games of tag and hide-and-seek to start frog-racing and frog-jumping contests with the more agreeable frogs.

But as frogs continued to flood into the town, even the children lost interest. A frog or two or seven in the street is one thing. But a frog floating languidly in your milk glass or curled up on your pillow or draped across your toothbrush is another.

By evening the frogs outnumbered the citizens by a thousandfold. And still the green plague continued.

"We need a piper!" the mayor whispered. A day of thundering had reduced his vocal chords to single notes. The councilors had to strain to hear him in a room now crowded with frogs who were peeping and thrumming and harrumphing with spring pleasure.

At that point, everyone on the council—and the mayor himself—trooped down to the village gift shop and tried tootling on the plastic piccolos. They hoped, one and all, that the legend might actually have some base in reality. But tootle as they might, it was soon quite clear that there was not a real piper among them.

A second day of frogs went by and the roadways were thronged with green. Beds were slimed. Kitchen floors uncrossable. The school yard was a mass of undulating froggery.

The locals began to pack up and move—slowly, because the one highway into the village was covered with both frogs and persons from the media trying to get in. The news organizations, at least, were delighted with the green plague.

"Maybe that will get us a piper," the mayor said to the council after one particularly grueling interview with CNN. And even the thin man had to agree.

And then down the side of Harlingberg Mountain, which being quite steep was relatively frogless, came a drummer. He was a tall, skinny, scruffy man with legs like a stork's. His clothes resembled a personal rummage sale: a green jacket that had once had some sort of emblem on the sleeve; dark pants that were neither black nor blue but somewhere in between; and a white shirt that had certainly seen better days, and probably a better night or two, for it was the tattered remnant of a fancy dress outfit. The drummer had been only partially successful in tucking his shirttails into the pants and one side hung down, obscuring the right-hand pocket, which was just as well as the pocket was no longer there. A pair of granny glasses were perched on his rather prominent nose and made his eyes seem to bulge, rather like those of *Trichobatrachus robustus.* He had a green swatch of cloth tied around his forehead, which did not succeed in keeping his scraggly yellow hair out of his mouth.

A bongo drum was strapped to the tattered man's back and he was carrying a bodhran, a Gaelic hand drum that is played in the best Irish bands.

Once he made his way down the mountainside and found himself right at the town gates, the tattered man marched on his long stork legs through the green swale of frogs, banging all the while on his bodhran. Unaccountably, the frogs opened a path for him, then fell in line behind, hopping feverishly in 4/4 time to keep up with his long strides.

He marched right up the stairs and into the town hall, marking time with the drum. Pushing aside the green invaders, clerks and secretaries opened their doors to stare at him.

"The mayor?" he cried, over the sound of his drum.

Two secretaries and the assistant in charge of weddings, funerals, and bank holidays pointed to the council room door.

Without losing a beat, the drummer stork-legged into the room with his hopping parade behind.

The mayor and council were once again hard at work arguing, but when they saw the drummer and what followed him in two precise lines, they stopped.

"Welcome indeed," said the mayor. "A drummer will do. Name your price." He really knew how to get to the point.

"A bag of gold bullion and a twice yearly gig at the amphitheater," said the tattered drummer. "For me and my band."

The mayor pulled out a piece of paper, swatting away a large guppyi frog from the pen drawer as he did so.

"It's from the Solomon Islands," remarked the thin councilor, pointing to the large frog. The mayor ignored him.

Pen in hand, the mayor asked the drummer, "What is the name of your band?"

"Frog," said the drummer. "Formerly known as Prince."

"Figures," said the mayor. He began to write.

"We'll want guarantees and merchandise rights as well," said the drummer. "And the ability to do a video of the concert intercut with frames from the frog parade."

"Done," said the mayor. He knew better than to argue. Or to go back on his promise. The town legend had taught him that much.

They both signed the paper and then the mayor had one of his secretaries run off copies in triplicate. The councilors put their own signatures in the margins and the mayor handed the drummer a bag of gold. He had, in his own way, done his homework.

The drummer carefully lifted his shirttail, tucked his copy of the agreement in his right pocket, and turned. Smiling, he began drumming in earnest on the bodhran; it was a rhythm in 5/8 time.

The frogs hopped about, forming two straight lines behind him.

Then they all marched out the door, down the steps, along the road, through the village gates, up over Grossmutter Mountain, and were gone, followed by the eager media.

Every last frog left behind the drummer.

For good.

Or for bad.

It depends on how you feel about frogs.

Back at the council room only the thin councilor had noticed that the signed contract the drummer put in his missing pocket had floated down onto the floor. Surreptitiously he picked it up and stuck it in his own pants, under the belt, for safekeeping. He knew how short memories were—for plagues and for promises. He ran against the mayor at the next election.

"We will not go from one plague to another!" was his rallying cry. The villagers knew what he meant. Frogs were one thing. A little bit of slime here, a pond full of tadpoles there. Rock-and-roll fests, however, were another: farmyards destroyed, garbage everywhere, and any number of hippies staying on in the village forever. It had happened to a dozen towns on the other side of the mountain.

The thin man won the election overwhelmingly. No one seemed to remember the tale of the piper and the rats when in the voting booth, except for the loud mayor.

"We must not break our promise," he warned.

"What promise?" retorted the thin man, patting the paper under his belt surreptitiously.

The mayor could not convince the voters that history and story have more in common than five letters. He lost in a landslide.

In the fall all the children in the village over the age of fourteen left in a school bus for a rock concert in the next town over the mountain. There was a group called Forever Green that was currently popular. The drummer was known to be toadally awesome.

Only the youngest three children ever returned. They said the others had found their little mountain village stifling. They said the others complained that there were no jobs for them except as tour guides. They said the others wanted to see the world.

The three who came back mentioned that the band had needed roadies.

"You mean toadies," thundered the ex-mayor. It was the line that would carry him back into politics. Into the winner's circle.

And into story.

If not into history.

REMEMBERING BOOKS

I remember certain special books by remembering exactly where I read them. I mark my childhood by the books and places. Little else from my childhood can I recall with such perfect clarity.

An eclectic reader, I was mesmerized by everything from adventure stories and horse books to fantasy epics and Victorian girl stories. But my all-time favorites were the colored fairy books edited by Andrew Lang—*The Lilac Fairy Book*, *The Crimson Fairy Book*, *The Olive Fairy Book*, *The Blue Fairy Book* (all Longmans Green originally, today in Dover Publications).

They came in a crayon-box assortment and I read through them filled with the special wonder that fairy tales impart.

> *Books Yellow, Red, and Green and Blue,*
> *All true or just as good as true...*

went the awful rhyme at the beginning of *The Yellow Fairy Book*. Yet I was not deterred by the jangling rhythm and forced scansion. I scarcely read Lang's twee introductions that dripped butter and honey and apologized in smarmy lines for bowdlerizing the tales or mixing folk and fakelore. I wanted the stories, and stories is what I got. There were stories from the Punjab and stories from Asbjørnsen & Moe's Scandinavian collection; Celtic and French sat side by side with German märchen and Japanese tales. Lang raided the annals of the folklore societies and the fairy tale collections of dozens of countries.

By his own admission, he said, "I do not write the stories out of my own head," then admits latterly that the tales were, in fact, "translated or adapted by Mrs. Lang." That is all the credit she, poor lady, got. It was *Andrew* Lang whose name is on the book's spine and "Another Andrew Lang fairy book, please," is what I begged the librarian for.

The color fairy books were my first (but not my last) foray into "guilty pleasures." I would take home the book from the library at P.S. 93, the school I attended in Manhattan, not daring to read anything along the way because Carl Switzer and his gang of unruly boys always trailed me home, singing out "Jane, Jane, Jane the Brain. Give me a kiss and I won't complain." (I only wanted to kiss Marcel Sislowitz, but that is another story altogether.) When I made it to my own block, my mother would lean out of the window of our fourth floor apartment and scold loudly, "Carl Switzer, you leave her alone or I'll have to call your mother."

I would run gratefully into our building, and before the elevator had even gotten to the fourth floor I was deep into the first of the tales.

The rest I would read on the window seat, overlooking Central Park. I would gallop through the stories in one sitting, barely stopping for dinner, homework, or to watch any of the frequent accidents that occurred outside on the 97th street crossing.

Later that night in bed, I would reread the stories, savoring the H.J. Ford illustrations. The color plates were gorgeous, but I actually preferred the black-and-white pictures which fell more or less at the proper places in each tale. Ford's work was my favorite, so much so that, when in 1950 Longman's came out with a *Yellow Fairy Book* edition with pictures by Janice Holland, I was so disappointed in them I could not read the stories with the same pleasure.

What made me, a child growing up in the 1940s and the 1950s in New York City, a sucker for these old books? They had first been brought out in England, after all, beginning in 1899 with *The Blue Fairy Book*, and were full of the stories that had been told for centuries before. As any American child living in a major city, I had no first-hand knowledge of goose girls or charcoal burners, herd boys or sultans, groac'hs or shepherds or any other of the old characters who peopled these tales. I knew apartment buildings and sidewalks, not castles or huts.

Maybe *because* I had no knowledge of those wonders I was drawn to them. Maybe *because* my life was so humdrum, I craved the adventures.

Or maybe, being human, I was mesmerized by the humanity in the tales. Because if the fairy stories of a hundred different cultures have one thing in common, it is this: they are simply sogged with humanity. Despite the fairies and brownies and elves and ogres and dragons and talking bears I found in them, the stories are about people and how people—the shy, the winsome, the frightened, the curious, the stubborn, the horrified, the careless and the careful—react to challenging situations.

So I read the colored fairy books at an impressionable age and, quite frankly, have never gotten over them. They taught me about honor and loyalty and truth. They taught me about courage and conviction and control. "Just as good as true" said Mr. Lang, but when I first read them they were *better* than true. They were in the deepest sense truth itself. They were about you and they were about me. They were humanity's history.

Over the years, I have read a lot of folk and fairy tales. I have written quite a few myself. Some I have written "out of my own head," like "The Girl Who Cried Flowers," and "The Seeing Stick," and "Greyling." Some I have retold, like "Wings" and "Tam Lin." But my long and passionate affair with such stories can be traced back to the time when I sat on that hard window seat, feet tucked up under me, and—ignoring all the excitement four stories below on Central Park West—read over and over the Andrew Lang fairy books. Years later—in 1992 actually—living in St. Andrews, Scotland, for my husband's sabbatical, I discovered Andrew Lang's grave.

"Thank you, Mr. Lang," I whispered to it, oblivious to the tourists around me. "Thank you for my living. And thank you for my life." He didn't, of course, answer. But then, he didn't have to. His books had been all the answers I needed, even before I knew how to frame the thanks.

THE HONEY-STICK BOY

Once in the middle of a honey forest there lived a man and woman. They wanted a child and had none, so they prayed to the spirit of the hive to give them a child. But through the years, though they wept and prayed, neither son nor daughter was ever sent them.

At last they grew old and bitter.

One day the old woman took three long sticks she had been saving for the cookfire and made a figure with them.

"If we had a child like that," she said, pointing to the stick figure, "even so would I be happy. But what is the good of praying to the spirit of the hive if it cannot grant us this one thing?"

"Old woman," cautioned her husband, "watch how your tongue wags. For the little honey bees are the ears of the forest. And I would not want the spirit of the hive to hear what you have said."

"May his honey become as bitter as I," said the old woman, turning from her man.

She looked at the stick figure and held it up. "See, I have made a child where the spirit of the hive has failed. Even thus shall I make my own happiness."

Then she went to a nearby hollow tree not far from their camp and thrust her arm into the honeybee's nest. She did not mind the buzzing and the stinging, and she brought a handful of honey home.

"The sticks shall make my new son strong," said the old woman. 'The honey shall make him sweet." And she shaped the sticks and honey into the figure of a slim boy, patting the sticky stuff into place.

"Where is it said that a boy should be sweet?" asked the old man gruffly.

"All people should be sweet," she replied.

And to this he had no answer. Yet still he feared that they had angered the spirit of the hive and he worried about this long into the night.

In the morning, when the two old people awoke, they found the fire had been laid, the dirt floor swept, and the table set for two.

"Who could have done such a thing?" asked the old man, marveling.

"Our son, of course," said the old woman. "For like all good sons, he helps his parents."

"You are mad," the old man began. But at that moment, the door swung open and a slim boy came through, his arms full of berries, flowers, and a jug of wild grape wine.

"Good morning, my parents," he said, with a smile so sweet and strong the old man knew at once who it was.

So they called him Mellis, for his honied disposition. He lived with them happily for many days, helping cook and gather food, watching for wild animals at night, and singing softly to send them to sleep. And in all things he was as a human son to them save for these two: He did not eat nor did he sleep.

But the spirit of the hive was angry. The old man and the old woman no longer prayed to him. It was Mellis who brought them berries and wine. It was Mellis who found them feathers and fur. And it was Mellis for whom they saved their praise.

"They no longer remember how many years I gave them life. They grow old and forgetful. They think that they exist by their own wits alone, making a mannikin of honey and sticks. But they forget whose honey it was that made him sweet and whose sticks it was that made him strong. I shall have to help them remember."

So the spirit of the hive sent a drone to listen while the old man and his new son talked. For surely there would fall from their lips some way to make the old people remember.

The bee flew high and the bee flew low and the bee flew in through the window of the hut. It hovered out of sight while Mellis served the old man and his woman their food.

"Today," the old man said to the boy, "we shall go down to the river. There I will teach you how to fish. A man must teach his son all he knows, for we do not live on berries alone. The forest and the river are as one in this life."

"But I do not dare go to the river, my father," replied Mellis.

"What is this?" asked the old man. "A boy does not disobey his father."

"In all things I am yours," said the boy, "save this. For should I fall in the river, the honey that makes me sweet will be washed away. And the sticks that make me strong will float downstream and out of sight."

"What nonsense," said the old woman angrily, for she had forgotten how she had made the boy and believed that he was as human as they.

"You will do as I say," said the old man.

And so Mellis did, for his nature was so sweet he could not disobey.

The drone heard all that was said, and sped back through the forest to the great hive. When it had danced out its message, the spirit of the hive nodded.

"You have done well," said the spirit. "For now I know how to make the old man and old woman remember." And the spirit flew on gauzy wings to the river's edge.

Mellis and the old man had just come down to the bank. The old man flung a vine net into the river, saying, "And thus, my son, goes the cast."

The vine net settled quietly in the stream. The little fish swam round and about it but they did not disturb the lines.

Then the spirit of the hive sent a small swarm of drones into the river. As they dropped into the water, they struggled in the waves. Down in the depth of the river a big black fish, looking for food, saw the movement and swam slowly to the top. It swam right into the waiting net. The fish felt the net close upon it and twisted and turned and pulled the net in many different ways.

The old man was not prepared for such a great fish. His hands were caught in the twisting and he was pulled into the river.

"Ae-i!" he cried out as he fell. "My son, my son, catch hold of my foot!"

Obediently, Mellis reached for the old man's foot and caught hold.

The old man kicked and the old man thrashed, and Mellis held tight to his foot. But with one final pull the old man pulled Mellis right into the river with a splash.

As the water swept over the boy, it tore his pants, his sandals, and his shirt and ripped them from his body. It washed and it washed at his flailing limbs till honey-sweet hair and flesh and all were washed away and nothing was left but three long sticks that bobbed up to the top of the river.

The old man reached out for the sticks and caught hold. The sticks kept his head above the waves and carried him safely to shore. He crept up on the bank and lay there gasping out his thanks. He called to the spirit of the hive and blessed it for bringing him out of the stream.

But the sticks did not hear the thanks nor care. Caught up in the current, they bobbed and danced and raced down the river and were soon lost to sight.

The old man stood up wearily, pushed his wet hair from his eyes, and went home.

"A brave son," he told his wife. "He gave his life to save me."

"Now once more we have no child," said the old woman sadly, but she did not say it bitterly. For she had her dear husband safe and she had her memories, and it was hard to say which she treasured more.

As for the sticks that had been Mellis, they eventually touched shore and rooted together and grew into a mighty tree. And long after the old man and the old woman had passed away, the honey from that tree was known throughout the forest as the strongest and the sweetest in the world.

THE FAERY FLAG

Long ago, when the wind blew from one corner of Skye to another without ever encountering a house higher than a tree, the faery folk lived on the land and they were called the Daoine Sithe, the Men of Peace. They loved the land well and shepherded its flocks, and never a building did they build that could not be dismantled in a single night or put up again in a single day.

But then human folk set foot upon the isles and scoured them with their rough shoeing. And before long both rock and tree were in the employ of men; the land filled with forts and houses, byres and pens. Boats plowed the seas and netted the fish. Stones were piled up for fences between neighbors.

The *Daoine Sithe* were not pleased, not pleased at all. An edict went out from the faery chief: *Have nothing to do with this humankind.*

And for year upon year it was so.

Now one day, the young laird of the MacLeod clan—Jamie was his name—walked out beyond his manor seeking a brachet hound lost outside in the night. It was his favorite hound, as old as he, which—since he was just past fifteen years—was quite old indeed.

He called its name. "Leoid. Leeeeeeoid." The wind sent back the name against his face but the dog never answered.

The day was chill, the wind was cold, and a white mist swirled about the young laird. But many days on Skye are thus, and he thought no more about the chill and cold than that he must find his old hound lest it die.

Jamie paid no heed to where his feet led him, through the bogs and over the hummocks. This was his land, after all, and he knew it well. He could not see the towering crags of the Black Cuillins, though he knew they were there. He could not hear the seals calling from the bay. Leoid was all he cared about. A MacLeod takes care of his own.

So without knowing it, he crossed over a strange, low, stone drochit, a bridge the likes of which he would never have found on a sunny day, for it was the bridge into Faerie.

No sooner had he crossed over than he heard his old dog barking. He would have known that sound were there a hundred howling hounds.

"Leoid!" he called. And the dog ran up to him, its hind end wagging, eager as a pup, so happy it was to see him. It had been made young again in the land of Faerie.

Jamie gathered the dog in his arms and was just turning to go home when he heard a girl calling from behind him.

"Leoid. Leoid." Her voice was as full of longing as his own had been just moments before.

He turned back, the dog still in his arms, and the fog lifted. Running toward him was the most beautiful girl he had ever seen. Her dark hair was wild with curls, her black eyes wide, her mouth generous and smiling.

"Boy, you have found my dog. Give it to me."

Now that was surely no way to speak to the young laird of the MacLeods, he who would someday be the chief. But the girl did not seem to know him. And surely he did not know the girl, though he knew everyone under his father's rule.

"This is my dog," said Jamie.

The girl came closer and put out her hand. She touched him on his bare arm. Where her hand touched, he felt such a shock, he thought he would die, but of love not of fear. Yet he did not.

"It is my dog now, Jamie MacLeod," she said. "It has crossed over the bridge. It has eaten the food of the *Daoine Sithe* and drunk our honey wine. If you bring it back to your world it will die at once and crumble into dust."

The young laird set the dog down and it frolicked about his feet. He put his hand into the girl's but was not shocked again.

"I will give it back to you for your name—and a kiss," he said.

"Be warned," answered the girl.

"I know about faery kisses," said Jamie, "but I am not afraid. And as you know my name, it is only fair that I should know yours."

"What we consider fair, you do not, young laird," she said. But she stood on tiptoe and kissed him on the brow. "Do not come back across the bridge, or you will break your parents' hearts."

He handed her the sprig of juniper from his bonnet.

She kissed the sprig as well and put it in her hair. "My name is Aizel and, like the red hot cinder, I burn what I touch." Then she whistled for the dog and they disappeared at once into the mist.

Jamie put his hand to his brow where Aizel had kissed him, and indeed she had burned him, it was still warm and sweet to his touch.

Despite the faery girl's warning, Jamie MacLeod looked for the bridge not once but many times. He left off fishing to search for it, and interrupted his hunting to search for it; and often he left his bed when the mist was thick to seek it. But even in the mist and the rain and the fog he could not find it. Yet he never stopped longing for the bridge to the girl.

His mother and father grew worried. They guessed by the mark on his brow what had occurred. So they gave great parties and threw magnificent balls that in this way the young laird might meet a human girl and forget the girl of the *Daoine Sithe*.

But never was there a girl he danced with that he danced with again. Never a girl he held that he held for long. Never a girl he kissed that he did not remember Aizel at the bridge. As time went on, his mother and father grew so desperate for him to give the MacLeods an heir, that they would have let him marry any young woman at all, even a faery maid.

On the eve of Jamie's twenty-first birthday, there was a great gathering of the clan at Dunvegan Castle. All the lights were set out along the castle wall and they twinned themselves down in the bay below.

Jamie walked the ramparts and stared out across the bogs and drums. "Oh Aizel," he said with a great sigh, "if I could but see you one more time. One more time and I'd be content."

And then he thought he heard the barking of a dog.

Now there were hounds in the castle and hounds in the town and hounds who ran every day under his horse's hooves. But he knew that particular call.

"Leoid!" he whispered to himself. He raced down the stairs and out the great doors with a torch in his hand, following the barking across the bog.

It was a misty, moisty evening, but he seemed to know the way. And he came quite soon to the cobbled bridge that he had so long sought. For a moment he hesitated, then went on.

There, in the middle, not looking a day older than when he had seen her six years before, stood Aizel in her green gown. Leoid was by her side.

"Into your majority, young laird," said Aizel. "I called to wish you the best."

"It is the best, now that I can see you," Jamie said. He smiled. "And my old dog."

Aizel smiled back. "No older than when last you saw us."

"I have thought of you every day since you kissed me," said Jamie. "And longed for you every night. Your brand still burns on my brow."

"I warned you of faery kisses," said Aizel.

He lifted his bonnet and pushed away his fair hair to show her the mark.

"I have thought of you, too, young laird," said Aizel. "And how the MacLeods have kept the peace in this unpeaceful land. My chief says I may bide with you for a while."

"How long a while?" asked Jamie.

"A faery while," replied Aizel. "A year or an heir, whichever comes first."

"A year is such a short time," Jamie said.

"I can make it be forever," Aizel answered.

With that riddle Jamie was content. And they walked back to Dunvegan Castle hand in hand, though they left the dog behind.

If Aizel seemed less fey in the starlight, Jamie did not mind. If he was only human, she did not seem to care. Nothing really mattered but his hand in hers, her hand in his, all the way back to his home.

The chief of the MacLeods was not pleased and his wife was not happy with the match. But that Jamie smiled and was content made them hold their tongues. So the young laird and the faery maid were married that night and bedded before day.

And in the evening Aizel came to them and said, "The MacLeods shall have their heir."

The days went fast and slow, warm and cold, and longer than a human it took for the faery girl to bear a child. But on the last day of the year she had lived with them, Aizel was brought to labor till with a great happy sigh she birthed a beautiful babe.

"A boy!" the midwife cried out, standing on a chair and showing the child so that all the MacLeods might see.

A great cheer ran around the castle then. "An heir. An heir to the MacLeods!"

Jamie was happy for that, but happier still that his faery wife was well. He bent to kiss her brow.

"A year or an heir, that was all I could promise. But I have given you forever," she said. "The MacLeods shall prosper and Dunvegan will never fall."

Before he could say a word in return, she had vanished and the bed was bare, though her outline could be seen on the linens for a moment more.

The cheer was still echoing along the stone passageways as the midwife carried the babe from room to room to show him to all the clan. But the young laird of the MacLeods put his head in his hands and wept.

Later that night, when the fires were high in every hearth and blackberry wine filled every cup; when the harp and fiddle rang throughout Dunvegan with their tunes; when the bards' mouths swilled with whisky and swelled with the old songs; and even the nurse was dancing with her man, the young laird Jamie MacLeod walked the castle ramparts seven times round, mourning for his lost faery wife.

The youngest laird of the MacLeods lay in his cradle all alone.

So great was the celebration that no one was watching him. And in the deepest part of the night, he kicked off his blankets as babies often do, and he cried out with the cold.

But no one came to cover him. Not the nurse dancing with her man, nor his grandam listening to the tunes, nor his grandfather drinking with his men, nor his father on the castle walk. No one heard the poor wee babe crying with the cold.

It was a tiny cry, a thin bit of sound threaded out into the dark. It went over hillock and hill, over barrow and bog, crossed the cobbled *drochit*, and wound its way into Faerie itself.

Now they were celebrating in the faery world as well, not for the birth of the child but for the return of their own. There was feasting and dancing and the singing of tunes. There was honey wine and faery pipes and the high, sweet laughter of the *Daoine Sithe*.

But in all that fine company, Aizel alone did not sing and dance. She sat in her great chair with her arms around her brachet hound. If there were tears in her eyes, you would not have known it, for the *Daoine Sithe* do not cry, and besides the hound had licked away every one. But she heard that tiny sound as any mother would. Distracted, she stood.

"What is it, my daughter?" asked the great chief of the *Daoine Sithe* when he saw her stand, when he saw a single tear that Leoid had not had time to lick away. But before any of the fey could tell her no, Aizel ran from the faery hall, the dog at her heels. She raced across the bridge, herself as insubstantial as the mist.

And behind her came the faery troops. And the dog.

The company of fey stopped at the edge of the bridge and watched Aizel go. Leoid followed right after. But no sooner had the dog's legs touched the earth on the other side than it crumbled into dust.

Aizel hesitated not a moment, but followed that thread of sound, winding her back into the world of men. She walked over bog and barrow, over hill and hillock, through the great wooden doors and up the castle stairs.

When she entered the baby's room, he was between one breath and another.

"There, there," Aizel said, leaning over the cradle and covering him with her shawl, "thy Mama's here." She rocked him till he fell back asleep, warm and content. Then she kissed him on the brow, leaving a tiny mark there for all to see, and vanished in the morning light.

The nurse found the babe sleeping soundly well into the day. He was wrapped in a cloth of stranger's weave. His thumb was in his mouth, along with a piece of the shawl. She did not know how the cloth got there, nor did his grandfather, the Great MacLeod. If his grandmother guessed, she did not say.

But the young laird Jamie knew. He knew that Aizel had been drawn back across the bridge by her son's crying, as surely as he had first been led to her by the barking of his hound.

"Love calls to love," he whispered softly to his infant son as he held him close. "And the fey, like the MacLeods, take care of their own."

The faery shawl still hangs on the wall at Dunvegan Castle on the Isle of Skye. Only now it is called a Faery Flag and the MacLeods carry it foremost into battle. I have seen it there. Like this story, it is a tattered remnant of stranger's weave and as true and warming as you let it be.

THE GOLDEN STAIR

I cut my hair last week;
all that long gold gone
in a single silent scissoring
after the king was buried.
My husband,
the new king,
wept when he saw it.
But he agreed
that with all I have to do—
the royal tea parties,
the ribbon-cuttings,
the hospital visits,
the endless trips
to factories,
football games,
day care centers—
a short bob is best.
It has been months
since he has noticed my hair.
The golden stair he called it.
It has been years since the tower.
Now that he is king
we cannot risk another fall,
at least until our sons are grown,
at least until
they have taken over the kingdom.

THE TOWER BIRD

There was once a king who sat all alone in the top of a high tower room. He saw no one all day long except a tiny golden finch who brought him nuts and seeds and berries out of which the king made a thin, bitter wine.

What magic had brought him to the room, what binding curse kept him there, the king did not know. The curving walls of the tower room, the hard-backed throne, the corbeled window, and the bird were all he knew.

He thought he remembered a time when he had ruled a mighty kingdom; when men had fought at his bidding and women came at his call. Past battles, past loves, were played again and again in his dreams. He found scars on his arms and legs and back to prove them. But his memory had no real door to them, just as the tower room had no real door, only a thin line filled in with bricks.

Each morning the king went to the window that stood head-high in the wall. The window was too small for anything but his voice. He called out, his words spattering into the wind.

> Little bird, little bird,
> Come to my hand.
> Sing me of my kingdom,
> Tell me of my land.

A sudden whirring in the air, and the bird was there, perched on the stone sill.

"O King," the bird began, for it was always formal in its address. "O King, what would you know?"

"Is the land green or sere?" asked the king.

The bird put its head to one side as if considering. It opened its broad little beak several times before answering. "It is in its proper season."

Color suffused the king's face. He was angry with the evasion. He stuttered his second question. "Is...is the kingdom at peace or is it at war?" he asked.

"The worm is in the apple," replied the bird, "but the apple is not yet plucked."

The king clutched the arms of his throne. Every day his questions met with the same kinds of answers. Either this was all a test or a jest, a dreaming, or an enchantment too complex for his understanding.

"One more question, O King," said the finch. Under its golden breast a tiny pulse quickened.

The king opened his mouth to speak. "Is... is..." No more words came out. He felt something cracking inside as if, with his heart, his whole world were breaking.

The little bird watched a fissure open beneath the king's throne. It grew wider, quickly including the king himself. Without a sound, the king and throne cracked into two uneven pieces. The king was torn between his legs and across the right side of his face. From within the broken parts a smell of soured wine arose.

The bird flew down. It pulled a single white hair from the king's mustache, hovered a moment, then winged out of the window. Round and round the kingdom it flew, looking for a place to nest, a place to build another tower and lay another egg. Perhaps the king that grew from the next egg would be a more solid piece of work.

Oh, God, Here Come the Elves

Since I am a storyteller, I will begin with a story. It is a creation story, an etiological tale:

> And it came to pass in the days of the Author that she was sitting before her typewriter and contemplating a plot gone awry. Her characters, astride horses, had been riding so long, both she and they had forgotten the mission. To rectify this, she entitled the chapter "The Long Riding"[1] and, thus satisfying all, was proceeding with the tale.
>
> The characters got off their horses at last and looked about the scene. There was a grove of aspen, trembling slightly in the breeze. Around was the forest with its layers of green. And beyond the line of trees lay a great road which, only lately, they had all been endlessly riding upon.
>
> The Author paused, waiting for inspiration, having settled those past weeks for perspiration instead, comforting herself with a mantra learned from William Faulkner: "I only write when I am inspired; fortunately I am inspired at 9 o'clock every morning."[2]
>
> Leaning back, the Author took a sip of tea, waiting.
>
> Sudden silence alerted her. The forest itself seemed to have stopped breathing. At first there was nothing. And then—there was a circle of some thirty mannikins, dressed all in green jerkin and trews, as if they had metamorphosed from the trees and brush. Half the size of men, with skin a greenish cast, like translucent glaze over fine bones, as if the land itself had been thinned down to its essence and given human form.[3]

> "Oh, God," the Author groaned, putting her hands over
> her eyes so as not to read the offending words on the page.
> "Here come the elves."

To understand the Author's agony, the reader must be reminded: the book *White Jenna* is not a book about elves. It is not a book in which little humanoid creatures of an unearthly attenuated beauty caper about making white fire and singing in tongues. There is but one kind of magic in White Jenna's land and it has absolutely nothing to do with unicorns or dragons or trolls or ents or sentient swords or philosophical bards or elves. Especially not elves.

And yet, with an arrogance born of centuries of misrule, the elves have casually—and without invitation—walked onto the scene.

There are three things any author can do at this point. The first is to take a Number 2 pencil or a red or green Flair pen and declare open war on elvery. A single deadly stroke, an airborne attack, delete signs rained from above—any of these will suffice. In that way the elves and all their faery accoutrement—bells, spells, and pointed ears—will disappear from the forest as if they had never been. It will be a clean surgical strike. And if it leaves a hole—we had to destroy the novel in order to save it—at least the author will not spend days agonizing over the battle. Like the wonderfully silly song about "Railroad Bill,"[4] in which the song writer finally destroys the recalcitrant eponymous hero with his pen, the author declares the novel belongs to her and no character or characters will do other than her explicit bidding. That's number one.

There is a second course, a compromise approach. The author gives a little to the elves and takes a little away. Like most political settlements, this ends up compromising everybody. For example, the author could say: okay, the elves can stay but they are going to have to wear red rather than green. Or the author could call them Oompa-loompahs or Red Injuns or Gildensterns or Thieves' World™ Thieves. Anything but *elves.* Or the author could declare that the elves may stay for tea and leave on the 8 o'clock ferry for Lothlorien. That's number two.

The third solution, while not nearly as neat as the surgical strike nor as balanced as the compromise, is the one to which I subscribe: *total, utter, and abject surrender to the elves.*

Let me explain.

Writers are creatures of layers, an uneasy yoking of conscious, subconscious, and unconscious. Almost like real people. The conscious dictates those endless revisions; the subconscious dictates the invention of characters that are pastiches of beloved and/or hated friends, relatives, and acquaintances of the author; and the unconscious does the intricate weaving together of plot and the gathering and distribution of subtext which is the GNP of any real novel.

A writer who lets her conscious dictate subtext and her unconscious the revisions is in serious trouble. Ministers, rabbis, and politicians consciously (and conscientiously—as well as sententiously) dictate subtext and what they write are sermons and position papers.[5] Unpublished writers allow the revisions to be done by their unconscious mind alone, which is to say they don't change a single word in real time. But the professional writer acknowledges the tripartite division and, like Gaul, manages to keep running nonetheless.

An aside: if the profession takes over the writer, a new equation emerges. Deadlines D and payments P are divided by the need to produce stories S and books B. After the equal signs you will find no more elves.

It is easy to see that I believe in the *elf factor,* that sudden appearance on the pages of heretofore unexpected characters or landscapes or pieces of plot machinery. It is what so often distinguishes a piece of writing. I further believe that when something wonderfully anarchic or surprising surfaces, it is the writer's duty to hear the thing out.

Storytelling is always a combination of what we know and what surprises us. But before any reader can be surprised, the author must be surprised, too. Like the sibyls before us, we must be overwhelmed by the vatic voice.

Vatic: the prophetic or oracular or inspired voice. The sibyls used drug-inducing leaves in a smudge pot and the resonant cave walls as conduits for their gnomic utterances. The author, lacking leaves, pot, and cave walls, uses black smudges on a page. I have often said that stories leak out of my fingertips. For me that is a shorthand statement, a metaphor (as in Ciardi's definition of a metaphor as an "exactly felt error") that describes the process of being possessed by the vatic voice.

I am not saying that writers need to put on Indian print dresses, wear dangling earrings, and channel Shirley MacLaine's next book. I am not even saying we need to sit in darkened rooms waiting—like some latter day William Butler Yeats—for the automatic writing to begin. But we do, indeed, always need to be prepared for serendipity.

Writers, according to Natalie Goldberg in her book *Writing Down the Bones,* "live twice."[6] But that is not entirely true. Writers live twice only when they are prepared to take that second breath, the one that sings out of the chest in the full bardic tones; the one that converses with elves, even when the elves were not in the character list, the plot outline, the 20-page synopsis, or the contract. Even then.

And see ye not that bonny road
That winds about the fernie brae?
That is the road to fair Elfland
Where thou and I this night maun gae.[7]

sings the Elf queen to Thomas of Ercildoune. *Maun* is the operative word here. It means *must*. "Where thou and I must go." He goes with her because he must. Past thorns and briars, past black skies and a sea of blood. Past time itself. Unless and until Thomas of Ercildoune goes with the Elf queen he cannot become the poet, the seer Thomas the Rhymer, he cannot speak truly. In order to become a truth teller, in order to speak *ferly*, you must go with the elf queen, kiss her and go.

Last year when I was living in Edinburgh, I took author Ellen Kushner—who was then working on a novel about Thomas the Rhymer[8]— on a tour of Erlston and the ruins of Melrose Abbey. We climbed the Eildon Hills as well. Overhead was the brilliant blue bowl of sky and beneath our feet the fern-covered hillside. Writers both, we *were* living twice. As twentieth century American women we were clambering up the gentle slope of the Eildon Hills above a modern farm, carefully avoiding cowpats. In the Rhymer's Tower Cafe we had come upon an elderly Scotswoman who had taken us to her home and recited the 61 verses of "True Thomas" in Broad Scots while her "auld man" slept by the fire. At the Abbey we had investigated the remarkably contemporary drainage system and explored the tiny Abbey museum. But we were also at the same time back in the misty moisty poetic past, 700 years before, when the Abbey had been filled with the voices of young men singing psalms, when the hills had been crossed with roads of thorn and briar, and the Rhymer himself—not the rhyme—had lived. In that setting neither of us would have been surprised by elves.

Story is a way of remembering, after all. Once upon a time is not a specific era; it stands for all time and all times. Just one letter difference is between *never-never-land* and *ever-ever-land*. And it is, after all, with exquisite care that someone once called the land of faerie the place where things never were but always are.

Grant me, then, that it is important to accept the entrance of elves. And further understand that if you grant that, you must be prepared for them as well.

Susan Shwartz, author and academic, has written about creative research as one way of being prepared. In a letter to me, she told me about a rather radical Holy Grail book she is writing in which she suddenly found herself in need of a sister whore for Mary Magdalene. But she had never read of any specifically. Something led her to purchase a translation of the Gnostic Gospels and there waiting was something she had no way of knowing existed: a gospel of Mary and a poem "Thunder: Perfect Mind" with a narrative voice that proclaimed itself to be both virgin and whore. "Just," she wrote to me, "what the plot line ordered."

This all sounds suspiciously and wonderfully like Susanne Langer's line about discoveries which she wrote of in *Philosophy in a New Key:*[9] "Most discoveries are suddenly seen things that were always there."

Suddenly seen things. Like Koestler's "shaking together of two previously unconnected matrices,"[10] like the Gestalt therapy's great a-ha, like Watson on the top level of the double-decker bus suddenly envisioning DNA's double helix. Writers need to be prepared for serendipity, must be ready for the entrance of the elves.

This has happened to me enough times so that I look forward to such things. But as they occur differently each time, I am sometimes not as prepared as I might like to be.

For example, in a humorous fantasy novel for children called *Hobo Toad & The Motorcycle Gang,*[11] I wrote about a hitchhiking toad called HT or Hopalong Toad, who gets a ride with a truck driver. Now the driver's truck was filled with—of all things—marbles. It was a throw-away line. I had to fill the truck with something. I had no plans for the truck's contents—at least as far as I knew consciously. But later on, when the motorcycle gang has kidnapped HT and the trucker and several other people along the way, it is that truck full of marbles that actually saves the day. I could have filled the truck with pizzas or chocolate milk or nitroglycerine for that matter. But I stuck a load of marbles, round and ready, in at the loading dock. And when I needed them, the marbles—like the elves—marched onto the scene.

Then there was a fairy tale I wrote called *The Seeing Stick.*[12] It is set in ancient Peking where a blind princess, unhappy with her lot, is taught to see with her fingers by an old man who comes up from the south. The old man carves his adventures into a walking stick and teaches the princess, finger on finger, to read this early braille. When I read the story to my writing group—a weekly critique group with which I have been meeting for 19 years—one member said, "I am sorry, did I miss it? Is the old man blind, too?" Stunned, I didn't answer for a second, then blurted out, "Well of course." Of course he hadn't been the moment before but all the clues had been put in by my unconscious mind. And the book *now* ends:

> As the princess grew, she grew eyes on the tips of her fingers, or at least that is what she told the other blind children whom she taught to see as she saw. And certainly it was as true as saying she had a seeing stick.
>
> But the little blind princess believed that both things were true.

And so did all the blind children in Peking.
And so did the blind old man.

I also had the experience with a children's novel[13] about the Holocaust, in which a modern-day American girl, Hannah Stern, travels back in time through the door that opens for that estimable time traveler Elijah. When Hannah and her new friends in the shtetl are rounded up by the Nazis and put in a concentration camp, she loses all sense of who she was and now only knows who she *is*, *Chaya Abramowitz*. Well within the nightmare months, she is told a story by the rabbi's daughter. When I got to that part of the novel, I knew I needed a powerful story, a folk tale or midrash tale that would speak to the horror in which they were all bound. I have a number of volumes of Jewish and Israeli folk material. The Yiddish Book Center is in the next town. The problem was to find the right story and yet not spend the next few months researching, because I was afraid of losing the flow of the book. I picked out all the volumes in my local library and piled them on my desk. Now this next will seem like mystical claptrap and yet it is exactly what happened. I shuffled through the books and picked out one of them—*Classic Hassidic Tales*.[14] I opened it up randomly and found a story called "Israel and the Enemy" about Rabbi Israel Baal Shem, who takes the heart out of a werewolf and sets it upon the ground. And I knew that I had found the story I needed without opening a single other book. With only slight paraphrasing, I set the story into the mouth of the rabbi's daughter and it summed up in horrifying detail what the people of Chaya's shtetl were going through.

> That night Fayge began to speak, as if the eords so long dammed up had risen to flood. She told a story she had heard from her father, about the great Ba'al Shem Tov. It was set in the time when he was a boy named Israel and *his* father warned him: "Know, my son, that the enemy will always be with you. He will be in the shadow of your dreams and in your living flesh, for he is the other part of yourself. There will be times when he will surround you with walls of darkness. But remember always that your soul is secure to you, for your soul is entire, and that he cannot enter your soul, for your soul is part of God." Fayge's voice rose and fell as she told how young Israel led a small band of children against a werewolf whose heart was Satan's. And in the end, when Israel walked straight into the werewolf's body and held its awful dark heart in his hand, "shivering and jerking like a fish out of water," Fayge said, her own hand moving in the same way, that awful heart

was filled with "immeasurable pain. A pain that began before time and would endure forever."

She whispered the story as the night enfolded them. "Then Israel took pity on the heart and gave it freedom. He placed it upon the earth and the earth opened and swallowed the black heart into itself."

A sigh ran around the barrack and Hannah's was the deepest of all. A *werewolf*, she thought. *That's where we are now. In the belly of the werewolf. But where, where is its dark pain-filled heart?* She was still sighing when she slipped into sleep.

A plot device, a character, and a story within a story that serves as metaphor for the entire book—that is what I had become used to.

So why, when the elves marched onto the scene in *White Jenna.* did I balk? For balk I did. I left Jenna and her companions surrounded by a ring of elves for three weeks while I went off and did the usual writer-not-working things. I cleaned the house, I baked cookies, I washed windows, I answered long overdue mail.

I think it has to do with the perception of elves and their place in the world of fantasy literature.

Elfy-welfy is a phrase often heard today in the reviewing of fantasy literature. It summarizes a tendency of rather ardent fans and collectors of badly wrought miniatures to rhapsodize over the Cute. When the line thins down between sentiment and the sentimental, it does not take seven-league boots to cross over.

But if a writer is one who first is an accurate observer and then a careful selector of details, what can we say about the sentimentalist except that he has neither a keen eye nor any understanding of how details work. The sentimentalist softens details or perhaps he first observes them through a fuzzy lens. For if we are to look back upon elves in the lore, we do not find anything cute about them at all.

Dr. H. R. Ellis Davidson in *Scandinavian Mythology*[15] links elves and the dead, suggesting also that their beauty and their dangerous personalities had to do with their being land spirits not always to be counted upon. Something of this latter, she further suspects, came down into the smaller "tricksy flower-loving creatures" of the Elizabethan plays.

Katherine Briggs, the dean of the British folklorists and surely the most knowledgeable folklorist in the realm of the faery folk, reminds us of faery morality, which is not like mortal choosing. Though they will never tell a direct lie, or break a promise, they may "often distort it." And, she further states, "Order more than morality is part of the fairy code. They are great lovers of cleanliness, tidiness and established ways. The second thing they require of human beings is liberality…[they] set high value on courtesy and respect… A flavor of bawdiness hung about them… and a genial rogue is as likely to receive their favours as anyone else." She further points out that elves and other faery folk have no respect for human goods, for "honesty means nothing to [them]. They consider that they have right to whatever they need or fancy, including the human beings themselves."[16]

This is a far cry from the coy pointy-eared creatures in fur loin clothes who have recently infested the shores of fantasy, a vulgarization encouraged by Victorian spiritualists, helped on by Walt Disney, and given a genial pat on the head by Mr. Spock.

Is it any wonder that an Author who discovers elves marching into her hitherto pristine glade chooses to run off to the kitchen and eat chocolate chip cookies until the pesky critters depart for Elfhame?

Three weeks is a long time to consider the inevitable. In the end, of course, I capitulated. Besides, I am nothing if not nosey. I wanted to know what the elves thought they were doing there. The only way to find out was to let them talk. And I could always delete them after. Being an *American* writer, I had to consider them innocent until otherwise proven. I let them walk and talk and lead my Jenna and her party down the primrose paths.

It should be no surprise at this point to any of us that the elves—or at least the forest folk or Green folk or Grenna as it seems they were called—turned out to be important to my book. In fact they turned out to be important to the book that immediately preceded *White Jenna* as well, a book called *Sister Light, Sister Dark,* a book already published.

The Grenna solved three problems raised in the two books: a problem of time, a problem of sociological structures, and a problem that had to do with pre-history metaphysics, if you will. Only one of these was a problem I knew I had.

The problem of time was clear. I had as my hero a fourteen-year-old girl. I was a third of the way through the second book and she needed to be much older. But I hadn't the time—literally—in the novel to let all that time pass. And it wasn't the kind of book where you could keep them on their horses for another five years. That would be a "Long Riding" indeed.

The first chapter in Katherine Briggs's book *The Vanishing People: Fairy Lore & Legends,* a book I consulted regularly when working on notes for my mammoth collection of *Folk Tales From Around the World* for Pantheon, is called "The Supernatural Passage of Time in Fairyland." It begins:

> All through the world, wherever the idea of Fairyland or of a
> supernatural country was evolved, it was accompanied by a strong
> feeling of the relativity of time. This may well have been founded
> on the experiences of a dream or a state of trance. It is common

> in a dream to pass through long and varied experiences in the
> mortal time occupied between, let us say, beginning to fall out
> of bed and landing with a bump on the floor. In a state of trance,
> on the other hand, the mental processes can be so retarded that
> one train of thought is slowly pursued for several hours. Both
> these psychological experiences are reproduced in legends of visits
> to fairyland or to the Other World.[17]

What better use of my new elven characters than to have them take Jenna
and company to their own world—below the hill or into the glade or through
the tunnel, all viable folkloric concepts—where time will move differently:
When my travelers emerge, it is five years (but only 14 pages) later.

The problem of sociologic structure was less clear, but somehow these
Green Folk did not live in a hierarchical society. Unlike the usual folkloric elves whose highly structured society always consists of a queen or
king at the top, a royal or seely (seelie) court, and fairy underlings, with
human or changeling others at the bottom, my elves announced: "We
have neither king nor captain. We have only the circle." And later adds
"Is the circle not the perfect form...? ...In it no one is higher. No one is
lower. No one is first. No one is last."[18]

It certainly sets up a different form in opposition to the hierarchies
within the books' other societal structures where a king reigns in the land,
a captain rules the armies, a priestess or Mother Alta rules the Hames,
and Jenna, unwillingly, commands.

The third problem the elves dealt with was to explain in a allegorical
way, in the trance state of time manipulation, who the great goddess of
the Dales was and how she came to know the magic she knows and why
she passed it on to the women of the Dales.

The one thing they do not explain is how and why there are elves. But
that is perhaps something to be left for another adventure, another trance,
another author. As the spokesman for the elves for that time says: "This
one speaks today. Tomorrow another. The circle moves on."[19]

When I listened to my elves, I discovered that they had indeed links
with the elven folk of fairy lore. They do have some connection with the
dead for Jenna cannot come back to the land-outside-of-time until she is
close to death herself. And the Grenna, while never telling a direct lie, do
avoid telling the complete truth. Their circle, being the perfect form, is as
neat and tidy as anything elves in the old woods might imagine. Yet they
are not simple clones of the old elves. They are couriers, they are trans-
porters, they are device rather than devisers. And as swiftly as they moved
onto the pages, they moved off again.

I don't want you to think that what I am talking about has anything
to do with New Age shamanism or Madame Blavatsky trance writing.

Rather I am trying to draw a distinction between conscious creation and what I term the *elf factor*, that is the Author's receptivity to surprise.

William Morris wrote: "The master of any trade can keep his eye on the work, what he wants to do, and leave his hand free to get it out. He has it in his mind's eye clearly enough. But when it is finished, his hands put a lot of things into it that his mind never thought of: that is exactly where inspiration comes in, if you want to call it so."[20]

In fact I call it so—at 9 o'clock every morning. And my gates remain open to any passing elves.

Footnotes

1. Yolen, Jane, *White Jenna,* Tor Books, 1989. pp. 43–82.
2. I have tried in vain to track down a citation for this wonderful bit of Faulknerian wisdom, something I have known for years.
3. Yolen, Jane, *White Jenna,* Tor Books, 1989. p. 58.
4. For the complete text of this song, ask Steve Brust, who sings it whenever asked (and sometimes when asked not to) with great glee.
5. Having been a speech writer for a political campaign, I am well aware of the difference between novels and position papers, though fiction is a heavy component of both!
6. Goldberg, Natalie, *Writing Down the Bones,* Shambhala, 1986, p. 4.
7. "Thomas the Rhymer," Child Ballad #37, *The English and Scottish Popular Ballads,* Dover, Vol. 1, 1882, 1965, pp. 317–329.
8. Kushner, Ellen, *Thomas the Rhymer,* Morrow, 1990.
9. Langer, Susanne, *Philosophy in a New Key,* Harvard University Press, 1951.
10. Koestler, Arthur, *The Act of Creation,* Macmillan, 1964.
11. Yolen, Jane, *Hobo Toad & the Motorcycle Gang,* World, 1970.
12. Yolen, Jane, *The Seeing Stick,* T.Y. Crowell, 1976.
13. Yolen, Jane, *The Devil's Arithmetic,* Viking, 1988.
14. Levin, Meyer, reteller, *Classic Hassidic Tales,* Dorset Press, 1931, 1959, 1985, pp. 10–16
15. Davidson, Dr. H. R. Ellis, *Scandinavian Mythology,* London, 1967.
16. Briggs, Katharine, *The Fairies in English Tradition and Literature,* University of Chicago Press, 1967, pp. 108–114.
17. Briggs, Katharine, *The Vanishing People,* Pantheon Books, 1978, p. 11.
18. Yolen, Jane, *White Jenna,* Tor Books, 1989. pp. 59–61.
19. Ibid, p. 61.
20. Sparling, H. Halliday, *The Kelmscott Press... William Morris, Master Craftsman.*

THE BARBARIAN AND THE QUEEN: THIRTEEN VIEWS

1.

Dax sat on the edge of his chair, uneasy with the cushion at the back. His people always said that "Comfort is the enemy of the warrior." He was always most careful when he felt most at ease.

He clutched the porcelain cup with one of his death grips. It was only by chance that he did not break the cup and spill the contents—a special blend of Angoran and Basilien tea flavored with tasmairn seeds—down his leather pants. They were his best leather, sewn by his favorite wife. He did not want to stain them.

This queen of the New People who invited him to drink, this old woman with the face of a frog. Did she mean him to come and discuss peace? Or did she mean to threaten more war?

He looked into the cup and saw the black leaves thick as bog at the bottom.

She meant him to die, then.

I will not, he thought—slowly drawing out his long blade—*go to the dark lands alone.*

2.

Prince Henry sat next to his mother and stared at the barbarian who perched on the edge of his seat, one enormous hairy hand wrapped around a teacup.

Rather like a vulture on a cliff's edge, Prince Henry thought. *Except, of course, for the teacup.*

"Excuse me, sir," Prince Henry said, "but why don't you lean back in the chair. You look terribly uncomfortable."

The barbarian grunted, a sound quite like the sound Prince Henry's prize pig made in labor.

"Comfortable warrior," the barbarian said in his grunt voice, "dead warrior."

"Yes, of course. But no one here is actually trying to kill you," Prince Henry said sensibly.

The barbarian stood up suddenly and looked about with hooded eyes. His muscles bunched alarmingly.

"He means," Prince Henry's mother put in tactfully, "that he must at all times be on his guard so as not to get into bad habits. And Henry—you do know about bad habits, don't you?"

Satisfied that no enemies were coming up from behind, the barbarian sat again. On the edge of the chair.

The queen smiled and poured some of the tasmairn-laced tea into the cup. She never showed—even for a moment—that she feared the barbarian might crush the cup, and it one of an important set sent to her by her godmother, the Sultana.

"Sugar?"

Prince Henry was too young to be impressed with his mother's calm demeanor. But he knew better than to say anything more. Bad habits was a subject best left unexplored.

3.

She crossed and uncrossed her legs three times just to hear the stockings squeak. She'd never actually owned a pair before, having to make do with drawing lines down the back of her legs. But then all the girls did that. At least they'd done it through the war. No one had ever known the difference. And since she had the best-looking legs in her little town, she'd never actually felt the need for the real thing.

Before now, that is.

She made the squeak again.

Catching a glimpse of herself in the full-length mirror, she checked her shoulder-length blonde hair.

"Looking good, Babs," she said, and winked at the reflection and took a sip of tea from the little pink flower cup. God, how she could have used a slug of something stronger.

Just then the queen came into the room and Babs stood at once. They had taught her well, all those nameless servants. And she was a fast learner, as long as it wasn't school stuff.

She wobbled ever so slightly on the high heels. Those were new for her, too, the height of them. But with the money the servants had doled out, she knew she had to have them. It made her taller than the prince, but then he didn't seem to mind.

The queen stood at the door waiting for something. A bow maybe. But Babs knew her rights. She was an American and they didn't need to bow to any old queen. Still she gave a quick little bob just in case.

"So you are this Barbie character," the queen said, looking down her long nose. "The girl my son has been seeing. The girl everyone is talking about." She said the word *everyone* as if it were dirty somehow. But necessary.

"I'm called Babs, your majesty."

"Babs? Don't be ridiculous. Babs is a cow's name." The queen signaled for her tea to be served. "I shall call you Barbie." She sat down on a chair that was covered with a fine raw silk the color of old milk.

Babs caught another glimpse of herself in the mirror beore sitting. Every golden hair was in place and her mouth was drawn on perfectly. On the other hand, the queen—with her long nose and bulging eyes, her dowdy dress and her blue hair—the queen was a mess.

And who's the cow here? Babs thought, crossing her legs slowly so that the queen could hear every little squeak.

4.

Queen Victoria stared over the flowered teacup at her new Prime Minister. Her nose twitched but she did not sniff at him. It would not do.

He was the barbarian, not she. All Jews were barbarians. Eastern, oily, brilliant, full of dark unpronounceable magic. However long they lived in England, they remained different, apart, unknowable. She did not trust him. She *could* not trust him. But she would never say so.

"More tea, Mr. Disraeli?"

Disraeli smiled an alarmingly brilliant smile, and nodded.

His lips moved but no words—no English words—could be heard. Across the rosewood table the queen slowly melted like butter on a hot skillet. A few more cabalistic phrases and she reformed into a toad.

"Yes, please, ma'am," Disraeli answered.

The toad, wearing a single crown jewel in her head, poured the tea.

"Ribbet," she said clearly.

"I agree, ma'am," said Disraeli. "I entirely agree." With a single word he turned her back. It was not an improvement. Such small distractions amused him on these state visits. He could not say as much for the queen.

5.

The queen had turned three that morning and had not gotten what she wanted for her birthday. At the moment she was lying on the floor and holding her royal breath and turning quite blue.

In any other household, Nanny Brown would have paddled her charge swiftly on her lovely pink bottom. Such a tempting target right now, on the Caucasian Dragon carpet. But one does not paddle a royal bottom whatever the cause.

Nanny Brown sighed and, holding the dimity cup filled with tasmairn tea—the best thing for her headaches—leaned back against the rocker waiting for the tantrum to wear itself out.

"I...want...a...barbarian," the little queen had screamed before flinging herself down.

Nanny Brown knew that tame barbarians from the Eastern Steppes were all the rage these days. Most castles had one or two. But the regent had said no.

And when that piece of "ordure" ("Best say shite where one means shite," Mr. Livermore, the butler, had told her, but she could never let such a word pass her lips) said no to something that the little queen wanted...

"Well, he does not have to deal with her tantrums," Nanny Brown said under her breath.

The tantrum finally passed, of course. They always did. The queen sat up, her face the color of one of her dear dead mother's prize roses. Her golden ringlets, so lovingly twirled around Nanny Brown's finger not an hour since, were now wet little yellow tangles. The lower lip stuck out more than was strictly necessary.

"Oh, Nanny," she cried. "My tummy hurts. I think I am going to swallow up again."

"Come to Nanny," Nanny Brown said. She put down the cup, the tasmairn having once again worked wonders, and held her arms out wide. "And I shall tell you a story about a big bad wolf. So much better than any old smelly barbarian, don't you think?" That was safe. They had a wolf down in the private zoo and she could spin out the tale till the little queen fell asleep and they could visit it after her nap. Wolves always went down well with this one.

The little queen stood up and wriggled into Nanny Brown's ample lap, her big, blue eyes still pooling.

"A story, Nanny," she said, "I want my story."

"And so you shall have it, my dove," said Nanny Brown, setting the rocker into motion.

The queen put her thumb in her mouth, like a stopper in a perfume bottle.

The barbarian was forgotten.

6.

The Barbarian, waist a solid 44, pecs nicely sculpted by recent days at the Uptown Gym, this week's special at $25 if you sign up the full year and use the coupons from Safeway, wrapped his hamfist around the dimity cup of tea carefully because the cup was frigging hot. He could smell the mint

leaves and something else as well, maybe a touch of tasmairn? Good for
what ails you and then some, as his old aunt used to say, his mother's sister
still in the old country or cuntry as Cappy put it. He'd always drink tasmairn
tea. As long as there was nothing else added. Nothing—you know—ille-
gal. Like some guys always wanted you to try. They tested you these days
after every match. He couldn't afford to be ruled off. Not with the house
payment coming due. And wanting to buy Jolie a real ring for putting up
with him without complaints or at least not a lot for so many years.

But this Queen dame who was fronting money for his training was—
Cappy said—an angel come from somewhere real far away, Connecticut
maybe, or Maine. Wanting to be part of the action. And he had to see her
for tea. She said a drink but Cappy said not during training though he
longed for a single malt something from Scotland where his mother—
God Rest her—had come from and even eighty years later had a brogue
could flay the skin off your cheeks. The ones both sides of your nose and
the other ones as well.

This Queen character wanted to know what she was buying for her
cash, touch the bod a bit, he guessed, the dames who came to watch him
always wanted that. Jolie didn't mind; she was used to it as long as it wasn't
anywhere serious. An arm, a calf, maybe even a thigh, though not higher
or Jolie really would kill him and if she left what would become of him he
didn't know but probably like some old cauliflower fighter just hang around
the gym not knowing his ass from...from a teacup.

He smiled, glad he'd put in the new bridge so the spaces between his
teeth didn't show. And the colored lenses which he wore out of the ring but
not in since a good blow to the head could lose them and them worth a
small fortune being colored and all not like glasses which were twelve bucks
at Safeway if you could find one to fit. Turned his head slightly to look at
her, the Queen character, out of the comer of his eye. Jolie liked that, said
it was cute which given he weighed in at 388 was something he supposed.

And the Queen smiled back, only her teeth were odd—even pointed
like, even filed if he didn't know better. Not Connecticut then, or Maine.
Somewhere across the pond maybe. Her accent was strange. Maybe Brook-
lyn, maybe further away. And he didn't or wouldn't ever know better because she leaned into him, over him, those teeth in his throat and razoring
down to his belly, slitting him open, the hot intestines falling out like so
many sausages, her eyes glittering, and he never laid a hand, Jolie, he swore.
Or a hold. Nothing serious at all, so who was the barbarian now?

7.

Since coming from East Jersey, the barbarian had been forced to be tea-
total, and never more so than when he had drinks with the Queen. She,
poor mad thing, was once again AA-ed and—he knew—that meant T.

Really, things were better before alphabet soup had been invented. He remembered fondly his illiterate days on the steppes and the fermented yak dung. It was why he liked Lapsang Souchong, it had the same slightly smoky, yakky taste. Not this tasmairn stuff. Crap with a capital K.

"Drink up, Queenie," he said to her, lifting the cup, the one with all the letters on it.

She raised her flower-sprigged cup back at him. It did—he thought—suit her to a T.

8.

Boobs the Barbarian sat and spread her thighs to let in a little breeze. Leather was hot this time of year, but the customers demanded it.

She'd been weeks without a paying gig, and this one—dancing for Randy Queen's birthday party—was easily a C-note, not counting tips, and could pay off her week's rent and with some over. Maybe get some new hardware. Her sword was looking a bit thin. The costumer who'd made it for her three years ago was out of business now. But a new place had opened up just down the street, promising fine edges and light-weights. She could do with a lighter blade.

The tea in her floral cup had gone cold, but she drank it anyway. Then she swirled her finger in the sugar at the bottom and sucked on the finger. A good sugar high right now was what she needed to get through the next couple of hours.

Behind the door the music started.

Usually she liked to dance to *Carmina Burana,* but this was a strictly bump-and-grind crowd, the men already well oiled and eager for some hot stuff. Which she could do, of course.

Hot.

The leather.

The tea.

And me, she thought.

Flinging the cup over her shoulder for luck—she hated those little sprigged flowers anyway—she stood and started for the kitchen door. As she walked, already swaying to the music, she began to loosen the strings on her jerkin.

When she strode into the room, the roar of the men was nearly over-powering. But with a smile, she drew her sword and quieted them all.

9.

The sky over Venice was the deep blue of a glass bead. No stars. No moon.

Ned Robertson shrugged his shoulders, and the costume he was wearing felt heavy and ill-fitting.

Like an old boot, he thought.

When he had complained, the costumer had smiled a gaptooth smile and said, "All barbarian costumes fit like dis, signor. Otherwise they would not be barbary. You capice?" Though of course his English was atrocious and Ned had had to talk rather more loudly to make him understand.

I should have worn a Pierrot, he thought. *Chalk to cheese.* Instead he had let Sofia talk him into the leather. She'd run her hand over his shoulder, down his back, and whispered in his ear, "I love the feel of this stuff."

He should have let *her* wear the leather.

Venice was too hot for such a costume on a man.

Sofia, of course, was dressed like Marie Antoinette, in a wig that made her almost as tall as he was. She was such a pretty little thing, a pocket Venus as his mother used to say.

He cursed the leather costume, the heat of Venice, his new wife's towering wig.

But what's a man to do?

He put on the mask with its permanent smile and went downstairs.

There were at least ten Marie Antoinettes in the milling tour group, and a dozen Pierrots. He could not see Sofia in the crowd.

But evidently all the Marie Antoinettes could see him. Or some part of him, anyway. For suddenly they were all laughing behind their fans and pointing and the Pierrots made a series of awful jokes at his expense.

Bugger this, he thought, and ran back upstairs where he shed the leather skins and swore he would not go back down there again.

Not for all the tasmairn tea in China.

10.

Dar sat uneasily by the northern queen and stared at the black spot high up on her cheekbone. It was not a god-spot, which all his wives had. It looked like a bit of a petal stuck there.

He wondered if he should point it out to her. He wondered if such things mattered to these brittle creatures from the north.

She lowered one eyelid at him.

Among his people, such a thing meant she wanted to fuck. But did it mean the same here? He did not want to offend. Not now. Not when his people and hers were deep in negotiations for the passage across the Great River. The cattle were unsettled and lowing their misery. As were his wives. He had to be certain.

There. She did it again.

Dar hesitated.

But then her unshod foot touched his under the table, the toes slowly rubbing up his leg, past the calf, along the inside of the thigh.

There was no mistaking her desire.

Dar stood up quickly, upended the table, teapot, flowered cups, and sachets of tea. Reaching the queen in a single step, he grabbed her up, flipped her over, slammed her onto the ground, and raised the massive skirts over her head. Momentarily flummoxed by the thing that hid her bum, he solved that problem by ripping the soft material apart.

Then he entered her.

She was harder than his wives, harder than any of his sheep. But she opened to him at last and let out only one stifled cry.

Dar was sure it was a cry of pleasure.

11.
EXT: HAMPTON COURT, day, 17th century

A COACH comes up the drive, driven by two HORSES. FOOTMEN run out and open the door. TWO COURTIERS in capes descend. They help out a YOUNG WOMAN dressed in the latest Elizabethan fashion. She is dark skinned. Her black hair is in braids. The COURTIERS, of course, are powdered whiter than white and wear wigs. The COURTIERS and YOUNG WOMAN all enter the building.

INT: PRESENCE ROOM. Even though it is day, there are torches and candles everywhere. QUEEN ELIZA-BETH I, well past middle age, her face whitened with powder, sits on a high carved chair on a dais, a large goblet decorated with flowers in her hand. She is speaking to SIR ROBERT CECIL, a middle-aged scribe/politician.

ELIZABETH

Is she a barbarian?

CECIL
(Cautiously)
How does one measure barbarity, Majesty?

ELIZABETH
(Testily)
Do not play words with me, Cecil. You will not win the game. Does she wear skins? Does she have a bone through her nose? Does she eat her enemies?

CECIL
(Bowing slowly, languidly)
She wears skins in her own home, Majesty. Here she is dressed in the latest
fashion. There is no bone through her nose. And as far as I know, she does
not cannibalize her neighbors.

ELIZABETH
(She sighs, looks bored, takes a sip from the cup)

CECIL
She does, however, use bear grease in her hair.

ELIZABETH
(Looking up eagerly)
Does she smell?

DOOR bursts open and TWO COURTIERS from the
carriage march in, stop, bow. FIRST COURTIER waves
in the dark-skinned YOUNG WOMAN to stand by
him. He takes her by the hand and forces her to bow.

ELIZABETH
(Looking interested, leans forward)
Come here. Come here, child.

FIRST COURTIER pushes the young woman forward. The
SECOND COURTIER with a flourish and bow, speaks.

SECOND COURTIER
She is a princess in her own country, Majesty.

ELIZABETH
(Aside to Cecil)
Better and better, Cecil. You did not tell me she was a barbarian *princess*.

CECIL
(Recovering quickly; clearly this is news to him)
It was meant to be a surprise, Majesty. I see we have been successful.

ELIZABETH
(Putting the goblet down on a side table)
What is your name, my lady?

> YOUNG WOMAN
> (Turns and looks at the two men for translation)

> FIRST COURTIER
> (He speaks in her own language a quick sentence)

> YOUNG WOMAN
> (Speaking directly to Elizabeth)

Pocahontas.

> ELIZABETH
> (Bringing a pomander ball to her nose)

Have her come closer. I would smell her.

> FIRST COURTIER
> (Speaking to Young Woman)

Go. Forward. Now.

YOUNG WOMAN goes reluctantly up to the steps of
the dais and when signaled by ELIZABETH, goes up
the three steps to stand by the queen.

ELIZABETH takes the pomander from her nose for a
moment, then sniffs YOUNG WOMAN, who, in turn,
sniffs her.

> YOUNG WOMAN
> (Turns and speaks to the First Courtier)

Feh! Feh! Feh!

> ELIZABETH

What did she say? What did she say?

> CECIL
> (Trying hard not to laugh)

Oh, I think she was perfectly clear, Majesty. She says you smell!

<Note to Producer—Pocahontas was actually brought
to England during the reign of King James I, several years
after Elizabeth died. But I doubt the public will know
this. Or care.>

12.

Do not, I beg thee, make me wait too long.
True love should yield the ground with little fight.
We stand here taking count of what is wrong,
When all but sense and reason have ta'en flight.
Then send them off, thy soldiers standing guard,
That all unrobed, thy beauty might be seen,
Till crying pax I come across your sward,
Barbarian to his unresisting queen.
Fling now the castle gates full open wide,
And with your fingers, offer up the store
That others have all cautioned you to hide;
Your royal jewels I richly will adore.
Pray let me roam your countryside full free
So that by love alone I ravage thee.

13.

Grax sat uneasily on the synth-hide stool waiting for the queen. He drank
tea because, after a night of bar-hopping, from the Wet End to the White
Horse, his stomach was tied up, knotted as neatly as a sailor's rope.

Running his fingers over the tensed muscles, he groaned. He could
hear the tea gurgling inside, complaining like the river Dee in full flood.
In the diner's mirror, his face was reflected back with a green tinge.

The queen would notice such things. Mean and green, she'd probably
say. If he was lucky she wouldn't sing.

He took another sip out of the chipped white cup with the flower de-
cals all along the rim. By-the-Powers-Tetley, he could have used something
stronger. Blackberry maybe. He whispered to himself:

> "Blackberry,
> Bayberry,
> Thistle and thorn.
> You'll rue the day
> That you were born."

But she'd smell it on him and say something. Her word alone could
make his stomachache last a full month.

When he took his third sip, she was there, sitting on a stool next to
him as if it were a throne. Her hair was gold today and piled in a high
crown, her lips rowanberry red.

"New in town, sailor?" she asked lightly. "What's a nice barbarian like
you doing in a place like this?"

He knew she didn't expect an answer. Not from a barbarian.

"Give us a kiss."

He did what was expected, on the cheek. But her cheek was rough, the beard already beginning to show through the rouge. It surprised him. She never used to be so careless.

"By the Green, Mab!" he said, incautiously. "I thought you could do a better job than that."

She smiled sadly at him. "The grid is going, Grax. The Magic is failing. An old queen just doesn't have the power to fool anymore."

He put down his cup and held her hands. "It doesn't matter," he said, and meant it. "It doesn't matter to me."

But of course it did matter, which is why Mab had come to him.

"You shall put the grid aright," she said. "A day's work."

A week at least, he knew.

And an eternity if I get it wrong. But he didn't say it aloud. Some things were best left unsaid, lest the wrong ears hear them. He said only what was expected. "I will go, my queen."

She smiled at him. There was a gap between her top front teeth that hadn't been there before. And a pimple on the side of her nose.

Oh-oh, mused Grax, *the grid is in worse shape than I thought.* He stood, bowed quickly, and was gone.

Mab watched him till he was no more than a point on the horizon, then sighed.

The counterman leaned over and said, "Mab, he's not the best any more."

She turned and raised an eyebrow. "He's all there is, Sid."

The counterman ran a nervous hand through his shaggy locks and rubbed one of his button horns. "What about Dar? What about Babs? What about...?"

"Gone," she said with an awful sigh that fluttered the wings of three pigeons in a nearby park. "All gone." Then she put her head on the counter and cried, her tears making deep runnels in her makeup, for once something was gone from her, it was gone from all the world.

THE ELF KING'S DAUGHTER

When he first saw her
She was drinking wine,
Her skin so pale
He could trace the path of it
Down her throat.
His mouth filled as if tasting
The rich full body
Though he had not yet brought
Cup to lips.

When she looked at him
He drank, the amber and the red,
Making his stay in Faerie
Nine times nine.

When they were done with him
He lay on the hillside,
Old, drained,
The print of her lips
On his whitened neck
So finely etched,
As if she had sucked
All ten pints of him
In a single draught.

WINTER'S KING

He was not born a king but the child of wandering players, slipping out ice-blue in the deepest part of winter, when the wind howled outside the little green caravan. The midwife pronounced him dead, her voice smoothly hiding her satisfaction. She had not wanted to be called to a birth on such a night.

But the father, who sang for pennies and smiles from strangers, grabbed the child from her and plunged him into a basin of lukewarm water, all the while singing a strange, fierce song in a tongue he did not really know.

Slowly the child turned pink in the water, as if breath were lent him by both the water and the song. He coughed once, and spit up a bit of rosy blood, then wailed a note that was a minor third higher than his father's last surprised tone.

Without taking time to swaddle the child, the father laid him dripping wet and kicking next to his wife on the caravan bed. As she lifted the babe to her breast, the woman smiled at her husband, a look that included both the man and the child but cut the midwife cold.

The old woman muttered something that was part curse, part fear, then more loudly said, "No good will come of this dead cold child. He shall thrive in winter but never in the warm and he shall think little of this world. I have heard of such before. They are called Winter's Kin."

The mother sat up in bed, careful not to disturb the child at her side. "Then he shall be a Winter King, more than any of his kin or kind," she said. "But worry not, old woman, you shall be paid for the live child as well as the dead." She nodded to her husband who paid the midwife twice over from his meager pocket, six copper coins.

The midwife made the sign of horns over the money, but still she kept it and, wrapping her cloak tightly around her stout body and a scarf round her head, she walked out into the storm. Not twenty steps from the caravan, the wind tore one cloak from her and pulled tight the scarf about her neck. An icy branch broke from a tree and smashed in the side of her head. In the morning when she was found, she was frozen solid. The money she had clutched in her hand was gone.

The player was hanged for the murder and his wife left to mourn even as she nursed the child. Then she married quickly, for the shelter and the food. Her new man never liked the winter babe.

"He is a cold one," the husband said. "He hears voices in the wind," though it was he who was cold and who, when filled with drink, heard the dark counsel of unnamed gods who told him to beat his wife and abuse her son. The woman never complained, for she feared for her child. Yet strangely the child did not seem to care. He paid more attention to the sounds of the wind than the shouts of his stepfather, lending his own voice to the cries he alone could hear, though always a minor third above.

As the midwife had prophesied, in winter he was an active child, his eyes bright and quick to laugh. But once spring came, the buds in his cheeks faded even as the ones on the boughs grew big. In the summer and well into the fall, he was animated only when his mother told him tales of Winter's Kin, and though she made up the tales as only a player can, he knew the stories all to be true.

When the winter child was ten, his mother died of her brutal estate and the boy left into the howl of a storm, without either cloak or hat between him and the cold. Drunk, his ten-year father did not see him go. The boy did not go to escape the man's beatings; he went to his kin who called him from the wind. Bare-footed and bare-headed, he crossed the snows trying to catch up with the riders in the storm. He saw them clearly. They were clad in great white capes, the hoods lined with ermine; and when they turned to look at him, their eyes were wind-blue and the bones of their faces were thin and fine.

Long, long he trailed behind them, his tears turned to ice. He wept not for his dead mother, for it was she who had tied him to the world. He wept for himself and his feet, which were too small to follow after the fast-riding Winter's Kin.

A woodcutter found him that night and dragged him home, plunging him into a bath of lukewarm water and speaking in a strange tongue that even he, in all his wanderings, had never heard.

The boy turned pink in the water, as if life were returned to him by both the bathing and the prayer, but he did not thank the old man when he woke. Instead he turned his face to the window and wept, this time like any child, the tears falling like soft rain down his cheeks.

"Why do you weep?" the old man asked.

"For my mother and for the wind," the boy said. "And for what I cannot have."

The winter child stayed five years with the old woodcutter, going out each day with him to haul the kindling home. They always went into the woods to the south, a scraggly, ungraceful copse of second-growth trees, but never to the woods to the north.

"That is the great Ban Forest," the old man said. "All that lies therein belongs to the king."

"The king," the boy said, remembering his mother's tales. "And so I am."

"And so are we all in God's heaven," the old man said. "But here on earth I am a woodcutter and you are a foundling boy. The wood to the south be ours."

Though the boy paid attention to what the old man said in the spring and summer and fall, once winter arrived, he heard only the voices in the wind. Often the old man would find him standing nearly naked by the door and have to lead him back to the fire where the boy would sink down into a stupor and say nothing at all.

The old man tried to make light of such times, and would tell the boy tales while he warmed at the hearth. He told him of Mother Holle and her feather bed, of Godfather Death, and of the Singing Bone. He told him of the Flail of Heaven and the priest whose rod sprouted flowers because the Water Nix had a soul. But the boy had ears only for the voices in the wind, and what stories he heard there, he did not tell.

The old man died at the tag-end of their fifth winter and the boy left, without even folding the hands of the corpse. He walked into the southern copse for that was the way his feet knew. But the Winter Kin were not about.

The winds were gentle here, and spring had already softened the bitter brown branches to a muted rose. A yellow-green haze haloed the air and underfoot the muddy soil smelled moist and green and new.

The boy slumped to the ground and wept, not for the death of the woodcutter nor for his mother's death, but for the loss once more of his kin. He knew it would be a long time till winter came again.

And then, from far away, he heard a final wild burst of music. A stray strand of cold wind snapped under his nose as strong as a smelling bottle. His eyes opened wide and, without thinking, he stood.

Following the trail of song, as clear to him as cobbles on a city street, he moved towards the great Ban Forest where the heavy trees still shadowed over winter storms. Crossing the fresh new furze between the woods, he entered the old dark forest and wound around the tall, black trees, in and out of shadows, going as true north as a needle in a waterfilled bowl. The path grew cold and the once-muddy ground gave way to frost.

At first all he saw was a mist, as white as if the hooves of horses had struck up dust from sheer ice. But when he blinked once and then twice, he saw coming toward him a great company of fair folk, some on steeds the color of clouds and some on steeds the color of snow. And he realized all at once that it was no mist he had seen but the breath of those great white stallions.

"My people," he cried at last. "My kin. My kind." And he tore off first his boots, then his trousers, and at last his shirt until he was free of the world and its possessions and could run toward the Winter Kin naked and unafraid.

On the first horse was a woman of unearthly beauty. Her hair was plaited in a hundred white braids and on her head was a crown of diamonds and moonstones. Her eyes were wind-blue and there was frost in her breath. Slowly she dismounted and commanded the stallion to be still. Then she took an ermine cape from across the saddle, holding it open to receive the boy.

"My king," she sang, "my own true love," and swaddled him in the cloud-white cloak.

He answered her, his voice a minor third lower than hers. "My queen, my own true love. I am come home."

When the king's foresters caught up to him, the feathered arrow was fast in his breast, but there was, surprisingly, no blood. He was lying, arms outstretched, like an angel in the snow.

"He was just a wild boy, just that lackwit, the one who brought home kindling with the old man," said one.

"Nevertheless, he was in the king's forest," said the other. "He knew better than that."

"Naked as a newborn," said the first. "But look!"

In the boy's left hand were three copper coins, three more in his right.

"Twice the number needed for the birthing of a babe," said the first forester.

"Just enough," said his companion, "to buy a wooden casket and a man to dig the grave."

And they carried the cold body out of the wood, heeding neither the music nor the voices singing wild and strange hosannas in the wind.

Women's Stories

There are two fathers I do not understand:
the one at the bridge,
devil's bargain still warm on his mouth,
kissing his daughter first, saying,
"Do I have a husband for you;"
and Abraham with his traitor's hand,
leading Isaac to the hill to God.

These are not women's stories.
Even before I birthed my three,
and the one bled out before its time,
and the one encysted in the tube,
even before that I would have thrust the knife
In my own breast, before God;
I would have swallowed the kiss,
gone back to the beast myself.

Job's wife has her own story.
Lot's pillar of salt cried tears
indistinguishable from her eyes.
Who invented a glass slipper
never had to dance.

Do not try to climb my hair.
Do not circle me with a hedge of thorns.
My stories are not your stories.
We women go out into the desert together,
or not at all.

EVIAN STEEL

Ynis Evelonia, the Isle of Women, lies within the marshy tidal river Tamor that is itself but a ribbon stretched between the Mendip and the Quantock hills. The isle is scarcely remarked from the shore. It is as if Manannan MacLir himself had shaken his cloak between.

On most days there is an unsettling mist obscuring the irregular coast of the isle; and only in the full sun, when the light just rising illuminates a channel, can any passage across the glass-colored waters be seen. And so it is that women alone, who have been schooled in the hidden causeways across the fen, mother to daughter down through the years, can traverse the river in coracles that slip easily through the brackish flood.

By ones and twos they come and go in their light skin boats to commerce with the Daughters of Eve who stay in holy sistership on the isle, living out their chaste lives and making with their magicks the finest blades mankind has ever known.

The isle is dotted with trees, not the great Druidic oaks that line the roadways into Godney and Meare and tower over the mazed pathways up to the high tor, but small womanish trees: alder and apple, willow and ash, leafy havens for the migratory birds. And the little isle fair rings with bird song and the clanging of hammer on anvil and steel.

But men who come to buy swords at Ynis Evelonia are never allowed farther inland than the wattle guest house with its oratory of wicker wands winded and twisted together under a rush roof. Only one man has ever slept there and is—in fact—sleeping there still. But that is the end of this story—which shall not be told—and the beginning of yet another.

Elaine stared out across the gray waters as the ferret-faced woman rowed them to the isle. Her father sat unmoving next to her in the prow of the little boat, his hands clasped together, his jaw tight. His only admonition so far bad been, "Be strong. The daughter of a vavasour does not cry." She had not cried, though surely life among the magic women on Ynis Evelonia would be far different from life in the draughty but familiar castle at Escalot. At home women were cosseted but no one feared them as they feared the Daughters of Eve, unless one had a sharp tongue like the ostler's wife or Nanny Bess.

Elaine bent over the rim of the hide boat and tried to see her reflection in the water, the fair skin and the black hair plaited with such loving care by Nanny Bess that morning. But all she could make out was a shadow boat skimming across the waves. She popped one of her braids into her mouth, remembering Nanny's repeated warning that some day the braid would grow there: "And what knight would wed a girl with hair agrowin' in 'er mouth, I asks ye?" Elaine could hear Nanny's voice, now sharp as a blade, now quiet as a lullay, whispering in her ear. She sighed.

At the sound her father looked over at her. His eyes, the faded blue of a late autumn sky, were pained and lines like runes ran across his brow.

Elaine let the braid drop from her mouth and smiled tentatively; she could not bear to disappoint him. At her small attempt at a smile he smiled back and patted her knee.

The wind spit river water into her face, as salty as tears, and Elaine hurriedly wiped her cheeks with the hem of her cape. By the time the boat rocked against the shore her face was dry.

The ferret-faced woman leaped over the side of the coracle and pulled it farther onto the sand so that Elaine and her father could debark without wading in the muddy tide. When they looked up, two women in gray robes had appeared to greet them.

"I am Mother Lisanor," said the tallest one to the vavasour. "You must be Bernard of Escalot."

He bowed his head, quickly removing his hat.

"And this," said the second woman, taking Elaine by the hand, "must be the fair Elaine. Come child. You shall eat with me and share my bed this night. A warm body shall keep away any bad dreams."

"Madam..." the vavasour began.

"Mother Sonda," the woman interrupted him.

"Mother Sonda, may my daughter and I have a moment to say goodbye? She has never been away from home before." There was the slightest suggestion of a break in his voice.

"We have found, Sir Bernard, that it is best to part quickly. I *had* suggested in my letter to you that you leave Elaine on the Shapwick shore. This is an island of women. Men come here for commerce sake alone. Ynis Evelonia is Elaine's home now. But fear you not. We shall train her well." She gave a small tug on Elaine's hand and started up the hill and Elaine, all unprotesting, went with her.

Only once, at the top of the small rise, did Elaine turn back. Her father was still standing by the coracle, hat in hand, the sun setting behind him. He was haloed against the darkening sky. Elaine made a small noise, almost a whimper. Then she popped the braid in her mouth. Like a cork in a bottle, it stoppered the sound. Without a word more, she followed Mother Sonda toward the great stone house that nestled down in the valley in the very center of the isle.

The room in the smithy was lit only by the flickering of the fire as Mother Hesta pumped the bellows with her foot. A big woman, whose right arm was more muscular than her left, Hesta seemed comfortable with tools rather than with words. The air from the bellows blew up a sudden large flame that had a bright blue heart.

"See, there. *There.* When the flames be as long as an arrow and the heart of the arrowhead be blue, thrust the blade in," she said, speaking to the new apprentice.

Elaine shifted from one foot to another, rubbing the upper part of her right arm where the brand of Eve still itched. Then she twisted one of her braids up and into her mouth, sucking on the end while she watched but saying nothing.

"You'll see me do this again and again, girl," the forge mistress said. "But it be a year afore I let you try it on your own. For now, you must watch and listen and learn. Fire and water and air make Evian steel, fire and water and air. They be three of the four majorities. And one last thing—though I'll not tell you that yet, for that be our dearest secret. But harken: what be made by the Daughters of Eve strikes true. All men know this and that be why they come here, crost the waters, for our blades. They come, hating it that they must, but knowing only at our forge on this holy isle can they buy this steel. It be the steel that cuts through evil, that strikes the heart of what it seeks."

The girl nodded and her attention blew upon the small fire of words.

"It matters not, child, that we make a short single edge, or what the old Romies called a *glady-us*. It matters not we make a long blade or a double edge. If it be Evian steel, it strikes true." She brought the side of her hand down in a swift movement which made the girl blink twice, but otherwise she did not move, the braid still in her mouth.

Mother Hesta turned her back on the child and returned to work, the longest lecture done. Her muscles under the short sleeved tunic bunched and flattened. Sweat ran over her arms like an exotic chain of water beads as she hammered steadily on the sword, flattening, shaping, beating out the swellings and bulges that only *her* eye could see, only her fingers could find. The right arm beat, the left arm, with its fine traceries of scars, held.

After a while, the girl's eyes began to blink with weariness and with the constant probings of the irritating smoke. She dropped the braid and it lay against her linen shirt limply, leaving a slight wet stain. She rubbed both eyes with her hands but she was careful not to complain.

Mother Hesta did not seem to notice, but she let the fire die down a bit and laid the partially finished sword on the stone firewall. Wiping her grimed hands on her leather apron, she turned to the girl.

"I'm fair famished, I am. Let's go out to garden where Mother Sonda's set us a meal."

She did not put her hand out to the girl as she was, herself, uncomfortable with such open displays. It was a timeworn joke on Evelonia that Hesta put all her love into pounding at the forge. But she was pleased when the girl trotted by her side without any noticeable hesitation or delay. *A slow apprentice is no apprentice,* Mother Hesta often remarked.

When they stepped out of the shed, the day burst upon them with noisy celebration. Hesta, who spent almost the entire day everyday in her dark forge, was always pleased for a few moments of birds and the colorful assault of the green landscape drifting off into the marshy river beyond. But she was always just as happy to go back into the dark fireroom where the tools slipped comfortably to hand and she could control the *whoosh-whoosh* sigh of the bellows and the loud clangorous song of metal on metal.

A plain cloth was spread upon the grass and a variety of plates covered with napkins awaited them. A jug of watered wine—Hesta hated the feeling heavy wines made in her head when she was working over the hot fire—and two stoneware goblets completed the picture.

"Come," Mother Hesta said.

The word seemed to release the child and she skipped over to the cloth and squatted down, but she touched nothing on the plate until Hesta had lowered herself to the ground and picked up the first napkin. Then the girl took up a slice of apple and jammed it into her mouth.

Only then did Hesta remember that it was mid-afternoon and the child, who had arrived late the evening before and slept comforted in Mother Sonda's bed, had not eaten since rising. Still, it would not do to apologize. That would make discipline harder. This particular girl, she knew, was the daughter of a vavasour, a man of some means in Escalot. She was not used to serving but to being served, so she must not be coddled now. Hesta was gentle in her chiding, but firm.

"The food'll not disappear, child," she said. "Slow and steady in these things. A buyer for the steel comes to guest house table and he be judging us and we he by what goes on there. A greedy man be a man who'll pay twice what a blade be worth. Discipline, discipline in all things."

The girl, trying to eat more slowly, began to choke.

Hesta poured the goblets halfway full and solemnly handed one to her. The child sipped down her wine and the choking fit ended suddenly. Hesta made no reference to the incident.

"When you be done, collect these plates and cups and take them to yon water house. Mother Argente will meet you there and read you the first chapter of the *Book of Brightness*. Listen well. The ears be daughters of the memory."

"I can read, Mother Hesta," the girl said in a quiet little voice. It was not a boast but information.

"Can you? Then on the morrow you can read to me from the chapter on fire." She did not mention that she, herself a daughter of a landless vassal, had never learned to read. However one came to the *Book*—by eye or ear—did not matter a whit. Some were readers and some were read-tos; each valued in the Goddess's sight, as Argente had promised her many years ago when they had been girls. So she comforted herself still.

"Yes, mother," the girl said. Her voice, though quiet, was unusually low and throaty for one her age. It was a voice that would wear well in the forge room. The last novice had had a whiny voice; she had not remained on the isle for long. But this girl, big eyed, deep voiced, with a face the shape of a heart under a waterfall of dark hair, was such a lovely little thing, she would probably be taken by the mothers of guest house, Sonda, Lisanor and Katwyn, no matter how fair her forging. Sometimes, Hesta thought, the Goddess be hard.

As she watched the girl eating, then wiping her mouth on the linen square with an easy familiarity, Hesta remembered how mortifying it had been to have to be taught not to use her sleeve for that duty. Then she smiled because that memory recalled another, that of a large, rawboned, parentless ten-year-old-girl she had been, plunging into the cold channel of the Tamor just moments ahead of the baron who had claimed her body as his property. He had had to let her go, exploding powerful curses at her back, for he could not himself swim. He had been certain that she would sink. But her body's desperate strength and her crazed determination had brought her safely across the brackish tide to the isle where, even in a boat, that powerful baron had not dared go, so fearful was he of the rumors of magic. And the girl, as much water in as without, had been picked up out of the rushes by the late forge mistress and laughingly called Moses after an old tale. And never gone back across the Tamor, not once these forty years.

In the middle of Hesta's musing, the girl stood up and began to clear away the dishes to the accompaniment of a trilling song sung by a modest little brown bird whose flute-like tunes came daily in spring from the apple bough. It seemed an omen. Hesta decided she would suggest it to Mother Sonda as the bird name for the vavasour's child—Thrush.

There were three other girls in the sleep room when Elaine was left there. Two of the girls were smoothing their beds and one was sitting under a corbeled window, staring out.

Elaine had the braid in her mouth again. Her wide gray eyes took in everything. Five beds stood in a row along the wall with wooden chests for linen and other possessions at each bed foot. A fine Eastern tapestry hung above the beds, its subject the Daughters of Eve. It depicted about thirty women at work on a large island surrounded by troubled waves. Against the opposite wall were five arched windows that looked out across the now placid Tamor. Beneath the windows stood two high-warp looms with rather primitive weavings begun on each.

One of the standing girls, a tall wraithy lass with hair the insubstantial color of mist, noticed that Elaine's eyes had taken in the looms.

"We have been learning to weave. It is something that Mother A learned from a traveler in Eastern lands. Not just the simple cloths the peasants make but true *tapisseries* such as the one over our beds. *That* was a gift of an admirer, Mother A said."

Elaine had met Mother Argente the night before. She was a small white-haired woman with soft, plump cheeks and hands that disguised the steel beneath. Elaine wondered who could admire such a firm soul. That kind of firmness quite frightened her.

She spun around to set the whole room into a blur of brown wood and blue coverlets and the bright spots of tapestry wool hanging on the wall. She spun until she was dizzy and had to stop or collapse. The braid fell from her mouth and she stood hands at her side, silently staring.

"Do you have a name yet?" the mist-haired girl asked.

After a moment came the throaty reply. "Elaine."

"No, no, your bird name, she means." The other standing girl, plump and whey-faced, spoke in a twittering voice.

Mist-hair added, "We all receive bird names, new names, like novices in nunneries, until we decide whether to stay. That's because the Druids have their trees and tree alphabet for *their* magic, but we have our little birds who make their living off the trees. That's what Mother A says. It's all in the *Book*. After that, if we stay, we get to have Mother names and live on Holy Isle forever."

"Forever," whispered Elaine. She could not imagine it.

"Do you want to know our bird names?" asked whey-face.

Before Elaine could answer, the tall girl said, "I'm Gale—for nightingale—because I sing so well. And this is Marta for house martin because she is our homebody, coming from Shapwick, across the flood. And over there—that..." she hesitated a moment, as much to draw a breath as to make a point, "that is Veree. That's because she's solitary like the vireo, and a rare visitor to our isle. At least she's rare in her own eyes." She paused. "We used to have Brambling, but she got sick from the dampness and had to go home or die."

"I didn't like Bram," Marta said. "She was too common and she whined all the time. Mother Hesta couldn't bear her, and that's why she had to leave."

"It was her chest and the bloody cough."

"It was her whine."

"Was not."

"Was."

"Was not."

"Was!"

Veree stood and came over to Elaine who had put the braid back into her mouth during the girls' argument. "Don't let their squabblings fright you," she said gently. "They are chickens scratching over bits of feed. Rumor and gossip excite them."

The braid dropped from Elaine's mouth.

"You think because you're castle born that you're better than we are," scolded Marta. "But all are the same on this holy isle."

Veree smiled. It was not an answer but a confirmation.

"We will see," hissed Gale. "There is still the forging."

"But she's *good* at forging," Marta murmured.

Gale pursed her mouth. "We will see."

Veree ignored them, putting a hand under Elaine's chin and lifting her face until they were staring at one another, gray eyes into violet ones. Elaine could not look away.

"You are quite, quite beautiful," Veree pronounced at last, "and you take in everything with those big eyes. But like the magpie, you give nothing away. I expect they'll call you Maggie, but *I* shall call you Pie."

Beyond the fingers of light cast by the hearth fire was a darkness so thick it seemed palpable. On the edges of the darkness, as it crowded them together, sat the nine Mothers of Ynis Evelonia. In the middle of the half circle, in a chair with a firm back, sat Mother Argente, smiling toward the flames, her fingers busy with needlework. She did not once look down to check the accuracy of her stitches but trusted her fingers to do their work.

"Young Maggie seems to be settling in quite nicely. No crying at night, no outlandish longings for home, no sighing or sniffles. We needn't have been so worried." Her comment did not name any specific worrier, but the Mothers who had voiced such fears to her in the privacy of their morning confessionals were chastized all the same.

Still chaffing over the rejection of her suggested name, Hesta sniffed. "She's too much like Veree—high-strung, coddled. And she fair worships the ground Veree treads which, of course, Veree encourages."

"Now, now, Hesta," Mother Sonda soothed. She made the same sounds to chickens agitated at laying time and buyers in the guest house, a response in tone rather than actual argument. It always worked. Hesta smoothed her skirts much like a preening bird and settled down.

Sonda rose to stack another log onto the embers and to relight a taper on the candlestand. A moth fluttered toward the flame and on reaching it, burst with a sudden bright light. Sonda swept the ashes onto the floor where they disappeared into shadows and rushes. Then, turning, she spoke with a voice as sweetly welcoming as the scent of roses and verbena in the room.

"Mother A has asked me to read the lesson for this evening." She stepped to the lectern where the great leatherbound *Book of Brightness* lay open. Above it, from the sconce on the wall, another larger taper beamed down to light the page. Sonda ran her finger along the text, careful not to touch either the words or the brightly colored illuminations. Halfway, she stopped, looked up, and judging the stilled expectant audience, glanced down again and began to read.

The lesson was short: a paragraph and a parable about constancy. The longer reading had been done before the full Company of women and girls at dinner. Those who could took turns with the readings. All others listened. Young Maggie, with her low, steady voice and ability to read phrases rather than merely piece together words, would some day make a fine reader. She would probably make a fine Mother, too. Time—and trial—would tell. That was the true magic on the isle: time and trial.

Sonda looked up from the text for a moment. Mother Argente always chose the evening's lesson. The mealtime reading was done from the *Book's* beginning straight through to the end. In that way the entire *Book of Brightness* was heard at least once a year by everyone on the isle.

As usual, Sonda was in full agreement with Mother A's choice of the parable on constancy. In the last few months the small community had been beset by inconstancy, as if there were a curse at work, a worm at the heart inching its way to the surface of the body. Four of the novices had left on one pretext or another, a large number in such a short time. One girl with the bloody flux whose parents had desired that she die at home. One girl beset by such lingering homesickness as to render her unteachable. One girl plainly too stupid to learn at all. And one girl summoned home to be married. Married! Merely a piece in her father's game, the game of royalty. Sonda had escaped that game on her own by fasting until her desperate father had given her permission to join the Daughters of Eve. But then, he had had seven other daughters to counter with. And if such losses of novices were not enough—girls were always coming and going—two of the fully vowed women had left as well, one to care for her aged and dying parents and take over the reins of landholding until her brothers might return from war. And one, who had been on the isle for twenty years, had run off with a Cornish miller, a widower only recently bereaved; run off to become his fourth wife. Constancy indeed!

Sonda stood for a moment after the reading was over, her hands lingering on the edges of the *Book*. She loved the feel of it under her fingers, as if the text could impress itself on her by the feel of the parchment alone. She envied mothers Morgan and Marie who could write and illumine the pages. They were at work on a new copy of the *Book* to be set permanently in the dining common so that this one, old and fragile and precious, would not have to be shifted daily.

Finally Sonda took her place again on a stool by Mother A's right hand.

Mother A shifted a moment and patted Sonda's knee. Then she looked to the right and left, taking in all eight women with her glance. "My sisters," she began, "tomorrow our beloved daughter Vireo will begin her steel."

Elaine awoke because someone was crying. She had been so near crying herself for a fortnight that the sound of the quiet weeping set her off, and before she could stop herself, she was snuffling and gulping, the kind of sobbing that Nanny Bess always called "bear grabbers."

She was making so much noise, she did not hear the other weeper stop and move onto her bed, but she felt the sudden warmth of the girl's body and the sturdy arms encircling her.

"Hush, hush, little Pie," came a voice, and immediately lifter her hair was smoothed down.

Elaine looked up through tear-blurred eyes. There was no moon to be seen through the windows, no candles lit. The dark figure beside her was faceless, but she knew the voice.

"Oh, Veree," she whispered, "I didn't *mean* to cry."

"Nor I, little one. You have been brave the long weeks here. I have seen that and admired it. And now, I fear that I have been the cause of your weeping."

"No, not you, Veree. Never you. It is just that I miss my father so much. And my brother Lavaine, who is the handsomest man in all the world."

Veree laughed and tousled the girl's hair. "Ah, there can be no *handsomest* man, Pie. All men be the same to the women who love and serve the bright goddess flame here."

"If I cannot still love my Lavaine, then I do not want to *be* here." She wiped at her eyes.

"You will get over such losses. I have." Veree sat back on the bed.

"Then why *were* you crying? It was that which woke me." Elaine would admit that much.

Veree shushed her fiercely and glanced around, but the other two girls slept on.

Elaine whispered, "You *were* weeping. By the window. Admit it."

"Yes, sweet Pie, I was crying. But not for the loss of father or brother. Nor yet for house and land. I cry about tomorrow and tomorrow's morrow, and especially the third day after when I must finish my steel." She rose and went towards the window.

Elaine saw the shadow of her passing betwixt dark and dark and shivered slightly. Then she got out of her bed and the shock of the cold stone beneath the rushes caused her to take quick, short steps over to Veree who sat by the open window.

Outside a strange moaning, part wind and part water, sighed from the Tamor. A night owl on the hunt cried, a soft ascending wheeze of sound.

Elaine put her hand out and touched Veree's shoulder, sturdy under the homespun shift. "But what are you afraid of? Do you fear being burned? Do you fear the blade? I had a maidservant once who turned white as hoarfrost when she had to look upon a knife, silly thing."

"I fear the hurting. I fear...the blood."

"What blood?"

In the dark Veree turned and Elaine could suddenly see two tiny points of light flashing out from the shadow eyes. "They have not told you yet about the blood?"

Elaine shook her head. Then realizing the motion might not be read in the blackness, she whispered, "No. Not yet."

Veree sighed, a sound so unlike her that Elaine swallowed with difficulty. "Tell me. Please."

"I must not."

"But *they* will soon."

"Then let *them*."

"But I must know now so that I might comfort you, who have comforted me these weeks." Elaine took her hand away from Veree's shoulder and reached for a lock of her own hair, unbound from its night plait, and popped it into her mouth, a gesture she had all but forgotten the last days.

"Oh, little Pie, you must not think I am a coward, but if I tell you when I should not...I would not have you think me false." Veree's voice was seeped in sadness.

"I never..."

"You will when I tell you."

"You are wonderful," Elaine said, proclaiming fealty. "You have been the one to take me in, to talk to me, to listen. The others are all common mouths chattering, empty beads like wooden whistles blowing common tunes." That was one of Nanny Bess's favorite sayings. "Nothing would make me think you false. Not now, not ever."

Veree's head turned back to the window again and the twin points of light were eclipsed. She spoke toward the river and the wind carried her soft words, away. Elaine had to strain to hear them.

"Our steel is forged of three of the four elements—fire and water and air."

"I know that."

"But the fourth thing that makes Evian steel, what makes it strike true, is a secret learned by Mother Morgan from a necromancer in the East where magic rides the winds and every breath is full of spirits."

"And what is the fourth thing?" whispered Elaine, though she feared she already knew.

Veree hesitated, then spoke. "Blood. The blood of a virgin girl, an unblemished child, or a childless old maid. Blood drawn from her arm where the vein runs into the heart. The left arm. Here." And the shadow held out its shadowy arm, thrusting it half out of the window.

Elaine shivered with more than the cold.

"And when the steel has been worked and pounded and beaten and shaped and heated, again and again, it is thrust into a silver vat that contains pure water from our well mixed through with the blood."

"Oh." Elaine sighed.

"And the words from the *Book of Brightness* are spoken over it by the mothers in the circle of nine. The sword is pulled from its bloody bath. Then the girl, holding up the sword, with the water flooding down her arm, marches into the Tamor, into the tidal pool that sits in the shadow of the high tor. She must go under the water with the sword, counting to nine times nine. Then thrusting the sword up and out of the water before her, she follows it into the light. Only then is the forging done."

"Perhaps taking the blood will not hurt, Veree. Or only a little. The mothers are gentle. I burned myself the third day here, and Mother Sonda soothed it with a honey balm and not a scar to show for it."

Veree turned back to the window. "It must be done by the girl all alone at the rising of the moon. Out in the glade. Into the silver cup. And how can I, little Pie, how can I prick my own arm with a knife, I who cannot bear to see myself bleed. Not since I was a small child, could I bear it without fainting. Oh, I can kill spiders, and stomp on serpents. I am not afraid of binding up another's wounds. But my own blood...if I had known...if my father had known...I never would have come."

Into the silence that followed her anguished speech, came the ascending cry of another owl, which ended in a shriek as the bird found its prey.

The cry seemed to agitate the two sleepers in their beds and they stirred noisily. Veree and Elaine stood frozen for the moment, and even after were tentative with their voices.

"Could you..." Elaine began.

"Yes?"

"Could you use an animal's blood instead?"

"Then the magic would not work and everyone would know."

Elaine let out a long breath. "Then I shall go out in your place. We shall use *my* blood and you will not have to watch." She spoke quite assuredly, though her heart beat wildly at her own suggestion.

Veree hugged her fiercely. "What *can* you think of me that you would believe I would let you offer yourself in my place, little one. But I shall love you forever just for making the suggestion."

Elaine did not quite understand why she should feel so relieved, but she smiled into the darkness. Then she yawned loudly.

"What *am* I thinking of?" Veree chastised herself. "You should be sleeping, little one, not staying up with me. But be relieved. You have comforted me. I think..." she hesitated for a little, then finished gaily, "I think I shall manage it all quite nicely now."

"Really?" asked Elaine.

"Really," said Veree. "Trust me."

"I do. Oh, I do," said Elaine and let herself be led back to bed where she fell asleep at once and dreamed of an angel with long dark braids in a white shift who sang, "verily, verily," to her and drew a blood-red crux on her forehead and breast and placed her, ever smiling, in a beautiful silk-lined barge.

If there was further weeping that night, Elaine did not wake to it, nor did she speak of it in the morn.

The morn was the first day of Veree's steel and the little isle buzzed with the news. The nine Mothers left the usual chores to the lesser women and the girls, marching in a solemn line to the forge where they made a great circle around the fire.

In due time Veree, dressed in a white robe with the hood obscuring her face, was escorted by two guides, Mothers who had been chosen by lot. They walked along the Path of Steel, the winding walkway to the smithy that was lined with water-smoothed stones.

As she walked, Veree was unaware of the cacophony of birds that greeted her from the budding apple boughs. She never noticed a flock of finches that rose up before her in a cloud of yellow wings. Instead her head was full of the chant of the sword.

> *Water to cool it,*
> *Forge to heat it,*
> *Anvil to form it,*
> *Hammer to beat it.*

She thought carefully of the points of the sword: hilt and blade, forte and foible, pommel and edge, quillon and grip. She rehearsed her actions. She thought of everything but the blood.

Then the door in front of her opened, and she disappeared inside. The girls who had watched like little birds behind the trees sighed as one.

"It will be your turn next full moon," whispered Marta to Gale. Gale smiled crookedly. The five girls from the other sleeping room added their silent opinions with fingers working small fantasies into the air. Long after the other girls slipped back to their housely duties, Elaine remained, rooted in place. She watched the forge and could only guess at the smoky signals that emerged from the chimney on the roof.

> *Water to cool it,*
> *Forge to heat it,*
> *Anvil to form it,*
> *Hammer to beat it.*

The mothers chanted in perfect unity, their hands clasped precisely over the aprons of their robes. When the chant was done, Mother Argente stepped forward and gently pushed Veree's hood back.

Released from its binding, Veree's hair sprang forward like tiny black arrows from many bowstrings, the dark points haloing her face.

She really is a magnificent child, Argente thought to herself, but aloud spoke coldly. "My daughter," she said, "the metal thanks us for its beating by becoming stronger. So by our own tempering we become women of steel. Will you become one of us?"

"Mother," came Veree's soft answer, "I will."

"Then you must forge well. You must pour your sweat and your blood into this sword that all who see it and any who use it shall know it is of excellent caliber, that it is of Evian Steel."

"Mother, I will."

The Mothers stood back then and only Hesta came forward. She helped Veree remove her robe and the girl stood stiffly in her new forging suit of tunic and trews. Hesta bound her hair back into a single braid, tying it with a golden twine so tightly that it brought tears to the girl's eyes. She blinked them back, making no sound.

"Name your tools," commanded Hesta.

Veree began. Pointing out each where it hung on its hook on the wall, she droned: "Top swage, bottom swage, flatter, cross peen, top fuller, bottom fuller, hot chisel, mandrel..." The catalogue went on and only half her mind was occupied with the rota. This first day of the steel was child's play, things she had memorized her first weeks on Ynis Evelonia and never forgot. They were testing the knowledge of her head. The second day they would test her hands. But the third day...she hesitated a moment, looked up, saw that Hesta's eyes on her were glittering. For the first time she understood that the old forge mistress was hoping that she would falter, fail. That startled her. It had never occurred to her that someone she had so little considered could wish her ill.

She smiled a false smile at Hesta, took up the list, and finished it flawlessly.

The circle of nine nodded.

"Sing us now the color of the steel," said Sonda.

Veree took a breath and began. "When the steel is red as blood, the surface is at all points good; and when the steel is rosy red, the top will scale, the sword is dead; and when the steel is golden bright, the time for forging is just right; and when the steel is white as snow, the time for welding you will know."

The plainsong accompaniment had helped many young girls remember the colors, but Veree sang it only to please the mothers and pass their test. She had no trouble remembering when to forge and when to weld, and the rest was just for show.

"The first day went splendidly," remarked Sonda at the table.

"No one ever questioned *that* one's head knowledge," groused Hesta, using her own head as a pointer toward the table where the girls sat.

Mother Argente clicked her tongue against the roof of her mouth, a sound she made when annoyed. The others responded to it immediately with silence, except for Mother Morgan who was so deep in conversation with a server she did not hear.

"We will discuss this later. At the hearth," Argente said.

The conversation turned at once to safer topics: the price of corn, how to raise the milling fee, the prospect of another visitor from the East, the buyer of Veree's sword.

Morgan looked over. "It shall be the arch-mage," she said. "He will come for the sword himself."

Hesta shook her head. "How do you know? How do you *always* know?"

Morgan smiled, the corners of her thin upper lip curling. There was a gap between her two front teeth, carnal, inviting. "I know."

Sonda reached out and stroked the back of Hesta's hand. "You know she would have you think it's magic. But it is the calendar, Hesta. I have explained all that."

Hesta mumbled, pushing the lentils around in her bowl. Her own calendar was internal and had to do with forging, when the steel was ready for the next step. But if Morgan went by any calendar, it was too deep and devious for the forge mistress's understanding. Or for any of them. Morgan always seemed to *know* things. Under the table, Hesta crossed her fingers, holding them against her belly as protection.

"It *shall* be the arch-mage," Morgan said, still smiling her gapped smile. "The stars have said it. The moon has said it. The winds have said it."

"And now you have said it, too." Argente's voice ended the conversation, though she wondered how many of her women were sitting with their fingers crossed surreptitiously under the table. She did not encourage them in their superstitions, but the ones who came from the outer tribes or the lower classes never really rid themselves of such beliefs. "Of course, it shall be a Druid. Someone comes once a year at this time to look over our handiwork. They rarely buy. Druids are as close with their gold as a dragon on its hoard."

"It shall be the arch-mage himself," intoned Morgan. "I know."

Hesta shivered.

"Yes," Argente smiled, almost sighing. When Morgan became stubborn it was always safest to cozen her. Her pharmacopeia was not to be trusted entirely. "But gloating over such arcane knowledge does not become you, a daughter of a queen. I am sure you have more important matters to attend to. Come mothers, I have decided that tonight's reading shall be about humility. And you, Mother Morgan, will do us all the honor of reading it." Irony, Argente had found, was her only weapon against Morgan, who seemed entirely oblivious to it. Feeling relieved of her anger by such petty means always made Argente full of nervous energy. She stood. The others stood with her and followed her out the door.

Elaine watched as Veree marched up to the smithy, this time with an escort of four guides. Veree was without the white robe, her forge suit unmarked by fire or smoke, her hair bound back with the golden string but not as tightly as when Hesta plaited it. Elaine had done the service for her soon after rising, gently braiding the hair and twine together so that they held but did not pull. Veree had rewarded her with a kiss on the brow.

"This day I dedicate to thee," Veree had whispered to her in the courtly language they had both grown up with.

Elaine could still feel the glow of that kiss on her brow. She knew that she would love Veree forever, the sister of her heart. She was glad now, as she had never been before, that she had had only brothers and no sisters in Escalot. That way Veree could be the only one.

The carved wooden door of the smithy closed behind Veree. The girls, giggling, went back to their chores. Only Elaine stayed, straining to hear something of the rites that would begin the second day of Veree's Steel.

Veree knew the way of the steel, bending the heated strips, hammering them together, recutting and rebending them repeatedly until the metal patterned. She knew the sound of the hammer on the hot blade, the smell of the glowing charcoal that made the soft metal hard. She enjoyed the hiss of the quenching, when the hot steel plunged into the water and emerged, somehow, harder still. The day's work was always difficult but satisfying in a way that other work was not. Her hands now held a knowledge that she had not had two years before when, as a pampered young daughter of a baron, she had come to Ynis Evelonia to learn "to be a man as well as a woman" as her father had said. He believed that a woman who might some day have to rule a kingdom (oh, he had such high hopes for her), needed to know both principles, male and female. A rare man, her father. She did not love him. He was too cold and distant and cerebral for that. But she admired him. She wanted him to admire her. And—except for the blood—she was not unhappy that she had come.

Except for the blood. If she thought about it, her hand faltered, the hammer slipped, the sparks flew about carelessly and Hesta boomed out in her forge-tending voice about the recklessness of girls. So Veree very carefully did *not* think about the blood. Instead she concentrated on fire and water, on earth and air. Her hands gripped her work. She *became* the steel.

She did not stop until Hesta's hand on her shoulder cautioned her.

"It be done for the day, my daughter," Hesta said, grudging admiration in her voice. "Now you rest. Tonight you must do the last of it alone."

And then the fear really hit her. Veree began to tremble.

Hesta misread the shivering. "You be aweary with work. You be hungry. Take some watered wine for sleep's sake. We mothers will wake you and lead you to the glade at moonrise. Come. The sword be well worked. You have reason to be proud."

Veree's stomach began to ache, a terrible dull pain. She was certain that, for the first time in her life, she would fail and that her father would be hurt and the others would pity her. She expected she could stand the fear, and she would, as always, bear the dislike of her companions, but what could not be borne was their pity. When her mother had died in the bloody aftermath of an unnecessary birth, the entire court had wept and everyone had pitied her, poor little motherless six-year-old Gwyneth. But she had rejected their pity, turning it to white anger against her mother who had gone without a word. She had not accepted pity from any of those peasants then; she would not accept it now. Not even from little Pie, who fair worshiped her. Especially not from Pie.

The moon's cold fingers stroked Veree's face but she did not wake. Elaine, in her silent vigil, watched from her bed. She strained to listen as well.

The wind in the orchard rustled the blossoms with a soft soughing. Twice, an owl had given its ascending hunting cry. The little popping hisses of breath from the sleeping girls punctuated the quiet in the room. And Elaine thought that she could also hear, as a dark counter to the other noises, the slapping of the Tamor against the shore, but perhaps it was only the beating of her own heart. She was not sure.

Then she heard the footsteps coming down the hall, hauled the light covers up to her chin, and slotted her eyes.

The Nine Mothers entered the room, their white robes lending a ghostly air to the proceedings. They wore the hoods up, which obscured their faces. The robes were belted with knotted golden twine; nine knots on each cincture. and the golden ornament shaped like a circle with one half filled in, the signet of Ynis Evelonia, hanging from the end.

The Nine surrounded Veree's bed, undid their cinctures, and lay the ropes over the girl's body as if binding her to a bier.

Mother Argente's voice floated into the room. "We bind thee to the isle. We bind thee to the steel. We bind thee to thy task. Blood calls to blood, like to like. Give us thine own for the work."

The Nine picked up their belts and tied up their robes once again. Veree, who had awakened some time during Argente's chant, was helped to her feet. The Mothers took off her shift and slipped a silken gown over her head. It was sleeveless and Elaine, watching, shivered for her.

Then Mother Morgan handed her a silver cup, a little grail with the sign of the halved circle on the side. Mother Sonda handed her a silken bandage. Marie bound an illumined message to her brow with a golden headband. Mothers Bronwyn and Matilde washed her feet with lilac water, while Katwyn and Lisanor tied her hair atop her head into a plaited crown. Mother Hesta handed her a silver knife, its tip already consecrated with wine from the Goddess Arbor.

Then Argente put her hands on Veree's shoulders. "May She guide your hand. May She guard your blood. May the moon rise and fall on this night of your consecration. Be you steel tonight."

They led her to the door and pushed her out before them. She did not stumble as she left.

Veree walked into the glade as if in a trance. She had drunk none of the wine but had spilled it below her bed knowing that the wine was drugged with one of Mother Morgan's potions. Bram had warned her of it before leaving. Silly, whiny Bram who, nonetheless, had had an instinct for gossip and a passion for Veree. Such knowledge had been useful.

The moon peeped in and out of the trees, casting shadows on the path, but Veree did not fear the dark. This night the dark was her friend.

She heard a noise and turned to face it, thinking it some small night creature on the prowl. There was nothing larger than a stoat or fox on Ynis Evelonia. She feared neither. At home she had kept a reynard, raised up from a kit, and had hunted with two ferrets as companions in her pocket.

Home! What images suddenly rose up to plague her, the same that had caused her no end of sleepless nights when she had first arrived. For she *had* been homesick, whatever nonsense she had told little Pie for comfort's sake. The great hearth at Carmelide, large enough to roast an ox, where once she had lost the golden ring her mother had given her and her cousin Cadoc had grabbed up a bucket of water, dousing the fire and getting himself all black with coal and grease to recover it for her. And the great apple tree outside her bedroom window up which young Jemmy, the ostler's son, had climbed to sing of his love for her even though he knew he would be soundly beaten for it. And the mews behind the main house where Master Thom had kept the hawks and let her sneak in to practice holding the little merlin that she had wanted for her own. But it had died tangled in its jesses the day before she'd been sent off to the isle, and one part of her had been glad that no one else would hunt the merlin now.

She heard the noise again, louder this time, too loud for a fox or a squirrel or a stoat. Loud enough for a human. She spoke out, "Who is it?" and held out the knife before her, trembling with the cold. Only the cold, she promised herself.

"It is I," came a small voice.

"Pie!" Her own voice took back its authority. "You are not supposed to be here."

"I saw it all, Veree. The dressing and undressing. The ropes and the knife. And I *did* promise to help." The childish form slipped out from behind the tree, white linen shift reflecting the moon's light.

"I told you all would be well, child. You did not need to come."

"But I *promised*." If that voice held pity, it was self-pity. The child was clearly a worshiper begging not to be dismissed.

Veree smiled and held out the hand with the cup: "Come, then. Thou shalt be my page."

Elaine put her hand to Veree's gown and held on as if she would never let go and, so bound, the two entered into the Goddess Glade.

The arch-mage came in the morning just as Morgan had foretold. He was not at all what Elaine had expected, being short and balding, with a beard as long and as thin as an exclamation mark. But that he was a man of power no one could doubt.

The little coracle, rowed by the same ferret-faced woman who had deposited Elaine on the isle, fair skimmed the surface of the waves and plowed onto the shore, leaving a furrow in which an oak could have been comfortably set.

The arch-mage stood up in the boat and greeted Mother Argente familiarly. *"Salve, mater. Visne somnia vendere?"*

She answered him back with great dignity. *"Si volvo, Merline, caveat emptor."*

Then they both laughed, as if this exchange were a great and long-standing joke between them. If it was a joke, they were certainly the only ones to understand it.

"Come, Arch-Mage," Mother Argente said, "and take wine with us in the guest house. We will talk of the purpose of your visit in comfort there."

He nodded and, with a quick twist of his wrist, produced a coin from behind the boat woman's right ear. With a flourish he presented it to her, then stepped from the coracle. The woman dropped the coin solemnly into the leather bag she wore at her waist.

Elaine gasped and three other girls giggled.

"The girls are, as always, amused by your tricks, Merlin," said Mother Argente, her mouth pursed in a wry smile.

"I like to keep in practice," he said. *"And* to amuse the young ones. Besides, as one gets older the joints stiffen."

"That I know, that I know," Argente agreed. They walked side by side like old friends, moving slowly up the little hill. The rest of the women and girls fell in behind them, and so it was, in a modest processional, that they came to the guest house.

At the door of the wattle pavilion which was shaded by a lean of willows, Mother Argente turned. "Sonda, Hesta, Morgan, Lisanor, enter and treat with our guest. Veree, ready yourself for noon. The rest of you, you know your duties." Then she opened the door and let Merlin precede them into the house.

The long table was already set with platters of cheese and fruit. Delicate goblets of Roman glass marked off six places. As soon as they were all seated with Argente at the head and Merlin at the table's foot, Mother A

poured her own wine and passed the silver ewer. Morgan, seated at
Argente's right hand, was the last to fill her glass. When she set the ewer
down, she raised her glass.

"I am Wind on Sea," Morgan chanted.

"I am Wind on Sea,
  I am Ocean-wave,
  I am Roar of Sea,
  I am Bull of Seven Fights,
  I am Vulture on Cliff,
  I am Dewdrop,
  I am Fairest of Flowers,
  I am Boar for Boldness,
  I am Salmon in Pool,
  I am Lake on Plain,
  I am a Word of Skill
  I am the Point of a Weapon—"

"Morgan," warned Argente.

"Do not stop her," commanded Merlin. "She is *vates,* afire with the
word of the Gods. My god or your god, they are the same. They speak
with tongues of fire and they sometimes pick a warped reed through which
to blow a particular tune."

Argente bowed her head once to him but Morgan was already finished.
She looked across the table at Hesta, her eyes preternaturally bright. "I
know things." she said.

"It is clear that I have come at a moment of great power," said Merlin.
" 'I am the point of a Weapon' say the gods to us. And my dreams these
past months have been of sword point, but swords that are neither *gladius*
nor *spatha* nor the far tribes' *ensis.* A new creation. And where does one
come for a sword of power, but here. Here to Ynis Evelonia."

Mother Argente smiled. "We have many swords ready, arch-mage."

"I need but one." He did not return her smile, staring instead into his
cup of wine.

"How will we know this sword of power?" Argente asked, leaning forward.

"I will know," intoned Morgan.

Sonda, taking a sip of her wine, put her head to one sidelike a little
bird considering a tasty worm. "And what payment, arch-mage?"

"Ah, Mother Sonda, that is always the question they leave to you.
What payment indeed." Merlin picked up his own glass and suddenly
drained it. He set the glass down gently, contemplating the rim. Then
he stroked his long beard. "If I dream true—and I have never been known

to have false dreams—then you shall *give* me this particular sword and its maker."

"*Give* you? What a notion, Merlin." Mother Argente laughed, but there was little amusement in it. "The swords made of Evian Steel are never given away. We have too many buyers vying for them. If you will not pay for it, there will be others who will."

There was a sudden, timid knock upon the door. Sonda rose quietly and went to it, spoke to the Mother who had interrupted them, then turned.

"It is nearing noon, Mother. The sun rides high. It is time." Sonda's voice was smooth, giving away no more than necessary.

Mother Argente rose and with her the others rose, too.

"Stay, Arch-Mage, there is food and wine enough. When we have done with our...obsequies...we shall return to finish our business with you."

The five Mothers left and so did not hear the man murmur into his empty cup, "This business will be finished before-times."

The entire company of women gathered at the river's edge to watch. The silver vat, really an overlarge bowl, was held by Mother Morgan. The blood-tinted water reflected only sky.

Veree, in the white silken shift, stood with her toes curling under into the mud. Elaine could see the raised goose bumps along her arms, though it was really quite warm in the spring sun.

Mother Hesta held a sword on the palms of her upturned hands. It was a long-bladed double edge sword, the quillon cleverly worked. The sword seemed afire with the sun, the shallow hollow down its center aflame.

Veree took the sword from Hesta and held it flat against her breast while Mother Argente anointed her forehead with the basin's water. With her finger she drew three circles and three crosses on Veree's brow.

"Blood to blood, steel to steel, thee to me," said Mother Argente.

Veree repeated the chant. "Blood to blood, steel to steel, I to thee." Then she took the sword and set it into the basin.

As the sword point and then the blade touched the water, the basin erupted in steam. Great gouts of fire burst from the sword and Mother Argente screamed.

Veree grabbed the sword by the handle and ran down into the tidal pool. She plunged in with it and immediately the flames were quenched, but she stayed under the water and Elaine, fearful for her life, began to cry out, running down to the water's edge.

She was pushed aside roughly by a strong hand and when she caught her breath, she saw it was the arch-mage himself, standing knee deep in water, his hands raised, palms down, speaking words she did not quite understand.

> "I'll take ye here
> Till Bedevere
> Cast ye back."

Bedevere? Did he mean Veree? Elaine wondered, and then had time to wonder no further for the waters parted before the arch-mage and the sword pierced up into the air before him.

He grasped the pommel in his left hand and with a mighty heave pulled the sword from the pool. Veree's hand, like some dumb, blind thing, felt around in the air, searching.

Elaine waded in, dived under, and wrapping her arms around Veree's waist, pushed her out of pool. They stood there, trembling, looking like two drowned ferrets, unable to speak or weep or wonder.

"This the sword I shall have," Merlin said to Mother Argente, his back to the two half-drowned girls.

"I do not understand..." began Mother Argente. "But I *will* know."

"I *know* things," said Morgan triumphantly.

Mother Argente turned and spoke through clenched teeth, "Will someone shut her up?"

Hesta smiled broadly. "Yes, Mother. Your will is my deed." Her large right hand clamped down on Morgan's neck and she picked her up and shook her like a terrier with a rat, then set her down. Morgan did not speak again but her eyes grew slotted and cold.

Marta began to sob quietly until nudged by Gale, but the other girls were stunned into silence.

"Now, now," murmured Sonda to no one in particular. "Now, now."

Mother Argente walked over to Veree who straightened up and held her chin high. "Explain this, child."

Veree said nothing.

"What blood was used to quench the sword?"

"Mother, it was my own."

Elaine interrupted. "It was. I saw it."

Mother Argente turned on her. "You *saw* it? Then it was your watching that corrupted the steel."

Merlin moved between them. "*Mater.* Think. Such power does not emanate from this child." He swung his head so that he was staring at Veree. "And where did the blood come from?"

Under his stare Veree lowered her eyes. She spoke to the ground. "It is a woman's secret. I cannot talk of it."

The arch-mage smiled. "I am man and woman, neither and both. The secrets of the body are known to me. Nothing is hidden from me."

"I have nothing to tell you if you know it already."

"Then I will tell it to thee," said Merlin. He shifted the sword to his left hand, turned to her, and put his right hand under her chin. "Look at me, Gwyneth, called here Vireo, and deny this if you can. Last night for the first time you became a woman. The moon called out your blood. And it was this flux that you used, the blood that flows from the untested womb, not the body's blood flowing to the heart. Is it so?"

She whispered, "It is so."

Argente put a hand to her breast. "That is foul. Unclean."

"It is the more powerful thereby," Merlin answered.

"Take the sword, arch-mage. And the girl. And go."

"*No!*" Elaine dropped to her knees by Veree's side and clasped her legs. "Do not go. Or take me with you. I could not bear to be here without you. I would die for you."

Merlin looked down at the little girl and shook his head. "You shall not die yet, little Elaine. Not so soon. But you shall give your life for her—that I promise you." He tucked the sword in a scabbard he suddenly produced from inside his cloak. "Come, Gwyneth." He held out his hand.

She took his hand and smiled at him. "There is nothing here to pity," she said.

"I shall never give you pity," he said. "Not now or ever. You choose and you are chosen. I see that you know what it is you do."

Mother Argente smoothed her skirts down, a gesture which seemed to return them all to some semblance of normality. "I myself will row you across. The sooner she is gone from here, the better."

"But my clothes, mother."

"They shall be sent to you."

The arch-mage swung the cape off his shoulders and enfolded the girl in it. The cape touched the ground, sending up little puffs of dirt.

"You shall never be allowed on this isle again," said Mother Argente. "You shall be denied the company of women. Your name shall be crossed off the book of the Goddess."

Veree still smiled.

"You shall be barren," came a voice from behind them. "Your womb's blood was given to cradle a sword. It shall not cradle a child. I *know* things."

"Get into the boat," instructed Merlin. "Do not look back, it only encourages her." He spoke softly to Mother Argente, "I am glad, *Mater* that *that* one is *your* burden."

"I give you no thanks for her," said Mother Argente as she pushed the boat off into the tide. She settled onto the seat, took up the oars, feathered them once, and began to pull.

The coracle slipped quickly across the river.

Veree stared out across the gray waters that gave scarcely any reflection. Through the mist she could just begin to see the far shore where the tops of thatched cottages and the smoky tracings of cook fires were taking shape.

"Shapwick-across-the-flood," mused Merlin. "And from there we shall ride by horse to Camlann. It will be a long and arduous journey, child. Your bones will ache."

"Pitying me already?"

"Pitying *you?* My bones are the older and will ache the more. No, I will not pity you. But we will all be pitied when this story is told years hence, for it will be a tale cunningly wrought of earth, air, fire—and blood."

The boat lodged itself clumsily against the Shapwick shore. The magician stood and climbed over the side. He gathered the girl up and carried her to the sand, huffing mightily. Then he turned and waved to the old woman who huddled in the coracle.

"Ave, mater."

"Ave, magister," she called back, "Until we must meet again."

Ynis Evelonia, the Isle of Women, lies within the marshy tidal river Tamor that is itself but a ribbon stretched between the Mendip and the Quantock hills. The isle is scarcely remarked from the shore. It is as if Manannan MacLir himself had shaken his cloak between.

On most days there is an unsettling mist obscuring the irregular coast of the isle; and only in the full sun, when the light just rising illuminates a channel, can any passage across the glass-colored waters be seen. And so it is that women alone, who have been schooled in the hidden causeways across the fen, mother to daughter down through the years, can traverse the river in coracles that slip easily through the brackish flood.

By ones and twos they come and go in their light skin boats to commerce with the Daughters of Eve who stay in holy sistership on the isle, living out their chaste lives and making with their magics the finest blades mankind has ever known.

The isle is dotted with trees, not the great Druidic oaks that line the roadways into Godney and Meare and tower over the mazed pathways up to the high tor, but small womanish trees: alder and apple, willow and ash, leafy havens for the migratory birds. And the little isle fair rings with bird song and the clanging of hammer on anvil and steel.

But men who come to buy swords at Ynis Evelonia are never allowed further inland than the wattle guest house with its oratory of wicker wands winded and twisted together under a rush roof. Only one man has ever slept there and is— in fact—sleeping there still. But that is the end of this story—which shall not be told—and the beginning of yet another.

THE GWYNHFAR

The *gwynhfar*—the white one, the pure one, the anointed one—waited. She had waited every day since her birth, it seemed, for this appointed time. Attended by her voiceless women in her underground rooms, the *gwynhfar's* limbs had been kept oiled, her bone-white hair had been cleaned and combed. No color was allowed to stain her dead-white cheeks, no *maurish* black to line her eyes. White as the day she had been born, white as the foam on a troubled sea, white as the lilybell grown in the wood, she waited.

Most of her life had been spent on her straw bed in that half-sleep nature spent on her. She moved from small dream to small dream, moment to moment, hour to hour, day to day, without any real knowledge of what awaited her. Nor did she care. The *gwynhfar* did not have even creature sense, nor had she been taught to think. All she had been taught was waiting. It was her duty, it was her life.

She had been the firstborn of a dour landholder and his wife. Pulled silently from between her mother's thighs, bleached as bone, her tiny eyes closed tight against the agonizing light, the *gwynhfar* cried only in the day—a high, thin, mewling call. At night, without the sun to torment her, she seemed content; she waited.

They say now that the old mage attended her birth, but that is not true. He did not come for weeks, even months, till word of the white one's birth had traveled mouth to ear, mouth to ear, over and over the intervening miles. He did not come at first, but his messengers came, as they did to every report of a marvel. They had visited two-headed calves, fish-scaled infants, and twins joined at the hip and heart. When they heard of the white one, they came to her, too.

She waited for them as she waited for everything else.

And when the messengers saw that the stories were true enough, they reported back to the stone hall. So the Old One himself came, wrapped in his dignity and the sour trappings of state.

He had to bend down to enter the cottage, for age had not robbed him of the marvelous height that had first brought him to the attention of the Oldest Ones, those who dwell in the shadows of the Circle of Stones. He bent and bent till it seemed he would bend quite in two, and still he broke his head on the lintel.

"A marvel," it was said. "The blood anointed the door." That was no marvel, but a failing of judgment and the blood a mere trickle where the skin broke apart. But that is what was said. What the Old One himself said was in a language far older than he and twice as filled with power. But no one reported it, for who but the followers of the oldest way even know that tongue?

As the Old One stood there, gazing at the mewling white babe in her half sleep before the flickering fire, he nodded and stroked his thin beard. This, too, they say, and I have seen him often enough musing in just that way, so it could have been so.

Then he stretched forth his hand, that parchment-colored, five-fingered magician's wand that could make balls and cards and silken banners disappear. He stretched forth his hand and touched the child. She shivered and woke fully for the first time, gazing at a point somewhere beyond his hand but not as far as his face with her watery pink eyes.

"So," he said in that nasal excuse for a voice. "So." He was never profligate with words. But it was enough.

The landholder gladly gave up the child, grateful to have the monster from his hearth. Sons could help till the lands. Only the royals crave girls. They make good counters in the bargaining games played across the castle boundary lines. But this girl was not even human enough to cook and clean and wipe the bottoms of her sisters and brothers to come. The landholder would have killed the moon-misbegotten thing on its emergence from his child-bride's womb had not the midwife stayed him. He sold the child for a single gold piece and thought himself clever in the bargain.

And did the Old One clear his throat then and consecrate their trade with words? Did he speak of prophesy or pronounce upon omens? If the landholder's wife had hoped for such to ease her guilt, she got short shrift of him. He had paid with a coin and a single syllable.

"So," he had said. And so it was.

The Old One carried the *gwynhfar* back over the miles with his own hands. "With his own hands," run the wonder tales, as if this were an awesome thing, carrying a tiny, witless babe. But think on it. Would he have trusted her to another, having come so far, across the years and miles, to find her? Would he have given her into clumsier hands when his own could still pull uncooked eggs from his sleeves without a crack or a drop?

Behind him, they say, came his people: the priests and the seers, a grand processional. But I guess rather he came by himself and at night. She would have been a noisy burden to carry through the bright, scalding light; squalling and squealing at the sun. The moon always quieted her. Besides, he wanted to surprise them with her, to keep her to himself till the end. For was it not written that the *gwynhfar* would arise and bind the kingdom:

> *Gwynhfar,* white as bone,
> Shall make the kingdom one.

Just as it had been written in the entrails of deer and the bloody leavings of carrion crow that the Tall One, blessed be, would travel the length of the kingdom to find her. Miracles are made by hands such as his, and prophesies can be invented.

And then, too, he would want to be sure. He would want time to think about what he carried, that small, white-haired marvel, that unnature. For if the Old One was anything, he was a planner. If he had been born better, he would have been a mighty king. So, wrapped in the cloak of night, keeping the babe from her enemy light, which drained even the small strength she had, and scheming—always scheming—the Old One moved through the land.

By day, of course, there would have been no mistaking him. His height ever proclaimed him. Clothes were no disguise. A mask but pointed the finger. At night, though, he was only a long shadow in a world of long shadows.

I never saw him then, but I know it all. I can sort through stories as a crow pecks through grain. And though it is said he rode a whirlwind home, it was a time of year for storms. They were no worse than other years. It is just that legend has a poor memory, and hope an even worse.

The Old One returned with a cough that wracked his long, thin body and an eye scratched out by a tree limb. The black patch he wore thereafter gave rise to new tales. They say he had been blinded in one eye at his first sight of her, the *gwynhfar.* But I have it from the physician who attended him that there was a great scar on his cheek and splinters still in the flesh around the eye.

And what did the Old One say of the wound?

"Clean it," he said. And then, "So!" There is no story there. That is why words of power have been invented for him.

The Old One had a great warren built for the child under the ground so the light would not disturb her rest. Room upon room was filled with things for a growing princess, but nothing there to speak to a child. How could he know what would interest a young one? It was said he had never been a babe. This was only partly a lie. He had been raised by the Oldest Ones himself. He had been young but he had never had a youth. So he waited impatiently for her to grow. He wanted to watch the unfolding of this white, alien flower, his only child.

But the *gwynhfar* was slow. Slow to sit, slow to crawl, slow to eat. Like a great white slug, she never did learn speech or to hold her bowels. She had to be kept wrapped in swaddling under her dresses to keep her clean, but who could see through the silk to know? She grew bigger but not much older, both a natural and unnatural thing. So she was never left alone.

It meant that the Old One had to change his plan. And so his plan became this. He had her beaten every day, but never badly. And on a signal, he would enter her underground chambers and put an end to her punishment. Again and again he arrived just as blood was about to be drawn. Then he would send away her tormentors, calling down horrid punishments upon them. It was not long before the *gwynhfar* looked only to him. She would turn that birch-white face toward the door waiting for him to enter, her watery eyes glistening. The over-big head on the weak neck seemed to strain for his words, though it was clear soon enough that she was deaf as well.

If he could have found another as white as she, he would likely have gotten rid of her. Perhaps. But there have been stranger loves. And only he could speak to her, a language of simple hand signs and finger plays. As she grew into womanhood, the two would converse in a limited fashion. It was some relief from statecraft and magecraft and the tortuous imaginings of history.

On those days and weeks when he did not come to see her, the *gwynhfar* often fell into a half sleep. She ate when fed, roused to go out into the night only when pulled from her couch. The women around her kept her exercised as if she were some exotic, half-wild beast, but they did take good care of her. They guessed what would happen if they did not.

What they did not guess was that they were doomed anyway. Her raising was to be the Old One's secret. Only one woman, who escaped with a lover, told what really happened. No one ever believed her, not even her lover, and he was soon dead in a brawl and she with him.

But I believed. I am bound to believe what cannot be true, to take fact from fancy, fashion fancy from fact,

The plan was changed, but not the promise.

Gwynhfar, white as bone,
Shall make the kingdom one.

The rhyme was known, sung through the halls of power and along the muddy country lanes. Not a man or woman or child but wished it to be so: for the kingdom to be bound up, its wounds cleansed. Justice is like a round banquet table—it comes full circle, and none should be higher or lower than the next. So the mage waited, for the *gwynhfar*'s first signs of womanhood. And the white one waited for the dark prince she had been promised, light and dark, two sides of the same coin. She of the old tribes, he of the new. She of the old faith and he of the new. He listened to new advisers, men of action, new gods. She had but one adviser, knew no action, had one god. That was the promise: old and new wedded together. How else can a kingdom be made one?

How did the mage tell her this, finger upon finger? Did she understand? I only know she waited for the day with the patience of the dreamer, with the solidity of a stone. For that was what she was, a white pebble in a rushing stream, which does not move but changes the direction of the water that passes over it.

I know the beginning of the tale, but not yet the end, Perhaps this time the wisdom of the Oldest Ones will miscarry. Naught may come of naught. Such miracles are often barren. There have been rumors of white ones before. Beasts sometimes bear them. But they are weak, they die young, they cannot conceive. A queen without issue is a dreadful thing. Unnatural.

And the mage has planned it all except for the dark prince. He is a young bear of a king and I think will not be bought so easily with handwrought miracles. His hunger for land and for women, his need for heirs, will not be checked by the mage's blanched and barren offering. He is, I fear, of a lustier mind.

And I? I am no one, a singer of songs, a teller of tales. But I am the one to be wary of, for I remake the past and call it truth. I leave others to the rote of history, which is dry, dull, and unbelievable. Who is to say which mouth's outpourings will lift the soul higher—that which *is* or that which could be? Did it really flood, or did Noah have a fine storymaker living in his house? I care not either way. It is enough for me to sing.

But stay. It is my turn on the boards. Watch. I stride to the rooms center, where the songs echo will linger longest. I lift my hands toward the young king, toward the old mage, toward the *gwynhfar* swaddled in silk who waits, as she waits for everything else. I bow my head and raise my voice.

"Listen," I say, my voice low and cozening.

"Listen, lords and ladies, as I sing of the coming days. I sing of the time when the kingdom will be one. And I call my song, the lay of the dark King Artos and of Guinevere the Fair."

JOHANNA

The forest was dark and the snow-covered path was merely an impression left on Johanna's moccasined feet.

If she had not come this way countless daylit times, Johanna would never have known where to go. But Hartwood was familiar to her, even in the unfamiliar night. She had often picnicked in the cool, shady copses and grubbed around the tall oak trees. In a hard winter like this one, a family could subsist for days on acorn stew.

Still, this was the first night she had ever been out in the forest, though she had lived by it all her life. It was tradition—no, more than that—that members of the Chevril family did not venture into the midnight forest. "Never, never go to the woods at night," her mother said, and it was not a warning so much as a command. "Your father went though he was told not to. He never returned."

And Johanna had obeyed. Her father's disappearance was still in her memory, though she remembered nothing else of him. He was not the first of the Chevrils to go that way. There had been a great-uncle and two girl cousins who had likewise "never returned." At least, that was what Johanna had been told. Whether they had disappeared into the maw of the city that lurked over several mountains to the west, or into the hungry jaws of a wolf or bear, was never made clear. But Johanna, being an obedient girl, always came into the house with the setting sun.

For sixteen years she had listened to that warning. But tonight, with her mother pale and sightless, breathing brokenly in the bed they shared, Johanna had no choice. The doctor, who lived on the other side of the wood, must be fetched. He lived in the cluster of houses that rimmed the far side of Hartwood, a cluster that was known as "the village," though it was really much too small for such a name. The five houses of the Chevril family that clung together, now empty except for Johanna and her mother, were not called a village, though they squatted on as much land.

Usually the doctor himself came through the forest to visit the Chevrils. Once a year he made the trip. Even when the grandparents and uncles and cousins had been alive, the village doctor came only once a year. He was gruff with them and called them "strong as beasts" and went away, never even offering a tonic. They needed none. They were healthy.

But the long, cruel winter had sapped Johanna's mother's strength. She lay for days silent, eyes cloudy and unfocused, barely taking in the acorn gruel that Johanna spooned for her. And at last Johanna had said: "I will fetch the doctor."

Her mother had grunted "no" each day, until this evening. When Johanna mentioned the doctor again, there had been no answering voice. Without her mother's no, Johanna made up her own mind. She would go.

If she did not get through the woods and back with the doctor before dawn, she felt it would be too late. Deep inside she knew she should have left before, even when her mother did not want her to go. And so she ran as quickly as she dared, following the small, twisting path through Hartwood by feel.

At first Johanna's guilt and the unfamiliar night were a burden, making her feet heavier than usual. But as she continued running, the crisp night air seemed to clear her head. She felt unnaturally alert, as if she had suddenly begun to discover new senses.

The wind molded her short dark hair to her head. For the first time she felt graceful and light, almost beautiful. Her feet beat a steady tattoo on the snow as she ran, and she felt neither cold nor winded. Her steps lengthened as she went.

Suddenly a broken branch across the path tangled in her legs. She went down heavily on all fours, her breath caught in her throat. As she got to her feet, she searched the darkness ahead. Were there other branches waiting?

Even as she stared, the forest seemed to grow brighter. The light from the full moon must be finding its way into the heart of the woods. It was a comforting thought.

She ran faster now, confident of her steps. The trees seemed to rush by. There would be plenty of time.

She came at last to the place where the woods stopped, and cautiously she ranged along the last trees, careful not to be silhouetted against the sky. Then she halted.

She could hear nothing moving, could see nothing that threatened. When she was sure, she edged out onto the short meadow that ran in a downward curve to the back of the village.

Once more she stopped. This time she turned her head to the left and right. She could smell the musk of the farm animals on the wind, blowing faintly up to her. The moon beat down upon her head and, for a moment, seemed to ride on her broad, dark shoulder.

Slowly she paced down the hill toward the line of houses that stood like teeth in a jagged row. Light streamed out of the rear windows, making threatening little earthbound moons on the graying snow.

She hesitated.

A dog barked. Then a second began, only to end his call in a whine.

A voice cried out from the house farthest on the right, a woman's voice, soft and soothing. "Be quiet, Boy."

The dog was silenced.

She dared a few more slow steps toward the village, but her fear seemed to proceed her. As if catching its scent, the first dog barked lustily again.

"Boy! Down!" It was a man this time, shattering the night with authority.

She recognized it at once. It was the doctor's voice. She edged toward its sound. Shivering with relief and dread, she came to the backyard of the house on the right and waited. In her nervousness, she moved one foot restlessly, pawing the snow down to the dead grass. She wondered if her father, her great-uncle, her cousins had felt this fear under the burning eye of the moon.

The doctor, short and too stout for his age, came out of the back door, buttoning his breeches with one hand.

In the other he carried a gun. He peered out into the darkness.

"Who's there?"

She stepped forward into the yard, into the puddle of light. She tried to speak her name, but she suddenly could not recall it. She tried to tell why she had come, but nothing passed her closed throat. She shook her head to clear the fear away.

The dog barked again, excited, furious.

"My God," the doctor said, "it's a deer."

She spun around and looked behind her, following his line of sight. There was nothing there.

"That's enough meat to last the rest of this cruel winter," he said. He raised the gun, and fired.

Into the Wood

Let us enter the wood.
Take my hand.
I feel your fear
rise on your palm,
a map beneath my fingers.
Can you decipher
the pulsing code
that beats at my wrist?
I do not need to see
dragons
to know there are
dragons here.
The back of my neck knows,
the skin of my inner thighs.
There, among the alders,
between twin beeches,
the gray-white pilasters
twined with wild grape,
stands a pavilion,
inferior Palladian in style.
Who sleeps on the antique couch?
I hear a thin scraping,
a belly through dead leaves,
a long, hollow good-by,
thin, full of scales,
modal, descending sounds.

In the dark
there will be eyes
thick as starshine,
a galaxy of watchers
beneath the trailing vine.
And trillium,
the red of heart's blood,
spills between rocks
to mark the path.
Do not, for God's sake,
let my hand go.
Do not, for God's sake,
speak.
I know what is here
and what is not,
and if we do not
name it aloud
it will do us no harm.
So the spells go,
so the tales go,
and I must believe it so.

THE MOON CHILD

There was once a land called Solin where all men worshipped the sun.

Children were born in the day and brought up in the sun's light. Lads and lasses courted at noon when the sun's power was at its height. And the dead were buried at the sun's waning and were afterward known only as shades.

All the people in Solin closed their doors when darkness fell. They gathered around their own homefires for food and for prayer. There they sang hymns to the "little sun," as they called the flames that flickered in every hearth.

Now in that kingdom was a great forest which all men feared, for it was dense and dark and so tangled with undergrowth and so arched over with trees that no one dared enter it. The Solinians called it Swartwood, and they named it only in whispers.

Year by year the trees of Swartwood tried to advance on the kingdom. And year by year the men of Solin cut the outermost trees back. It was those cut trees that burned in every hearth as a tribute to the sun.

Now it happened once in that kingdom that a baby was born, not at noon as was the custom, but at night in the light of the moon. Pale and wan, she grew tired in the sun and seemed to flourish only in the evening. And because of this, she was known as Mona, which meant "Moon Child."

Mona was a lonely girl, for her paleness frightened the other Solinians. They were all tanned and strong from the sun, while she seemed weakened by each day's light. They warned their children to leave her alone, and so the children did. For strangeness begets fear. Even Mona's own parents seemed to shun her, seeking out their own friends to walk with and work with in the sun.

So Mona learned to play by herself, seeking out the few shady places in Solin. And on the day she turned thirteen, forsaken by the children of her own age, she discovered the darkling woods.

Swartwood was a name used to frighten bad children. It was a place to make the strongest men in Solin tremble. But, to Mona, Swartwood was cool and inviting.

At first she had merely strolled by its edge, testing her fear of the stories told about the wood against her desire to know what lay hidden in its shade. And then, on her birthday, the thirteenth one she had celebrated all by herself, she resolved to enter the dark woods. If some evil befell her there, she thought it would just serve to show her parents and neighbors what her loss would mean to them.

She drew in a hasty breath, closed her eyes, and walked down an arched-over path into the very heart of the wood.

Nothing happened but the whisper of wind in her ears and the cool shadows on her face. Mona opened her eyes and looked around wonderingly.

There were soft mosses underfoot and climbing flowers that bloomed when the sun started down. There were ferns with fleshy leaves and fruit like faded grapes. And on the bank of a transparent pool, Mona discovered a large plant with brilliant purple flowers and pods that were as clear as the water nearby. At evening, refreshed and cooled, Mona returned to her home. No one, in fact, had missed her, and where she had been she did not tell.

Soon Mona was slipping away from her house early every morning and running into the woods when she thought no one watched. She gave each plant a name.

"This one," she said, pointing to a fragrant white blossom, "shall be Moonflower. And this one Moonseed," she said, pointing to a climbing vine with heart-shaped leaves. "And that fern I shall call Moonwort." For the idea of the Moon would not leave her.

Mona built a bower of trailing vines and lined a path to the door with milky white rocks she called Moonstones. And for the first time in her life, Mona was content.

It was not long before the other children noticed that Mona was wandering down to the overshadowed paths. And after a while, the bravest of them followed her. By ones and by twos and by threes they crept to the edge of the forest to watch for her, though they did not dare go into the woods. Some called her names and some mocked her, but they waited a long time to see if she would return.

Return she did, in the late afternoon just before dusk, with a strange, contented smile.

The first day, the children who had waited laughed at her, and teased her with questions about the dark wood. Mona merely smiled. She pressed on them some of the cool white milky stones she had gathered from the woods. But they did not dare to take the stones and ran from her in fright.

The next day when Mona returned from the forest, the children taunted her and called her names. Again she said nothing but smiled and offered them fragile blossoms such as they had never seen before. And though many of the children ran away, a few of the girls thought the blossoms pretty and put them in their hair, where they seemed to grow and open with the coming night.

The third day all the children waited at the forest line. This time, when Mona appeared they questioned her again, and now, although they were still frightened they were also eager. And this time Mona answered them, the smile still playing on her mouth.

"There is a place," she said, "deep in the wood where it is neither night nor day, where sunlight and shadows meet and dance together in ever-changing ways."

The children repeated this to themselves, over and over and over again, until it became a chant. And they accepted her presents and brought them home.

But such angry scenes greeted them there. Fathers and mothers gathered the stones and blossoms and, in a crowd, marched to the edge of the darkling woods. There they threw the moon gifts as far as they could into the deepening shade.

"Lie there, devil rocks," they cried as the milky white stones went flying. "Grow there, devil seeds," they called as the fragile blossoms were caught by the wind.

The children did not understand their anger and were saddened by the loss of the gifts.

But the mothers and fathers of Solin could not throw away Mona's tale of the secret place in the wood or the impression her strange smile had made.

So the men of Solin gathered in angry councils, for fear begets anger. They argued before the safe bright hearthfires, first in one home and then the other. "She will bring the evil spell of Swartwood to our homes," they declared.

Their wood piles grew taller than before as they cut back even more trees from the forest. But still it did not seem enough to make them feel safe.

"Her heart is as dark as the woods," they decided. And it was then that the people of Solin knew that Mona must be driven from their land, for anger seeks a victim.

So the men met and armed themselves. Their women formed behind them in a thin row. And behind them were the children, in scattered bunches, some weeping and some crying out, and all very much afraid.

Only Mona's mother and father remained at home. They were mourning that such a thing had come to pass, though at the same time they were secretly relieved to be rid of her.

And late that afternoon, when the sun's shadows were beginning to lengthen on the land and Mona came out of the woods, she was met not by ones and by twos and by threes of curious children but by an angry mob of Solinians. They shouted and shook their fists and ran toward her, their raised axes gleaming dully in the sun.

The pale girl looked at them for a long moment, and then quickly turned and ran, ran back to the tree-arched, shadowy wood.

The people of Solin were, by that time, so angry that they chased right after her, waving their axes and fists at her back. They threw rocks and called out and hooted and made so much noise that before they realized it, they had run right into the woods.

But when the first trees had blotted out the sun, the men in the first rank grew frightened and stopped short. And the running women and children behind them bumped into them. The townspeople were shaken. They looked about uneasily at the trees above them and at the way the shadows crawled across their bodies.

Then the darkness was too much. With a single shout, the men and women turned around and ran back the way they had come. After a quick glance around, the children ran after them.

The little suns—the fires that burned that night in all the hearths of the village—seemed brighter and warmer than they ever had before.

Mona never returned. Fearing the axes and fists, she stayed and lived in her bower for the rest of her life. She learned which ferns made a balm and which made a meal. She fished in deep pools and farmed in small meadows. And if occasionally she missed the powerful sun or the bright sunflowers or the laughter of others, she did not say.

But strange—or was it?—one day years later, when she was old past fearing the axes and fists, she heard human voices in the forest. Some she almost recognized, for they were the other children, grown old as she. They came tentatively into the woods, by ones and by twos and by threes.

As they walked they talked of her, of Mona the pale girl, the child of the moon. And they saw the Moonstones, and the Moonflowers and Moonwort growing wild by the path. But though they searched for Mona in the green glades and in the hidden meadows, and they looked for her in the coppice, they never really found her where she waited, further out, always further out, in the place past the darkness where the sunlight and shadows met and danced together in ever-changing ways.

GREAT SELKIE

When he came courting, Jesus,
he was a lovely man,
his face smooth and sly,
his hair the color of plums.
I plucked yarrow to keep me safe.
"May I be an isle in the sea,
May I be a hill on the shore."
We danced on heather all in darkness,
his body against mine,
till we were wet as water,
till I breathed in salt.
"May I be a star in waning of the
            moon."

The yarrow wilted before dawn.
All crested and furred,
he returned to the sea.
I was not honest with him;
he was not my first.
But I will a child of him,
webbings between its fingers
gray as storm air.
Then we shall see who is queen of
            the isle.
We shall see who claims the
            Selkie's trove.

INSCRIPTION

Father, they have burned your body,
Set your ashes in the cairn.
Still I need your advice.
Magnus sues for me in marriage,
Likewise McLeod of the three farms.
Yet would I wait for Iain the traveler,
Counting each step of his journey
Till the sun burns down behind Galan
Three and three hundred times;
Till he has walked to Steornabhagh
And back the long, hard track,
Singing my praises at every shieling
Where the lonely women talk to the east wind
And admire the ring he is bringing
To place on my small white hand.
—Inscription on Callanish Stones, Isle of Lewis

It is a lie, you know, that inscription. From first to last. I did not want my father's advice. I had never taken it when he was alive, no matter how often he offered it. Still I need to confess what's been done.

If I do not die of this thing, I shall tell my son himself when he is old enough to understand. But if I cannot tell him, there will still be this paper to explain it: who his mother was, what she did for want of him, who and what his father was, and how the witch cursed us all.

Magnus Magnusson did ask for me in marriage, but he did not really want me. He did not want me though I was young and slim and fair. His eye was to the young men, but he wanted my father's farm and my father was a dying man, preferring a dram to a bannock.

And McLeod had the richest three farms along the machair, growing more than peat and sand. Still he was ugly and old, older even than my father, and as pickled, though his was of the brine where my father's was the whiskey.

Even Iain the traveler was no great catch, for he had no money at all. But ach—he was a lovely man, with hair the purple brown of heather in the spring or like a bruise beneath the skin. He was worth the loving but not worth the waiting for. Still I did not know it at the time.

I was nursed not by my mother, who died giving birth to me, but by brown-haired Mairi, daughter of Lachlan, who was my father's shepherd. And if she had married my father and given him sons, these troubles would not have come upon me. But perhaps that, too, is a lie. Even as a child I went to trouble as a herring to the water, so Mairi always said. Besides, my father was of that rare breed of man who fancied only the one wife; his love once given was never to be changed or renewed, even to the grave.

So I grew without a brother or sister to play with, a trouble to my dear nurse and a plague to my father, though neither ever complained of it. Indeed, when I stumbled in the bog as the household dug the peat, and was near lost, they dragged me free. When I fell down a hole in the cliff when we went for birds' eggs, they paid a man from St. Kilda's to rescue me with ropes. And when the sea herself pulled me from the sands the day I went romping with the selchies, they got in the big boat that takes four men and a bowman in normal times, and pulled me back from the clutching tide. Oh I was a trouble and a plague.

But never was I so much as when I came of age to wed. That summer, after my blood flowed the first time and Mairi showed me how to keep myself clean—and no easy job of it—handsome Iain came through on his wanderings. He took note of me I am sure, and not just because he told me the summer after. A girl knows when a man has an eye for her: she knows it by the burn of her skin; she knows it by the ache in her bones. He said he saw the promise in me and was waiting a year to collect on it. He had many such collections in mind, but I wasn't to know.

His eyes were as purple brown as his hair, like wild plums. And his skin was dark from wandering. There is not much sun on Leodhas, summer to winter, but if you are constantly out in it, the wind can scour you. Iain the traveler had that color; while others were red as rowan from the wind, he was brown as the roe. It made his teeth the whiter. It made the other men look boiled or flayed and laughable.

No one laughed at Iain. No woman laughed, that is.

So of course I loved him. How could I not? I who had been denied nothing by my father, nothing by my nurse. I loved Iain and wanted him, so I was certain to have him. How was I to know the count of days would be so short?

When he came through the next summer to collect on that promise, I was willing to pay. We met first on the long sea loch where I had gone to gather periwinkles and watch the boys come in from the sea, pulling on the oars of the boat which made their new young muscles ripple.

Iain spoke to all of the women, few of the men, but for me he took out his whistle and played one of the old courting tunes. We had a laugh at that, all of us, though I felt a burn beneath my breastbone, by the heart, and could scarcely breathe.

I pretended he played the tune because I was watching out for the boys. He pretended he was playing it for Jennie Morrison, who was marrying Jamie Matheson before the baby in her belly swelled too big. But I already knew, really, he was playing just for me.

The pipes told me to meet him by the standing stones and so I did. He acted surprised to see me, but I knew he was not. He smoothed my hair and took me in his arms, and called me such sweet names as he kissed me I was sure I would die of it.

"Come tomorrow," he whispered, "when the dark finally winks," by which he meant well past midnight. And though I thought love should shout its name in the daylight as well as whisper at night, I did as he asked.

Sneaking from our house was not easy. Like most island houses, it was small and with only a few rooms, and the door was shared with the byre. But father and nurse and cows were all asleep, and I slipped out, barely stirring the peat smoke as I departed.

Iain was waiting for me by the stones, and he led me down to a place where soft grasses made a mat for my back. And there he taught me the pain of loving as well as the sweetness of it. I did not cry out, though it was not from wanting. But bred on the island means being strong, and I had only lately given over playing shinty with the boys. Still there was blood on my legs and I cleaned myself with grass and hurried back as the sun—what there was of it—was rising, leaving Iain asleep and guarded by the stones.

If Mairi noticed anything, she said nothing. At least not that day. And as I helped her at the quern preparing meal, and gave a hand with the baking as well, all the while suppressing the yawns that threatened to expose me, perhaps she did not know.

When I went back to the stones that night, Iain was waiting for me and this time there was neither blood nor pain, though I still preferred the kisses to what came after.

But I was so tired that I slept beside him all that night, or what was left of it. At dawn we heard the fishermen calling to one another as they passed by our little nest on the way to their boats. They did not see us: Iain knew how to choose his places well. Still I did not rise, for no fisherman dares meet a woman as he goes toward the sea for fear of losing his way in the waves. So I was forced to huddle there in the shelter of Iain's arms till the fishermen—some of them the boys I had lately played shinty with—were gone safely on their way.

This time when I got home Mairi was already up at the quern, her face as black as if it had been rinsed in peat. She did not say a word to me, which was even worse, but by her silence I knew she had said nothing to my father, who slept away in the other room.

That was the last but one I saw of Iain that summer, though I went night after night to look for him at the stones. My eyes were red from weeping silently as I lay in the straw by Mairi's side, and she snoring so loudly, I knew she was not really asleep.

I would have said nothing, but the time came around and my blood did not flow. Mairi knew the count of it since I was so new to womanhood. Perhaps she guessed even before I did, for I saw her looking at me queer. When I felt queasy and was sick behind the house, there was no disguising it.

"Who is it?" she asked. Mairi was never one for talking too much.

"Iain the traveler," I said. "I am dying for love of him."

"You are not dying," she said, "lest your father kill you for this. We will go to Auld Annie who lives down the coast. She practices the black airt and can rid you of the child."

"I do not want to be rid of it," I said. "I want Iain."

"He is walking out with Margaret MacKenzie in her shieling. Or if not her, another."

"Never! He loves me," I said. "He swore it."

"He loves," Mairi said, purposefully coarse to shock me, "the cherry in its blossom but not the tree. And his swearing is done to accomplish what he desires."

She took me by the hand, then, before I could recover my tongue, and we walked half the morning down the strand to Auld Annie's croft, it being ten miles or so by. There was only a soft, fair wind and the walking was not hard, though we had to stop every now and again for me to be quietly sick in the sand.

Auld Annie's cottage was much the smallest and meanest I had seen, still it had a fine garden both in front and again in back in the long rig. Plants grew there in profusion, in lazybeds, and I had no name for many of them.

"She can call fish in by melted lead and water," Mairi said. "She can calm the seas with seven white stones."

I did not look impressed, but it was my stomach once more turning inside me.

"She foretold your own dear mother's death."

I looked askance. "Why didn't I know of this?"

"Your father forbade me ever speak of it."

"And now?"

"Needs does as needs must." She knocked on the door.

The door seemed to open of itself because when we got inside, Auld Annie was sitting far from it, in a rocker, a coarse black shawl around her shoulders and a mutch tied under her chin like any proper wife. The croft was lower and darker than ours, but there was a broad mantel over the fire and on it sat two piles of white stones with a human skull, bleached and horrible, staring at the wall between them. On the floor by a long table were three jugs filled with bright red poppies, the only color in the room. From the rafters hung bunches of dried herbs, but they were none of them familiar to me.

Under her breath, Mairi muttered a charm:

> I trample upon the eye
> As tramples the duck upon the lake,
> In the name of the secret Three,
> And Brigid the Bride...

and made a quick sign against the *Droch Shùil,* the evil eye.

"I knew it, I knew ye were coming, Molly," Auld Annie said.

How she knew that—or my name—I could not guess.

"I knew it as I knew when yer mam was going to die." Her voice was low, like a man's.

"We haven't come for prophecy," I said.

"Ye have come about a babe."

My jaw must have gone agape at that for I had told no one but Mairi— and that only hours before. Surely Auld Annie *was* a witch, though if she threw no shadow one could not tell in the dark of her house. Nevertheless I shook my head. "I will keep the babe. All I want is the father to come to me."

"Coming is easy," Auld Annie said in her deep voice. "Staying is hard."

"If you get him to come to me," I answered, suddenly full of myself, "I will get him to stay."

From Mairi there was only a sharp intake of breath in disapproval, but Auld Annie chuckled at my remark, dangerous and low.

"Come then, girl," she said, "and set yer hand to my churn. We have butter to take and spells to make and a man to call to yer breast."

I did not understand entirely, but I followed her to the churn, where she instructed me in what I had to do.

"As ye churn, girl, say this: *Come, butter, come. Come, butter, come.*"

"I know this charm," I said witheringly. "I have since a child."

"Ah—but instead 'a saying 'butter,' ye must say yer man's name. Only—" she raised her hand in warning, "not aloud. And ye must not hesitate even a moment's worth between the words. Not once. Ye must say it over and over till the butter be done. It is not easy, for all it sounds that way."

I wondered—briefly—if all she was needing was a strong young girl to do her chores, but resolved to follow her instructions. It is a dangerous thing to get a witch angry with you. And if she could call Iain to me, so much the better.

So I put my hands upon the churn and did as she bid, over and over and over without a hesitation till my arms ached and my mind was numb and all I could hear was Iain's name in my head, the very sound of it turning my stomach and making me ill. Still I did not stop till the butter had come.

Auld Annie put her hands upon mine, and they were rough and crabbed with time. "Enough!" she said, "or it will come sour as yer belly, and we will have done all for nought."

I bit back the response that it was not *we* but *I* who had done the work and silently put my aching arms down at my sides. Only then did I see that Annie herself had not been idle. On her table lay a weaving of colored threads.

"A framing spell," Mairi whispered by my side. "A *deilbh buidseachd.*"

I resisted crossing myself and spoiling the spell and went where Annie led me, to the rocking chair.

"Sit ye by the fire," she said.

No sooner had I sat down, rubbing my aching arms and trying not to jump up and run outside to be sick, when a piece of the peat broke off in the hearth and tumbled out at my feet.

"Good, good," Auld Annie crooned. "Fire bodes marriage. We will have success."

I did not smile. Gritting my teeth, I whispered, "Get on with it."

"Hush," cautioned Mairi, but her arms did not ache as mine did..

Auld Annie hastened back to the churn and, dipping her hand into it, carved out a pat of butter the size of a shinty ball with her nails. Slapping it down on the table by the threads, she said: "Name three colors, girl, and their properties."

"Blue like the sea by Galan's Head," I said.

"Good, good, two more."

"Plum—like his eyes."

"And a third."

I hesitated, thinking. "White," I said at last. "White—like...like God's own hair. "

Auld Annie made a loud *tch* sound in the back of her throat and Mairi, giving a loud explosive exhalation, threw her apron up over her head.

"Not a proper choice, girl," Auld Annie muttered. "But what's said cannot be unsaid. Done is done."

"Is it spoiled?" I whispered.

"Not spoiled. Changed." She drew the named colors of thread from the frame and laid them, side by side, across the ball of butter. "Come here."

I stood up and went over to her, my arms all a-tingle.

"Set the two threads at a cross for the name of God ye so carelessly invoked, and one beneath for yer true love's name."

I did as she bid, suddenly afraid. What had I called up or called down, so carelessly in this dark house?

Auld Annie wrapped the butter in a piece of yellowed linen, tying the whole up with a black thread, before handing it to me.

"Take this to the place where ye wish to meet him and bury it three feet down, first drawing out the black thread. Cover it over with earth and while doing so recite three times the very words ye said over the churn. He will come that very evening. He will come—but whether he will stay is up to ye, my girl."

I took the sachet in my right hand and dropped it carefully into the pocket of my apron.

"Come now, girl, give me a kiss to seal it."

When I hesitated, Mairi pushed me hard in the small of the back and I stumbled into the old woman's arms. She smelled of peat and whiskey and age, not unlike my father, but there was something more I could put no name to. Her mouth on mine was nothing like Iain's, but was bristly with an old woman's hard whiskers and her lips were cracked. Her sour breath entered mine and I reeled back from her, thankful to be done. As I turned, I glanced at the mantel. To my horror I saw that between the white stones, the skull was now facing me, its empty sockets black as doom.

Mairi opened the cottage door and we stumbled out into the light, blinking like hedgehogs. I started down the path, head down. When I gave a quick look over my shoulder, Mairi was setting something down by Auld Annie's door. It was a payment, I knew, but for what and how much I did not ask, then or ever.

We walked back more slowly than we had come, and I chattered much of the way, as if the charming had been on my tongue to loosen it. I told Mairi about Iain's hair and his eyes and every word he had spoken to me, doling them out a bit at a time because, truth to tell, he had said little. I recounted the kisses and how they made me feel and even—I blush to think of it now—how I preferred them to what came after. Mairi said not a word in return until we came to the place where the path led away to the standing stones.

When I made to turn, she put her hand on my arm. "No, not there," she said. "I told you he has gone up amongst the shielings. If you want him to come to you, I will have your father send you up to the high pasture today."

"He will come wherever I call him," I said smugly, patting the pocket where the butter lay.

"Do not be more brainless than you have been already," Mairi said. "Go where you have the best chance of making him stay."

I saw at last what she meant. At the stones we would have to creep and hide and lie still lest the fishermen spy us. We would have to whisper our love. But up in the high pasture, along the cliffside, in a small croft of our own, I could bind him to me by night and by day, marrying him in the old way. And no one—especially my father—could say no to such a wedding.

So Mairi worked her own magic that day, much more homey than Auld Annie's, with a good hot soup and a hearty dram and a word in the ear of my old father. By the next morning she had me packed off to the shieling, with enough bannocks and barley and flasks of water in my basket to last me a fortnight, driving five of our cows before.

The cows knew the way as well as I, and they took to the climb like weanlings, for the grass in the shieling was sweet and fresh and greener than the overgrazed land below. In another week Mairi and I would have gone up together. But Mairi had my father convinced that I was grown enough to make the trip for the first time alone. Grown enough—if he had but known!

Perhaps it was the sea breeze blowing on my face, or the fact that I knew Iain would be in my arms by dark. Or perhaps it was just that the time for such sickening was past, but I was not ill at all on that long walk, my step as jaunty as the cows'.

It was just coming on late supper when we turned off the path to go up and over the hill to the headland where our little summer croft sits.

The cows followed their old paths through the matted bog with a quiet satisfaction, but I leaped carelessly from tussock to tuft behind them.

I walked—or rather danced—to the cliff's edge where the hummocks and bog and gray-splattered stone gave way to the sheer of cliff. Above me the gannets flew high and low, every now and again veering off to plummet into the sea after fish. A solitary seal floated below, near some rocks, looking left, then right, then left again but never once up at me.

With the little hoe I had brought along for the purpose, I dug a hole, fully three feet down, and reverently laid in the butter pat. Pulling the black thread from the sachet, I let the clods of dirt rain back down on it, all the while whispering, "Come, Iain, come. Come, Iain, come." Then loudly I sang out, "Come, Iain, come!" without a hesitation in between. Then I packed the earth down and stood, rubbing the small of my back where Mairi had pushed me into the sealing kiss.

I stared out over the sea, waiting.

He did not come until past dark, which in summer is well into the mid of the night. By then I had cooked myself a thin barley gruel, and made the bed up, stuffing it with soft grasses and airing out the croft.

I heard his whistle first, playing a raucous courting tune, not the one he had played on the beach when first I had noticed him, but "The Cuckoo's Nest," with words that say the one thing, but mean another.

In the dim light it took him a minute to see me standing by the door. Then he smiled that slow, sure smile of his. "Well...Molly," he said.

I wondered that he hesitated over my name, almost as if he could not recall it, though it had been but a few short weeks before that he had whispered it over and over into my tumbled hair.

"Well, Iain," I said. "You have come to me."

"I have been called to you," he said airily. "I could not stay away."

And then suddenly I understood that he did not know there was magic about; that these were just words he spoke, part of his lovemaking, that meant as little to him as the kisses themselves, just prelude to his passion.

Well, I had already paid for his pleasure and now he would have to stay for mine. I opened my arms and he walked into them as if he had never been away, his kisses the sweeter now that I knew what he was and how to play his game.

In the morning I woke him with the smell of barley bread. I thought if I could get him to stay a second night, and a third, the charm would have a chance of really working. So I was sweet and pliant and full of an ardor that his kisses certainly aroused, though that which followed seemed to unaccountably dampen it. Still, I could dissemble when I had to, and each time we made love I cried out as if fulfilled. Then while he slept I tiptoed out to the place where I had buried the butter sachet.

"Stay, Iain, stay. Stay, Iain, stay," I recited over the little grave where my hopes lay buried.

For a day and another night it seemed to work. He did stay—and quite happily—often sitting half-dressed in the cot watching me cook or lying naked on the sandy beach, playing his whistle to call the seals to him. They rose up out of the water, gazing long at him, as if they were bewitched.

We made love three and four and five times, day and night, till my thighs ached the way my arms had at the churn, and I felt scrubbed raw from trying to hold on to him.

But on the third day, when he woke, he refused both the barley and my kisses.

"*Enough,* sweet Moll," he said. "I am a traveler, and I must travel." He got dressed slowly, as if almost reluctant to leave but satisfying the form of it. I said nothing till he put his boots on, then could not stop myself.

"On to another shieling, then?"

"Perhaps."

"And what of the babe—here." It was the first time I had mentioned it. From the look on his face, I knew it made no matter to him, and without waiting for an answer, I stalked out of the croft. I went to the headland and stood athwart the place where the butter lay buried.

"Stay, Iain," I whispered. "Stay..." but there was neither power nor magic nor desire in my calling.

He came up behind me and put his arms around me, crossing his hands over my belly where the child-to-be lay quiet.

"Marry another," he whispered, nuzzling my ear, "but call him after me."

I turned in his arms and pulled him around to kiss me, my mouth wide open as if to take him in entire. And when the kiss was done, I pulled away and pushed him over the cliff into the sea.

Like most men of Leodhais, he could not swim, but little it would have availed him, for he hit the rocks and then the water, sinking at once. He did not come up again till three seals pushed him ashore onto the beach, where they huddled by his body for a moment as if expecting a tune, then plunged back into the sea when there was none.

I hurried down and cradled his poor broken body in my arms, weeping not for him but for myself and what I had lost, what I had buried up on that cliff, along with the butter, in a boggy little grave. Stripping the ring from his hand, I put it on my own, marrying us in the eyes of the sea. Then

I put him on my back and carried him up the cliffside to bury him deep beneath the heather that would soon be the color of his hair, of his eyes.

Two weeks later, when Mairi came, I showed her the ring.

"We were married in God's sight," I said, "with two selchies as brides-maids and a gannet to cry out the prayers."

"And where is the bridegroom now?" she asked.

"Gone to Steornabhagh," I lied, "to whistle us up money for our very own croft." She was not convinced. She did not say so, but I could read her face.

Of course he never returned and—with Mairi standing up for me—I married old McLeod after burying my father, who had stumbled into a hole one night after too much whiskey, breaking both his leg and his neck.

McLeod was too old for more than a kiss and a cuddle—as Mairi had guessed—and too pigheaded to claim the child wasn't his own. When the babe was born hale and whole, I named him Iain, a common-enough name in these parts, with only his nurse Mairi the wiser. At McLeod's death a year later, I gave our old farm over to her. It was a payment, she knew, but exactly for what she never asked, not then or ever.

Now I lie abed with the pox, weakening each day, and would repent—of the magic and the rest—though not of the loving which gave me my child. Still I would have my Iain know who his mother was and what she did for want of him, who and what his father was, and how the witch cursed us all. I would not have my son unmindful of his inheritance. If ever the wind calls him to travel, if ever a witch should tempt him to magic, or if ever a cold, quiet rage makes him choose murder, he will understand and, I trust, set all those desires behind.

Written this year of our Lord 1539, Tir a' Gheallaidh, Isle of Lewis.

THE FISHERMAN'S WIFE

John Merton was a fisherman. He brought up eels and elvers, little finny creatures and great sharp-toothed monsters from the waves. He sold their meat at markets and made necklaces of their teeth for the fairs.

If you asked him, he would say that what he loved about the ocean was its vast silence, and wasn't that why he had married him a wife the same. Deaf she was, and mute too, but she could talk with her hands, a flowing syncopation. He would tell you that, and it would be no lie. But there were times when he would go mad with her silences, as the sea can drive men mad, and he would leave the house to seek the babble of the marketplace. As meaningful as were her finger fantasies, they brought his ear no respite from the quiet.

There was one time, though, that he left too soon, and it happened this way. It was a cold and gray morning, and he slammed the door on his wife, thinking she would not know it, forgetting there are other ways to hear. And as he walked along the shore, singing loudly to himself—so as to prime his ears—and swinging the basket of fish pies he had for the fair, he heard only the sound of his own voice. The hush of the waves might have told him something. The silence of the sea-birds wheeling overhead.

"Buy my pies," he sang out in practice, his boots cutting great gashes like exclamation marks in the sand.

Then he saw something washed up an the beach ahead.

Now fishermen often find things left along the shore. The sea gives and it takes and as often gives back again, There is sometimes a profit to be turned on the gifts of the sea. But every fisherman knows that when you have dealings with the deep you leave something of yourself behind.

It was no flotsam lying on the sand. It was a sea-queen, beached and gasping. John Merton stood over her, and his feet were as large as her head. Her body had a pale-greenish cast to it. The scales of her fishlike tail ran up past her waist, and some small scales lay along her sides, sprinkled like shiny gray-green freckles on the paler skin. Her breasts were as smooth and golden as shells. Her supple shoulders and arms looked almost boneless. The green-brown hair that flowed from her head was the color and texture of wrackweed. There was nothing lovely about her at all, he thought, though she exerted an alien fascination. She struggled for breath and, finding it, blew it out again in clusters of large, luminescent bubbles that made a sound as of waves against the shore,

And when John Merton bent down to look at her more closely still, it was as if he had dived into her eyes. They were ocean eyes, blue-green, and with golden flecks in the iris like minnows darting about. He could not stop staring. She seemed to call to him with those eyes, a calling louder than any sound could be in the air. He thought he heard his name, and yet he knew that she could not have spoken it. And he could not ask the mermaid about it, for how could she tell him? All fishermen know that mermaids cannot speak. They have no tongues.

He bent down and picked her up and her tail wrapped around his waist, quick as an eel. He unwound it slowly, reluctantly, from his body and then, with a convulsive shudder, threw her from him back into the sea. She flipped her tail once, sang out in a low ululation, and was gone.

He thought, wished really, that that would be the end of it, though he could not stop shuddering. He fancied he could still feel the tail around him, coldly constricting. He went on to the fair, sold all his pies, drank up the profit and started for home.

He tried to convince himself that he had seen stranger things in the water. Worse—and better. Hadn't he one day brought up a shark with a man's hand in its stomach? A right hand with a ring on the third finger, a ring of tourmaline and gold that he now wore himself, vanity getting the better of superstition. He could have given it to his wife, Mair, but he kept it for himself, forgetting that the sea would have its due. And hadn't he one night seen the stars reflecting their cold brilliance on the water as if the ocean itself stared up at him with a thousand eyes? Worse—and better. He reminded himself of his years culling the tides that swept rotting boards and babies' shoes and kitchen cups to his feet. And the fish. And the eels. And the necklaces of teeth. Worse—and better.

By the time he arrived home he had convinced himself of nothing but the fact that the mermaid was the nastiest and yet most compelling thing he had yet seen in the ocean. Still, he said nothing of it to Mair, for though she was a fisherman's daughter and a fisherman's wife; since she had been deaf from birth no one had ever let her go out to sea. He did not want her to be frightened; as frightened as he was himself.

But Mair learned something of it, for that night when John Merton lay in bed with the great down quilt over him, he swam and cried and swam again in his sleep, keeping up stroke for stroke with the sea-queen. And he called out, "Cold, oh God, she's so cold," and pushed Mair away when she tried to wrap her arms around his waist for comfort. Oh, yes, she knew, even though she could not hear him, but what could she do? If he would not listen to her hands on his, there was no more help she could give.

So John Merton went out the next day with only his wife's silent prayer picked out by her fingers along his back. He did not turn for a kiss.

And when he was out no more than half a mile, pulling strongly on the oars and ignoring the spray, the sea-queen leaped like a shot across his bow. He tried to look away, but he was not surprised. He tried not to see her webbed hand on the oarlock or the fingers as sure as wrackweed that gripped his wrist. But slowly, ever so slowly, he turned and stared at her, and the little golden fish in her eyes beckoned to him. Then he heard her speak, a great hollow of sound somewhere between a sigh and a song, that came from the grotto that was her mouth.

"I will come," he answered, now sure of her question, hearing in it all he had longed to hear from his wife. It was magic, to be sure, a compulsion, and he could not have denied it had he tried. He stood up, drew off his cap and tossed it onto the waves. Then he let the oars slip away and his life on land slip away and plunged into the water near the bobbing cap just a beat behind the mermaid's flashing tail.

A small wave swamped his boat. It half sank, and the tide lugged it relentlessly back to the shore where it lay on the beach like a bloated whale.

When they found the boat, John Merton's mates thought him drowned. And they came to the house, their eyes tight with grief and their hands full of unsubtle mimings.

"He is gone," said their hands. "A husband to the sea." For they never spoke of death and the ocean in the same breath, but disguised it with words of celebration.

Mair thanked them with her fingers for the news they bore, but she was not sure that they told her the truth. Remembering her husband's night dreams, she was not sure at all. And as she was a solitary person by nature, she took her own counsel. Then she waited until sunrise and went down to the shore.

His boat was now hers by widow's right. Using a pair of borrowed oars, she wrestled it into the sea.

She had never been away from shore, and letting go of the land was not an easy thing. Her eyes lingered on the beach and sought out familiar rocks, a twisted tree, the humps of other boats that marked the shore. But at last she tired of the landmarks that had become so unfamiliar, and turned her sights to the sea.

Then, about half a mile out, where the sheltered bay gave way to the open sea, she saw something bobbing on the waves. A sodden blue knit cap. John Merton's marker.

"He sent it to me," Mair thought. And in her eagerness to have it, she almost loosed the oars. But she calmed herself and rowed to the cap, fishing it out with her hands. Then she shipped the oars and stood up. Tying a great strong rope around her waist, with one end knotted firmly through the oarlock—not a sailor's knot but a loveknot, the kind that she might have plaited in her hair—Mair flung herself at the ocean.

Down and down and down she went, through the seven layers of the sea.

At first it was warm, with a cool, light-blue color hung with crystal teardrops. Little spotted fish, green and gold, were caught in each drop. And when she touched them, the bubbles burst and freed the fish, which darted off and out of sight.

The next layer was cooler, an aquamarine with a fine, falling rain of gold. In and out of these golden strings swam slower creatures of the deep: bulging squid, ribboned sea snakes, knobby five fingered stars. And the strands of gold parted before her like a curtain of beads and she could peer down into the colder, darker layers below.

Down and down and down Mair went until she reached the ocean floor at last. And there was a path laid out, of finely colored sands edged round with shells, and statues made of bone. Anemones on their fleshy stalks waved at her as she passed, for her passage among them was marked with the swirlings of a strange new tide.

At last she came to a palace that was carved out of coral. The doors and windows were arched and open, and through them passed the creatures of the sea,

Mair walked into a single great hall. Ahead of her, on a small dais, was a divan made of coral, pink and gleaming. On this coral couch lay the sea-queen. Her tail and hair moved to the sway of the currents, but she was otherwise quite still. In the shadowed, filtered light of the hall, she seemed ageless and very beautiful.

Mair moved closer, little bubbles breaking from her mouth like fragments of unspoken words. Her movement set up countercurrents in the hall. And suddenly, around the edges of her sight, she saw another movement. Turning, she saw ranged around her an army of bones, the husbands of the sea. Not a shred or tatter of skin clothed them, yet every skeleton was an armature from which the bones hung, as surely connected as they had been on land. The skeletons bowed to her, one after another, but Mair could see that they moved not on their own reckoning, but danced to the tunes piped through them by the tides. And though on land they would have each looked different, without hair, without eyes, without the subtle coverings of flesh, they were all the same.

Mair covered her eyes with her hands for a moment, then she looked up. On the couch, the mermaid was smiling down at her with her tongue-less mouth. She waved a supple arm at one whole wall of bone men and they moved again in the aftermath of her greeting.

"Please," said Mair, "please give me back my man." She spoke with her hands, the only pleadings she knew. And the tongueless sea-queen seemed to understand, seemed to sense a sisterhood between them and gave her back greetings with fingers that swam as swiftly as any little fish.

Then Mair knew that the mermaid was telling her to choose, choose one of the skeletons that had been men. Only they all looked alike, with their sea-filled eye sockets and their bony grins.

"I will try," she signed, and turned toward them.

Slowly she walked the line of bitter bones. The first had yellow min-nows fleeting though its hollow eyes. The second had a twining of green vines round its ribs. The third laughed a school of red fish out its mouth. The fourth had a pulsing anemone heart. And so on down the line she went, thinking with quiet irony on the identity of flesh.

But as long is she looked, she could not tell John Merton from the rest. If he was there, he was only a hanging of bones indistinguishable from the others.

She turned back to the divan to admit defeat, when a flash of green and gold caught her eye. It was a colder color than the rest—yet warmer, too. It was alien under the sea, as alien as she, and she turned toward its moving light.

And then, on the third finger of one skeleton's hand, she saw it—the tourmaline ring which her John had so prized. Pushing through the water toward him, sending dark eddies to the walls that set the skeletons writh-ing in response, she took up his skeletal hand. The fingers were brittle and stiff under hers.

Quickly she untied the rope at her waist and looped it around the bones. She pulled them across her back and the white remnants of his fingers tightened around her waist.

She tried to pull the ring from his hand, to leave something there for the sea. But the white knucklebones resisted. And though she feared it,

Mair went hand over hand, hand over hand along the rope, and pulled them both out of the sea.

She never looked back. And yet if she had looked, would she have seen the sea replace her man layer by layer? First it stuck the tatters of flesh and blue-green rivulets of veins along the bones. Then it clothed muscle and sinew with a fine covering of skin. Then hair and nails and the decorations of line. By the time they had risen through the seven strata of sea, he looked like John Merton once again.

But she, who had worked so hard to save him, could not swim, and so it was John Merton himself who untied the rope and got them back to the boat. And it was John Merton himself who pulled them aboard and rowed them both to shore.

And a time later, when Mair Merton sat up in bed ready at last to taste a bit of the broth he had cooked for her, she asked him in her own way what it was that had occurred.

"John Merton," she signed, touching his fine strong arms with their covering of tanned skin and fine golden hair. "Tell me..."

But he covered her hands with his, the hand that was still wearing the gold and tourmaline ring. He shook his head and the look in his eyes was enough. For she could suddenly see past the sea-green eyes to the sockets beneath, and she understood that although she had brought home, a part of him would be left in the sea forever, for the sea takes its due.

He opened his mouth to her then, and she saw it was hollow, as dark black as the deeps, and filled with the sound of waves.

"Never mind, John Merton," she signed on his hand, on his arms around her, into his hair. "The heart can speak, though the mouth be still. I will be loving you all the same."

And, of course, she did.

PRINCE CHARMING COMES

The goose flies past the setting sun, plums roasting in her breast;
Sleeping Beauty lays her head a hundred years to rest.
Then fee, fi, fo the giant fums
And to my dark Prince Charming comes
A ride, a ride, a ride, a riding,
Into my night of darkness, my own Prince Charming comes.

The witch is popped into the oven, rising into cake;
The swan queen glides her downy form to the enchanted lake.
And rum-pum-pum the drummer drums
As into the darkness my love comes
A ride, a ride, a ride, a riding,
Into my night of darkness, my own Prince Charming comes.

But do you come to take me out
Or come to put me in?
But do you come to yield to me
Or do you come to win?

It's half past twelve and once again the shoe of glass is gone,
And magic is as magic was and vanished with the dawn.
For Pooh has hummed his final hums,
The giant finished off his fums,
                                        they've drawn their final breath.
For into darkness my prince comes
A ride, a ride, a ride, a riding,
For into darkness my prince comes
On his bony horse called death.

AMERICA'S "CINDERELLA"

It is part of the American creed, recited subvocally along with the pledge of allegiance in each classroom, that even a poor boy can grow up to become president. The unliberated corollary is that even a poor girl can grow up and become the president's wife. This rags-to-riches formula was immortalized in American children's fiction by the Horatio Alger stories of the 1860s and by the Pluck and Luck nickel novels of the 1920s.

It is little wonder, then, that Cinderella should be a perennial favorite in the American folktale pantheon.

Yet how ironic that this formula should be the terms on which "Cinderella" is acceptable to most Americans. "Cinderella" is *not* a story of rags to riches, but rather riches recovered; *not* poor girl into princess but rather rich girl (or princess) rescued from improper or wicked enslavement; *not* suffering Griselda enduring but shrewd and practical girl persevering and winning a share of the power. It is really a story about the "stripping away of a disguise that conceals the soul from the eyes of others..."

We Americans have it wrong. "Rumpelstiltskin," in which a miller tells a whopping lie and his docile daughter acquiesces in it to become queen, would be more to the point.

But we have been initially seduced by the Perrault cinder-girl, who was, after all, the transfigured folk creature of a French literary courtier. Perrault's "Cendrillon" demonstrated the well-bred seventeenth-century female traits of gentility, grace, and selflessness, even to the point of graciously forgiving her wicked stepsisters and finding them noble husbands.

The American "Cinderella" is partially Perrault's. The rest is a spun-sugar caricature of her hardier European and Oriental forbears, who made their own way in the world, tricking the stepsisters with double-talk, artfully disguising themselves, or figuring out a way to win the king's son. The final bit of icing on the American Cinderella was concocted by that master candy-maker, Walt Disney, in the 1950s. Since then, America's Cinderella has been a coy, helpless dreamer, a "nice" girl who awaits her rescue with patience and a song. This Cinderella of the mass market books finds her way into a majority of American homes while the classic heroines sit unread in old volumes on library shelves.

Poor Cinderella. She has been unjustly distorted by storytellers, misunderstood by educators, and wrongly accused by feminists. Even as late as 1975, in the well-received volume *Womenfolk and Fairy Tales,* (American author) Rosemary Minard writes that Cinderella "would still be scrubbing floors if it were not for her fairy godmother." And Ms. Minard includes her in a sweeping condemnation of folk heroines as "insipid beauties waiting passively for Prince Charming."

Like many dialecticians Ms. Minard reads the fairy tales incorrectly. Believing—rightly—that the fairy tales, as all stories for children, acculturate young readers and listeners, she has nevertheless gotten her target wrong. Cinderella is not to blame. Not the real, the true Cinderella. Ms. Minard should focus her sights on the mass-market Cinderella. She does not recognize the old Ash-girl for the tough, resilient heroine. The wrong Cinderella has gone to the American ball.

HISTORY OF THE CINDERELLA TALE

The story of Cinderella has endured for over a thousand years, surfacing in a literary source first in ninth-century China. It has been found from the Orient to the interior of South America and over five hundred variants have been located by folklorists in Europe alone. This best-beloved tale has been brought to life over and over and no one can say for sure where the oral tradition began. The European story was included by Charles Perrault in his 1697 collection *Histoires ou Contes du temps passé* as "Cendrillon." But even before that, the Italian Straparola had a similar story in a collection, Since there had been twelve editions of the Straparola book printed in French before 1694, the chances are strong that Perrault had read the tale *"Peau d'Ane"* (Donkey Skin).

(Australian folklorist) Joseph Jacobs. the indefatigable Victorian collector. once said of a Cinderella story he printed that it was "an English version of an Italian adaptation of a Spanish translation of a Latin version of a Hebrew translation of an Arabic translation of an Indian original."

Perhaps it was not a totally accurate statement of that particular variant but Jacobs was making a point about the perils of folktale-telling: each teller brings to a tale something of his/her own cultural orientation. Thus in China. where the "lotus foot," or tiny foot was such a sign of a woman's worth that the custom of foot-binding developed, the Cinderella tale lays emphasis on an impossibly small slipper as a clue to the heroine's identity. In seventeenth-century France, Perrault's creation sighs along with her stepsisters over the magnificent "gold flowered mantua" and the "diamond stomacher." In the Walt Disney American version, both movie and book form, Cinderella shares with the little animals a quality of "lovableness," thus changing the intent of the tale and denying the heroine her birthright of shrewdness, inventiveness, and grace under pressure.

Notice, though, that many innovations—the Chinese slipper, the Perrault godmother with her midnight injunction and her ability to change pumpkin into coach—become incorporated in later versions. Even a slip of the English translator's tongue (de vair, fur, into de verre, glass) becomes immortalized. Such cross fertilization of folklore is phenomenal. And the staying power, across countries and centuries, of some of these inventions is notable. Yet glass slipper and godmother and pumpkin coach are not the common incidents by which a "Cinderella" tale is recognized even though they have become basic ingredients in the American story. Rather, the common incidents recognized by folklorists are these: an ill-treated though rich and worthy heroine in Cinders-disguise; the aid of a magical gift or advice by a beast/bird/mother substitute; the dance/festival/church scene where the heroine comes in radiant display; recognition through a token. So "Cinderella" and her true sister tales, (English variant) "Cap o'Rushes" with its King Lear judgment and "Catskin" wherein the father unnaturally desires his daughter, are counted.

(Scottish scholar and author) Andrew Lang's judgment that "a naked shoeless race could not have invented Cinderella," then, proves false. Variants have been found among the fur-wearing folk of Alaska and the native tribes in South Africa where shoes were not commonly worn.

"Cinderella" speaks to all of us in whatever skin we inhabit: the child mistreated, a princess or highborn lady in disguise bearing her trials with patience and fortitude. She makes intelligent decisions for she knows that wishing solves nothing without the concomitant action. We have each of us been that child. It is the longing of any youngster sent supperless to bed or given less than a full share at Christmas. It is the adolescent dream,

To make Cinderella less than she is, then, is a heresy of the worst kind. It cheapens our most cherished dreams. and it makes a mockery of the true magic inside us all—the ability to change our own lives, the ability to control our own destinies.

CINDERELLA COMES TO AMERICA

Cinderella first came to America in the nursery tales the settlers remembered from their own homes and told their children. Versions of these tales can still be found. Folklorist Richard Chase. for example, discovered "Rush Cape," an exact parallel of "Cap o'Rushes" with an Appalachian dialect in Tennessee, Kentucky, and South Carolina among others.

But when the story reached print, developed, was made literary, things began to happen to the hardy Cinderella. She suffered a sea change, a sea change aggravated by social conditions,

In the 1870s, for example, in the prestigious magazine for children *St. Nicholas,* there are a number of retellings or adaptations of "Cinderella." The retellings which merely translate European variants contain the hardy heroine. But when a new version is presented, a helpless Cinderella is born. G.B. Bartlett's "Giant Picture-Book," which was considered a curious novelty [that] can be produced...by children for the amusement of their friends..." presents a weepy, prostrate young blonde (the instructions here are, quite specific) who must be "aroused from her sad revery" by a godmother. Yet in the truer Cinderella stories, the heroine is not this catatonic. For example, in the Grimm "Cinder-Maid," though she weeps, she continues to perform the proper rites and rituals at her mother's grave instructing the birds who roost there to:

> Make me a lady fair to see,
> Dress me as splendid as can be.

And in "The Dirty Shepherdess," a "Cap o'Rushes" variant from France "...she dried her eyes, and made a bundle of her jewels and her best dresses and hurriedly left the castle where she was born." In the *St. Nicholas* "Giant Picture Book" she has none of this strength of purpose. Rather, she is manipulated by the godmother until the moment she stands before the prince where she speaks "meekly" and "with downcast eyes and extended hand." *St. Nicholas* was not meant for the mass market. It had, in (American children's writer) Selma Lanes' words, "a patrician call to a highly literate readership." But nevertheless, Bartlett's play instructions indicate how even in the more literary reaches of children's books a change was taking place.

However, to truly mark this change in the American "Cinderella," one must turn specifically to the mass-market books, merchandised products that masquerade as literature but make as little lasting literary impression as a lollipop. They, after all, serve the majority the way the storytellers of the village used to serve. They find their way into millions of homes.

Mass market books are almost as old as colonial America. The chapbooks of the eighteenth and nineteenth century, crudely printed tiny paperbacks, were the source of most children's reading in the early days of our country. Originally these were books imported from Europe. But slowly American publishing grew. In the latter part of nineteenth century one firm stood out—McLoughlin Bros. They brought bright colors to the pages of children's books. In a series selling for twenty-five cents per book, Aunt Kate's Series, bowdlerized folk tales emerged. "Cinderella" was there, with "Red Riding Hood," "Puss in Boots," and others. Endings were changed, innards cleaned up, and good triumphed with very loud huzzahs. Cinderella is the weepy, sentimentalized, pretty girl incapable of helping herself. In contrast, one only has to look at the girl in "Cap o'Rushes" who comes to a great house and asks "Do you want a maid?" and when refused, goes on to say "...I ask no wages and do any sort of work." And she does. In the end, when the master's young son is dying of love for the mysterious lady, she uses her wits to work her way out of the kitchen. Even in Perrault's "Cinderella," when the fairy godmother runs out of rats for enchantment and "was at a loss for a coach-man, I'll go and see, says Cinderella, if there be never a rat in the rat trap, we'll make a coachman of him. You are in the right, said her godmother, go and see."

Hardy, helpful, inventive, that was the Cinderella of the old tales but not of the mass market in the nineteenth century. Today's mass-market books are worse. These are the books sold in supermarket and candystore, even lining the shelves of many of the best bookstores. There are pop-up Cinderellas, coloring-book Cinderellas, scratch-and-sniff Cinderellas, all inexpensive and available. The point in these books is not the story but the *gimmick*. These are books which must "interest 300,000 children, selling their initial print order in one season and continuing strong for at least two years after that." Compare that with the usual trade publishing house print order of a juvenile book—10,000 copies—which an editor hopes to sell out in a lifetime of that title.

THE ORIGINAL CINDERELLA TALE

All the folk tales have been gutted. But none so changed, I believe, as "Cinderella." For the sake of Happy Ever After, the mass-market books have brought forward a good, malleable, forgiving little girl and put her in Cinderella's slippers. However, in most of the Cinderella tales there is no forgiveness in the heroine's heart. No mercy. Just justice. In "Rushen Coatie" and "The Cinder-Maid," (a European variant identified by Jacobs) the elder sisters hack off their toes and heels in order to fit the shoe. Cinderella never stops them, never implies that she has the matching slipper. In fact, her tattletale birds warn the prince in "Rushen Coatie":

> Hacked Heels and Pinched Toes
> Behind the young prince rides,
> But Pretty Feet and Little Feet
> Behind the cauldron bides.

Even more graphically, they call out in "Cinder-Maid"

> Turn and peep, turn and peep,
> There's blood within the shoe:
> A bit is cut from off the heel
> And a bit from off the toe.

Cinderella never says a word of comfort. And in the least bowdlerized of the German and Nordic tales. the two sisters come to the wedding "the elder was at the right side and the younger at the left, and the pigeons pecked out one eye from, each of them. Afterwards, as they came back. the elder was on the left. and the younger at the right and then the pigeons pecked out the other eye from each. And thus. for their wickedness and falsehood. they were punished with blindness all their days." That's a far cry from Perrault's heroine who "gave her sisters lodgings in the palace, and married them the same day to two great lords of the court." And further still from (American author) Nola Langner's Scholastic paperback "Cinderella,"

> (The sisters) began to cry.
> They begged Cinderella to forgive them for being so mean to her.
> Cinderella told them they were forgiven.
> "I am sure you will never be mean to me again," she said.
> "Oh, never," said the older sister.
> "Never, ever," said the younger sister.

Missing, too, from the mass-market books is the shrewd, even witty Cinderella. In a Wonder Book entitled "Bedtime Stories." a 1940s adaptation from Perrault, we find a Cinderella who talks to her stepsisters "in a shy little voice." Even Perrault's heroine bantered with her stepsisters, asking them leading questions about the ball while secretly and deliciously knowing the answers. In the Wonder Book, however, the true wonder is that Cinderella ever gets to be princess. Even face-to-face with the prince, she is unrecognized until she dons her magic ballgown. Only when her clothes are transformed does the prince know his true love.

WALT DISNEY'S *CINDERELLA*

In 1949, Walt Disney's film *Cinderella* burst onto the America scene. The story in the mass market has not been the same since.

The film came out of the studio at a particularly trying time for Disney: He had been deserted by the intellectuals who had been champions of this art for some years: Because of World War II, the public was more interested in war films than cartoons. But when *Cinderella,* lighter than light, was released it brought back to Disney—and his studio—all of his lost fame and fortune. The film was one of the most profitable of all time for the studio, grossing $4.247 million dollars in the first release alone. The success of the movie opened the floodgates of "Disney Cinderella" books. Golden Press's *Walt Disney's Cinderella* set the new pattern for America's Cinderella. This book's text is coy and condescending. (Sample: "And her best friends of all were—guess who—the mice!") The illustrations are poor cartoons. And Cinderella herself is a disaster. She cowers as her sisters rip her homemade ball gown to shreds. (Not even homemade by Cinderella, but by the mice and birds.) She answers her stepmother with whines and pleadings. She is a sorry excuse for heroine, pitiable and useless. She cannot perform even a simple action to save herself, though she is warned by her friends, the mice. She does not hear them because she is "off in a world of dreams." Cinderella begs, she whimpers, and at last has to be rescued by—guess who—the mice!

There is also an easy-reading version published by Random House, *Walt Disney's Cinderella.* This Cinderella commits the further heresy of cursing her luck. "How I did wish to go to the ball," she says. "But it is no use. Wishes never come true."

But in the fairy tales wishes have a habit of happening—*wishes accompanied by the proper action,* bad wishes as well as good. That is the beauty of the old stories and their wisdom as well.

Take away the proper course of action, take away Cinderella's ability to think for herself and act for herself, and you are left with a tale of wishes-come-true-regardless. But that is not the way of the fairy tale. As (Australian-born folklorist and children's book writer) P. L. Travers so wisely puts it, "If that were so, wouldn't we all be married to princes?"

The mass-market American "Cinderellas" have presented the majority of American children with the wrong dreams. They offer the passive princess, the "insipid beauty waiting...for Prince Charming" that Rosemary Minard objects to, and thus acculturate millions of girls and boys. But it is the wrong Cinderella and the magic of the old tales has been falsified, the true meaning lost, perhaps forever.

KNIVES

Love can be as sharp
as the point of a knife,
as piercing as a sliver of glass.
My sisters did not know this.
They thought love was an old slipper:
pull it on and it fits.
They did not know this secret of the world:
the wrong word can kill.
It cost them their lives.

Princes understand the world,
they know the nuance of the tongue,
they are bred up in it.
A shoe is not a shoe:
it implies miles, it suggests length,
it measures and makes solid.
It wears and is worn.
Where there is one shoe, there must be a match.
Otherwise the kingdom limps along.

Glass is not glass
in the language of love:
it implies sight, it suggests depth,
it mirrors and makes real,
it is sought and is seen.
What is made of glass reflects the gazer.
A queen must be made of glass.

I spoke to the prince in that secret tongue,
the diplomacy of courting,
he using shoes, I using glass,
and all my sisters saw was a slipper,
too long at the heel,
too short at the toe,
What else could they use but a knife?
What else could he see but the declaration of war?

Princes understand the world,
they know the nuance of the tongue,
they are bred up to it.
In war as in life they take no prisoners
And they always marry the other shoe.

THE MOON RIBBON

There was once a plain but good-hearted girl named Sylva whose sole possession was a ribbon her mother had left her. It was a strange ribbon, the color of moonlight, for it had been woven from the grey hairs of her mother and her mother's mother and her mother's mother's mother before her.

Sylva lived with her widowed father in a great house by the forest's edge. Once the great house had belonged to her mother, but when she died, it became Sylva's father's house to do with as he willed. And what he willed was to live simply and happily with his daughter without thinking of the day to come.

But one day, when there was little enough to live on, and only the great house to recommend him, Sylva's father married again, a beautiful widow who had two beautiful daughters of her own.

It was a disastrous choice, for no sooner were they wed when it was apparent the woman was mean in spirit and meaner in tongue. She dismissed most of the servants and gave their chores over to Sylva, who followed her orders without complaint. For simply living in her mother's house with her loving father seemed enough for the girl.

After a bit, however, the old man died in order to have some peace, and the house passed on to the stepmother. Scarcely two days had passed, or maybe three, when the stepmother left off mourning the old man and turned on Sylva. She dismissed the last of the servants without their pay.

"Girl," she called out, for she never used Sylva's name, "you will sleep in the kitchen and do the charring." And from that time on it was so.

Sylva swept the floor and washed and mended the family's clothing. She sowed and hoed and tended the fields. She ground the wheat and kneaded the bread, and she waited on the others as though she were a servant. But she did not complain.

Yet late at night, when the stepmother and her own two daughters were asleep, Sylva would weep bitterly into her pillow, which was nothing more than an old broom laid in front of the hearth.

One day, when she was cleaning out an old desk, Sylva came upon a hidden drawer she had never seen before. Trembling, she opened the drawer. It was empty except for a silver ribbon with a label attached to it. *For Sylva* read the card. *The Moon Ribbon of Her Mother's Hair.* She took it out and stared at it. And all that she had lost was borne in upon her. She felt the tears start in her eyes, and so as not to cry she took the tag off and began to stroke the ribbon with her hand. It was rough and smooth at once and shone like the rays of the moon.

At that moment her stepsisters came into the room. "What is that?" asked one. "Is it nice? It is mine."

"I want it. I saw it first," cried the other.

The noise brought the stepmother to them. "Show it to me," she said.

Obediently, Sylva came over and held the ribbon out to her. But when the stepmother picked it up, it looked like no more than strands of grey hair woven together unevenly. It was prickly to the touch.

"Disgusting," said the stepmother dropping it back into Sylva's hand. "Throw it out at once."

"Burn it," cried one stepsister.

"Bury it," cried the other.

"Oh, please. It was my mother's. She left it for me. Please let me keep it," begged Sylva.

The stepmother looked again at the grey strand. "Very well," she said with a grim smile. "It suits you." And she strode out of the room, her daughters behind her.

Now that she had the silver ribbon, Sylvia thought her life would be better. But instead it became worse. As if to punish her for speaking out for the ribbon, her sisters were at her to wait on them both day and night. And whereas before she had to sleep by the hearth, she now had to sleep outside with the animals. Yet she did not complain or run away, for she was tied by her memories to her mother's house.

One night, when the frost was on the grass turning each blade into a silver spear, Sylva threw herself to the ground in tears. And the silver ribbon, which she had tied loosely about her hair, slipped off and lay on the ground before her. She had never seen it in the moonlight. It glittered and shone and seemed to ripple.

Sylva bent over to touch it and her tears fell upon it. Suddenly the ribbon began to grow and change, and as it changed the air was filled with a woman's soft voice speaking these words:

> *"Silver ribbon, silver hair,*
> *Carry Sylva with great care,*
> *Bring my daughter home."*

And there at Sylva's feet was a silver river that glittered and shone and rippled in the moonlight.

There was neither boat nor bridge, but Sylva did not care. She thought the river would wash away her sorrows, and without a single word, she threw herself in.

But she did not sink. Instead she floated like a swan and the river bore her on, on past houses and hills, past high places and low. And strange to say, she was not wet at all.

At last she was carried around a great bend in the river and deposited gently on a grassy slope that came right down to the water's edge. Sylva scrambled up onto the bank and looked about. There was a great meadow of grass so green and still, it might have been painted on. At the meadow's rim, near a dark forest, sat a house that was like and yet not like the one in which Sylva lived.

Surely someone will be there who can tell me where I am and why I have been brought here, she thought. So she made her way across the meadow and only where she stepped down did the grass move. When she moved beyond, the grass sprang back and was the same as before. And though she passed larkspur and meadowsweet, clover and rye, they did not seem like real flowers, for they had no smell at all.

Am I dreaming? she wondered, *or am I dead?* But she did not say it out loud, for she was afraid to speak into the silence.

Sylva walked up to the house and hesitated at the door. She feared to knock and yet feared equally not to. As she was deciding, the door opened of itself and she walked in.

She found herself in a large, long, dark hall with a single crystal door at the end that emitted a strange glow the color of moonlight. As she walked down the hall, her shoes made no clatter on the polished wood floor. And when she reached the door, she tried to peer through into the room beyond, but the crystal panes merely gave back her own reflection twelve times.

Sylva reached for the doorknob and pulled sharply. The glowing crystal knob came off in her hand. She would have wept then, but anger stayed her; she beat her fist against the door and it suddenly gave way.

Inside was a small room lit only by a fireplace and a round, white globe that hung from the ceiling like a pale, wan moon. Before the fireplace stood a tall woman dressed all in white. Her silver-white hair was unbound and cascaded to her knees. Around her neck was a silver ribbon.

"Welcome, my daughter," she said.

"Are you my mother?" asked Sylva wonderingly, for what little she remembered of her mother, she remembered no one as grand as this.

"I am if you make me so," came the reply.

"And how do I do that?" asked Sylva.

"Give me your hand."

As the woman spoke, she seemed to move away, yet she moved not at all. Instead the floor between them moved and cracked apart. Soon they were separated by a great chasm which was so black it seemed to have no bottom.

"I cannot reach," said Sylva.

"You must try," the woman replied.

So Sylva clutched the crystal knob to her breast and leaped, but it was too far. As she fell, she heard a woman's voice speaking from behind her and before her and all about her, warm with praise.

"Well done, my daughter. You are halfway home."

Sylva landed gently on the meadow grass, but a moment's walk from her house. In her hand she still held the knob, shrunk now to the size of a jewel. The river shimmered once before her and was gone, and where it had been was the silver ribbon, lying limp and damp in the morning frost.

The door to the house stood open. She drew a deep breath and went in.

"What is that?" cried one of the stepsisters when she saw the crystalline jewel in Sylva's hand.

"I want it," cried the other, grabbing it from her.

"I will take that," said the stepmother, snatching it from them all. She held it up to the light and examined it. "It will fetch a good price and repay me for my care of you. Where did you get it?" she asked Sylva.

Sylva tried to tell them of the ribbon and the river, the tall woman and the black crevasse. But they laughed at her and did not believe her. Yet they could not explain away the jewel. So they left her then and went off to the city to sell it. When they returned, it was late. They thrust Sylva outside to sleep and went themselves to their comfortable beds to dream of their new riches.

Sylva sat on the cold ground and thought about what had happened. She reached up and took down the ribbon from her hair. She stroked it, and it felt smooth and soft and yet hard, too. Carefully she placed it on the ground.

In the moonlight, the ribbon glittered and shone. Sylva recalled the song she had heard, so she sang it to herself:

> *"Silver ribbon, silver hair,*
> *Carry Sylva with great care,*
> *Bring my daughter home."*

Suddenly the ribbon began to grow and change, and there at her feet was a silver highway that glittered and glistened in the moonlight.

Without a moment's hesitation, Sylva got up and stepped out onto the road and waited for it to bring her to the magical house.

But the road did not move.

"Strange," she said to herself. "Why does it not carry me as the river did?"

Sylva stood on the road and waited a moment more, then tentatively set one foot in front of the other. As soon as she had set off on her own, the road set off, too, and they moved together past fields and forests, faster and faster, till the scenery seemed to fly by and blur into a moon-bleached rainbow of yellows, greys, and black.

The road took a great turning and then quite suddenly stopped, but Sylva did not. She scrambled up the bank where the road ended and found herself again in the meadow. At the far rim of the grass, where the forest began, was the house she had seen before.

Sylva strode purposefully through the grass, and this time the meadow was filled with the song of birds, the meadowlark and the bunting and the sweet *jug-jug-jug* of the nightingale. She could smell fresh-mown hay and the pungent pine.

The door of the house stood wide open, so Sylva went right in. The long hall was no longer dark but filled with the strange moonglow. And when she reached the crystal door at the end, and gazed at her reflection twelve times in the glass, she saw her own face set with strange grey eyes and long grey hair. She put her hand up to her mouth to stop herself from crying out. But the sound came through, and the door opened of itself.

Inside was the tall woman, all in white, and the globe above her was as bright as a harvest moon.

"Welcome, my sister," the woman said.

"I have no sister," said Sylva, "but the two stepsisters I left at home. And you are none of those."

"I am if you make me so.

"How do I do that?"

"Give me back my heart, which you took from me yesterday."

"I did not take your heart. I took nothing but a crystal jewel."

The woman smiled. "It was my heart."

Sylva looked stricken. "But I cannot give it back. My stepmother took it from me."

"No one can take unless you give."

"I had no choice."

"There is always a choice," the woman said.

Sylva would have cried then, but a sudden thought struck her. "Then it must have been your choice to give me your heart."

The woman smiled again, nodded gently, and held out her hand.

Sylva placed her hand in the woman's, and there glowed for a moment on the woman's breast a silvery jewel that melted and disappeared.

"Now will you give me your heart?"

"I have done that already," said Sylva, and as she said it, she knew it to be true.

The woman reached over and touched Sylva on her breast and her heart sprang out onto the woman's hand and turned into two fiery red jewels. "Once given, twice gained," said the woman. She handed one of the jewels back to Sylva. "Only take care that you give each jewel with love."

Sylva felt the jewel warm and glowing in her hand, and at its touch felt such comfort as she had not in many days. She closed her eyes and a smile came on her face. And when she opened her eyes again, she was standing on the meadow grass not two steps from her own door. It was morning, and by her feet lay the silver ribbon, limp and damp from the frost.

The door to her house stood open.

Sylva drew in her breath, picked up the ribbon, and went in.

"What has happened to your hair?" asked one stepsister.

"What has happened to your eyes?" asked the other.

For indeed Sylva's hair and eyes had turned as silver as the moon.

But the stepmother saw only the fiery red jewel in Sylva's hand. "Give it to me," she said, pointing to the gem.

At first Sylva held out her hand, but then quickly drew it back. "I *can* not," she said.

The stepmother's eyes became hard. "Girl, give it here."

"I *will* not," said Sylva.

The stepmother's eyes narrowed. "Then you shall tell me where you got it."

"That I shall, and gladly," said Sylva. She told them of the silver ribbon and the silver road, of the house with the crystal door. But strange to say, she left out the woman and her words.

The stepmother closed her eyes and thought. At last she said, "Let me see this wondrous silver ribbon, that I may believe what you say."

Sylva handed her the ribbon, but she was not fooled by her stepmother's tone.

The moment the silver ribbon lay prickly and limp in the stepmother's hand, she looked up triumphantly at Sylva. Her face broke into a wolfish grin. "Fool," she said, "the magic is herein. With this ribbon there are jewels for the taking." She marched out of the door and the stepsisters hurried behind her.

Sylvia walked after them, but slowly, stopping in the open door.

The stepmother flung the ribbon down. In the early morning sun it glowed as if with a cold flame.

"Say the words, girl," the stepmother commanded.

From the doorway Sylva whispered:

> *"Silver ribbon, silver hair,*
> *Lead the ladies with great care,*
> *Lead them to their home."*

The silver ribbon wriggled and writhed in the sunlight, and as they watched, it turned into a silvered stair that went down into the ground.

"Wait," called Sylva. "Do not go." But it was too late.

With a great shout, the stepmother gathered up her skirts and ran down the steps, her daughters fast behind her. And before Sylva could move, the ground had closed up after them and the meadow was as before.

On the grass lay the silver ribbon, limp and dull. Sylva went over and picked it up. As she did so, the jewel melted in her hand and she felt a burning in her breast. She put her hand up to it, and she felt her heart beating strongly beneath. Sylva smiled, put the silver ribbon in her pocket, and went back into her house.

After a time, Sylva's hair returned to its own color, except for seven silver strands, but her eyes never changed back. And when she was married and had a child of her own, Sylva plucked the silver strands from her own hair and wove them into the silver ribbon, which she kept in a wooden box. When Sylva's child was old enough to understand, the box with the ribbon was put into her safekeeping, and she has kept them for her own daughter to this very day.

SNOW IN SUMMER

They call that white flower that covers the lawn like a poplin carpet Snow in Summer. And because I was born in July with a white caul on my head, they called me that, too. Mama wanted me to answer to Summer, which is a warm, pretty name. But my Stepmama, who took me in hand just six months after Mama passed away, only spoke the single syllable of my name, and she didn't say it nicely.

"Snow!" It was a curse in her mouth. It was a cold, unfeeling thing. "Snow, where are you, girl? Snow, what have you done now?"

I didn't love her. I couldn't love her, though I tried. For Papa's sake I tried. She was a beautiful woman, everyone said. But as Miss Nancy down at the postal store opined, "Looks ain't nothing without a good heart." And she was staring right at my Stepmama when she said it. But then Miss Nancy had been Mama's closest friend ever since they'd been little ones, and it nigh killed her, too, when Mama was took by death.

Papa was besot with my Stepmama. He thought she couldn't do no wrong. The day she moved into Cumberland he said she was the queen of love and beauty. That she was prettier than a summer night. He praised her so often, she took it ill any day he left off complimenting, even after they was hitched. She would have rather heard those soft nothings said about her than to talk of any of the things a husband needs to tell his wife: like when is dinner going to be ready or what bills are still to be paid.

I lived twelve years under that woman's hard hand, with only Miss Nancy to give me a kind word, sweet pop, and a magic story when I was

blue. Was it any wonder I always went to town with a happier counte-
nance than when I had to stay at home?

And then one day Papa said something at the dinner table, his mouth
greasy with the chicken I had cooked and his plate full with the taters I
had boiled. And not a thing on that table that my Stepmama had made.
Papa said, as if surprised by it, "Why Rosemarie..." which was my
Stepmama's Christian name..."why Rosemarie do look at what a beauty
that child has become."

And for the first time my Stepmama looked—really looked—at me.

I do not think she liked what she saw.

Her green eyes got hard, like gems. A row of small lines raised up on
her forehead. Her lips twisted around. "Beauty," she said. "Snow," she said.
She did not say the two words together. They did not fit that way in her
mouth.

I didn't think much of it at the time. If I thought of myself at all those
days, it was as a lanky, gawky, coltish child. Beauty was for horses or grown
women, Miss Nancy always said. So I just laughed.

"Papa, you are just fooling," I told him. "A daddy *has* to say such things
about his girl." Though in the thirteen years I had been alive he had never
said any such over much. None in fact that I could remember.

But then he added something that made things worse, though I wasn't
to know it that night. "She looks like her Mama. Just like her dear Mama."

My Stepmama only said, "Snow, clear the dishes."

So I did.

But the very next day my Stepmama went and joined the Holy Roller
Mt. Hosea Church which did snake handling on the fourth Sunday of
each month and twice on Easter. Because of the Bible saying "Those who
love the Lord can take up vipers and they will not be killed," the Mt.
Hosea folk proved the power of their faith by dragging out rattlers and
copperheads from a box and carrying them about their shoulders like a
slippery shawl. Kissing them, too, and letting the pizzen drip down on
their checks.

Stepmama came home from church, her face all flushed and her eyes
all bright and said to me, "Snow, you will come with me next Sunday."

"But I love Webster Baptist," I cried. "And Reverend Bester. And the
hymns." I didn't add that I loved sitting next to Miss Nancy and hearing
the stories out of the Bible the way she told them to the children's class
during the Reverend's long sermon. "Please Papa, don't make me go."

For once my Papa listened. And I was glad he said no. I am feared of
snakes, though I love the Lord mightily. But I wasn't sure any old Mt.
Hosea rattler would know the depth of that love. Still, it wasn't the snakes
Papa was worried about. It was, he said, those Mt. Hosea boys.

My Stepmama went to Mt. Hosea alone all that winter, coming home later and later in the afternoon from church, often escorted by young men who had scars on their cheeks where they'd been snakebit. One of them, a tall blonde fellow who was almost handsome except for the meanness around his eyes, had a tattoo of a rattler on his bicep with the legend "Love Jesus Or Else" right under it.

My Papa was not amused.

"Rosemarie," he said, "you are displaying yourself. That is not a reason to go to church."

"I have not been doing this for myself," she replied. "I thought Snow should meet some young men now she's becoming a woman. A *beautiful* woman." It was not a compliment in her mouth. And it was not the truth, either, for she had never even introduced me to the young men nor told them my true name.

Still Papa was satisfied with her answer, though Miss Nancy, when I told her about it later, said, "No sow I know ever turned a boar over to her litter without a fight."

However, the blonde with the tattoo came calling one day and he didn't ask for my Stepmama. He asked for me. For Snow. My Stepmama smiled at his words, but it was a snake's smile, all teeth and no lips. She sent me out to walk with him, though I did not really want to go. It was the mean eyes and the scars and the rattler on his arm, some. But more than that, it was a feeling I had that my Stepmama wanted me to be with him. And that plum frightened me.

When we were in the deep woods, he pulled me to him and tried to kiss me with an open mouth and I kicked him in the place Miss Nancy had told me about, and while he was screaming, I ran away. Instead of chasing me, he called after me in a voice filled with pain. "That's not even what your Stepmama wanted me to do to you." But I kept running, not wanting to hear any more.

I ran and ran even deeper into the woods, long past the places where the rhododendron grew wild. Into the dark places, the boggy places, where night came upon me and would not let me go. I was so tired from all that running, I fell asleep right on a tussock of grass. When I woke there was a passel of strangers staring down at me. They were small, humpbacked men, their skin blackened by coal dust, their eyes curious. They were ugly as an unspoken sin.

"Who are you?" I whispered, for a moment afraid they might be more of my Stepmama's crew.

They spoke together, as if their tongues had been tied in a knot at the back end. "Miners," they said. "On Keeperwood Mountain."

"I'm Snow in Summer," I said. "Like the flower."

"Summer," they said as one. But they said it with softness and a kind of dark grace. And they were somehow not so ugly anymore. "Summer."
So I followed them home.

And there I lived for seven years, one year for each of them. They were as good to me and as kind as if I was their own little sister. Each year, almost as if by magic, they got better to look at. Or maybe I just got used to their outsides and saw within. They taught me how to carve out jewels from the black cave stone. They showed me the secret paths around their mountain. They warned me about strangers finding their way to our little house.

I cooked for them and cleaned for them and told them Miss Nancy's magic stories at night. And we were happy as can be. Oh, I missed my Papa now and then, but my Stepmama not at all. At night I sometimes dreamed of the tall blonde man with the rattler tattoo, but when I cried out one of the miners would always comfort me and sing me back to sleep in a deep, gruff voice that sounded something like a father and something like a bear.

Each day my little men went off to their mine and I tidied and swept and made-up the dinner. Then I'd go outside to play. I had deer I knew by name, grey squirrels who came at my bidding, and the sweetest family of doves that ate cracked corn out of my hand. The garden was mine, and there I grew everything we needed. I did not mourn for what I did not have.

But one day a stranger came to the clearing in the woods. Though she strived to look like an old woman, with cross-eyes and a mouth full of black teeth, I knew her at once. It was my Stepmama in disguise. I pretended I did not know who she was, but when she inquired, I told her my name straight out.

"Summer," I said.

I saw "Snow" on her lips.

I fed her a deep-dish apple pie and while she bent over the table shoveling it into her mouth, I felled her with a single blow of the fry pan. My little men helped me bury her out back.

Miss Nancy's stories had always ended happy-ever-after. But she used to add every time, "Still you must make your own happiness, Summer dear."

And so I did. My happiness—and hers.

I went to the wedding when Papa and Miss Nancy tied the knot. I danced with some handsome young men from Webster and from Elkins and from Canaan. But I went back home alone. To the clearing and the woods and the little house with the eight beds. My seven little fathers needed keeping. They needed my good stout meals. And they needed my stories of magic and mystery. To keep them alive.

To keep me alive, too.

THE GOLDEN BALLS

Not all princesses are selfish. No. But it is an occupational hazard. Perhaps it is even in the genes, inbred along with fine, thin noses and high arches, along with slender fingers and a swanlike neck.

There was a princess once endowed with all those graces at birth. Her father—a robust sort, given to hunting and sharing bones with his dogs—had married well. That meant his wife came with property and looks, and was gracious enough to expire after producing an heir. The heir was a boy who looked a lot like his father and screamed in similar lusty tones from one wet nurse to another until he found an ample breast that pleased him.

The heir was not the firstborn, however. He came second, after a sister. But primogeniture ruled him first. First at school, first at play, first in the hearts of his countrymen.

His sister turned her attention to golden balls.

She dallied with these golden balls in all manner of places: behind the cookstove, in the palace garden, under privet hedges, and once—just once—on the edge of a well deep in the forest. That was a mistake.

The splash could be heard for no more than a meter, but her cries could be heard for a mile.

No doubt she might have remained hours weeping by the well, unheard, unsung in song or story, had not an ambitious, amphibious hero climbed flipper after flipper to the rim of his world.

He gave her back what she most desired. He took from her what she did not wish to give.

"And will we meet again?" he whispered at last, his voice as slippery as kitchen grease, as bubbly as beer.

"By the wellspring," she gasped, putting him off, pushing his knobby body from hers.

"In your bed," he said. It was not a frog's demand.

To escape him, to keep him, she agreed. Then raising her skirts to show her slim ankles and high arches, she made a charming moue with her mouth and fled.

He leaped after her but was left behind. By the hop, it was many miles to the palace door. He made it in time for dinner.

By then the princess had changed her dress. The dampness had left a rash on her swanlike neck. The front of the skirt had been spotted with more than tears. She smiled meaningfully at the table, blandly at her brother who was now the king. He recognized the implications of that smile.

"Answer the door," said the king before there was a knock. He knew it would come, had come, would come again. "Answer the door," he said to his sister, ignoring the entire servant class.

She went to the door and lifted the latch, but the frog had already slipped in.

Three hops, seven hops, nine hops, thirteen; he was at the table. He dragged one frogleg, but he was on time.

The princess would have fed him tidbits under the table. She would have put her foot against his. She would have touched him where no one could see. But the king leaned down and spoke to the frog. "You are well suited," he said lifting the creature to her plate.

"Eat," commanded the king.

It was a royal performance. The frog's quick tongue darted around the princess's plate. Occasionally it flicked her hand, between her fingers, under her rings.

"After dinner comes bed," said the king, laughing at his sister's white face. He guessed at hidden promises. She had never shared her golden balls with him.

"I am not tired," she said to her plate. "I have a headache," she said to her bowl. "Not tonight," she said to her cup.

The frog led the way up the stairs. It was very slow going.

Her bed was too high for a hop. She lay upon it, trembling, moist as a well.

The frog stood at the foot of the bed. He measured the draperies for flipper-holds. He eyed the bell pull for a rope ladder. He would have been all night on the floor but for the king, who picked him up between thumb and finger and flung him onto the bed.

The bedclothes showed no signs in the morning, but a child grew in her like a wart.

Marriage transformed the frog but not the princess. He became a prince, Prince Grenouille. She became colder than a shower to him. She gave the child her golden balls. And she gave herself to cooks and choirboys, to farriers and foresters, but never again to a frog.

And Prince Grenouille suffers from her love for others. He wanders from his desk down to the wellspring in the forest. He dips his hand into the water and drinks a drop or two. The air is full of moist memories, and his burdens, like an ill-fitting skin, drop from him while he is there.

Frogs lust, but they do not love. Human beings have a choice. And, oh, a princess is a very large and troublesome golden ball indeed.

THE MIRROR SPEAKS

I have reflected upon abuse
all of my life,
and the vanity of loving.
Mothers see their worth
in the bones of a child,
in soft lineaments, gentle curves
like new-formed planets
not yet jutting into rock.
"Was I ever so fair?" they ask.
"Was I ever so new?"

—I cannot speak lies,
—but each truth is half-told;
—hot is not warm but warming,
—Age by planet's count not old.

Where does the threat begin—
in the cradle? In the heart?
Under the breastbone?
Behind the eyes,
where the time-crow plants
its uncaring feet, toes splayed,
etching the fine lines?
I show you what you would see:
bleached eyes, yellow teeth,
the lines of gray hair.
You were never so fair.

—I cannot speak lies,
—but each truth is half-told;
—hot is not warm but warming
—green is but part of gold.

Is it the child's fault?
Is it the glass?
Is it the fault of winter
and summer and winter again?
All childhoods pass.
I have reflected upon abuse
all of my life,
the answer is truth:
oh queen, all Snow Whites
are fairer still,
as you were, in your youth.

—I cannot speak lies,
—but each truth is half-told:
—hot is not warm but warming,
—death is but cool, not cold.

RIDE ME LIKE A WAVE

Hide me in your hollows
Taste the salt that clings to me
shipwrecked your shallows
scented by the sea
Hide me in the wisdom of your thighs
Ride me like a wave...
    —from "Ride Me Like A Wave" by Janis Ian

There is no profit in fishing, less in building boats. Tam knew that. But still he loved the shape of the wood under his hand, rising into a prow, a stern, a long keel. No one could afford the boats he built, no one could pay him what they were worth. So he gave them away to the fishermen of his village, for they made even less than he.

Each boat had an Eye painted on the prow, a red and blue and wide-open Eye, to prosper the catch. Then each boat was blessed by the priest, who gave away his blessings as well.

What they were all after—Tam, the priest, the fisherfolk—was food for the hungry of the village. And as they themselves were the hungry, it was an exchange that was, if not profit, at least something to keep their bellies from crying out, even in the winter after months of dried cod.

Tam did not begrudge the fishermen his boats. Indeed, he often went down to the shore to watch the fleet come in, knowing that every boat riding the whitecaps was known to his hand.

There was pride in that knowing.

And a full creel of fish for him when they were docked and dry, left by the grateful sailors.

When the spring storms raged, and some of the boats came back bit by bit, board by board, Tam gathered the pieces on the shore below his cottage and shaped coffins for the sailors whose bodies were found, and for the handful of dirt and seafoam for those who were not.

To be honest, Tam was a lonely man, but he did not know it. His love was for the wood and the wave, the one to shape, the one to watch. Strangely, for a man who had always lived by the seaside, he did not go out on the water himself. He feared the cold, green deep. It was enough that the salt clung to him, that he was well scented by its smell.

Can lives that are merely constant be happy?

You asked Tam how he felt, he would have counted these out: Wood, wind, waves. Not happy, perhaps, but content.

Now one day, a day of great wind and water the color of flotsam, a day of foam as filthy as the guts of fish, something other than driftwood came to the shore below Tam's cottage.

He found the thing in the dawn, lying on his part of the beach.

Thing. Not human, not fish.

Thing. Not beautiful, not ugly.

Thing. A mer creature.

The hair on its head was a yellow-green, encrusted with broken shells and sea drift. Its breasts stuck up like two small teacups, the nipples inverted. There was a ridge of hard skin, like a scab, running between the breasts and down to a bifurcated gray-green tail. A darker green were the little cuticle-shaped scales that covered the tail. The creature's arms and its chest were scaled, too, but those scales were like feathers, so light-colored they all but disappeared into the green-gold skin.

Tam did not know what to do with it, the dead thing from the sea. He didn't want to touch it, half fish, half human, all horrible. It smelled, too, a heavy musk, like something pulled up from the great deep. All he could do was stand over it and stare.

Then the mer gave a frothy cough and water and blood spilt out of the gill slits along the neck, slits Tam hadn't even noticed before. The creature's right hand, webbed with a lining like silk, reached up to its mouth. It coughed again and opened its eyes.

They were not a human's eyes, but more fishlike, dark, unfathomable. A shark's eyes. Turning its head, the mer stared at Tam with those black, mirrorless eyes.

He wondered what it saw.

Then drops of water began to fall from the mer's eyes, crawling down its cheeks, mixing with the seawater that puddled in its hair.

Suddenly Tam did not care that it was inhuman, alien, ghastly. She—for the creature was surely a she—was in distress. He took off his shirt, knelt beside her, wrapped her in it, and carried her to his home. There he placed her gently on a pallet by the hearth.

She refused fresh water cold or boiled into tea. She would not eat cress, salted or plain. The fish stew he'd made the night before caused her to moan and look away. She'd already torn off the shirt, once more exposing her tiny breasts with the odd inverted nipples. In the firelight the breasts seemed to shift color, from green to gray to gold.

He picked up the shirt and put it back on himself, buttoning it, slowly, aware that it smelled of her, and was wet clear through. Then he squatted by her side and stared.

The problem was, Tam was a doer, and he did not know what to do. They might have stayed that way for hours, days, but she suddenly opened her mouth and began to sing. At least it sounded like a song, though wordless, and without the kind of melody he was used to. Not a reel, not a ballad, not quite a lament.

The song caught him, pulled him to his knees, then propelled him toward her. He could not have stopped then had he wanted to.

And he did not want to.

He lay down by her side, careful not to touch her, as the song went on.

She reached out and rested her strange webbed fingers on his face. The touch was not so much hesitant as searching. She seemed repelled and as drawn as he.

Suddenly, she pulled at his shirt, so hard the horn buttons broke apart. The wet linen ripped.

"Hey!" he cried, but it did not frighten her.

Then she grabbed at his trousers, her touch oddly frantic, as if she had only now understood the clothes were not his skin. Her fingers raced across his waist, his thighs.

He pushed the trousers down to his ankles, taking no time to get out of his boots.

She made a funny, gasping sound, then cupped him between her hands, her touch both gentle and electric. He shuddered as if chilled, as if in cold water, as if shocked by an eel, then closed his eyes.

When he opened them again, she had spread herself, the tail forked as if two limbs, and then she reeled him in.

Not having done any such thing but once before, with a whore from the town, who had lain under him like a beached whale, he let himself come into her, riding her like a wave. It was a rising and a falling, a swelling and a cresting. When he put his mouth on hers, her lips were soft and slippery. Then he put his head in her hair and smelled the seaweed there.

He was, at last, more than content.

When Tam woke, the mer was gone, a trail of jingle shells out the door where she must have struggled alone. Pulling his pants up, he rose from the pallet, grabbed his Sunday shirt from the cupboard. He could see in the dirt floor where her tail had left a serpentine path and he followed it all the way down to the sea.

He wondered suddenly why she had come. A gift, from some sea god for all the boats he had made? For all the sailors he had helped? For the ones he had buried?

Or was she instead a sea god's curse? He touched himself, fearing he would find himself diseased, changed. There was no electricity in his touch, and no comfort either.

Wading into the sea, up to his knees, he strained to see across the now placid water for some sign of her.

"Come back. Come back," he called.

But no one—no thing—answered his cry.

Every few weeks there were gifts of fish left at his door. Not the kind of fish that the sailors gave him after a good catch—cod and ling and halibut. These were large-eyed, deep sea, hideous creatures he was afraid to eat. He used them to fertilize his vegetable garden.

After a while the gifts stopped.

The years passed. If he remembered the mer and the night he rode her like a wave, he thought it but a dream. Or a nightmare. Or a bit of both. He never spoke of it to anyone, except once in his cups after a long night gathering the bits of broken boats from the sea.

The sailors thought he was yarning, telling a tall tale, and they dragged him back to his house where, with grateful thanks, they put him to bed.

He never spoke of it again.

Nor did they.

One day, when Tam was very old and the pain in his chest too strong to be ignored, he did what many of the sailors of that village did when they could no longer put out to sea. He got into his best clothes, left a note on the table, held down with his carving knife, and walked into the sea.

The sea wrapped him in its cold arms.

At first he trembled, like a boy with his first lover. Then he smiled for the cold had pushed away the pain. So, taking in a last gulp of air, he walked even farther in.

The sea took away his breath and cradled him in green. Memories rushed in like a wave.

In the last moments, he saw the mer again, holding her hand out to him, drawing him in.

He went to her gladly, letting her touch him again, letting her kiss him with her slippery mouth until he died, content, surrounded by the green world and his dozens of mourning children.

IMPEDIMENTA:
FOR DELIA AND ELLEN

True minds, two minds,
to minds married
there is no impediment.
  (Latin—*impedire*, to ensnare.)
But have we got it wrong
all this time?
What is finer than to be
tangled in love's snares,
to be taken unawares
by long looks, dark hairs.
To climb the tower stairs
and see Rapunzel with the witch,
breast to breast on the bed,
love to love,
tongue to tongue,
head to head.

True minds, two minds,
mind you, without impediment
become this day married.
  (Latin—*maritus*, husband.)
But have we got it wrong
all this time?
What is truer than two,
coming in the ark,
coming in the dark,

and through till morning's single lark
sings lustily from the park
to waken Cinderella from
her sister's bed, breast to breast,
love to love,
tongue to tongue,
head to head.

THE FOXWIFE

It was the spring of the year. Blossoms sat like painted butterflies on every tree. But the student Jiro did not enjoy the beauty. He was angry. It seemed he was always angry at something. And he was especially angry because he had just been told by his teachers that the other students feared him and his rages.

"You must go to a far island," said the master of his school.

"Why?" asked Jiro angrily.

"I will tell you if you listen," said his master with great patience.

Jiro shut his mouth and ground his teeth but was otherwise silent.

"You must go to the furthest island you can find. An island where no other person lives. There you must study by yourself. And in the silence of your own heart you may yet find the peace you need."

Raging, Jiro packed his tatami mat, his book, and his brushes. He put them in a basket and tied the basket to his back. Though he was angry—with his master and with all the teachers and students in his school—he really *did* want to learn how to remain calm. And so he set out.

Sometimes he crossed bridges. Sometimes he waded rivers. Sometimes he took boats across the wild water. But at last he came to a small island where, the boatman assured him, no other person lived.

"Come once a week and bring me supplies," said Jiro, handing the boatman a coin. Then Jiro went inland and walked through the sparse woods until he came to a clearing in which he found a deserted temple.

"Odd," thought Jiro. "The boatman did not mention such a thing." He walked up the temple steps and was surprised to find the temple clean.

He set his basket down in one corner, pulled out his mat, and spread it on the floor.

"This will be my home," he said. He said it out loud and there was an edge still to his voice.

For many days Jiro stayed on the island, working from first light till last. And though once in a while he became angry—because his brush would not write properly or because a dark cloud dared to hide the sun—for the most part he was content.

One day, when Jiro was in the middle of a particularly complicated text and having much trouble with it, he looked up and saw a girl walking across the clearing toward him.

Every few steps she paused and glanced around. She was not frightened but rather seemed alert, as if ready for flight.

Jiro stood up. "Go away," he called out, waving his arm.

The girl stopped. She put her head to one side as if considering him. Then she continued walking as before.

Jiro did not know what to do. He wondered if she were the boatman's daughter. Perhaps she had not heard him. Perhaps she was stupid. Perhaps she was deaf. She certainly did not belong on *his* island. He called out louder this time, "Go away. I am a student and must not be disturbed." He followed each statement with a movement of his arms.

But the girl did not go away and she did not stop. In fact, at his voice, she picked up her skirts and came toward him at a run.

Jiro was amazed. She ran faster than anyone he had ever seen, her dark russet hair streaming out behind her like a tail. In a moment she was at the steps of the temple.

"Go away!" cried Jiro for the third time.

The girl stopped, stared, and bowed.

Politeness demanded that Jiro return her bow. When he looked up again, she was gone.

Satisfied, Jiro smiled and turned back to his work. But there was the girl, standing stone-still by his scrolls and brushes, her hands folded before her.

"I am Kitsune," she said. "I care for the temple."

Jiro could contain his anger no longer. "Go away," he screamed. "I must work alone. I came to this island because I was assured no other person lived here."

She stood as still as a stone in a river and let the waves of his rage break against her. Then she spoke. "No other person lives here. I am Kitsune. I care for the temple."

After that, storm as he might, there was nothing Jiro could do. The girl simply would not go away.

She did care for the temple—and Jiro as well. Once a week she appeared and swept the floors. She kept a bowl filled with fresh camellias by his bed. And once, when he had gone to get his supplies and tripped and hurt his legs, Kitsune found him and carried him to the temple on her back. After that, she came ever day, as if aware Jiro needed constant attention. Yet she never spoke unless he spoke first, and even then her words were few.

Jiro wondered at her. She was little, lithe, and light. She moved with a peculiar grace. Every once in a while, he would see her stop and put her head to one side in that attitude of listening. He never heard what it was she heard, and he never dared ask.

At night she disappeared. One moment she would be there and the next moment gone. But in the morning Jiro would wake to find her curled in sleep at this feet. She would not say where she had been.

So spring passed, and summer too. Jiro worked well in the quiet world Kitsune helped him maintain, and he found a kind of peace beginning to bud in his heart.

On the first day of fall, with leaves being shaken from the trees by the wind, Jiro looked up from his books. He saw that Kitsune sat on the steps trembling.

"What is it?" he asked.

"The leaves. Aieee, the leaves," she cried. Then she jumped up and ran down to the trees. She leapt and played with the leaves as they fell about her. They caught in her hair. She blew them off her face. She rolled in them. She put her face to the ground and sniffed the dirt. Then, as if a fever had suddenly left her, she was still. She stood up, brushed off her clothing, smoothed her hair, and came back to sit quietly on the steps again.

Jiro was enchanted. He had never seen any woman like this before. He left his work and at down on the steps beside her. Taking her hand in his, he stroked it thoughtfully, then brought it slowly to his cheek. Her hand was warm and dry.

"We must be married," he said at last. "I would have you with me always."

"Always? What is always?" asked Kitsune. She tried to pull away.

Jiro held her hand tightly and would not let her go. And after a while she agreed.

The boatman took them across to the mainland, where they found a priest who married them at once, though he smiled behind his hand at their haste. Jiro was supremely happy and he knew that Kitsune must be, too, though all the way in the boat going there and back again, she shuddered and would not look out across the waves.

That night Kitsune shared the tatami mat with Jiro. When the moon was full and the night whispered softly about the temple, Jiro awoke. He turned to look at Kitsune, his bride. She was not there.

"Kitsune," he called out fearfully. He sat up and looked around. He could not see her anywhere. He got up and searched around the temple, but she was not to be found. At last he fell asleep, sitting on the temple steps. When he awoke again at dawn, Kitsune was curled in sleep on the mat.

"Where were you last night?" he demanded.

"Where I should be," she said and would say no more.

Jiro felt anger flowering inside, so he turned sharply from her and went to his books. But he did not try to calm himself. He fed his rage silently. All day he refused to speak. At night, exhausted by his own anger, he fell asleep before dark. He woke at midnight to find Kitsune gone.

Jiro knew he had to stay awake until she returned. A little before dawn he saw her running across the clearing. She ran up the temple steps and did not seem to be out of breath. She came right to the mat, surprised to see Jiro awake.

Jiro waited for her explanation, but instead of speaking she began her morning chores. She had fresh camellias in her hands, which she put in a bowl as if nothing were wrong.

Jiro sat up. "Where do you go at night?" he asked. "What do you do?"

Kitsune did not answer.

Jiro leaped up and came over to her. He took her by the shoulders and began to shake her. "Where? Where do you go?" he cried.

Kitsune dropped the bowl of flowers and it shattered. The water spread out in little islands of puddles on the floor. She looked down and her hair fell around her shoulders, hiding her face.

Jiro could not look at the trembling figure so obviously terrified of him. Instead, he bent to pick up the pieces of the bowl. He saw his own face mirrored a hundred times in the spilled drops. Then he saw something else. Instead of Kitsune's face or her russet hair, he saw the sharp-featured head of a fox reflected there. The fox's little pointed ears were twitching. Out of its dark eyes tears began to fall.

Jiro looked up but there was no fox. Only Kitsune, beginning to weep, trembling at the sight of him, unable to move. And then he knew. She was a *nogitsone*, a were-fox, who could take the shape of a beautiful woman. But the *nogitsone's* reflection in the water was always that of a beast.

Suddenly Jiro's anger, fueled by his terror, knew no bounds. "You are not human," he cried. "Monster, wild thing, demon, beast. You will rip me or tear me if I let you stay. Some night you will gnaw upon my bones. Go away."

As he spoke, Kitsune fell to her hands and knees. She shook herself once, then twice. Her hair seemed to flow over her body, covering her completely. Then twitching her ears once, the vixen raced down the temple steps, across the meadow, and out of sight.

Jira stood and watched for a long, long time. He thought he could see the red flag of her tail many hours after she had gone.

The snows came early that year, but the season was no colder than Jiro's heart. Every day he thought he heard the barking of a fox in the woods beyond the meadow, but he would not call it in. Instead he stood on the steps and cried out, "Away. Go away." At night he dreamed of a woman weeping close by his mat. In his sleep he called out, "Away. Go away."

Then when winter was full and the nights bitter cold, the sounds ceased. The island was deadly still. In his heart Jiro knew the fox was gone for good. Even his anger was gone, guttered in the cold like a candle. What had seemed so certain to him, in the heat of his rage, was certain no more. He wondered over and over which had been human and which had been beast. He even composed a haiku on it.

> Pointed ears, red tail,
> Wife covered in fox's skin,
> The beast hides within.

He said it over many times to himself but was never satisfied with it.

Spring came suddenly, a tiny green blade pushing through the snow. And with it came a strange new sound. Jiro woke to it, out of a dream of snow. He followed the sound to the temple steps and saw prints in the dust of white. Sometimes they were fox, sometimes girl, as if the creature who made them could not make up its mind.

"Kitsune," Jiro called out impulsively. Perhaps she had not died after all.

He looked out across the meadow and thought he saw again that flag of red. But the sound that had wakened him came once more, from behind. He turned, hoping to see Kitsune standing again by the mat with the bowl of camellias in her hands. Instead, by his books, he saw a tiny bundle of russet fur. He went over and knelt by it. Huddled together for warmth were two tiny kit foxes.

For a moment Jiro could feel the anger starting inside him. He did not want these two helpless, mewling things. He wanted Kitsune. Then he remembered that he had driven her away. Away. And the memory of that long, cold winter without her put out the budding flames of his new rage.

He reached out and put his hands on the foxlings. At his touch, they sprang apart on wobbly legs, staring up at him with dark, discerning eyes. They trembled so, he was afraid they might fall.

"There, there," he crooned to them." This big, rough beast will not hurt you. Come. Come to me." He let them sniff both his hands, and when their trembling ceased, he picked them up and cradled them against his body, letting them share his warmth. First one, then the other, licked his fingers. This so moved Jiro that, without meaning to, he began to cry.

The tears dropped onto the muzzles of the foxlings and they looked as if they, too, were weeping. Then, as Jiro watched, the kits began to change. The features of a human child slowly superimposed themselves on each fox face. Sighing, they snuggled closer to Jiro, closed their eyes, put their thumbs in their mouths, and slept.

Jiro smiled. Walking very carefully, as if afraid each step might jar the babies awake, he went down the temple steps. He walked across the clearing leaving man-prints in the unmarked snow. Slowly, calmly, all anger gone from him, he moved toward the woods where he knew Kitsune waited. He would find her before evening came again.

DEIRDRE

She was a woman of wheat and sea,
A woman of corn and sky,
In whose eyes a man might live for long,
In whose eyes a man might die.
    So they died, they died, they died, and they died
    In the hour of their desire,
    For she was a woman of wheat and sea
    With a heart that was made of fire.

She was a woman of laughter and tears,
And she was a woman of night,
In whose thighs a man might rest for years,
From whose thighs he might take flight.
    So they ran, they ran, they ran, and they ran
    In the hour of their desire,
    For she was a woman of wheat and sea
    With a heart that was made of fire.

chorus:
    And all of Ulster mourns her still,
    And all of Ulster cries,
    And all of Ulster bleeds the years,
    And all of Ulster dies.

She was a woman of rose and briar,
A woman of snow and blood,
In whose heart a man might drown forever
Or float upon the flood.
    So they drowned, they drowned, they drowned, they burned,
    In the hour of their desire,
    For she was a woman of wheat and sea
    With a heart that was made of fire.

chorus:
    And all of Ulster mourns her still,
    And all of Ulster cries,
    And all of Ulster bleeds the years,
    And all of Ulster dies.

THE MAIDEN MADE OF FIRE

Once on the edge of a great Eastern forest there lived a charcoal burner named Ash. He was a kind of poet. Surrounded by the gray reminders of his trade, he did not see the dust. Instead, he spent most of his time staring into the heart of the fire where he saw of world of bright, fierce beauty.

And when the kiln was all burnt and opened up, Ash would sit and talk to the scattered coals in rhyme as sharp and as bright as flames. The woodsmoke was intoxicating, and he was always slightly addled by its smell.

But seeing him squatting in the dust and talking to the burned-out ends of fire, the villagers thought Ash more than a little mad, a summoner of demons. And so the poor lad got himself an evil name and was friendless because of it.

Yet if he was lonely, he never talked of it. He continued building his kilns like his father before him, making charcoal for the village, and talking fancies into the smoke-filled air.

One evening as he sat and stared into the heart of his fire, Ash thought he saw a maiden lying on the coals, glowing red and gold. He shook his head vigorously to shake the dream from it, but when he looked again, the girl was still there

So he leaped up and reached into the fire, heedless of the flames that licked his wrists, and pulled the firemaid out.

She came slowly up from the coals and stood before him. Her hair hung below her shoulders in blackened wisps and her eyes were brilliant points of light. She was wrapped in nothing but smoke.

"Who are you?" whispered Ash.

The girl was silent except with her hands. And when she moved them, little tendrils of smoke hovered in the air between them.

"Who are you?" Ash asked again.

Still the girl did not speak.

"Shall I answer for you?" he said and, when she nodded slightly, added, "Since you are a maiden made of fire, Brenna shall be your name."

Shyly he held out his grimed hand to her, but when she moved toward him, the heat that came from her was so intense that he stepped back. Only then did he realize that his hands had been burned by the flames, and he put them behind him as if ashamed of some weakness.

"You need something to wear. You will be chilled."

At that, the girl threw her head back and laughed, and her laughter was light and crackling.

Then Ash laughed too, for he realized that Brenna was not cold. Wrapped in her mantle of smoke, she was far warmer than he.

He signaled her towards him again. This time with his head, and she stepped forward suddenly. Just as suddenly she stopped and put up her hands before her, feeling the air as if it were a wall.

Looking at the ground to see what hindered her, Ash saw the outlines of he kiln. Around the entire inside of the burned-out kiln she stepped, and was stopped again and again by a wall neither of them could see.

Brenna sank to her knees. Drops of fire rained from her eyes. She pointed helplessly to the coals. The embers were the borders of her world. She could not cross over.

She turned her face up at last and it was ashen and desolate. She signaled for him to come to her instead. But the charcoal burner was too afraid of her fires.

Then Ash had a thought. "I shall make you more room," he cried.

Quickly he built little beehive-shaped kilns side by side, small fiery alcoves that burned swiftly and were soon no more than mounds of glowing coals. By night's end, he had made Brenna a palace of embers, large and rambling, where she could run like mist through the smoke-filled halls.

Brenna thanked him again and again with her brilliant smile and tendrils of smoke she signed with her hands. And though Ash did not dare go close to her, with that smile and those thanks he was content.

For days they lived that way. Ash neglected his charcoal kilns and instead told Brenna stories and rhymes and sang her songs which she accepted with her crackling, light laugh. He brought her little offerings: shiny leaves, smooth nuts, woven baskets which she turned to flame with her touch. At each blaze she clapped her hands together in delight and Ash clapped with her.

In turn, Brenna danced for him, leaping high over the heaped up coals. And she drew pictures in the dust and smoke, pictures of a fierce bright country where firebirds flew through blazing trees and incandescent flowers flared upward toward a glowing sky.

And so the days passed for them, burning out into nights filled with fiery stars. But at last the village elders came, with their coal-black robes and their bitter mouths. They stood in a circle around him, their voices brittle.

"Where is our charcoal?" one asked, his voice rising in pitch. "While you sing and dance here in the clearing, you neglect your work."

The second joined in. "Your work is to build kilns and tend the fires and set the charcoal aside for our needs. Yet for a week you have done nothing but posture before the flames and talk wild fancies into the air."

Ash tried to escape from the circle of elders, but they moved closer to him, like a tightening noose. He tried to explain. "I am talking to Brenna, my love, my bride."

The elders whispered to one another. "What is he saying? What does he mean?"

The oldest one silenced them with his hand. "He is quite mad. He is in love with the fire."

Ash turned round and round pleading with the circle of men. "But she is there. Can you not see her? Her hair is black and her eyes are bright and she is like a steady flame."

The oldest one spoke coldly. "There is nothing there. No girl. And no charcoal either."

"But she is there. Brenna. She is there." Ash pointed towards the embered palace. Yet even as he spoke there was doubt in his voice, and at that doubt the maiden made of fire began to fade. Slowly, like a candle guttering out, her outline wavered. She held her arms, mere outlines now, towards Ash. She sighed and it was the sound of a fire being extinguished.

Ash looked again at the circle of villagers around him. Then back again at Brenna who was but a soft glow. With an effort, he thrust his doubt from him and pushed through the elders.

"Brenna," he called.

At his voice, she grew brighter, clearer. With a hand that dripped fragile tears of flame, she signaled him to her.

He leaped over the low embers and ran straight into Brenna's arms. They flared up in a brilliant burst of light, a star in nova, that singed the robes of the watching men. Then in a moment, the firemaid and the charcoal burner were gone. All that was left was a pile of ashes that smoldered for years, sending up a pale spiral of smoke.

No one from the village was ever able to put it out.

MÄRCHEN

Wilhelm Grimm loved words,
not stories,
they waterfalled from his pen.
He was deaf to the telling,
only the told.

Words like *camphor*,
goblet, *ruby*, *anvil*
waxed and waned in him.
He was tidal
with words.

I, on the other hand,
drink in tales,
giving them out again
in mouth-to-ear
resuscitation.

It does not matter
if the matter of the stories
is the coast of Eire
or the Inland Sea,
I swim—ah—ever deeper in them

THE STORY BETWEEN

When I am in my fiat-issuing mood, I am tempted to announce that there is no one right way to read a story. Only, I add under my breath, plenty of wrong ways to teach it. That is because there is no real story on the page, only that which is created in between the writer and the reader.

Just as the writer brings a lifetime to the creation of the tale, so the reader carries along a different lifetime with which to recreate it. Even the author may reread her own story days, weeks, months later and understand it on another level. I once wrote a poem called "The Storyteller" (proving again that I am always smartest when I am writing and not when I am thinking):

A story must be worn again
before the magic garment
fits the ready heart.

Thus, there is no way an author can write to an audience. Oh, perhaps we may—as they say in faerie—be *guiled* about audience profile for a while. We may be tempted to write for that mythical "5–7 year old" or "8–12 year old," each as wily a shape-shifter as ever roamed the unicorn's garden. But there is only one real audience for the writer of tales: the child within.

How can I be sure that each reader has a hand in the creation of a tale, shaped to his or her own "ready heart?" I can only offer as proof the many letters and confrontations of stories that I have had over a twenty-year span. The storyteller in California who tells me a young couple chose to have my story "Dawn Strider" told at their wedding. "Dawn Strider"? It is a tale about a giant who steals the sun. Or the college student who asked her professor if my story "The Lady and the Merman" was about taking drugs. And this a fairy tale about a unloved young woman who dives after a merman into the sea. Then there was the young woman who, after hearing my story "The Face in the Cloth," was able to say the name of her famous mother out loud and start her own life. And the line in my own story "The Boy Who Sang for Death," written ten years after my own mother died: "Any gift I have I would give to get my mother back." When I reread that line, some months after having penned it, I began to weep, bringing to a close a long-drawn-out formal mourning period.

Therapy? Healing? Self-recognition? The "holistic" powers of stories have long been part of the ritual of tale telling. And today many therapists are using stories with their patients. But I am not talking about that. It is merely that we *bring* to tales that most complex of constructs—ourselves. And we *take* from them what we need. It is as true with the writer as the reader.

When I wrote "The Girl Who Loved the Wind," I wrote it with two emotional agendas, one I recognized at the time, one I understood only long after. That is not an unusual occurrence with my stories. I wrote about a girl who was overprotected, bound in, literally, by the walls of her father's great house and kept a prisoner of his desire to save her from the evils of the world. So it had been, figuratively, with my own father. But the story is also about a wind that blows in over the garden wall and tells the young woman about the ever-changing world. And in the end, she chooses to leave her father's house by spreading her cloak on the ocean, lifting one end, and being blown out into that world by the wind. It took me years to realize, to remember that, when I met my husband, he climbed in the window of the first floor apartment I shared with two other girls in Greenwich Village. It was during a party where so many of our friends were standing in line at the door, that this enterprising young man took a shortcut. "The Girl Who Loved the Wind" memorializes that meeting in a metaphoric way.

But years later a child came to that tale with another agenda altogether. Her way of hearing that story was as "right," was as valid, as any other. Yet had I tried to write a story *for* her, I would have failed, awash in sentiment and tears. I heard of Ann Marie through a letter from a stranger:

Nov. 7, 1984

Dear Jane:

I was working at a children's hospital as the person coordinating the child activity program. My main work with patients was to be with children who were gravely ill, having chemotherapy, or in some other way needing real support. I often used play therapy techniques or puppets, but if children were too sick I would read to them.

Ann Marie was an eleven-year-old girl who had been admitted by a doctor who didn't usually work with us. She had been sick for quite a while but not diagnosed, so by the time her therapy started, she had many tumors. As the therapy started to kill the tumors, her kidneys and then cardiac system were also affected, so that she had to be transferred to the ICU.

It appeared that she had always been an isolated and protected child and the nurses referred to her as "young for her age."

The day I was to see her I was apprehensive. The times I had been in before she had been so sick and was filled with IVs and tubes and monitors. It was hard to think about the person inside that ailing repository of technology. I picked at random a couple of books from the shelf and went down to ICU.

At first all I could think of was how sick she was. Her eyes were half open and her skin was yellow. She hardly moved except to turn her eyes toward me when I came in. I was in gown and mask, as were all three nurses there. They were just finishing her peritoneal dialysis and preparing to leave.

I asked her what she would like me to read and she didn't answer. "Would you like me to choose?" She nodded.

And then, Jane, when I started reading "The Girl Who Loved the Wind" the whole scene changed. The humming and beeping machines receded; the fear and pain stepped back into the corners of the room; I read this child a story that was all about her life and leaving.

She was a child who had grown up behind protective walls. She too had felt the summons of the wind. "Not always good, not always kind" and was deciding to leave her overly protected life.

When I finished reading the story, we just sat for a while in silence.

Two days later she was dead, her doctor and family shocked because it seemed so sudden, not expected. The date she died was Nov. 5.

I have always since then loved that story. I went to the ICU to search for it, but it was gone. It wasn't until two years later, to the day, that I found it again.

I know it truly served to comfort the departure of that child.

The morning after her death, after we had cried and talked and wept about it, a beautiful stellar jay flew into our patio, came

*and sat on the arm of a chair and looked into the bedroom at me,
still in bed. He sat there almost a minute and I was filled then
with a sense of peace. He seemed to say, "I come from Ann Marie
and she's alright now."*

These are things that you should know.

So two people met, with a story between them. The story I wrote was not exactly the story that Ann Marie took with her. But she took it with her because she needed it and I am not so selfish about the meaning of my tales to deny all the Ann Maries in the world that garment for the trip.

THE LADY AND THE MERMAN

"Wheresoever love goes, the lover follows."

Once in a house overlooking the cold northern sea a baby was born. She was so plain, her father, a sea captain, remarked on it.

"She shall be a burden," he said. "She shall be on our hands forever." Then without another glance at the child he sailed off on his great ship.

His wife, who had longed to please him, was so hurt by his complaint that she soon died of it. Between one voyage and the next, she was gone.

When the captain came home and found this out, he was so enraged, he never spoke of his wife again. In this way he convinced himself that her loss was nothing.

But the girl lived and grew as if to spite her father. She looked little like her dead mother but instead had the captain's face set round with mouse-brown curls. Yet as plain as her face was, her heart was not. She loved her father but was not loved in return.

And still the captain remarked on her looks. He said at every meeting, "God must have wanted me cursed to give me such a child. No one will have her. She shall never be wed. She shall be with me forever." So he called her Borne, for she was his burden.

Borne grew into a lady and only once gave a sign of this hurt.

"Father," she said one day when he was newly returned from the sea, "what can I do to heal this wound between us?"

He looked away from her, for he could not bear to see his own face mocked in hers, and spoke to the cold stone floor. "There is nothing between us, daughter," he said. "But if there were, I would say *salt for such wounds.*"

"Salt?" Borne asked.

"A sailor's balm," he said. "The salt of tears or the salt of sweat or the final salt of the sea." Then he turned from her and was gone next day to the farthest port he knew of, and in this way he cleansed his heart.

After this, Borne never spoke of it again. Instead, she carried it silently like a dagger inside. For the salt of tears did not salve her, and so she turned instead to work. She baked bread in her ovens for the poor, she nursed the sick, she held the hands of the sea widows. But always, late in the evening, she walked on the shore looking and longing for a sight of her father's sail. Only less and less often did he return from the sea.

One evening, tired from the work of the day, Borne felt faint as she walked on the strand. Finding a rock half in half out of the water, she climbed upon it to rest. She spread her skirts about her, and in the dusk they lay like great gray waves.

How long she sat there, still as the rock, she did not know. But a strange pale moon came up. And as it rose, so too rose the little creatures of the deep. They leaped free for a moment of the pull of the tide. And last of all, up from the deeps, came the merman.

He rose out of the crest of the wave, seafoam crowning his green-black hair. His hands were raised high above him, and the webbings of his fingers were as colorless as air. In the moonlight he seemed to stand upon his tail. Then, with a flick of it, he was gone, gone back to the deeps. He thought no one had remarked his dive.

But Borne had. So silent and still, she saw it all, his beauty and his power. She saw him and loved him, though she loved the fish half of him more. It was all she could dare.

She could not tell what she felt to a soul, for she had no one who cared. Instead she forsook her work and walked by the sea both morning and night. Yet, strange to say, she never once looked for her father's sail.

That is why one day her father returned without her knowing. He watched her pacing the shore for a long while through slotted eyes, for he would not look straight upon her. At last he said, "Be done with it. Whatever ails you, give it over." For even he could see this wound.

Borne looked up at him, her eyes shimmering with small seas. Grateful for his attention, she answered, "Yes, Father, you are right. I must be done with it."

The captain turned and left her then, for his food was cold. But Borne went directly to the place where the waves were creeping onto the shore. She called out in a low voice, "Come up. Come up and be my love."

There was no answer except the shrieking laughter of the birds as they dived into the sea.

So she took a stick and wrote the same words upon the sand for the merman to see should he ever return. Only, as she watched, the creeping tide erased her words one by one. Soon there was nothing left of her cry on that shining strand.

So Borne sat herself down on the rock to cry. And each tear was an ocean.

But the words were not lost. Each syllable washed from the beach was carried below, down, down, down to the deeps of the cool, inviting sea. And there, below on his coral bed, the merman saw her call and came.

He was all day swimming up to her. He was half the night seeking that particular strand. But when he came, cresting the currents, he surfaced with a mighty splash below Borne's rock.

The moon shone down on the two, she a grave shadow perched upon a stone and he all motion and light.

Borne reached down with her white hands and he caught them in his. It was the only touch she could remember. She smiled to see the webs stretched taut between his fingers. He laughed to see hers webless, thin, and small. One great pull between them and he was up by her side. Even in the dark she could see his eyes on her under the phosphoresence of his hair.

He sat all night by her. And Borne loved the man of him as well as the fish, then, for in the silent night it was all one.

Then, before the sun could rise, she dropped his hands on his chest. "Can you love me?" she dared to ask at last.

But the merman had no tongue to tell her above the waves. He could only speak below the water with his hands, a soft murmuration. So, wordlessly, he stared into her eyes and pointed to the sea.

Then, with the sun just rising beyond the rim of the world, he turned, dived arrow slim into a wave, and was gone.

Gathering her skirts, now heavy with ocean spray and tears, Borne stood up. She cast but one glance at the shore and her father's house beyond. Then she dived after the merman into the sea.

The sea put bubble jewels in her hair and spread her skirts about her like a scallop shell. Tiny colored fish swam in between her fingers. The water cast her face in silver, and all the sea was reflected in her eyes.

She was beautiful for the first time. And for the last.

Dawn-Strider

Far, far to the East, before the sun had settled firmly on a route, there lived a giant who walked at night.

His black head seemed crowned with the stars. The earth thundered where he stepped. And all who saw or heard him were afraid.

Night after lonely night the giant made his rounds. Up the mountains and down. By hill towns and valleys. Through low places and high. His footsteps warned of his coming, and the ways were empty where he walked.

Some people said that it was his nature to walk at night. Others, older, who remembered beginnings even as they forgot endings, recalled how the giant had once walked by day. But one morning, by chance, he had seen his own reflection in a still mountain lake. He had been so dismayed by his own rough image that he had taken to the night and had walked in darkness ever since.

One night, lost in a waking dream, the giant missed the crowing of the cock that warned of the coming sun. Instead of going straightaway to his castle which was hollowed in a cave, he stopped by the side of a stream to drink.

As he knelt, he heard a whisper of grass. Then he heard a soughing of wind. At last he heard the sound of early morning flowers opening.

Turning quickly, the giant saw a child dressed in red and gold. "Who are you?" he asked.

Before the child could answer, the giant growled: "Don't you know that I am Night-Walker? All who hear and see me are afraid." He stood up against the sky and his shadow put out the lingering stars.

The child answered, "And why should I be afraid?"

"They say my face withers the eyes. They say the sound of my coming turns hearers to stone."

"I have seen and I have heard," said the child. "But I am here still."

"Who are you?" the giant asked again.

"I am Dawn-Strider. And where I come, the sun comes, too."

"The sun!" cried the giant, and he looked about fearfully.

"And are you afraid of me?" asked the child with a laugh.

But the giant did not hear. He had already started to run, leaving hollows in the ground where he stepped.

For two nights the giant cowered in his cave and thought about the child who was not afraid. But on the third night, a night of dark shadows, he ventured out. He was determined to capture Dawn-Strider. For, in his own way, the giant had fallen in love with the child, the only being who did not hide at his coming. He wanted to carry Dawn-Strider to his cave-castle home.

Slowly the giant walked to the stream where he had seen the child and knelt down by the bank. First with his hand he scooped out a large deep basin in the earth near the side of the stream. He lined it with the softest mosses and made a breakfall of pine and fern. Finally, he covered the hole with juniper and trailed wild grapevines over the boughs.

Then Night-Walker lay down beside the trap to wait for the dawn.

When he heard the grass whisper and the wind sough through the juniper, and when he heard the sounds of flowers opening, the giant knew that Dawn-Strider would soon be there. So he began to moan.

Before long, Dawn-Strider appeared by the stream. "Why do you lie so still? Why do you cry?" the child asked.

The giant made no answer but continued to moan.

Dawn-Strider came over to his side and knelt down to see what was wrong. But as he came close to the giant, the child broke through the grapevines and juniper and fell into the hole.

Immediately the giant leaped up and looked into the trap. Then, smiling for the first time, he reached down and picked the child up in one hand. With great thundering steps, he ran back to his castle in the cave. Once they were inside, he rolled a huge stone over the entrance.

"Why did you trick me? Why did you carry me off to this dark castle?" asked the child when they were seated in the cave.

"Because I want you to stay with me always," replied the giant.

"But if you had asked," said the child, " I would have come by myself."

"Oh, no," the giant answered, shaking his massive head. "No one comes to me. I am Night-Walker. All who see and hear me are afraid."

Then Dawn-Strider laughed, and each sound was a spark of light in the dark. "I am not afraid."

But the giant did not understand. For seven days and seven nights he kept the stone rolled across the entrance to his cave. And for seven days and seven nights no sun shone upon the earth. For without Dawn-Strider to lead the way, the sun did not know which road to follow and so stayed hidden beyond the rim of the world.

Outside the cave it was as dark as within. Up the mountains and down, through hill towns and valleys, in low places and high, darkness reigned. And the world was dimly lit by the moon and flickering stars.

Plants withered and began to die. Trees shed their leaves. The little animals huddled in their burrows. And by their dying hearthfires the people shivered, waiting for the sun.

Only Night-Walker was happy in his cave, listening to Dawn-Strider's light-filled laughter and watching the bright child dressed in red and gold.

Finally, after seven days as dark as seven nights, the people bundled themselves into their clothes. They met in the courtyards and doorways of the towns or talked in the meadows.

Some said it was a curse. Others said it was the end of the world. But then someone said, "It is the giant. It is Night-Walker. *He* has stolen the sun." And everyone agreed.

But they could not agree how they could make the giant return the sun. None of them dared face him. They believed that to look upon his face or to hear his voice would turn them to stone.

After many cold meetings, the people decided to choose someone by lot. The chosen one would go up to the giant's cave and beg for the return of the sun. Then he would run back as fast as he could. If he were lucky, he would not have to see or hear Night-Walker at all.

The lots were drawn, and the short stick fell to a small child. His mother wept and his father cursed, but neither was allowed to take the child's place. "After all, it was fairly chosen," said the villagers. So the child had to go, alone, up to the giant's cave.

Behind him, safely hidden by bushes and trees, yet close enough so they could watch the child's progress, were all the people.

With his head down and feet scuffling the ground before him, the child trudged up the hill toward the cave. When he stood at last before the stone door, the child called out in a tiny voice, "Night-Walker, giant, return our sun."

For a few moments nothing happened. The child sighed, and started to turn back down the hill. But suddenly a grumbling was heard from the cave's entrance, and the stone started to roll aside.

Shaking his shaggy hair in the light of the moon, Night-Walker stepped out. He glared at the miserable child. The child was so frightened, he could not move. He stood like stone. And the people who had come to watch ran screaming and stumbling back to their homes.

The giant looked down and picked up the child in his hand. "What do you mean by disturbing me? Don't you know I am Night-Walker? I am the Watcher in the Gloom?"

The child was amazed that he could still blink and twitch after gazing on Night-Walker's face and hearing his voice. He managed to cry out, "Our...our sun. Give us back our sun."

"Bah! I do not have your sun," said Night-Walker.

"But you have me," said a small voice by the giant's side. "And with me comes the sun." It was Dawn-Strider, stepping out of the cave.

The child from the lottery looked down over the giant's cupped hand. And when he saw another child moving and laughing by the giant's side, he was no longer afraid. He smiled at Dawn-Strider. He even smiled at the giant.

Night-Walker was so surprised that, without thinking, he smiled back. And as he smiled, the sun so long hidden from the world rose up over the mountains.

The people who had been hastily stumbling back to their homes were stopped by the unexpected dawn. "The giant has given us back our sun," they called joyously to one another, and they turned back to the cave.

When they got to the top of the hill, they found the giant still standing there. He was smiling, with a child in each hand. The three new friends were laughing and talking—even singing in their joy.

Now that he had friends who did not find him fearsome to look upon, the giant gave up walking at night. He lived for the coming of the sun each day. And Dawn-Strider always visited the giant's cave-castle home first, bringing the sun there before anywhere else in the whole world.

The giant gave rides to all the children of the village in his outstretched palms every morning of the year. And he was known as Sun-Walker ever after.

BEANS

Jack, you see, went hand over hand
To a land beyond understanding:
Streets paved with gold, gold bedsteads,
Gold bidets, golden harps, golden geese,
Eggs the color of wedding bands.
He hated being poor, having jack all.
So he stole a gigantic load, jacked the big man.
Has-been no longer, he unhanded himself
Down the beanstalk, fled home, kissed mom,
Drank a quick cup of something strong
Made from beans, then chopped down the stalk.
Sometimes a boy hits the jackpot,
Becomes a man with one lucky whack.
Believe it. Would a story lie?

THE LAD
WHO STARED EVERYONE DOWN

Once there was a lad who was so proud, he was determined to stare everyone in the world down.

He began in the farmyard of his father's house. He stared into the eyes of the chickens until the cock's feathers drooped and the hens ran cackling from his gaze.

"What a fine eye," thought the lad. "They are all afraid of me." And he went to stare down the cows.

The cows turned their velvety eyes to watch the boy approach. He never turned his head but stared and stared until the herd turned away in confusion and clattered down to the meadow gate.

"They are all afraid. See them run," thought the lad. And he went to stare down his mother and father.

At the table he glared at his parents until his father dropped his knife and his mother started to weep.

"Why are you doing this?" they cried. "No good can come of such staring."

But the lad never said a word. He packed his handkerchief with a few provisions—a loaf of brown bread, some cheese, and a flask of ginger beer —and went out to stare down the world.

He walked a day and a night and came at last to the walls of a great town.

"Let me in," he called out to the old watchman, "for I have stared down fathers and mothers, I have stared down a host of herdsmen. I have stared down strangers in a farmyard, and I can stare you down, too."

The watchman trembled when he heard this, but he did not let the lad come in. "Stare away," he said in a wavery voice.

The lad came nearer to the watchman and stared into the old man's watery eyes. He stared steadily till the old man felt weak with hunger and faint with standing, and at last the old man glanced away.

Without another word, the lad marched in through the gate and on into the town.

He walked until he came to the door of the castle where two handsome soldiers in their bright red coats stood at attention and gazed into space.

The lad looked at them and thought, "I have stared down a mighty watchman, I have stared down fathers and mothers, I have stared down a host of herdsmen, I have stared down strangers in a farmyard, and I can stare down these two."

The soldiers glanced the lad's way. The lad stared back. He stared and stared until a passing fly caused one of the soldiers to sneeze.

"That mere lad stared you down," whispered the other soldier to his companion, out of the side of his mouth.

"No, he didn't," said the one who had looked away.

"Yes, he did!" said the other.

And soon they fell to fighting.

While they were squabbling and quarreling, the lad slipped in through the door and marched till he came to a great hall. There was the king, sitting on his throne.

The lad marched right up to the king who was sitting silent in all his majesty. He stared at the king and the king stared back.

As the lad stared, he thought, "I have stared down quarrelsome soldiers. I have stared down a mighty watchman, I have stared down fathers, I have stared down mothers, I have stared down a host of herdsmen, I have stared down strangers in the farmyard, and I can stare you down, too."

As the lad stared, the king thought, "What a strange, mad lad. He must be taken away." And he turned to speak to his councilor about the staring lad.

"See, see," thought the lad, "I have stared down the king himself. They are all afraid of me."

And without a word, he marched out the door and into the courtyard, through the courtyard and out into the town square.

"Hear ye, hear ye," he shouted to the crowd that quickly gathered. "I am the lad who stared everyone down. I have stared down the king of kings, I have stared down quarrelsome soldiers, I have stared down a mighty watchman, I have stared down fathers, I have stared down mothers, I have stared down a host of herdsmen, I have stared down strangers in the farmyard. I have stared everyone down. There is no one greater than I."

The crowd oohed and the crowd aahed, and the crowd made a thousand obeisances. Except for one old man who had seen everything and believed nothing.

"No good will come of all this staring," said the old man.

The lad merely stared at the old man and laughed. "And I can stare you down, too," he said.

"I am sure you can," said the old man. "But staring down an old man is no problem at all for a lad who has stared *everyone* down."

The lad looked uneasy for the first time.

Then the old man pointed to the sun that glowered like a red eye in the sky. "But if you can stare that down," he said, "I will believe your boast."

"Done," said the proud lad, and he turned his face to the sky.

All that day the lad stared at the sun. And as he stared, the sun seemed to grow and change and blossom. He stared until the sun had burned its image into his eyes.

And when at last night came, the sun went down. Yet still the boy kept staring.

The crowd shouted, "He has done it. He has done it. He has stared the sun down, too."

Even the old man nodded his head at the marvel and turned to shake the lad's hand.

But the proud lad thrust the hand aside. "Quiet, you fools. Quiet. Can't you see the sun? It is shining still. It shines on and on. Quiet, for I must keep on staring until I have stared it down. I am the lad who stares everyone down."

The sun came up again and the sun went down again, but the boy never moved. And as far as anyone knows, the proud lad is staring still.

CROWS

Crows, dusky reapers of corn,
Calculating fliers, speakers of the true,
About whom all good farmers warn,
Who over the brand new plantings flew;
Those birds, in gossiping, chattering flocks
Blanketed fields with upstart ways,
Looking like children's building blocks,
Black imprints on a green emblaze.
Crows—raining down fierce black motes,
Ebony markers spread on the lawn,
Animate letters, unreadable notes,
Messages sent, in a moment gone.
Here into this brief poem I throw
Enough short metaphors to pluck a crow.

THE SINGER OF SEEDS

There was once a minstrel named Floren who had never held a piece of earth in his hand. He could sing birds out of the trees and milk from a maiden's breast, but of the strong brown soil he knew nothing.

One day, when he came into a small fertile valley named Plaisant and heard the surrounding mountains sing his name, he was more than a little surprised. Still, being a man who believed in signs, he sold his harp for a plow and a plot of land—a poor plow and a strip of earth running close by the mountain foot—and sowed the field.

No one thought he had a hope of a crop, but his strip of land soon began to sprout. He walked up and down the rows singing to his grain, and this was his song:

> "Sunlight and moonbright
> And wind through the weeds
> Come up and come over,
> Come up and come over,
> Come up and come over
> My swift-growing seeds."

At first the neighboring farmers had laughed at Floren and his strange songs. They knew him to be a minstrel, and a good one. He had entertained at their fairs. But he was not a man of the land. His father's father's father had not put in long sweaty years at the plow. So they mocked him, even to his face, and called him Singer of Seeds.

Floren had returned their mockery with a smile, for even he was amused at the dirt under his nails and the way the grain seemed to spring up under his feet. He expected—as they all did—that the few rows would give him no real harvest and that by winter's edge he would be singing in their houses for food. Still, the mountain had called to him and it would have been impolite not to have answered. So he walked the rows of small tender shoots and sang:

> *"Sunlight and moonbright*
> *And wind through the weeds.*
> *Come up and come over,*
> *Come up and come over,*
> *Come up and come over*
> *My swift-growing seeds."*

After a while he found he loved the sound of his song in the open air, the way it fell against the mountainside and returned to him, the way it seemed to rain down on the new young leaves. After a while, he was content and the soil under his nails seemed natural and good.

But the farmers grew envious of Floren. For though he was no farmer, his plants were growing higher, his corn hardier, his grain fuller than theirs. Though his father and his father's father had been wandering minstrels, he was proving to be a better man of the soil than those who had lived all their lives with the soil of Plaisant under their feet. They began to mutter among themselves.

"He does not sing a mere song," one farmer said. "He sings hymns to the devil."

"He does not sing mere hymns to the devil," said another. "He sings an incantation for his crops."

"He does not sing a mere incantation for his own crops," said a third. "He calls out curses on our crops as well."

And so it grew, this seed of envy that the neighboring farmers planted. And by the following spring it was in full flower in their hearts. All they could think of was Floren's luck, for as he flourished so they seemed to decline. And when their early plantings died, flooded out by unusual rains, while Floren's field high on the mountain foot was saved, they knew where to lay the blame.

"It is *his* fault," they said, staring at the drowned crops, as if by not saying his name aloud they would not be accountable for anything that happened.

So they blamed Floren, but they could not decide what they should do.

"Perhaps we should raze his fields," said one.

"We should set his crops ablaze," said another.

"We should send our cattle to trample on his grain."

But though each of them desired revenge, they could not agree on the means. So in the end they agreed to visit the witch who lived in a cave high up in the mountains. She was an old woman who gave nothing but evil advice, and such was their mood, they wanted to hear only the worst.

It was a long climb to her home. For each man the climb seemed endless. Their backs were furrowed with sweat long before they reached the top. And though it was hard enough to climb up alone, each man feared to be left behind, so he held on to the shirt of the man in front and, in this way, doubled the agony.

The old witch woman was nearly blind, but the men made enough noise with their curses and cries to tell her they were coming. And so often did they now mix Floren's name in their loud talk, she also knew why they had come. She greeted them when they rounded the last curve, saying, "So you wish to know what to do with that cursed Singer of Seeds."

The men were hot and tired and so their marvel grew. Surely this was a mighty witch, nearly blind yet seeing with such a clear inner eye she had known they were coming and seen their purpose. They did not understand that their own lips and hearts had already betrayed them.

"We wish..." they began and then, to a man, stopped.

The old witch smiled at them, waiting. Fear and envy were common enough coins to her. She could afford to wait.

Then one man, braver than the rest, said, "We would end his song."

"Then thrust him from you," advised the witch.

Muttering amongst themselves, the farmers could come to no agreement. At last the same man spoke up again. "He would only return. He claims the mountain sings his name. He says he has sworn to the mountain that he will be with us forever."

They agreed at last. Though none had heard Floren say it, all believed it had been said. "He swore he would be with us forever," they concurred.

"Then thrust him where he cannot return," said the old woman, making a downward motion with her hand. "Seal his lips with his own mountain and then see if he can sing." She turned her back on the farmers and went into her cave. None of them dared follow.

So there was nothing the tired men could do but go back down the mountain. They grumbled all the way.

Now all the while the farmers had made their way up and then down the mountain, Floren had been at work. He had plowed and furrowed his fields. He had sown his seed. He had weeded and watered and waited for sprouts. And all the while he sang:

"Sunlight and moonbright
And wind through the weeds
Come up and come over,
Come up and come over,
Come up and come over
My swift-growing seeds."

Floren's song rose over the fields, over the meadows, up and over the mountain standing jagged against the sky.

The angry farmers, angered even further by their difficult trip down the mountainside, reached their homes late at night. And though they thought it was the ending of that same long day, it had been a season. Such is the way with magic; such is the way with madness.

In the morning when the sun rose, the men rose, too. Each by his own hearth dressed in surly silence. They met by the crossroads that led to Floren's farm.

No one spoke to any other except in growls and signs, for they had almost lost their human tongues. And if by chance a traveler had met them on the path then, he would have thought them a pack of feral men, so fierce were their faces, so wild their eyes.

They came to Floren's farm but he was up before them. It was the time of harvest and he was out with his crops at the sun's first rays. The men were amazed—was it harvest time already? Yet they had left right after planting. They thought the hasty season was magic of Floren's making, though in fact it was they who had climbed throughout the whole growing season, and what they had grown now lay rotted in their hearts.

The farmers lifted their faces to the late summer sun, shrouded in clouds. They sniffed the air. The sounds of Floren's song drifted to them.

"Come up and come over," he sang. "Come up and come over."

The music hurt their ears. One after another they cried out their distress, and the sound was a howling in the wind.

Then they ran into Floren's field, surprising him by his corn, which was full and golden and ripe. Surrounding him, they snapped at him with their teeth and tore at him with their nails. They watched as his life's blood poured out upon the rich dark soil.

Then suddenly the beast in them departed and the sun came out from behind the clouds. Horrified at what they had done, they buried Floren under the field, under the glowing corn. They sealed his lips with the dirt of his own mountain and left, no man daring to look at his neighbor.

The next morning when the sun rose, it was pale and thin like a worn copper penny. Every farmer in Plaisant rose, too, hurrying to his own field. But the growing time was over, and what little had sprung up in their fields was weedy and scant. Only Floren's field, at the mountain's foot, was full of ripened corn.

As each man looked across his fields, a wind came sighing down the mountainside. It blew a song across Floren's cornfield as if on a giant reed pipe. The song was wordless, but each farmer in his field recognized it at once. Floren's corn sang in a thousand voices, as clear as doom:

> *"Sunlight and moonbright*
> *And wind through the weeds*
> *Come up and come over,*
> *Come up and come over,*
> *Come up and come over*
> *My swift-growing seeds."*

It sang on and on that year and every year for the rest of their lives.

Every season from that time on, the corn grew without planting in Floren's field, and every season it sang his song. The wind whistled his song across the valley of Plaisant. And though passersby thought it a pleasant, cheerful song, the farmers heard a different tune. Floren was indeed with them forever.

THE GIRL WHO CRIED FLOWERS

In ancient Greece, where the spirits of beautiful women were said to dwell in trees, a girl was born who cried flowers. Tears never fell from her eyes. Instead blossoms cascaded down her cheeks: scarlet, gold, and blue in the spring, and snow-white in the fall.

No one knew her real mother and father. She had been found one day wrapped in a blanket of woven grasses in the crook of an olive tree. The shepherd who found her called her Olivia after the tree and brought her home to his childless wife. Olivia lived with them as their daughter, and grew into a beautiful girl.

At first her strangeness frightened the villagers. But after a while, Olivia charmed them all with her gentle, giving nature. It was not long before the villagers were showing her off to any traveler who passed their way.

For every stranger, Olivia would squeeze a tiny tear-blossom from her eyes. And that is how her fame spread throughout the land.

But soon a tiny tear-blossom was not enough. Young men wanted nosegays to give to the girls they courted. Young women wanted garlands to twine in their hair. The priests asked for bouquets to bank their altars. And old men and women begged funeral wreaths against the time of their deaths.

To all these requests, Olivia said yes. And so she had to spend her days thinking sad thoughts, listening to tragic tales, and crying mountains of flowers to make other people happy. Still, she did not complain, for above all things Olivia loved making other people happy—even though it made her sad.

Then one day, when she was out in her garden looking at the far mountains and trying to think of sad things to fill her mind, a young man came by. He was strong enough for two, but wise enough to ask for help when he needed it. He had heard of Olivia's magical tears and had come to beg a garland for his own proud sweetheart.

But when he saw Olivia, the thought of his proud sweetheart went entirely out of the young man's mind. He sat down by Olivia's feet and started to tell her tales, for though he was a farmer, he had the gift of telling that only true storytellers have. Soon Olivia was smiling, then laughing in delight, as the tales rolled off his tongue.

"Stop," she said at last. "I do not even know your name."

"I am called Panos," he said.

"Then, Panos, if you must tell me tales—and indeed I hope you never stop—tell me sad ones. I must fill myself with sorrow if I am to give you what you want."

"I want only you," he said, for his errand had been long forgotten. "And that is a joyous thing."

For a time it was true. Panos and Olivia were married and lived happily in a small house at the end of the village. Panos worked long hours in the fields while Olivia kept their home neat and spotless. In the evenings they laughed together over Panos' stories or over the happenings of the day, for Panos had forbidden Olivia ever to cry again. He said it made him sad to see her sad.

And as she wanted only to make him happy, Olivia never let even the smallest tear come to her eyes.

But one day, an old lady waited until Panos had gone off to the fields and then came to Olivia's house to borrow a cup of oil.

"How goes it?" asked Olivia innocently, for since her marriage to Panos, she had all but forsaken the villagers. And indeed, since she would not cry flowers for them, the villagers had forsaken her in return.

The old lady sighed. She was fine, she explained, but for one small thing. Her granddaughter was being married in the morning and needed a crown of blue and gold flowers. But, the crafty old lady said, since Olivia was forbidden to cry any more blossoms her granddaughter would have to go to the wedding with none.

"If only I could make her just one small crown," thought Olivia. She became so sad at the thought that she could not give the girl flowers without hurting Panos that tears came unbidden to her eyes. They welled up, and as they started down her cheeks, they turned to petals and fluttered to the floor.

The old lady quickly gathered up the blossoms and, without a word more, left for home.

Soon all the old ladies were stopping by for a cup of oil. The old men, too, found excuses to stray by Olivia's door. Even the priest paid her a call and, after telling Olivia all the troubles of the parish, left with a bouquet for the altar of his church.

All this time Panos was unaware of what was happening. But he saw that Olivia was growing thin, that her cheeks were furrowed, and her eyes rimmed with dark circles. He realized that she barely slept at night. And so he tried to question her.

"What is it, dear heart?" he asked out of love.

But Olivia did not dare answer.

"Who has been here?" he roared out of fear.

But Olivia was still. Whatever she answered would have been wrong. So she turned her head and held back the tears just as Panos wished, letting them go only during the day when they would be useful to strangers.

One day, when Olivia was weeping a basket full of Maiden's Breath for a wedding, Panos came home unexpectedly from the fields. He stood in the doorway and stared at Olivia who sat on the floor surrounded by the lacy blossoms.

Panos knew then all that had happened. What he did not know was why. He held up his hands as if in prayer, but his face was filled with anger. He could not say a word.

Olivia looked at him, blossoms streaming from her eyes. "How can I give you what you want?" she asked. "How can I give *all* of you what you want?"

Panos had no answer for her but the anger in his face. Olivia jumped up and ran past him out the door.

All that day Panos stayed in the house. His anger was so fierce he could not move. But by the time evening came, his anger had turned to sadness, and he went out to look for his wife.

Though the sun had set, he searched for her, following the trail of flowers. All that night the scent of the blossoms led him around the village and through the olive groves. Just as the sun was rising, the flowers ended at the tree where Olivia had first been found.

Under the tree was a small house made entirely of flowers, just large enough for a single person. Its roof was of scarlet lilies and its walls of green ivy. The door was blue Glory-of-the-snow and the handle a blood-red rose.

Panos called out, "Olivia?" but there was no answer. He put his hand to the rose handle and pushed the door open. As he opened the door, the rose thorns pierced his palm, and a single drop of his blood fell to the ground.

Panos looked inside the house of flowers, but Olivia was not there. Then he felt something move at his feet, and he looked down.

Where his blood had touched the ground, a small olive tree was beginning to grow. As Panos watched, the tree grew until it pushed up the roof of the house. Its leaves became crowned with the scarlet lilies. And as Panos looked closely at the twisted trunk of the tree, he saw the figure of a woman.

"Olivia," he cried, for indeed it was she.

Panos built a small hut by the tree and lived there for the rest of his life. The olive tree was a strange one, unlike any of the others in the grove. For among its branches twined every kind of flower. Its leaves were covered with the softest petals: scarlet, gold, and blue in the spring, and snow-white in the fall. There were always enough flowers on the tree for anyone who asked, as well as olives enough for Panos to eat and to sell.

It was said by the villagers—who guessed what they did not know—that each night a beautiful woman came out of the tree and stayed with Panos in his hut until dawn.

When at last Panos grew old and died, he was buried under the tree. Though the tree grew for many years more, it never had another blossom. And all the olives that it bore from then on were as bitter and salty as tears.

THE BIRD OF TIME

Once there was a miller who was named Honest Hans because he never lied or gave false weight. He had an only son called Pieter, whom many considered a fool.

Pieter often sat long hours looking steadily at the sky or a bird or a flower, saying nothing and smiling softly to himself. At such times he would not answer a question, even if someone asked him the time of day or the price of a sack of flour.

Yes, many considered Pieter a fool. But his father did not.

"Pieter is a dreamer," he said. "He knows beyond things. He understands the songs of the birds. And if he prefers the company of dumb plants and animals to that of people, perhaps it is a wise choice. It is not for me to say."

But the people of the village felt it was for them to say. They said so many unkind things about Pieter that the miller grew sad. At last Pieter said to him, "Father, I will go and seek my fortune. Then, perhaps, both you and I will have peace from this ceaseless wagging of mischievous tongues."

And so Pieter made his way into the wide, wide world.

He had traveled only two days and three nights into the wide, wide world when he heard a weak cry. It sounded like a call for help. Immediately, and without a thought for his own safety, Pieter rushed in the direction of the sound and found a tiny brown bird caught in a trap. He opened the trap and set the bird free. But the bird was so weak from lack of water and food that it only had time for a few faint chirps before it folded its tired wings and died.

However, since Pieter could speak the language of the birds, those few chirps were enough to tell him something of great importance. He hurried off to a nearby tree, where a nest lay concealed in the topmost branches.

In the nest was a single egg, gleaming like marble, white and veined with red and gold. Pieter picked it up. He thought about what the dying bird had told him: "In the egg lives the bird of time. When the egg is broken open, the bird will emerge singing. As long as it continues to sing, time will flow onward like a river. But if you should hold the bird and say, *'Bird of time, make time go fast,'* time will speed up for everyone except yourself and those you hold until you loose the bird again. And," the dying bird had continued, "if you say, *'Bird of time, make time go slow,'* time will slow down for everyone around. And you and those you hold will run through time like the wind through leafless trees."

Then the little brown bird had shivered all over. "But never say, *'Bird of time, make time stop,'* for then there will be a great shaking and a great quaking, and time will stop for you and those you hold forevermore."

With that, the bird had cried out, "Good friend, goodbye," and died.

Pieter was awed by this. But not overawed, for he was a dreamer, and dreamers believe in miracles, both large and small. So he put the egg in his cap, his cap on his head, and journeyed farther into the wide, wide world.

He had hardly been gone another night and day when suddenly there came a second cry for help. This time it was not a little cry, but a great weeping and a wailing and a terrible sobbing that filled the entire kingdom through which he was traveling.

Once again, without a thought for his own safety, Pieter ran toward the sound. Soon he came upon a large palace. Before it was a crowd of men and women and children. They were all crying and moaning, twisting their kerchiefs or stomping on their caps.

"What is the matter?" asked Pieter. "Is there something wrong?"

"You must be worse than a fool," said an old man. "For even a fool could see that we weep and cry because the wicked giant has just now stolen the king's daughter dear and carried her off to Castle Gloam. And none of us is brave enough or smart enough or strong enough to rescue her."

"Well, then, I must," said Pieter.

"Indeed you *are* a fool," said another man. "For if we, who are the people of the mightiest king in the world, are not brave enough or smart enough or strong enough to rescue the princess, then only a fool would try."

"Fool I may be," said Pieter, "or worse. But I think you are more foolish than I if you will not try at all."

And off he went with not a word more toward Castle Gloam to rescue the king's beautiful daughter.

Pieter walked and walked seven days and seven nights to Castle Gloam, which teetered on the edge of the world (for in those days the world was flat). At last he found the castle and pushed through the enormous door.

It was nearly dark inside the castle, and cold. A single light shone dimly at the end of a long hall. It was toward that light that Pieter walked. When he came to where the light began and the hall ended, he saw the King's daughter. She was sitting on a golden throne in a golden cage and weeping as though her tears could wash away the bars.

"Do not cry," said Pieter when he was quite close to the cage. "I am here to bring you home." He spoke bravely, although he had no idea how to accomplish what he promised.

When she heard him, the king's daughter looked up, her eyes shimmering with tears. And when she looked at him Pieter felt her gaze go straight to his heart; he had never seen anyone so beautiful. He knelt before her and took off his cap. And the egg, which had been hidden there, nestled in his hair.

Just then he heard loud footsteps and a giant voice shouting.

And before Pieter could move, the floors shook and the walls trembled and the giant of Castle Gloam stomped into the room.

Pieter turned around to stare at the giant. And as he turned, the egg, which had been nestled in his hair, fell off his head and broke upon the floor. A little brown bird arose singing from the broken egg and alighted on Pieter's hand.

Pieter stood up. Reaching into the cage, he took the hand of the king's daughter gently in his. Then he said, *"Bird of time, make time go slow."*

Immediately the little brown bird began singing a very slow, measured song. And time, which had been flowing along like a swift river, suddenly became muddy and slow for the giant. And he moved awkwardly through the air as though it were water.

Without letting go of the princess's hand, Pieter quickly opened the cage with a golden key he found hanging nearby. The king's daughter ran out. Then hand in hand they raced out into the countryside, like the wind through leafless trees. There they danced and laughed. And Pieter threw his arms up into the air with joy, and the bird of time was loosed.

At once time began to move normally again. In a moment Pieter and the princess heard the loud, rattling footsteps of the giant as he searched through Castle Gloam for the king's daughter.

"Quickly," said Pieter, taking the princess by the hand. "We must run."

But run as fast as they could, they could not run faster than the giant. With loud, earth-shattering footsteps, he gained at every stride.

"Save yourself!" cried the king's daughter. "It is foolish to stay with me."

But Pieter merely held out his hand, and the bird of time flew down and nestled in it.

"Lie down," said Pieter to the king's daughter. And he lay down by her side in the tall meadow grass.

"Bird of time, make time go fast," commanded Pieter.

The little brown bird began to sing a light, quick song. And time sped up for everyone but Pieter and the lovely princess.

The giant fairly flew over to the two bodies lying side by side on the ground. He twirled around and about them. To his speeded-up eyes they seemed dead, so measured and slow was their breathing. The giant gnashed his teeth in rage at having lost his beautiful captive. Hastily he pounded his fists on the ground. Then he noticed the bird of time in Pieter's hand singing a light, quick song. Forgetting the princess, he tore the bird out of Pieter's hand with a swift, sharp, angry movement.

Gloating, the giant ran back to Castle Gloam with the bird. Pieter and the princess watched him go.

Now the giant had heard what Pieter had said to the bird, and he realized that there was magic about. He thought that if the bird could make time speed up or make time slow down, it could help him conquer the world. And because he was evil and exceptionally greedy, the giant thought what a great fortune he could gather and how many beautiful princesses he could steal, if time could be stopped altogether and no one but he could move at all.

He put out his hand as he had seen Pieter do, and the bird nestled into it, almost disappearing in his vast palm.

"Bird of time," he commanded, "make time stop!"

And the bird of time stopped singing.

The giant did not know that this was a calamitous thing to say. He had not heard the dying bird's warning that no one can make time stop altogether. And he was too wicked to worry about it on his own.

Suddenly there was a great quaking. And a great shaking. The rocks that Castle Gloam stood upon began to crack. Fissures appeared in the walls. The roof began to tremble. Then, very slowly, Castle Gloam slid over the edge of the world and disappeared.

And inside the lost castle the giant and the silent bird of time were caught forever in a timeless scream.

Pieter and the king's daughter watched as the castle sank out of sight. As soon as the castle disappeared over the edge of the world, the world returned to normal again. Once more time flowed onward like a river.

Then Pieter and the princess looked at one another and smiled. And hand in hand they walked back for seven days and seven nights until they reached the palace of the king.

There Pieter and the princess were married amidst great singing and dancing. In due time, Pieter himself became king, and lived a long and full life with his beautiful wife always at his side.

And though Pieter had found another egg veined with red and gold nestled in his cap right after the bird and the giant had disappeared, he was never fool enough to tell. Instead he gave the egg into the keeping of his father, Honest Hans. And the old miller buried it under the mill in a wooden box, where it has remained safe and unbroken to this very day.

BLACK DOG TIMES

*"The world will end when the old woman finishes her
porcupine quill blanket, though her black dog unpicks it
whenever her back is turned."*—Lakota legend

What can you do in these black dog times?
When the world is close to done,
And only the dog's teeth stand between us
And the ending? What can you do?
Choose to be born, stand up, pick the quills,
See through the mist, through the dark.
Sew yourself a robe, not a shroud.
Age gracefully. Take your medicine.
Have a colonscopy. Do not complain.
Pick up your skirts, bend your aching knees,
And dance.

Words of Power

Late Blossoming Flower, the only child of her mother's old age, stared sulkily into the fire. A homely child, with a nose that threatened to turn into a beak and a mouth that seldom smiled, she was nonetheless cherished by her mother and the clan. Her loneness, the striking rise of her nose, the five strands of white hair that streaked through her shiny black hair, were all seen as the early sign of great power, the power her mother had given up when she had chosen to bear a child.

"I would never have made such a choice," Late Blossoming Flower told her mother. "I would never give up *my* power."

Her mother, who had the same fierce nose, the white streak of hair, and the bitter smile but was a striking beauty, replied gently, "You do not have that power yet. And if I had not given up mine, you would not be here now to make such a statement and to chide me for my choice." She shook her head. "Nor would you now be scolded for forgetting to do those things which are yours by duty."

Late Blossoming Flower bit back the reply that was no reply but merely angry words. She rose from the fireside and went out of the cliff house to feed the milk beast. As she climbed down the withy ladder to the valley below, she rehearsed that conversation with her mother as she had done so often before. Always her mother remained calm, her voice never rising into anger. It infuriated Flower, and she nursed that sore like all the others, counting them up as carefully as if she were toting them on a notch stick. The tally by now was long indeed.

But soon, she reminded herself, soon she would herself be a woman of power, though she was late coming to it. All the signs but one were on her. Under the chamois shirt her breasts had finally begun to bud. There was hair curling in the secret places of her body. Her waist and hips were changing to create a place for the Herb Belt to sit comfortably, instead of chafing her as it did now. And when at last the moon called to her and her first blood flowed, cleansing her body of man's sin, she would be allowed at last to go on her search for her own word of power and be free of her hated, ordinary chores. Boys could not go on such a search, for they were never able to rid themselves of the dirty blood-sin. But she took no great comfort in that, for not all girls who sought found. Still, Late Blossoming Flower knew she was the daughter of a woman of power, a woman so blessed that even though she had had a child and lost the use of the Shaping Hands she still retained the Word That Changes. Late Blossoming Flower never doubted that when she went on her journey she would find what it was she sought.

The unfed milk beast lowed longingly as her feet touched the ground. She bent and gathered up bits of earth, cupped the fragments in her hand, said the few phrases of the *Ke-waha,* the prayer to the land, then stood.

"I'm not *that* late," she said sharply to the agitated beast, and went to the wooden manger for maize.

It was the first day after the rising of the second moon, and the florets of the night-blooming panomom tree were open wide. The sickly sweet smell of the tiny clustered blossoms filled the valley, and all the women of the valley dreamed dreams.

The women of power dreamed in levels. Late Blossoming Flower's mother passed from one level to another with the ease of long practice, but her daughter's dream quester had difficulty going through. She wandered too long on the dreamscape paths, searching for a ladder or a rope or some other familiar token of passage.

When Late Blossoming Flower had awakened, her mother scolded her for her restless sleep.

"If you are to be a true woman of power, you must force yourself to lie down in the dream and fall asleep. Sleep within sleep, dream within dream. Only then will you wake at the next level." Her head had nodded gently every few words and she spoke softly, braiding her hair with quick and supple hands. "You must be like a gardener forcing an early bud to bring out the precious juices."

"Words. Just words," said Late Blossoming Flower. "And none of those words has power." She had risen from her pallet, shaking her own hair free of the loose night braiding, brushing it fiercely before plaiting it up again. She could not bear to listen to her mother's advice any longer and had let her thoughts drift instead to the reed hut on the edge of the valley, where old Sand Walker lived. A renegade healer, he lived apart from the others and, as a man, was little thought of. But Late Blossoming Flower liked to go and sit with him and listen to his stories of the time before time, when power had been so active in the world it could be plucked out of the air as easily as fruit from a tree. He said that dreams eventually explained themselves and that to discipline the dream figure was to bind its power. To Late Blossoming Flower that made more sense than all her mother's constant harping on the Forcing Way.

So intent was she on visiting the old man that day, she had raced through her chores, scanting the milk beast and the birds who squatted on hidden nests. She had collected only a few eggs and left them in the basket at the bottom of the cliff. Then, without a backward glance at the withy ladders spanning the levels or the people moving busily against the cliff face, she raced down the path toward Sand Walker's home.

As a girl child she had that freedom, given leave for part of each day to walk the many trails through the valley. On these walks she was supposed to learn the ways of the growing flowers, to watch the gentler creatures at their play, to come to a careful understanding of the way of predator and prey. It was time for her to know the outer landscape of her world as thoroughly as she would, one day, know the inner dream trails. But Late Blossoming Flower was a hurrying child. As if to make up for her late birth and the crushing burden of early power laid on her, she refused to take the time.

"My daughter," her mother often cautioned her, "a woman of true power must be in love with silence. You must learn all the outward sounds in order to approach the silence that lies within."

But Flower wanted no inner silence. She delighted in tuneless singing and loud sounds: the sharp hoarse cry of the night herons sailing across the marsh; the crisp howl of the jackals calling under the moon; even the scream of the rabbit in the teeth of the wolf. She sought to imitate *those* sounds, make them louder, sing them again in her own mouth. What was silence compared to sound?

And when she was with old Sand Walker in his hut, he sang with her. And told stories, joking stories, about the old women and their silences.

"Soon enough," Sand Walker said, "soon enough it will be silent and dark. In the grave. Those old *bawenahs*"—he used the word that meant the unclean female vulture—"those old *bawenahs* would make us rehearse for our coming deaths with their binding dreams. Laugh *now*, child. Sing out. Silence is for the dead ones, though they call themselves alive and walk the trails. But you and I, ho"—he poked her in the stomach lightly with his stick—"we know the value of noise. It blocks out thinking, and thinking means pain. Cry out for me, child. Loud. Louder."

And as if a trained dog, Late Blossoming Flower always dropped to her knees at this request and howled, scratching at the dirt and wagging her bottom. Then she would fall over on her back with laughter and the old man laughed with her.

All this was in her mind as she ran along the path toward Sand Walker's hut.

A rabbit darted into her way, then zagged back to escape her pounding feet. A few branches, emboldened by the coming summer, strayed across her path and whipped her arm, leaving red scratches. Impatient with the marks, she ignored them.

At the final turning the old man's hut loomed up. He was sitting, as always, in the doorway, humming, and eating a piece of yellowed fruit, the juices running down his chin. At the noise of her coming he looked up and grinned.

"Hai!" he said, more sound than greeting.

Flower skidded to a stop and squatted in the dirt beside him.

"You look tired," he said. "Did you dream?"

"I tried. But dreaming is so slow," Flower admitted.

"Dreaming is not living. You and I—we live. Have a bite?" He offered her what was left of the fruit, mostly core.

She took it so as not to offend him, holding the core near her mouth but not eating. The smell of the overripe, sickly sweet fruit made her close her eyes, and she was startled into a dream.

> The fruit was in her mouth and she could feel its sliding passage down her throat. It followed the twists of her inner pathways, dropping seeds as it went, until it landed heavily in her belly. There it began to burn, a small but significant fire in her gut.
>
> Bending over to ease the cramping, Flower turned her back on the old man's hut and crept along the trail toward the village. The trees along the trail and the muddle of gray-green wildflowers blurred into an indistinct mass as she went, as if she were seeing them through tears, though her cheeks were dry and her eyes clear.
>
> When she reached the cliffside she saw, to her surprise, that the withy ladders went down into a great hole in the earth instead of up toward the dwellings on the cliff face.
>
> It was deathly silent all around her. The usual chatter of children at their chores, the chant of women, the hum-buzz of men in the furrowed fields were gone. The cliff was as blank and as smooth as the shells of the eggs she had gathered that morning.

And then she heard a low sound, compounded of moans and a strange hollow whistling, like an old man's laughter breathed our across a reed. Turning around, she followed the sound. It led her to the hole. She bent over it, and as she did, the sound resolved itself into a single word: *bawenah*. She saw a pale, shining face looking up at her from the hole, its mouth a smear of fruit. When the mouth opened, it was as round and as black as the hole. There were no teeth. There was no tongue. Yet still the mouth spoke: *bawenah*.

Flower awoke and stared at the old man. Pulpy fruit stained his scraggly beard. His eyes were filmy. Slowly his tongue emerged and licked his lips.

She turned and without another word to him walked home. Her hands cupped her stomach, pressing and releasing, all the way back, as if pressure alone could drive away the cramps.

Her mother was waiting for her at the top of the ladder, hands folded on her own belly. "So," she said, "it is your woman time."

Flower did not ask how she knew. Her mother was a woman of great power still and such knowledge was well within her grasp, though it annoyed Flower that it should be so.

"Yes," Flower answered, letting a small whine creep into her voice. "But you did not tell me it would hurt so."

"With some," her mother said, smiling and smoothing back the white stripe of hair with her hand, "with some, womanhood comes easy. With some it comes harder." Then, as they walked into their rooms, she added with a bitterness uncharacteristic of her, "Could your *healer* not do something for you?"

Flower was startled at her mother's tone. She knew that her association with the old man had annoyed her mother. But Flower had never realized it would hurt her so much. She began to answer her mother, then bit back her first angry reply. Instead, mastering her voice, she said. "I did not think to ask him for help. He is but a man. *I* am a woman."

"You are a woman today, truly," her mother said. She went over to the great chest she had carved before Flower's birth, a chest made of the wood of a lightning-struck panomom tree. The chest's sides were covered with carved signs of power: the florets of the tree with their three-foil flowers, the mouse and hare who were her mother's personal signs, the trailing arbet vine which was her father's, and the signs for the four moons: quarter, half, full, and closed faces.

When she opened the chest, it made a small creaking protest. Flower went over to look in. There, below her first cradle dress and leggings, nestled beside a tress of her first, fine baby hair, was the Herb Belt she had helped her mother make. It had fifteen pockets, one for each year she had been a girl.

They went outside, and her mother raised her voice in that wild ululation that could call all the women of power to her. It echoed around the clearing and across the fields to the gathering streams beyond, a high, fierce yodeling. And then she called out again, this time in a gentler voice that would bring the women who had borne and their girl children with them.

Flower knew it would be at least an hour before they all gathered; in the meantime she and her mother had much to do.

They went back into the rooms and turned around all the objects they owned, as a sign that Flower's life would now be turned around as well. Bowls, cups, pitchers were turned. Baskets of food and the drying racks were turned. Even the heavy chest was turned around. They left the bed pallets to the very last, and then, each holding an end, they walked the beds around until the ritual was complete.

Flower stripped in front of her mother, something she had not done completely in years. She resisted the impulse to cover her breasts. On her leggings were the blood sign. Carefully her mother packed those leggings into the panomom chest. Flower would not wear them again.

At the bottom of the chest, wrapped in a sweet-smelling woven grass covering, was a white chamois dress and leggings. Flower's mother took them out and spread them on the bedding, her hand smoothing the nap. Then, with a pitcher of water freshened with violet flowers, she began to wash her daughter's body with a scrub made of the leaves of the sandarac tree. The nubby sandarac and the soothing rinse of the violet water were to remind Flower of the fierce and gentle sides of womanhood. All the while she scrubbed, Flower's mother chanted the songs of Woman: the seven-fold chant of Rising, the Way of Power, and the Praise to Earth and Moon.

The songs reminded Flower of something, and she tried to think of what it was as her mother's hands cleansed her of the sins of youth. It was while her mother was braiding her hair, plaiting in it reed ribbons that ended in a dangle of shells, that Flower remembered. The chants were like the cradle songs her mother had sung her when she was a child, with the same rise and fall, the same liquid sounds. She suddenly wanted to cry for the loss of those times and the pain she had given her mother, and she wondered why she felt so like weeping when anger was her usual way.

The white dress and leggings slipped on easily, indeed fit her perfectly, though she had never tried them on before, and that, too, was a sign of her mother's power.

And what of her own coming power, Flower wondered as she stood in the doorway watching the women assemble at the foot of the ladder. The women of power stood in the front, then the birth women, last of all the girls. She could name them all, her friends, her sisters in the tribe, who only lately had avoided her because of her association with the old man. She tried to smile at them, but her mouth would not obey her. In fact, her lower lip trembled and she willed it to stop, finally clamping it with her teeth.

"She is a woman," Flower's mother called down to them. The ritual words. They had known, even without her statement, had known from that first wild cry, what had happened. "Today she has come into her power, putting it on as a woman dons her white dress, but she does not yet know her own way. She goes now, as we all go at our time, to the far hills and beyond to seek the Word That Changes. She may find it or not, but she will tell of that when she has returned."

The women below began to sway and chant the words of the Searching Song, words which Flower had sung with them for fifteen years without really understanding their meaning. Fifteen years—far longer than any of the other girls—standing at the ladder's foot and watching another Girl-Become-Woman go off on her search. And that was why—she saw it now—she had fallen under Sand Walker's spell.

But now, standing above the singers, waiting for the Belt and the Blessing, she felt for the first time how strongly the power called to her. This was *her* moment, *her* time, and there would be no other. She pictured the old man in his hut and realized that if she did not find her word she would be bound to him forever.

"Mother," she began, wondering if it was too late to say all the things she should have said before, but her mother was coming toward her with the Belt and suddenly it was too late. Once the Belt was around her waist she could not speak again until the Word formed in her mouth, with or without its accompanying power. Tears started in her eyes.

Her mother saw the tears, and perhaps she mistook them for something else. Tenderly she placed the Belt around Flower's waist, setting it on the hips, and tying it firmly behind her. Then she turned her daughter around, the way every object in the house had been turned, till she faced the valley again where all the assembled women could read the fear on her face.

> Into the valley, in the fear we all face,
> Into the morning of your womanhood,
> Go with our blessing to guide you,
> Go with our blessing to guard you,
> Go with our blessing and bring back your word.

The chant finished, Flower's mother pushed her toward the ladder and went back into the room and sat on the chest to do her own weeping.

Flower opened her eyes, surprised, for she had not realized that she had closed them. All the women had disappeared, back into the fields, into the woods; she did not know where, nor was she to wonder about them. Her journey had to be made alone. Talking to anyone on the road this day would spell doom to them both, to her quest for her power, to the questioner's very life.

As she walked out of the village, Flower noticed that everything along the way seemed different. Her power had, indeed, begun. The low bushes had a shadow self, like the moon's halo, standing behind. The trees were filled with eyes, peering out of the knotholes. The chattering of animals in the brush was a series of messages, though Flower knew that she was still unable to decipher them. And the path itself sparkled as if water rushed over it, tumbling the small stones.

She seemed to slip in and out of quick dreams that were familiar pieces of her old dreams stitched together in odd ways. Her childhood was sloughing off behind her with each step, a skin removed.

Further down the path, where the valley met the foothills leading to the far mountains, she could see Sand Walker's hut casting a long, dark, toothy shadow across the trail. Flower was not sure if the shadows lengthened because the sun was at the end of its day or because this was yet another dream. She closed her eyes, and when she opened them again, the long shadows were still there, though not nearly as dark or as menacing.

When she neared the hut, the old man was sitting silently out front. His shadow, unlike the hut's black shadow, was a strange shade of green

She did not dare greet the old man, for fear of ruining her quest and because she did not want to hurt him. One part of her was still here with him, wild, casting green shadows, awake. He had no protection against her power. But surely she might give him one small sign of recognition. Composing her hands in front of her, she was prepared to signal him with a finger, when without warning he leaped up, grinning.

"*Ma-hane,* white girl," he cried, jumping into her path. "Do not forget to laugh, you in your white dress and leggings. If you do not laugh, you are one of the dead ones."

In great fear she reached out a hand toward him to silence him before he could harm them both, and power sprang unbidden from her fingertips. She had forgotten the Shaping Hands. And though they were as yet untrained and untried, still they were a great power. She watched in horror as five separate arrows of flame struck the old man's face, touching his eyes, his nostrils, his mouth, sealing them, melting his features like candle wax. He began to shrink under the fire, growing smaller and smaller, fading into a gray-green splotch that only slowly resolved itself into the form of a *sa-hawa,* a butterfly the color of leaf mold.

Flower did not dare speak, not even a word of comfort. She reached down and shook out the crumpled shirt, loosing the butterfly. It flapped its wings, tentatively at first, then with more strength, and finally managed to flutter up toward the top of the hut.

Folding the old man's tattered shirt and leggings with gentle hands, Flower laid them on the doorstep of his hut, still watching the fluttering *sa-hawa*. When she stood again, she had to shade her eyes with one hand to see it. It had flown away from the hut and was hovering between patches of wild onion in a small meadow on the flank of the nearest foothill.

Flower bit her lip. How could she follow the butterfly? It was going up the mountainside and her way lay straight down the road. Yet how could she not follow it? Sand Walker's transformation had been her doing. No one else might undo what she had so unwillingly, unthinkingly created.

To get to the meadow was easy. But if the butterfly went further up the mountainside, what could she do? There was only a goat track, and then the sheer cliff wall. As she hesitated, the *sa-hawa* rose into the air again, leaving the deep green spikes of onions to fly up toward the mountain itself.

Flower looked quickly down the trail, but the shadows of oncoming evening had closed that way. Ahead, the Path of Power—her Power—was still brightly lit.

"Oh, Mother," she thought. "Oh, my mothers, I need your blessing indeed." And so thinking, she plunged into the underbrush after the *sa-hawa,* heedless of the thorns tugging at her white leggings or the light on the Path of Power that suddenly and inexplicably went out.

The goat path had not been used for years, not by goats or by humans either. Briars tangled across it. Little rock slides blocked many turnings, and in others the pebbly surface slid away beneath her feet. Time and again she slipped and fell; her knees and palms bruised, and all the power in her Shaping Hands seemed to do no good. She could not call on it. Once when she fell she bit her underlip so hard it bled. And always, like some spirit guide, the little gray-green butterfly fluttered ahead, its wings glowing with five spots as round and marked as fingerprints.

Still Flower followed, unable to call out or cry out because a new woman on her quest for her Power must not speak until she has found her word. She still hoped, a doomed and forlorn hope, that once she had caught the *sa-hawa* she might also catch her Power or at least be allowed to continue on her quest. And she would take the butterfly with her and find at least enough of the Shaping Hands to turn him back into his own tattered, laughing, dismal self.

She went on. The only light now came from the five spots on the butterfly's wings and the pale moon rising over the jagged crest of First Mother, the leftmost mountain. The goat track had disappeared entirely. It was then the butterfly began to rise straight up, as if climbing the cliff face.

Out of breath, Flower stopped and listened, first to her own ragged breathing, then to the pounding of her heart. At last she was able to be quiet enough to hear the sounds of the night. The butterfly stopped, too, as if it was listening as well.

From far down the valley she heard the rise and fall of the running dogs, howling at the moon. Little chirrups of frogs, the pick-buzz of insect wings, and then the choughing of a nightbird's wings. She turned her head for a moment, fearful that it might be an eater-of-bugs. When she looked back, the *sa-hawa* was almost gone, edging up the great towering mountain that loomed over her.

Flower almost cried out then, in frustration and anger and fear, but she held her tongue and looked for a place to start the climb. She had to use hands and feet instead of eyes, for the moonlight made this a place of shadows—shadows within shadows—and only her hands and feet could see between the dark and dark.

She felt as if she had been climbing for hours, though the moon above her spoke of a shorter time, when the butterfly suddenly disappeared. Without the lure of its phosphorescent wings, Flower was too exhausted to continue. All the tears she had held back for so long suddenly rose to swamp her eyes. She snuffled loudly and crouched uncertainly on a ledge. Then, huddling against the rockface, she tried to stay awake, to draw warmth and courage from the mountain. But without wanting to, she fell asleep.

In the dream she spiraled up and up and up into the sky without ladder or rope to pull her, and she felt the words of a high scream fall from her lips, a yelping *kya*. She awoke terrified and shaking in the morning light, sitting on a thin ledge nearly a hundred feet up the mountainside. She had no memory of the climb and certainly no way to get down.

And then she saw the *sa-hawa* next to her and memory flooded back. She cupped her hand, ready to pounce on the butterfly, when it fluttered its wings in the sunlight and moved from its perch. Desperate to catch it, she leaned out, lost her balance, and began to fall.

"Oh, Mother," she screamed in her mind, and a single word came back to her. *Aki-la.* Eagle. She screamed it aloud.

As she fell, the bones of her arms lengthened and flattened, cracking sinew and marrow. Her small, sharp nose bone arched outward and she watched it slowly form into a black beak with a dull yellow membrane at the base. Her body, twisting, seemed to stretch, catching the wind, first beneath, then above; she could feel the swift air through her feathers and the high, sweet whistling of it rushing past her head. Spiraling up, she pumped her powerful wings once. Then, holding them flat, she soared.

Aki-la. Golden eagle, she thought. It was her Word of Power, the Word That Changes, hers and no one else's. And then all words left her and she knew only wind and sky and the land spread out far below.

How long she coursed the sky in her flat-winged glide she did not know. For her there was no time, no ticking off of moment after moment, only the long sweet soaring. But at last her stomach marked the time for her and, without realizing it, she was scanning the ground for prey. It was as if she had two sights now, one the sweeping farsight that showed her the land as a series of patterns and the other that closed up the space whenever she saw movement or heat in the grass that meant some small creature was moving below.

At the base of the mountain she spied a large mouse and her wings knew even before her mind, even before her stomach. They cleaved to her side and she dove down in one long, perilous swoop toward the brown creature that was suddenly still in the short grass.

The wind rushed by her as she dove, and a high singing filled her head, wordless visions of meat and blood.

Kya, she called, and followed it with a whistle. *Kya,* her hunting song.

Right before reaching the mouse, she threw out her wings and backwinged, extending her great claws as brakes. But her final sight of the mouse, larger than she had guessed, standing upright in the grass as if it had expected her, its black eyes meeting her own and the white stripe across its head gleaming in the early sun, stayed her. Some memory, some old human thought teased at her. Instead of striking the mouse, she landed gracefully by its side, her great claws gripping the earth, remembering ground, surrendering to it.

Aki-la. She thought the word again, opened her mouth, and spoke it to the quiet air. She could feel the change begin again. Marrow and sinew and muscle and bone responded, reversing themselves, growing and shrinking, folding and forming. It hurt, yet it did not hurt; the pain was delicious.

And still the mouse sat, its bright little eyes watching her until the transformation was complete. Then it squeaked a word, shook itself all over, as if trying to slough off its own skin and bones, and grew, filling earth and sky, resolving itself into a familiar figure with the fierce stare of an eagle and the soft voice of the mouse.

"Late Blossoming Flower," her mother said, and opened welcoming arms to her.

"I have found my word," Flower said as she ran into them. Then, unaccountably, she put her head on her mother's breast and began to sob.

"You have found much more," said her mother. "For see—I have tested you, tempted you to let your animal nature overcome your human nature. And see—you stopped before the hunger for meat, the thirst for blood, mastered you and left you forever in your eagle form."

"But I might have killed you," Flower gasped. "I might have eaten you. I was an eagle and you were my natural prey."

"But you did not," her mother said firmly. "Now I must go home,"

"Wait," Flower said. "There is something... something I have to tell you."

Her mother turned and looked at Flower over her shoulder. "About the old man?"

Flower looked down.

"I know it already. There he is." She pointed to a gray-green butterfly hovering over a blossom. "He is the same undisciplined creature he always was."

"I must change him back. I must learn how, quickly, before he leaves."

"He will not leave," said her mother. "Not that one. Or he would have left our village long ago. No, he will wait until you learn your other powers and change him back so that he might sit on the edge of power and laugh at it as he has always done, as he did to me so long ago. And now, my little one who is my little one no longer, use your eagle wings to fly. I will be waiting at our home for your return."

Flower nodded, and then she moved away from her mother and held out her arms. She stretched them as far apart as she could. Even so—even farther—would her wings stretch. She looked up into the sky, now blue and cloudless and beckoning.   .

"Aki-la!" she cried, but her mouth was not as stern as her mother's or as any of the other women of power, for she knew how to laugh. She opened her laughing mouth again. *"Aki-la."*

She felt the change come on her, more easily this time, and she threw herself into the air. The morning sun caught the wash of gold at her beak, like a necklace of power. *Kya,* she screamed into the waiting wind, *kya,* and, for the moment, forgot mother and butterfly and all the land below.

THE BOY WHO DREW UNICORNS

There was once a boy who drew unicorns. Even before he knew their names, he caught them mane and hoof and horn on his paper. And they were white beasts and gray, black beasts and brown, galloping across the brown supermarket bags. He didn't know what to call them at first but he knew what they called him: Phillip, a lover of horses, Philly, Phil.

Now, children, there is going to be a new boy in class today. His name is Philadelphia Carew.

Philadelphia? That's a city name not a kid's name.

Hey, my name is New York.

Call me Chicago.

I got a cousin named India, does that count?

Enough, children. This young man is very special. You must try to be kind to him. He'll be very shy. And he's had a lot of family problems.

I got family problems too, Ms. Wynne. I got a brother and he's a big problem. Joseph, that's enough.

He's six feet tall. That's a very big problem.

Now you may all think you have problems, but this young man has more than most. You see, he doesn't talk.

Not ever?

No. Not now. Not for several years. That's close enough to ever, I think.

Bet you'd like it if we didn't talk. Not for several years.

No, I wouldn't like that at all, though if I could shut you up for several hours, Joseph...

Ooooooh, Joey, she's got you!

"What is the good of such drawing, Philadelphia?" his mother said. "If you have to draw, draw something useful. Draw me some money or some groceries or a new man, one who doesn't beat us. Draw us some better clothes or a bed for yourself. Draw me a job."

But he drew only unicorns: horse-like, goat-like, deer-like, lamb-like, bull-like, things he had seen in books. Four-footed, silken swift, with the single golden horn. His corner of the apartment was papered with them.

When's he coming, Ms. Wynne?
Today. After lunch.
Does he look weird, too?
He's not weird, Joseph. He's special. And I expect you—all of you—to act special.
She means we shouldn't talk.
No, Joseph, I mean you need to think before you talk. Think what it must like, not to be able to express yourself.
I'd use my hands.
Does he use his hands, Ms. Wynne?
I don't know.
Stupid, only deaf people do that. Is he deaf?
No.
Is there something wrong with his tongue?
No.
Why doesn't he talk, then?
Why do you think?
Maybe he likes being special.
That's a very interesting idea, Joseph.
Maybe he's afraid.
Afraid to talk? Don't be dumb.
Now, Joseph, that's another interesting idea, too. What are you afraid of, children?
Snakes, Ms. Wynne.
I hate spiders.
I'm not afraid of anything!
Nothing at all, Joseph?
Maybe my big brother. When he's mad.

In school he drew unicorns down the notebook page, next to all his answers. He drew them on his test papers. On the bathroom walls. They needed no signature. Everyone knew he had made them. They were his thumbprints. They were his heartbeats. They were his scars.

Oooooh, he's drawing them things again.
Don't you mess up my paper, Mr. Philadelphia Carew.
Leave him alone. He's just a dummy.

Horses don't have horns, dummy.

Here comes Ms. Wynne.

If you children will get back in your seats and stop crowding around Philly. You've all seen him draw unicorns before. Now listen to me, and I mean you, too, Joseph. Fold your hands and lift those shining faces to me. Good. We are going on a field trip this afternoon. Joseph, sit in your seat properly and leave Philly's paper alone. A field trip to Chevril Park. Not now, Joseph, get back in your seat. We will be going after lunch. And after your spelling test.

Ooooh, what test, Ms. Wynne?

You didn't say there was going to be a test.

The park was a place of green glades. It had trees shaped like popsicles with the chocolate running down the sides. It had trees like umbrellas that moved mysteriously in the wind. There were hidden ponds and secret streams and moist pathways between, lined with rings of white toadstools and trillium the color of blood. Cooing pigeons walked boldly on the pavement. But in the quiet underbrush hopped little brown birds with white throats. Silent throats.

From far away came a strange, magical song. It sounded like a melody mixed with a gargle, a tune touched by a laugh. It creaked, it hesitated, then it sang again. He had never heard anything like it before.

I hear it, Ms. Wynne. I hear the merry-go-round.

And what does it sound like, children?

It sounds lumpy.

Don't be dumb. It sounds upsy-downsy.

It sounds happy and sad.

Joseph, what do you think it sounds like?

Like another country. Like "The Twilight Zone."

Very good, Joseph. And see, Philly is agreeing with you. And strangely, Joseph, you are right. Merry-go-rounds or carousels are from another country, another world. The first ones were built in France in the late 1700s. The best hand-carved animals still are made in Europe. What kind of animals do you think you'll see on this merry-go-round?

Horses.

Lions.

Tigers.

Camels.

Don't be dumb—camels.

There are too! I been here before. And elephants.

He saw unicorns, galloping around and around, a whole herd of them. And now he saw his mistake. They were not like horses or goats or deer or

lambs or bulls. They were like—themselves. And with the sun slanting on them from beyond the trees, they were like rainbows, all colors and no colors at all.

Their mouths were open and they were calling. That was the magical song he had heard before. A strange, shimmery kind of cry, not like horses or goats or deer or lambs or bulls; more musical, with a strange rise and fall to each phrase.

He tried to count them as they ran past. Seven, fifteen, twenty-one...he couldn't contain them all. Sometimes they doubled back and he was forced to count them again. And again. He settled for the fact that it was a herd of unicorns. No. *Herd* was too ordinary a word for what they were. Horses came in herds. And cows. But unicorns—there had to be a special word for them all together. Suddenly he knew what it was, as if they had told him so in their wavery song. He was watching a *surprise* of unicorns.

Look at old weird Philly. He's just staring at the merry-go-round. Come on, Mr. Phildelphia Chicago New York L.A. Carew. Go on up and ride. They won't bite.

Joseph, keep your mouth shut and you might be able to hear something.

What, Ms. Wynne?

You might hear the heart's music, Joseph. That's a lot more interesting than the flapping of one's own mouth.

What does that mean, Ms. Wynne?

It means shut up, Joseph.

Ooooh, she got you, Joey.

It means shut up, Denise, too, I bet.

All of you, mouths shut, ears open. We're going for a ride.

We don't have any money, Ms. Wynne.

That's all taken care of. Everyone pick out a horse or a whatever. Mr. Frangipanni, the owner of this carousel, can't wait all day.

Dibs on the red horse.

I got the gray elephant.

Mine's the white horse.

No, Joseph, can't you see Philly has already chosen that one.

But heroes always ride the white horse. And he isn't any kind of hero.

Choose another one, Joseph.

Aaaah, Ms. Wynne, that's not fair.

Why not take the white elephant, Joseph. Hannibal, a great hero of history, marched across the high Alps on elephants to capture Rome.

Wow—did he really?

Really, Joseph.

Okay. Where's Rome?

Who knows where Rome is? I bet Mr. Frangipanni does.

Then ask Mr. Frangipanni!
Italy, Ms. Wynne.
Italy is right. Time to mount up. That's it. We're all ready, Mr. Frangipanni.

The white flank scarcely trembled, but he saw it. "Do not be afraid," he thought. "I couldn't ever hurt you." He placed his hand gently on the tremor and it stopped.

Moving up along the length of the velvety beast, he saw the arched neck ahead of him, its blue veins like tiny rivers branching under the angel-hair mane.

One swift leap and he was on its back. The unicorn turned its head to stare at him with its amber eyes. The horn almost touched his knee. He flinched, pulling his knee up close to his chest. The unicorn turned its head back and looked into the distance.

He could feel it move beneath him, the muscles bunching and flattening as it walked. Then with that strange wild cry, the unicorn leaped forward and began to gallop around and around the glade.

He could sense others near him, catching movement out of the corners of his eyes. Leaning down, he clung to the unicorn's mane. They ran through day and into the middle of night till the stars fell like snow behind them. He heard a great singing in his head and heart and he suddenly felt as if the strength of old kings were running in his blood. He threw his head back and laughed aloud.

Boy, am I dizzy.
My elephant was the best.
I had a red pony. Wow, did we fly!
Everyone dismounted? Now, tell me how you felt.

He slid off the silken side, feeling the solid earth beneath his feet. There was a buzz of voices around him, but he ignored them all. Instead, he turned back to the unicorn and walked toward its head. Standing still, he reached up and brought its horn down until the point rested on his chest. The golden whorls were hard and cold beneath his fingers. And if his fingers seemed to tremble ever so slightly, it was no more than how the unicorn's flesh had shuddered once under the fragile shield of its skin.

He stared into the unicorn's eyes, eyes of antique gold so old, he wondered if they had first looked on the garden where the original thrush had sung the first notes from a hand-painted bush.

Taking his right hand off the horn, he sketched a unicorn in the air between them.

As if that were all the permission it needed, the unicorn nodded its head. The horn ripped his light shirt, right over the heart. He put his left palm over the rip. The right he held out to the unicorn. It nuzzled his hand and its breath was moist and warm.

Look, look at Philly's shirt.
Ooooh, there's blood.
Let me through, children. Thank you, Joseph, for helping him get down. Are you hurt, Philly? Now don't be afraid. Let me see. I could never hurt you. Why, I think there's a cut there. Mr. Frangipanni, come quick. Have you any bandages? The boy is hurt. It's a tiny wound but there's lots of blood so it may be very deep. Does it hurt, dear?

No.

Brave boy. Now be still till Mr. Frangipanni comes.
He spoke, Ms. Wynne. Philly spoke.
Joseph, do be still, I have enough trouble without you...
But he spoke, Ms. Wynne. He said "no."
Don't be silly, Joseph.
But he did. He spoke. Didn't you, Philly?
Yes.

Yes.
He turned and looked.
The unicorn nodded its head once and spoke in that high, wavering magical voice.
"THE HORN HEALS."
He repeated it.

Yes. The horn heals.
He spoke! He spoke!
I'll just clean this wound, Philly, don't move. Why—that's strange. There's some blood, but only an old scar. Are you sure you're all right, dear?
Yes.

Yes.
As he watched, the unicorn dipped its horn to him once, then whirled away, disappearing into the dappled light of the trees. He wondered if he would ever capture it right on paper. It was nothing like the sketch he had drawn before. Nothing. But he would try.

Yes, Ms. Wynne, an old scar healed. I'm sure.

ORKNEY LAMENT

When Magnus swam easy in his blood
And the selkies sang his passing,
No one in the islands was surprised.
Living is the miracle, not death.
Between the ice and axe
Lies but little space.

There were dolphins at the bow,
And tunny down below.
Earl Magnus is the sea.

When Magnus flew silent in his blood
And the curlews cried his passing,
No one on the islands was surprised.
Peace is the awkwardness, not war.
Between hawk and hand
Lies but a shield of skin.

There were eagles at the prow,
And osprey at the oars.
Earl Magnus is the dove.

When Magnus fell saintly in his blood
And the oxen wept his passing,
No one on the islands was surprised.

Growing is the prodigy, not rot.
Between stalk and root
Lies but a shaft of green.

There were blossoms on the bough
And petals on the ground.
Earl Magnus is the seed.

ROSECHILD

There once lived an old woman who longed for a child, though she was neither widow nor wed.

One day when she was out in the woods gathering herbs, she heard a cry. She saw nothing nearby but a flowering bush, so she went over to that. There, nestled in the petals of a wild rose, was a tiny babe.

Quickly the old woman picked the child up between her forefinger and thumb, and, wrapping it in her linen kerchief, she brought it to her home. There she made it a cradle from a walnut and lined the shell with soft wool. Then she sat back and wondered how to make the child grow.

"If it were a real child," thought she, "I would feed it pieces of bread sopped in honey and milk till it was quite grown up. But as it is a Rosechild, goodness alone knows what I must do, for I do not."

At last she got up and went to her neighbor Farmer Brow. For surely if anyone would know about raising a child who was born in a flower, a farmer would. So she knocked on his door, and when Brow threw it open, she called:

> *"Farmer Brow, answer me now,*
> *How shall my Rosechild grow?"*

Farmer Brow scratched his head up under his hat and said, "Turn its soil and water it well," for he thought she meant a flowering bush.

So the old woman went home and turned the child around in its cradle and sprinkled it with water from the well. Then she sat down and watched the child for a day. But the Rosechild did not grow.

At last the old woman got up and went to her other neighbor, Squire Bray. For surely if anyone would know how to raise a child born in a flower, a squire would. So she knocked on his door, and when Bray answered it she called:

"Squire Bray, tell me the way
To make my Rosechild grow."

Squire Bray struck his riding stick against his boot and said, "Feed it mash and turn it out to pasture," for he thought she was talking about a horse.

So the old woman went home and fed the Rosechild a meal of mash and put it out into the meadow. Then she settled down on the grass beside it and watched for a day. But the Rosechild did not grow.

At last she got up and put the child back in its walnut cradle and went to see the village priest, Father Bree. For surely if anyone would know how to raise a child born in a flower, a priest would. So she knocked on the vestry door. And when Father Bree came to see who was there, she called:

"Father Bree, tell to me
How shall my Rosechild grow?"

Father Bree fingered his beads and said, "Place it on the Good Book and make a cross on its forehead," for he thought the old woman was beset by a devil.

So the old woman went home and set the Rosechild upon the Good Book and made the sign of the cross on its forehead. Then she settled down and watched the child for a day. But still the Rosechild did not grow.

However, there was no one left to ask. So the old woman threw her apron up over her head and cried out loud:

"Oh me, oh my,
My Rosechild will die."

Just then a small wee voice called out from the walnut shell, "Mama."

The old woman took her apron off her head and saw the Rosechild holding up its hands. She reached over and plucked it up between her forefinger and thumb and cradled it to her cheek. She felt her love flowing out to the tiny child. And she loved it so much, it began to grow and grow and grow till it was old enough and big enough to care for the little old woman. It fed her pieces of bread sopped in milk and honey and anything else she needed or wanted. And from that day on, the house was always filled with the lovely scent of roses.

THE SEVENTH MANDARIN

Once in the East, where the wind blows gently on the bells of the temple, there lived a king of the highest degree. He was a good king. And he knew the laws of his land. But of his people he knew nothing at all, for he had never been beyond the high stone walls that surrounded his palace.

All day long the king read about his kingdom in the books and scrolls that were kept in the palace. And all day long he was guarded and guided by the seven mandarins who had lived all their lives, as the king had, within the palace walls.

These mandarins were honorable men. They dressed in silken robes and wore embroidered slippers. They ate from porcelain dishes and drank the most delicate teas.

Now, while it was important that the mandarins guarded and guided their king throughout his days, they had a higher duty still. At night they were the guardians of the king's soul.

It was written in the books and scrolls of the kingdom that each night the king's soul left his body and flew into the sky on the wings of a giant kite. And the king and the seven mandarins believed that what was written in the books and scrolls was true. And so, each mandarin took turns flying the king's kite through the long, dark hours, keeping it high above the terrors of the night.

This kite was a giant dragon. Its tail was of silk with colored tassels. Its body was etched with gold. And when the sun quit that kingdom in the East, the giant kite rose like a serpent in the wind, flown by one of the seven mandarins.

And for uncounted years it was so.

Now, of all the mandarins, the seventh was the youngest. He was also the most simple. While the other mandarins enjoyed feasting and dancing and many rich pleasures, the seventh mandarin loved only three things in all the world. He loved the king, the books and scrolls of the law, and the king's giant kite.

That he loved his king there was no doubt, for the seventh mandarin would not rest until the king rested.

That he loved the books and scrolls there was also no doubt. Not only did the seventh mandarin believe that what was written therein was true. He also believed that what was *not* written was *not* true.

But more than his king and more than the books and scrolls of the law, the seventh mandarin loved the king's kite, the carrier of the king's soul. He could make it dip and soar and crest the currents of air like a falcon trained to his hand.

One night, when it was the turn of the seventh mandarin to fly the king's kite, the sky was black with clouds. A wild wind like no wind before it entered the kingdom.

The seventh mandarin was almost afraid to fly the kite, for he had never seen such a wind. But he knew that he had to send it into the sky. The king's kite *must* fly, or the king's soul would be in danger. And so the seventh mandarin sent the kite aloft.

The minute the giant kite swam into the sky, it began to rage and strain at the string. It twisted and turned and dived and pulled. The wind gnawed and fretted and goaded the kite, ripping at its tender belly and snatching at its silken tail. At last, with a final snap, the precious kite string parted.

Before the seventh mandarin's eyes, the king's kite sailed wildly over the palace spires, over the roofs of the mandarins' mansions, over the high walls that surrounded the courtyards, and out of sight.

"Come back, come back, O Magnificent Wind Bird," cried the seventh mandarin. "Come back with the king's soul, and I will tip your tail with gold and melt silver onto your wings."

But the kite did not come back.

The seventh mandarin ran down the steps. He put his cape about his face so that no one would know him. He ran through the echoing corridors. He ran past the mandarins' mansions and through the gates of the high palace walls. Then he ran where he had never been before—past the neat houses of the merchants, past the tiny homes of the workers, past the canals that held the peddlers' boats, past the ramshackle, falling-down huts and hovels of the poor.

At last, in the distance, hovering about the hills that marked the edge of the kingdom, the seventh mandarin saw something flutter like a wounded bird in the sky. And though the wind pushed and pulled at his cape and at last tore it from his back, the seventh mandarin did not stop. He ran and ran until he came to the foot of the mountain.

There he found the king's kite. But what a terrible sight met his eyes. The wings of the dragon were dirty and torn. Its tail was shredded and bare. The links of its body were broken apart.

It would never fly again.

The seventh mandarin did not know what to do. He was afraid to return to the palace. It was not that he feared for his own life. He feared for the life of his king. For if the king's soul had flown on the wings of the kite, the king was surely dead.

Yet, much as he was afraid to return, the seventh mandarin was more afraid not to. And so he gathered the king's kite in his arms and began the long, slow journey back.

He carried the king's kite past the canals and the ramshackle, falling-down huts and hovels of the poor. And as he passed with the broken kite in his arms, it came to him that he had never read of such things in the books and scrolls of the kingdom. Yet the cries and groans he heard were not made by the wind.

At last, as the first light of the new day touched the gates of the high palace walls, the seventh mandarin entered the courtyard. He climbed the stairs to his chamber and placed the battered, broken kite on his couch.

Then he sat down and waited to hear of the death of the king.

Scarcely an hour went by before all seven of the mandarins were summoned to the king's chamber. The king lay on his golden bed. His face was pale and still. His hands lay like two withered leaves by his side.

Surely, thought the seventh mandarin, I have killed my king. And he began to weep.

But slowly the king opened his eyes.

"I dreamed a dream last night," he said, his voice low and filled with pain. "I dreamed that in my kingdom there are ramshackle hovels and huts that are falling down."

"It is not so," said the six mandarins, for they had never been beyond the high palace walls and so had never seen such things.

Only the seventh mandarin was silent.

"I dreamed that in my kingdom," continued the king, "there are people who sigh and moan—people who cry and groan when the night is dark and deep."

"It is not so," said the six mandarins, for they had never read of such things in the books and scrolls.

The seventh mandarin was silent.

"If it is not so," said the king, slowly raising his hand to his head, "then how have I dreamed it? For is it not written that the dream is the eye of the soul? And if my soul was flying on the wings of my kite and these things are not so, then how did my dream see all this?"

The six mandarins were silent.

Then the seventh mandarin spoke. He was afraid, but he spoke. And he said, "O King, I saw these same things last night, and I did not dream!"

The six mandarins looked at the seventh mandarin in astonishment.

But the seventh mandarin continued. "The wind was a wild, mad beast. It ripped your kite from my hands. And the kite flew like an angel in the night to these same huts and hovels of which you dreamed. And there are many who moan and sigh, who groan and cry beyond the high palace walls. There are many—although it is not written in any of the books or scrolls of the kingdom."

Then the seventh mandarin bowed his head and waited for his doom. For it was death to fail the king. And it was death to damage his kite. And it was death to say that what was *not* written in the books and scrolls was so.

Then the king spoke, his voice low and crackling like the pages of an ancient book. "For three reasons that you already know, you deserve to die."

The other mandarins looked at one another and nodded.

"But," said the king, sitting up in his golden bed, "for discovering the truth and not fearing to reveal it, you deserve to live." And he signaled the seventh mandarin to stand at his right hand.

That very night, the king and his seven mandarins made their way to the mountain at the edge of the kingdom. There they buried the king's kite with honors.

And the next morning, when the kingdom awoke, the people found that the high walls surrounding the palace had been leveled to the ground.

As for the king, he never again relied solely upon the laws of the land, but instead rode daily with his mandarins through the kingdom. He met with his people and heard their pleas. He listened and looked as well as read.

The mandarins never again had to fly the king's kite as a duty. Instead, once a year, at a great feast, they sent a giant dragon kite into the sky to remind themselves and their king of the folly of believing only what is written.

And the king, with the seventh mandarin always by his side, ruled a land of good and plenty until he came to the end of his days.

Song of the Cailleach Bheur

Do you see her, there, her staff in hand,
Calling the deer behind her.
They come like sheep to the shepherd's pipe,
Running on their toes to find her.

Come down frae the hills you wolves, you swine,
Come down frae the highlands and hollows,
Come down frae the snow-capped mountain fasts
The Cailleach Bheur to follow.

She is the winter, the wind, the snow,
Her breath both warm and chilling.
A single word from her icy lips,
A single kiss is killing.

I kenned her once in the winter tide,
When snow lay on the heather
I saw her dance with the lithesome goats
And the snoutish boar together.

I kenned her wrapped in a winter storm
Like a white shawl on her shoulders,
With icicle drops for earring bobs
Her hair as grey as boulders.

She is the winter, the wind, the snow,
Her breath both warm and chilling.
A single word from her icy lips,
A single kiss is killing.

I have heard that upon the May Day Eve,
Her staff will lie under the holly.
Then she will turn to a standing stane,
Like a tall, indomitable folly.

But I dare ye to gae—as I will not
For fear of hurt and dying—
To gambol beside that great grey stane
The winds aboot ye sighing.

She is the winter, the wind, the snow,
Her breath both warm and chilling.
A single word from her icy lips,
A single kiss is killing.

THE WIND CAP

There was once a lad who would be a sailor but his mother would not let him go to the sea.

"Tush, lad, what do you know of sailing?" she would say. "You are a farmer's son, and the grandson of a farmer. You know the turn of the seasons and the smell of the soil and the way to gentle a beast. You do not know the sea."

Now the boy, whose name was Jon, had always listened to his mother. Indeed, he knew no one else, for his father had died long ago. If his mother said he did not know the sea, then he believed he did not. So he went about his farm work with a heart that longed for sailing but he did not again mention the sea.

One day as he walked behind the plow, he all but ran over a tiny green turtle on a clod of dirt. He picked the turtle up and set it on his head, where he knew the tiny creature would be safe.

When at last he was done with his plowing, Jon led the horse to pasture and then plucked the turtle from his head. To his surprise, he found it had turned into a tiny green fairy man that stood upon his palm and bowed.

"I thank you for your kindness," said the mannikin.

Jon bowed back but said nothing. For his mother had warned him that, when addressed by the fairies, it is best to be still.

"For saving my life, I will give you your heart's desire," said the green mannikin.

Still Jon was silent, but his heart sent out a glory to the sea.

The mannikin could read a heart as easily as a page of a book, so he said, "I see you wish to go sailing."

Jon's face answered for him, though his tongue did not.

"Since you put me on your head like a hat to keep me safe, I shall give you a different kind of cap in return, the kind that sailors most desire. A cap full o' wind. But this one warning: Never a human hand will ever be able to take it off."

Then with a wink and a blink, the fairy man was gone, leaving a striped cap behind.

Young Jon clapped the cap on his head and ran home to tell his mother.

When she heard Jon's story, his mother wept and cried and threw her apron up over her head, for a fairy gift is not altogether a blessing.

"No good will come of this wind cap," she said.

But the lad would have none of her cautions. The sailor's cap had bewitched him utterly. The very next day, without even saying farewell to his mother, he ran off to the sea.

Well, the wind cap worked as the fairy had said, and young Jon could summon breezes at will. But still there was that one condition: Never a human hand could take the cap off.

Now, that was bad and that was good. It was bad because Jon could not take his cap off before his captain nor could he take it off for bed. But it was also good. For neither could he lose the cap nor could it be stolen from him.

And since it was wind that sailors called for, and wind that Jon could supply, he soon was a most popular lad, although he had never before been away from shore. For if he twisted the cap to the right, he summoned the east wind. And if he twisted it to the left, he summoned the west. He could turn the cap to call both north and south winds and all the breezes between.

But if that was good, it was also bad. It was good because it made Jon a popular lad. But it was also bad. For once on board ship, he was not again let ashore. The captain would not part with such a prize.

For a year and a day, young Jon did not set foot on land. He saw neither the turn of the seasons nor the turning of the soil. Nothing but the churning of the waves. And there grew in his heart such a yearning to see the land, that it was soon too much for him to bear.

"Oh, let me go ashore just one day," he begged the captain when they had sighted land. "One day, and I swear I will return."

The captain did not answer.

"Just an hour," cried Jon.

But the captain was still.

"Then may you never see land again just as I cannot," shouted Jon.

The captain called his strongest men and they carried Jon belowdecks. And from that time on he was allowed up above neither night nor day, neither near shore nor on the deepest seas.

But Jon could not stop dreaming of the land. He even talked of it in his sleep. As much as he had once longed for sailing, he now longed for farming.

One quiet afternoon, when the sea was as calm and glassy as a mirror and all the sky reflected in its blue, Jon lay fast asleep in his hammock in the hold. And he fell to dreaming again of the land. Only this dream was brighter and clearer than the others, for though he did not know it, the ship stood offshore from his old farm. In Jon's dream the seasons turned rapidly one into the next. And as each turned, so did Jon in his bed, and the cap on his head was twisted round and about, round and about, round and about again. It called up a squall from the clear sky that hit the ship without a warning.

The wind whirled about the boat from this side and that, ripping and fretting and gnawing the planks. It tore the sails and snapped the spars like kindling.

"It is *his* fault," the sailors cried, dragging Jon up from below. "He has called this wind upon us." And they fell upon Jon, one and another. They shouted their anger and fear. And they tried to rip the cap from his head.

Well, they could not take it from him, for it was a fairy cap. But they pulled it and twisted it one way and the next, and so the squall became a storm, the mightiest they had ever seen.

The ship's sides gave out a groan that was answered by the wind. And every plank and board shuddered.

Then the captain cried out above his terrified men. "Bring me that cap boy. I shall rid the ship of him." And when Jon was brought before him, the captain grabbed him by the tail of his striped cap and twisted Jon three times and flung him far out to sea.

But the winds called up by the cap spun the ship those same three times around. It turned turtle, its hull to the sky, and sank to the bottom of the sea.

As Jon went under the waves, fingers of foam snatched off the cap. And as it came off, the storm stopped, the sea became calm, and Jon swam ashore. The cap followed in his wake.

When he got to land, Jon picked up the cap and tucked it into his shirt. Then, without a backward glance at the sea, he found his way home to his mother and his farm. He was a farmer's son, no doubt.

But in the winter, when the crops lay gathered in the barn and the snow lay heavy on the fields, he began to dream again of the sea. Of the sea when he had stood his watch and the world rocked endlessly and smelled of salt.

So Jon went to the wardrobe and got out the fairy cap and stood a long moment staring at it.

Then he tucked the cap into his shirt and went out to the field where he had found the fairy man. Looking up the field and down, over the furrows lined with snow, Jon smiled. He placed the wind cap under a stone where he knew the mannikin would find it. For magic is magic and not for men. Then he left again for the sea.

And this set the pattern of his days. For the rest of his life Jon spent half the year on a ship and half on the shore, 'til at last he owned his own boat and a hundred-acre farm besides. And he was known far and wide as Captain Turtle, for, as all his neighbors and shipmates knew, he was as much at home on the water as he was on the land.

THE KING'S DRAGON

There was once a soldier who had fought long and hard for his king. He had been wounded in the war and sent home for a rest.

Hup and one. Hup and two. He marched down the long, dusty road, using a crutch.

He was a member of the Royal Dragoons, His red-and-gold uniform was dirty and torn. And in the air of the winter's day, his breath plumed out before him like a cloud.

Hup and one. Hup and two. Wounded or not, he marched with a proud step. For the Royal Dragoons are the finest soldiers in the land and—they always obey orders.

After a bit, the soldier came upon a small village. House after house nestled together in a line.

"Just the place to stop for the night," thought the dragoon to himself. So he hupped and one, hupped and two, up to the door of the very first house. He blew the dust from his uniform, polished the medals on his chest with his sleeve till they clinked and clanked together and shone like small suns. Then he knocked on the door with his crutch.

Now that very first house belonged to a widow and she, poor woman, was slightly deaf. When she finally heard the sound of the knock, she called out in a timid voice, "Who is there?"

The soldier puffed out his chest. He struck his crutch smartly on the ground. "I am a Royal Dragoon," he said, "and I am tired and hungry and would like to come in."

The woman began to shake. "The royal *dragon?*" she cried, for she had not heard him clearly. "I did not know the king had one. But if it is a dragon, and hungry besides, I certainly do not want him here. For he will eat up all l have and me as well!" She so frightened herself that she threw her apron up over her head and called out, *"Go away!"* Then weeping and wailing, she ran out her back door to her neighbor's home.

The Royal Dragoon did not see her leave, of course. But as she had told him to go, go he did, for the Royal Dragoons are the finest soldiers in the land and—they always obey orders.

Hup and one. Hup and two. He marched to the second house and knocked on the door. He stood at attention, his chest puffed out, and in the cold, wintry air, his breath plumed out before him like a cloud.

Now that second house belonged to the widow's father, and he, poor man, was nearly blind. He listened to his daughter's story, and when the knock came, the two of them crept up to the window. She still had her apron up over her head, and he could see no farther than the end of his nose. They peered out, and all they saw was the great plume of breath coming from the soldier's mouth.

"See," said the daughter, "it *is* a dragon. And he is breathing smoke."

"Who is there?" called out the old man in a timid voice.

"I am a Royal Dragoon," said the soldier. As he spoke, even more clouds streamed from his mouth. "I am tired and hungry and would like to come in."

"Go *away!*" cried the old man. "No one is here." Then he and his daughter ran out the back way to their neighbor's house, weeping as they went.

The Royal Dragoon did not see them leave, of course. But as he had been told to go, go he did, for the Royal Dragoons are the finest soldiers in the land and—they always obey orders.

Hup and one. Hup and two. He marched to the third house and knocked on the door. He stood at attention, his chest puffed out, and saluted so smartly his medals clinked and clanked together.

Now the third house belonged to the mayor, and a very smart young mayor he was, He could see perfectly well. He could hear perfectly well. And when the widow and her father finished their story, the mayor said: "The king's dragon, eh? And just listen to that! I hear his scales clinking and clanking together. He must be terribly hungry indeed and ready to pounce."

So the mayor called out the door, *"Wait,* Sir Dragon." Then the mayor and the widow and the widow's father ran out the back. They gathered together all the other people in the town, and without even taking time to pick up their belongings, they ran and ran as fast as they could, until they came to the mountains, where a very real dragon lived. When it came out and ate them all up, not a one of them was surprised. They were already convinced of dragons, you see.

As for the Royal Dragoon, he stood waiting at attention in front of the third house for a very, very, very long time. He may be standing there still. For the Royal Dragoons are the finest soldiers in the land. And— they always obey orders.

326

WHEN RAVEN SANG

When Raven sang among the constellations,
fathers plucked their newborns,
red with birthblood,
from between the mothers' thighs,
saying, "He is already dying,"
to fool the messengers of death.

My father did not see me
till the day after I was born;
did not hold me wrapped and diapered
till the day after that.

What is it about our men:
they cannot contain chaos,
they dare not trick the angels,
fearing to trade their own short lives
for the life of the newborn child.

THE RIVER MAID

There was once a rich farmer named Jan who decided to expand his holdings. He longed for the green meadow that abutted his farm with a passion that amazed him. But a swift river ran between the two. It was far too wide and far too deep for his cows to cross.

He stood on the river bank and watched the water hurtle over its rocky course.

"I could build a bridge," he said aloud. "But, then, any fool could do that. And I am no fool."

At his words the river growled, but Jan did not heed it.

"No!" Jan said with a laugh, "I shall build no bridge across this water. I shall make the river move aside for me." And so he planned how he would dam it up, digging a canal along the outer edge of the meadow, and so allow his cows the fresh green grass.

As if guessing Jan's thoughts, the river roared out, tumbling stones in its rush to be heard. But Jan did not understand it. Instead, he left at once to go to the town where he purchased the land and supplies.

The men Jan hired dug and dug for weeks until a deep ditch and a large dam had been built. Then they watched as the river slowly filled up behind the dam. And when, at Jan's signal, the gate to the canal was opened, the river was forced to move into its new course and leave its comfortable old bed behind.

At that, Jan was triumphant. He laughed and turned to the waiting men. "See!" he called out loudly, "I am not just Jan the Farmer. I am Jan the River Tamer. A wave of my hand, and the water must change its way."

His words troubled the other men. They spat between their fingers and made other signs against the evil eye. But Jan paid them no mind. He was the last to leave the river's side that evening and went home well after dark.

The next morning, Jan's feeling of triumph had not faded and he went down again to the path of the old river which was now no more than mud and mire. He wanted to look at the desolation and dance over the newly dried stones.

But when he got to the river's old bed, he saw someone lying face up in the center of the waterless course. It was a girl clothed only in a white shift that clung to her body like a skin.

Fearing her dead, Jan ran through the mud and knelt by her side. He put out his hand but could not touch her. He had never seen anyone so beautiful.

Fanned out about her head, her hair was a fleece of gold, each separate strand distinguishable. Fine gold hairs lay molded on her forearms and like wet down upon her legs. On each of her closed eyelids a drop of river water glistened and reflected back to him his own staring face.

At last Jan reached over and touched her cheek, and at his touch, her eyes opened wide. He nearly drowned in the blue of them.

He lifted the girl up in his arms, never noticing how cold her skin or how the mud stuck nowhere to her body or her shift, and he carried her up onto the bank. She gestured once towards the old river bank and let out a single mewling cry. Then she curled in towards his body, nestling, and seemed to sleep.

Not daring to wake her again, Jan carried her home and put her down by the hearth. He lit the fire, though it was late spring and the house already quite warm. Then he sat by the sleeping girl and stared.

She lay in a curled position for some time. Only the slow pulsing of her back told him that she breathed. Then, as dusk settled about the house, bringing with it a half-light, the girl gave a sudden sigh and stretched. Then she sat up and stared. Her arms went out before her as if she were swimming in the air. Jan wondered for a moment if she were blind.

Then the girl leaped up in one fluid movement and began to sway, to dance upon the hearthstones. Her feet beat swiftly and she turned round and round in dizzying circles. She stopped so suddenly that Jan's head still spun. He saw that she was now perfectly dry except for one side of her shift; the left hem and skirt were still damp and remained molded against her.

"Turn again," Jan whispered hoarsely, suddenly afraid.

The girl looked at him and did not move.

When he saw that she did not understand his tongue, Jan walked over to her and led her back to the fire. Her hand was quite cold in his. But she smiled shyly up at him. She was small, only chest high, and Jan himself was not a large man. Her skin, even in the darkening house, was so white it glowed with a fierce light. Jan could see the rivulets of her veins where they ran close to the surface, at her wrists and temples.

He stayed with her by the fire until the heat made him sweat. But though she stood silently, letting the fire warm her first one side and then the other, her skin remained cold, and the left side of her shift would not dry.

Jan knelt down before her and touched the damp hem. He put his cheek against it.

"Huttah!" he cried at last. "I know you now. You are a river maid. A water spirit. I have heard of such. I believed in them when I was a child."

The water girl smiled steadily down at him and touched his hair with her fingers, twining the strands round and about as if weaving a spell.

Jan felt the touch, cold and hot, burn its way down the back of his head and along his spine. He remembered with dread all the old tales. To hold such a one against her will meant death. To love such a one meant despair.

He shook his head violently and her hand fell away. "How foolish," Jan thought. "Old wives and children believe such things. I do not love her, beautiful as she is. And as for the other, how am I to know what is her will? If we cannot talk the same tongue, I can only guess her wants." He rose and went to the cupboard and took out bread and cheese and a bit of salt fish which he put before her.

The river maid ate nothing. Not then or later. She had only a few drops of water before the night settled in.

When the moon rose, the river maid began to pace restlessly about the house. Wall to wall, she walked. She went to the window and put her hand against the glass. She stood by the closed door and put her shoulder to the wood, but she would not touch the metal latch.

It was then that Jan was sure of her. "Cold iron will keep her in." He was determined she would stay at least until the morning.

The river maid cried all the night, a high keening that rose and fell like waves. But in the morning she seemed accommodated to the house and settled quietly to sleep by the fire. Once in a while, she would stretch and stand, the damp left side of her shift clinging to her thigh. In the half-light of the hearth she seemed even more beautiful than before.

Jan left a bowl of fresh water near the fire, with some cress by it, before he went to feed the cows. But he checked the latch on the windows and set a heavy iron bar across the outside of the door.

"I will let you go tonight," he promised slowly. *"Tonight,"* he said, as if speaking to a child. But she did not know his language and could not hold him to his vow.

By the next morning, he had forgotten making it.

For a year Jan kept her. He grew to like the wavering sounds she made as she cried each night. He loved the way her eyes turned a deep green when he touched her. He was fascinated by the blue veins that meandered at her throat, along the backs of her knees, and laced each small breast. Her mouth was always cold under his.

Fearing the girl might guess the working of window or gate, Jan fashioned iron chains for the glass and an ornate grillwork for the door. In that way, he could open them to let in air and let her look out at the sun and moon and season's changes. But he did not let her go. And as she never learned to speak with him in his tongue and thereby beg for release, Jan convinced himself that she was content.

Then it was spring again. Down from the mountains came the swollen streams, made big with melted snow. The river maid drank whole glasses of water now, and put on weight. Jan guessed that she carried his child, for her belly grew, she moved slowly and no longer tried to dance. She sat by the window at night with her arms raised and sang strange, wordless tunes, sometimes loud and sometimes soft as a cradle song. Her voice was as steady as the patter of the rain, and underneath Ian fancied he heard a growing strength. His nights became as restless as hers, his sleep full of watery dreams.

The night of the full moon, the rain beat angrily against the glass as if insisting on admission. The river maid put her head to one side, listening. Then she rose and left her window place. She stretched and put her hands to her back, then traced them slowly around her sides to the front. She moved heavily to the hearth and sat. Bracing both hands on the stones behind her, she spread her legs, crooked at the knees.

Jan watched as her belly rolled in great waves under the tight white shift.

She threw her head back, gasped at the air, and then, with a great cry of triumph, expelled the child. It rode a gush of water between her legs and came to rest at Ian's feet. It was small and fishlike, with a translucent tail. It looked up at him with blue eyes that were covered with a veil of skin. The skin lifted once, twice, then closed again as the child slept.

Jan cried because it was a beast.

At that very moment, the river outside gave a shout of release. With the added waters from the rain and snow, it had the strength to push through the earth dam. In a single wave, that gathered force as it rolled, it rushed across the meadow. through the farmyard and barn, and overwhelmed the house. It broke the iron gates and grilles as if they were brittle sticks, washing them away in its flood. Then it settled back into its old course, tumbling over familiar rocks and rounding the curves it had cut in its youth.

When the neighbors came the next day to assess the damage, they found no trace of the house or of Jan. "Gone," said one.

"A bad end," said another.

"Never change a river," said a third.

They spat through their fingers and made other signs against evil. Then they went home to their own fires and gave it no more thought.

But a year later, in a pocket of the river, in a quiet place said to house a great fish with a translucent tail, an inquisitive boy found a jumble of white bones.

His father and the other men guessed the bones to be Jan's, and they left them to the river instead of burying them.

When the boy asked why, his father said, "Huttah! Hush, boy, and listen."

The boy listened and heard the river playing merrily over the bones. It was a high, sweet, bubbling song. And anyone with half an ear could hear that the song, though wordless, or at least in a language unknown to men, was full of freedom and a conquering joy.

Swan/Princess

1.

When the change came
she was sitting in the garden
embroidering an altar cloth,
thin gold thread working the crown of Christ.
First her neck
arching like cathedral vaultings.
Dress ripping at the shoulders accommodated wings:
white-vaned, white-feathered like Oriental smocking.
Hands and feet tangling into orange legs,
inelegant, powerful as camshafts.
When her head went, she cried,
not for pain but for the loss
of her soft, thin lips
so recently kissed by the prince.
Not even the sweet air,
not even earth unfolding beneath her
recompensed for those lost kisses
or the comfort of his human arms.

2.

When the change came
she was floating in the millpond,
foam like white lace tracing her wake.
First her neck shrinking,
candle to candleholder,
the color of old, used wax.
Wings collapsing like fans;
one feather left,
floating memory on the churning water.
Powerful legs devolving;
powerful beak dissolving.
She would have cried for the pain of it
had not remembrance of sky sustained her.
A startled look on the miller's face
as she rose, naked and dripping,
recalled her to laughter,
the only thing she had really missed as a swan.

FLIGHT

I cannot tell you when I first heard about the winged horse. I can only tell you about the first time I rode him. It was a dark, moonless night in Corinth, for I dared not chance Athena spying me in her horse's field. She is not the kind to let such daring go unpunished. The gods only allow favors to those already favored, haven't you noticed? So, what chance had I, being neither well bred nor good looking but rather scrawny, small, and poor. The gods swat such mortals like horseflies.

The field was cut through by several streams. Later it was said that Peg himself had stamped a foot and forced a fountain. The fountain even had a name—Hippocrene. Storytellers like to make specific what they do not know. It lends a certain authenticity to the tale. But even for a god's horse, that was assuming much too much. He merely drank at one particular stream more often than at any of the others, for it had a well aerated flow of water. I expect the bubbles tickled his nose. Horses can have a sense of humor, you know, though that may be difficult for most people to understand. Peg certainly did. He liked the kind of jokes that manifested in snorting and drooling prodigiously over someone's new clothes, or dumping an unsuspecting rider into a still-warm pile of droppings. Not very sophisticated, of course. But he was only a horse, after all. I have known shopkeepers and temple virgins who had even coarser ideas of fun. And my stepfather, cursed be, used to laugh uproariously whenever he beat me, as if each stripe on my back were a laugh line.

I found all the streams in Peg's field by wading through each and everyone unexpectedly. They were cold and rocky, and my sandals were no proof against either. But I had never thought that getting through the night was going to be easy, so I didn't complain. At least not out loud. I might have caught my breath once or twice at the chill in the water, let out a whispered curse now and then when I slipped off a stone. But my heart was already racing just by being in Athena's field uninvited. "No man who is not a god's son may ride," was what was said about her horse. That warning was even posted on signs at the field's perimeters. So what was a bit of wet, a bit of cold, a twisted ankle, such minor shocks to the system, compared to the things an angry goddess might come up with if she caught you out?

After the fifth stream, I found myself in the main part of the field at last. I stopped still and listened hard. Horses are not quiet creatures, not even at night, not even in sleep. I could hear the harsh rales of his breathing from halfway across the green. I took my bearings by that sound, as might a sailor by the stars.

He could have heard me coming. He certainly showed no fear. But as I drew closer, his breathing never changed, though my own did. I could hear it moving deeper and deeper into my chest. I tried holding my breath so as not to alarm him, though I am sure the *swish-swash* of the grass at my feet had already done enough to alert him. Still, I held my breath as I held my entire body, in a kind of watchful readiness.

And then, before I was quite prepared for it, I was by his side. He was a great furnace of a creature, his white body exuding warmth. Without moonlight he was still aglow, as if lit up from within. I hadn't seen that coming across the field, yet it was all I *could* see now. The whiteness of him. The purity. The glow.

I put out my hand to touch his white flank. He shuddered a bit under my touch, live flesh crawling. But it was just a momentary shiver, and then the skin was still.

His big head slowly turned my way, and he sniffed me all over, starting down at my knees and working his way up until we were finally nose to nose. I put both hands on either side of his big muzzle, and breathed into each nostril. It was something my stepfather, a horse coper, had taught me. Something the poorest of us knows and yet kings never seem to have heard of. Breath to breath with a horse, and he is yours.

Actually, he would *never* be mine. He was Athena's. And one day he would be a hero's. There was no denying that. But tonight—breath in, breath out—he belonged to poor, scrawny me.

He finished his examination at the top of my head, then took a piece of my hair—my long, stringy, no-color hair—into his teeth and yanked. See—that horse sense of humor again.

It hurt, of course, but I laughed. I had to. It really *was* funny. He whinnied back, appreciating my appreciation. Comics do like their bit of applause.

I ran my hand over his head, scratched behind his ears, stroked his neck. Then I spent long minutes untangling the strands of his mane, thinking as I did so how ill-kept this god's horse was when even the meanest of peasants will spend hours braiding his horse's mane for a fair.

"If you were mine," I whispered, "you would have blue ribbons every day and red ones for the holy days." Though of course I had no coins to do any such thing.

He nuzzled me as I worked and I began to sing, one of the old songs from before even Athena's time. My mother's mother had taught it to me. It had to do with the rule of women, and the chorus went

> *"Maiden came I and crone I go,*
> *The wisdom of water is what I know."*

It was not a song I dared sing at home, for it would have meant another beating. My stepfather was not a man who appreciated women, except in his bed. And those he liked well enough. as long as he could master them.

Peg seemed to like the sound of the song. though, and he leaned into me as I sang. Either that or he liked the feel of my fingers in his mane. Or maybe a bit of both.

When at last his hair was untangled, I braided it into twenty small. braids, all by feel as there was no light but his own white coat to guide by. And then when he was ready, I led him by the forelock to a large stone I had stumbled over on my way across the field. He stood quietly while I climbed up, first on to the stone, and then onto his back. I was expecting an explosion once I was atop, for he had never been ridden before, but surprisingly he did not move. He did not even tremble.

"Oh, mighty Peg," I whispered, leaning forward and putting my cheek down against the arch of his neck.

In response, he lifted his great feathered wings till they stretched out on either side of us. He pumped them once, then twice. The wind from those wings was both warm and cold. Still wet from the streams I had crossed, I began to shiver.

But before I could dismount, before I could even *think* about dismounting, he had lifted up, straight up, hovering for a moment like a kestrel over a meadow. Then he took off into the air straight as an arrow. I had barely time to grab hold of his mane and wrap my legs tight around the great vaulted barrel that was his body.

We flew up and up and up above the field, a solid black space below us. Then we flew above the nearby mountains, their jagged peaks black against the blacker sky, with only the flickering stars showing the outlines.

And then we were above the clouds themselves, the air about us so cold I could scarcely breathe. I could not call out his name. But I smiled and kept my fingers wound in his mane, my legs clamped to his sides.

The world, which I had always known as dangerous and mean, was far away. For the first time in my life I felt powerful and pure and out of reach. Tears froze on my cheeks, but still I smiled.

Then, suddenly, like a stooping hawk, Peg clipped his wings back and we fell straight down, down, down, the wind screaming against our ears. I thought it was to be my death, but for the life of me could not care.

At the very last moment, Peg unfurled his wings again, like a flag over battle. We floated down to land in the field, so lightly I did not really know when we had reached ground except that he flung his head back, neighed, then trotted over to the stone, to wait patiently for me to dismount.

When I got off, stunned and sore, there was Athena standing tall, grim, unsmiling, her baleful face furious. Even in the dark I could see how she looked, for it was as if she, too, were lighted from within, only it was with a goddess' righteous anger. I thought suddenly how easy and glorious it would have been to have died falling out of the sky and how painful and ugly it was going to be to die on the point of her spear.

"No man who is not a god's son may ride my horse," she said in her doom-filled voice: "I do not think you can make that claim."

I did not speak. Indeed I could not even if I'd wanted to. But Peg whinnied and moved his head close to my body. With his teeth he ripped down the top of my chiton. Another bit of his humor, I supposed as I shivered in the cold. This time I did not smile but put my hands up over my goosefleshed breasts.

"A girl!" Athena cried. "By my father, then. You are no *man* at all, and so are under my protection." She had the grace to laugh. It was a golden sound, like a full descending scale on the lyre.

She disappeared, still laughing, leaving me to the cold and to a long, wet walk back over the field, and streams to Corinth. I had plenty of time to make up an explanation for my torn chiton, but none came to me. I told my stepfather the simple truth of it but he, used to my lying, did not believe a word of it. Certain another man had had me, he died of his rage, face purple, head down in a manure pile.

I was never certain if that was part of Athena's protection, or her idea of a cosmic joke. She had her horse's sense of humor. But either way it served me well. And that was only my *first* ride.

SOMEWHEN

Once, and it does not matter what the day, a young boy named Tom was traveling down a road to seek his fortune. The road was long, the sun was hot, and finally, where the road forked, the boy saw a tree.

"There," thought he, "I will rest a while and think about my fortune. For whether it is good or bad, it is certain that it lies ahead of me."

And so thinking, the boy made his way to the tree. Only, when he came to it, he found its shadow occupied by an old man who lay asleep. Being a good boy, Tom sat down in the sun quietly and waited for the old man to waken and share the cooling shade with him.

At last the old man opened his eyes and signaled with them for Tom to come closer. And if by then the sun was down and shadows lay all about, Tom did not complain, for he knew his fortune lay ahead while the old man's lay behind.

"I am seeking my fortune, old man," said Tom. "Can you point which way is best?"

The old man looked up the road and down. He looked east and he looked west. Then he shook his head. "My eyes are poor," he said to Tom. "Used to be I could see the wind."

"Well then, grandfather," continued Tom, "perhaps you have heard which way the wide world lies."

The old man put his head to one side and listened. Then he put his head to the other. Then he shook it. "My ears are poor, too," said he. "Used to be I could hear the grass."

Tom sat down and puzzled over this for a while. "Old father," he said at last, "do you know of a place I could go? A place to seek my fortune?"

"*Somewhen* is the best I can say," said the old man. Then he looked strangely at Tom and added, "Three's enough." He creaked to his feet, stretched, and disappeared behind the tree. Tom, being a good boy, did not follow. Instead he settled himself under the branches and slept until morning. When the sun rose slowly in the east, Tom rose, too. And he chose the fork in the road he hoped would lead him to *Somewhen*.

Tom traveled many days and did many deeds. He dug gold in the hills and dived for pearls in the sea. He climbed mountains and descended into caves. He slept hungry and he slept full. And he saw all there was to see in the world, and a lot more, too. But still he searched for *Somewhen*.

At last, however, he met a lovely girl whose hair was brushed with sunlight and whose hands were meant to rock cradles. And so Tom put *Somewhen* aside, planted grass and grain, and grew a world around his house.

And if he thought about *Somewhen,* it was as if it had been a tale he read one time as a child. It never troubled his mind at all.

Only one day, when he had grown old and his grandchildren sat by his side at the hearth and asked about the wide world, Old Tom told them about his travels.

"Yes," he said, "I roamed the world when I was young. Searching for things—I do not remember what. Found some. Didn't find others. But what was important was that I traveled some when I was young."

And then he stopped, for a memory caught him. "I traveled *some when* I was young. *Somewhen.*" Was that what the old man had meant? In the seeking was the finding? But Old Tom did not say that out loud.

And a few days later, Old Tom was sitting under a tree when a young lad, dusted with the road's winding, stopped a bit.

"Old man," said the lad, "I am seeking my fortune. Can you tell me which way to go?"

Old Tom settled his back against the tree and gazed at the sky. The clouds were passing quickly by. "Why," he replied, knowing it might take the lad years to puzzle out the answer—hard years but good years— *"Somewhen's* the best I know."

And then he closed his eyes and slept.

MY FATHER DIED SEVEN TIMES

My father died seven times before the end.
Each time I sat by his bedside,
A vigil in the lowering dark,
Except for the last, except for the very last.
If there really is a god,
He is Loki, Coyote, Anansi, Puck,
Stirring the world's pot, spitting in the stew.
Six times I sat there through the night,
Like a new mother by her infant's crib,
Watching his chest rise and fall and rise—
My own private corn god—and never saw him die
As he did in the daylight, after I had gone home,
To snatch my own sleep in a curtained room.
My father died on the seventh try,
Between two breaths, as the nurse took his pulse,
Which beat so strongly till the very end,
One moment here, then gone. Then gone.

THE FACE IN THE CLOTH

There was once a king and queen so in love with one another that they could not bear to be parted, even for a day. To seal their bond they desperately wanted a child. The king had even made a cradle of oak for the babe with his own hands and placed it by their great canopied bed. But year in and year out the cradle stood empty.

At last one night, when the king was fast asleep, the queen left their bed. She cast one long, lingering glance at her husband, then, disguising herself with a shawl around her head, she crept out of the castle, for the first time alone. She was bound for a nearby forest where she had heard three witch-sisters lived. The queen had been told that they might give her what she most desired by taking from her what she least desired to give.

"But I have so much," she thought as she ran through the woods. "Gold and jewels beyond counting. Even the diamond which the king himself put on my hand and from which I would hate to be parted. But though it is probably what I would least desire to give, I would give it gladly to have a child."

The witches' hut squatted in the middle of the wood and through its window the queen saw the three old sisters sitting by the fire, chanting a spell as soft as a cradle song:

> *Needle and scissors,*
> *Scissors and pins,*
> *Where one life ends,*
> *Another begins.*

And suiting their actions to the words, the three snipped and sewed, snipped and sewed with invisible thread over and over and over again.

The night was so dark and the three slouching sisters so strange that the queen was quite terrified. But her need was even greater than her fear. She scratched upon the window and the three looked up from their work.

"Come in," they called out in a single voice.

So she had to go, pulled into the hut by that invisible thread.

"What do you want, my dear?" said the first old sister to the queen through the pins she held in her mouth.

"I want a child," said the queen.

"When do you want it?" asked the second sister, who held a needle high above her head.

"As soon as I can get it," said the queen, more boldly now.

"And what will you give for it?" asked the third, snipping her scissors ominously.

"Whatever is needed," replied the queen. Nervously, she turned the ring with the diamond around her finger.

The three witches smiled at one another. Then they each held up a hand with the thumb and forefinger touching in a circle.

"Go," they said. "It is done. All we ask is to be at the birthing to sew the swaddling cloth."

The queen stood still as stone, a river of feelings washing around her. She had been prepared to gift them a fortune. What they asked was so simple, she agreed at once. Then she turned and ran out of the hut all the way to the castle. She never looked back.

Less than a year later the queen was brought to childbed. But in her great joy she forgot to mention her promise to the king. And then in her great pain, and because it had been such a small promise after all, she forgot it altogether.

As the queen lay in labor in her canopied bed, there came a knock on the castle door. When the guards opened it, who should be standing there but three slouching old women.

"We have come to be with the queen," said the one with pins in her mouth.

The guards shook their heads.

"The queen promised we could make the swaddling cloth," said the second, holding her needle high over her head.

"We must be by her side," said the third, snapping her scissors.

One guard was sent to tell the king.

The king came to the castle door, his face red with anger, his brow wreathed with sweat.

"The queen told me of no such promise," he said. "And she tells me everything. What possesses you to bother a man at a time like this? Be gone." He dismissed them with a wave of his hand.

But before the guards could shut the door upon the ancient sisters, the one with the scissors called out: "Beware, oh king, of promises given."

Then all three chanted:

> *Needle and scissors,*
> *Scissors and pins,*
> *Where one life ends.*
> *Another begins.*

The second old woman put her hands above her head and made a circle with her forefinger and thumb. But the one with the pins in her mouth thrust a piece of cloth into the king's hand.

"It is for the babe," she said. "Because of the queen's desire."

Then the three left the castle and were not seen there again.

The king started to look down at the cloth, but there came a loud cry from the bed chamber. He ran back, along the corridors, and when he entered the bedroom door the doctor turned around, a newborn child still red with birthblood in his hands.

"It is a girl, sire," he said.

There was a murmur of praise from the attending women.

The king put out his hands to receive the child and, for the first time really noticed the cloth he was holding. It was pure white, edged with lace. As he looked at it, his wife's likeness began to appear on it slowly as if being stitched in with a crimson thread. First the eyes he so loved, then the elegant nose, the soft, full mouth, the dimpled chin.

The king was about to remark on it when the midwife cried out. "It is the queen, sire. She is dead." And at the same moment, the doctor put the child into his hands.

The royal funeral and the royal christening were held on the same day and no one in the kingdom knew whether to laugh or cry except the babe, who did both.

Since the king could not bear to part with his wife entirely, he had the lace-edged cloth with her likeness sewn into the baby's cloak so that wherever she went, the princess carried her mother's face.

As she grew out of one cloak, the while lace cloth was cut away from the old and sewn into the new. And in this way the princess was never without the panel bearing her mother's portrait nor was she ever allowed to wander far from her father's watchful eyes. Her life was measured by the size of the cloaks, which were cut bigger each year, and the likeness of her mother, which seemed to get bigger as well.

The princess grew taller but she did not grow stronger. She was like a pale copy of her mother. There was never a time that the bloom of health sat on her cheeks. She remained the color of skimmed milk, the color of ocean foam, the color of second-day snow. She was always cold, sitting huddled for warmth inside her picture cloak even on the hottest days, and nothing could part her from it.

The king despaired of his daughter's health, but neither the royal physicians nor the royal philosophers could help. He turned to necromancers and star-gazers, to herbalists and diviners. They pushed and prodded and prayed over the princess. They examined the soles of her feet and the movement of her stars. But still she sat cold and whey-colored, wrapped in her cloak.

At last one night, when everyone was fast asleep, the king left his bed and crept out of the castle alone. He had heard that there were three witch sisters who lived nearby who might give him what he most desired by taking from him what he least desired to give. Having lost his queen, he knew there was nothing else he would hate losing, not his fortune, his kingdom, or his throne. He would give it all up gladly to see his daughter, who was his wife's pale reflection, sing and dance and run.

The witchs' hut squatted in the middle of the wood and through its window the king saw the three old sisters. He did not recognize them but they knew him at once.

"Come in, come in," they called out, though he had not knocked. And he was drawn into the hut as if pulled by an invisible thread.

"We know what you want," said the first.

"We can give you what you most desire," said the second.

"By taking what you least wish to give," said the third.

"I have already lost my queen," he said. "So anything else I have is yours so long as my daughter is granted a measure of health." And he started to twist off the ring he wore on his third finger, the ring his wife had been pledged with, to give to the three sisters to seal his part of the bargain.

"Then you must give us—your daughter," said the three.

The king was stunned. For a moment the only sound in the hut was the crackle of fire in the hearth.

"*Never!*" he thundered at last. "What you ask is impossible."

"What *you* ask is impossible," said the first old woman. "Nonetheless we promise it will be so." She stood. "But if your daughter does not come to us, her life will be worth no more than this." She took a pin from her mouth and held it up. It caught the firelight for a moment. Only a moment.

The king stared. "I know you," he said slowly. "I have seen you before."

The second sister nodded. "Our lives have been sewn together by a queen's desire," she said. She pulled the needle through a piece of cloth she was holding and drew the thread through in a slow, measured stitch.

The third sister began to chant, and at each beat her scissors snapped together:

> Needle and scissors,
> Scissors and pins,
> Where one life ends,
> Another begins.

The king cursed them thoroughly, his words hoarse as a rote of war, and left. But partway through the forest, he thought of his daughter like a waning moon asleep in her bed, and wept.

For days he raged in the palace and his courtiers felt his tongue as painfully as if it were a whip. Even his daughter, usually silent in her shroudlike cloak, cried out.

"Father," she said, "your anger unravels the kingdom, pulling at its loosest threads. What is it? What can I do?" As she spoke, she pulled the cloak more firmly about her shoulders and the king could swear that the portrait of his wife moved, the lips opening and closing as if the image spoke as well.

The king shook his head and put his hands to his face. "You are all I have left of her," he mumbled. "And now 1 must let you go."

The princess did not understand, but she put her small faded hands on his. "You must do what you must do, my father," she said.

And though he did not quite understand the why of it, the king brought his daughter into the wood the next night after dark. Setting her on his horse and holding the bridle himself, he led her along the path to the hut of the three crones.

At the door he kissed her once on each cheek and then tenderly kissed the image on her cloak. Then, mounting his horse, he galloped away without once looking back.

Behind him, the briars closed over the path and the forest was still.

Once her father had left, the princess looked around the dark clearing. When no one came to fetch her, she knocked upon the door of the little hut. Getting no answer, she pushed the door open and went in.

The hut was empty, though a fire burned merrily in the hearth. The table was set and beside the wooden plate were three objects: a needle, a scissors, and a pin. On the hearth wall, engraved in the stone, was a poem. The princess went over to the fire to read it:

Needle and scissors,
Scissors and pins,
Where one life ends
Another begins.

"How strange," thought the princess, shivering inside her cloak.

She looked around the little hut, found a bed with a wooden head-board shaped like a loom, lay down upon the bed and, pulling the cloak around her even more tightly, slept.

In the morning when the princess woke, she was still alone, but there was food on the table, steaming hot. She rose and made a feeble toilette, for there were no mirrors on the wall, and ate the food. All the while, she toyed with the needle, scissors, and pin by her plate. She longed for her father and the familiarity of the court, but her father had left her at the hut and, being an obedient child, she stayed.

As she finished her meal, the hearth fire went out and soon the hut grew chilly. So the princess went outside and sat on a wooden bench by the door. Sunlight illuminated the clearing and wrapped around her shoulders like a golden cloak. Alternately she dozed and woke and dozed again until it grew dark.

When she went inside the hut, the table was once more set with food and this time she ate eagerly, then went to sleep, dreaming of the needle and scissors and pin. In her dream they danced away from her, refusing to bow when she bade them. She woke to a cold dawn.

The meal was ready and the smell of it, threading through the hut, got her up. She wondered briefly what hands had done all the work but, being a princess and used to being served, she did not wonder about it very long.

When she went outside to sit in the sun, she sang snatches of old songs to keep herself company. The sound of her own voice, tentative and slightly off key, was like an old friend. One tune kept running around and around in her head and though she did not know where she had heard it before, it fitted perfectly the words carved over the hearth:

Needle and scissors,
Scissors and pins,
Where one life ends
Another begins.

"That is certainly true," she told herself, "for my life here in the forest is different than my life in the castle, though I myself do not feel changed." And she shivered and pulled the cloak around her.

Several times she stood and walked about the clearing, looking for the path that led out. But it was gone. The brambles were laced firmly together like stitches on a quilt, and when she put a hand to them, a thorn pierced her palm and the blood dripped down onto her cloak, spotting the portrait of her mother and making it look as if she were crying red tears.

It was then the princess knew that she had been abandoned to the magic in the forest. She wondered that she was not more afraid and tried out different emotions: first fear, then bewilderment, then loneliness, but none of them seemed quite real to her. What she felt, she decided at last, was a kind of lightness, a giddiness, as if she had lost her center, as if she were a balloon, untethered and ready—at last—to let go.

"What a goose I have become," she said aloud. "One or two days without the prattle of courtiers and I am talking to myself."

But her own voice was a comfort and she smiled. Then, settling her cloak more firmly about her shoulders, she went back to the hut.

She counted the meager furnishings of the hut as if she were telling beads on a string: door, window, hearth, table, chair, bed. "I wish there were something to *do*," she thought to herself. And as she turned around, the needle on the table was glowing as if a bit of fire had caught in its eye.

She went over to the table and picked up the needle, scissors, and pin and carried them to the hearth. Spreading her cloak on the stones, though careful to keep her mother's image facing up, she sat.

"If I just had some thread," she thought.

Just then she noticed the panel with her mother's portrait. For the first time it seemed small and crowded, spotted from the years. The curls were old-fashioned and overwrought, the mouth a little slack, the chin a touch weak.

"Perhaps if I could borrow a bit of thread from this embroidery," she whispered, "just a bit where it will not be noticed. As I am alone, no one will know but me."

Slowly she began to pick out the crimson thread along one of the tiny curls. She heard a deep sigh as she started as if it came from the cloak, then realized it had been her own breath that had made the sound. She wound up the thread around the pin until she had quite a lot of it. Then she snipped off the end, knotted it, threaded the needle—and stopped.

"What am I to sew upon?" she wondered. All she had was what she wore. Still, as she had a great need to keep herself busy and nothing else to do, she decided to embroider designs along the edges of her cloak. So she began with what she knew. On the gray panels she sewed a picture of her own castle. It was so real, it seemed as if its banners fluttered in a westerly wind. And as it grew, turret by turret, she began to feel a little warmer, a little more at home.

She worked until it was time to eat but, as she had been in the hut all the while, no magical servants had set the table. So she hunted around the cupboards herself until she found bread and cheese and a pitcher of milk. Making herself a scanty meal, she cleaned away the dishes, then lay down on the bed and was soon asleep.

In the morning she was up with the dawn. She cut herself some bread, poured some milk, and took the meal outside where she continued to sew. She gave the castle lancet windows, a Lady Chapel, cows grazing in the outlying fields, and a moat in which golden carp swam about, their fins stroking the water and making little waves that moved beneath her hand.

When the first bit of thread was used up, she picked out another section of the portrait, all of the curls and a part of the chin. With that thread she embroidered a forest around the castle, where brachet hounds, noses close to the ground, sought a scent; a deer started; and a fox lay hidden in a rambling thicket, its ears twitching as the dogs coursed by. She could almost remark their baying, now near, now far away. Then, in the middle of the forest—with a third piece of thread—the princess sewed the hut. Beneath the hut, as she sewed, letters appeared though she did not touch them.

> Needle and scissors,
> Scissors and pins,
> Where one life ends
> Another begins.

Stretching, she stood and went into the little house. The bread was gone. She searched the cupboards and could find no more, but there was flour and salt and so she made herself some flat cakes which she baked in an oven that was set into the stone of the fireplace. She knew that the smoke from her baking was sending soft clouds above the hut.

While the bread baked and the sweet smell embroidered the air, the princess went back outside. She unraveled more threads from her mother's image: the nose, the mouth, the startled eyes. And with that thread she traced a winding path from the crimson castle with the fluttering banners to the crimson hut with the crown of smoke.

As she sewed, it seemed to her that she could hear the sound of birds: the rapid flutings of a thrush and the jug-jug-jug of a nightingale, and they came not from the real forest around her but from the cloak. Then she heard, from the very heart of her lapwork, the deep brassy voice of a hunting horn summoning her home.

Looking up from her work, she saw that the brambles around the hut were beginning to part and there was a path heading north towards the castle.

She jumped up, tumbling needle and scissors and pin to the ground, and took a step towards the beckoning path. Then she stopped. The smell of the fresh bread stayed her. The embroidery was not yet done. She knew that she had to sew her own portrait onto the white laced panel of the cloak: a girl with crimson cheeks and hair tumbled to her shoulders, walking the path alone. She had to use up the rest of her mother's thread before she was free.

Turning back towards the hut, she saw three old women standing in the doorway, their faces familiar. They smiled and nodded to her, holding out their hands.

The first old woman had the needle and pin nestled in her palm. The second held the scissors by the blades, handles offered. The third old woman shook out the cloak and, as she did so, a breeze stirred the trees in the clearing.

The princess smiled back at them. She held out her hands to receive their gifts. When she was done with the embroidery, though it would be hard to part with, she would give them the cloak. She knew that once it was given, she could go.

ALLERLEIRAUH

Her earliest memory was of rain on a thatched roof, and surely it was a true one, for she had been born in a country cottage two months before time, to her father's sorrow and her mother's death. They had sheltered there, out of the storm, and her father had never forgiven himself nor the child who looked so like her mother. So like her, it was said, that portraits of the two as girls might have been exchanged and not even Nanny the wiser.

So great had been her father's grief at the moment of his wife's death, he might even have left the infant there, still bright with birth blood and squalling. Surely the crofters would have been willing, for they were child-less themselves. His first thought was to throw the babe away, his wife's Undoing as he called her ever after, though her official name was Allerleirauh. And he might have done so had she not been the child of a queen. A royal child, whatever the crime, is not to be tossed aside so lightly, a feather in the wind.

But he had made two promises to the blanched figure that lay on the rude bed, the woolen blankets rough against her long, fair legs. White and red and black she had been then. White of skin, like the color of milk after the whey is skimmed out. Red as the toweling that carried her blood, the blood they could not staunch, the life leaching out of her. And black, the color of her eyes, the black seas he used to swim in, the black tendrils of her hair.

"Promise me." Her voice stumbled between those lips, once red, now white.

He clasped her hands so tightly he feared he might break them, though it was not her bones that were brittle, but his heart. "I promise," he said. He would have promised her anything, even his own life, to stop the words bleeding out of that white mouth. "I promise."

"Promise me you will love the child," she said, for even in her dying she knew his mind, knew his heart, knew his dark soul. "Promise."

And what could he do but give her that coin, the first of two to close her dead eyes?

"And promise me you will not marry again, lest she be..." and her voice trembled, sighed, died.

"Lest she be as beautiful as thee," he promised wildly in the high tongue, giving added strength to his vow. "Lest she have thy heart, thy mind, thy breasts, thy eyes..." and his rota continued long past her life. He was speaking to a dead woman many minutes and would not let himself acknowledge it, as if by naming the parts of her he loved, he might keep her alive, the words bleeding out of him as quickly as her lost blood.

"She is gone, my lord," said the crofter's wife, not even sure of his rank except that he was clearly above her. She touched his shoulder for comfort, a touch she would never have ventured in other circumstances, but tragedy made them kin.

The king's litany continued as if he did not hear, and indeed he did not. For all he heard was the breath of death, that absence made all the louder by his own sobs.

"She is dead, Sire," the crofter said. He had known the king all along, but had not mentioned it till that one moment. Blunter than his wife, he was less sure of the efficacy of touch. "Dead."

And this one final word the king heard.

"She is not dead!" he roared, bringing the back of his hand around to swat the crofter's face as if he were not a giant of a man but an insect. The crofter shuddered and was silent, for majesty does make gnats of such men, even in their own homes. Even there.

The infant, recognizing no authority but hunger and cold, began to cry at her father's voice. On and on she bawled, a high, unmusical strand of sound till the king dropped his dead wife's hand, put his own hands over his ears, and ran from the cottage screaming, "I shall go mad!"

He did not, of course. He ranged from distracted to distraught for days, weeks, months, and then the considerations of kingship recalled him to himself. It was his old self recalled: the distant, cold, considering king he had been before his marriage. For marriage to a young, beautiful, foreign-born queen had changed him. He had been for those short months a better man, but not a better ruler. So the counselors breathed easier, certainly. The barons and nobles breathed easier, surely. And the peasants—well, the peasants knew a hard hand either way, for the dalliance of kings has no effect on the measure of rain nor the seasons in the sun, no matter what the poets write or the minstrels pluck upon their strings.

Only two in the kingdom felt the brunt of his neglect. Allerleirauh, of course, who would have loved to please him; but she scarcely knew him. And her Nanny, who had been her mother's Nanny, and was brought across the seas to a strange land. Where Allerleirauh knew hunger, the nurse knew hate. She blamed the king as he blamed the child for the young queen's death, and she swore in her own dark way to bring sorrow to him and his line.

The king was mindful in his own way of his promises. Kingship demands attention to be paid. He loved his daughter with the kindness of kings, which is to say he ordered her clothed and fed and educated to her station. But he did not love her with his heart. How could he, having seen her first cloaked in his wife's blood? How could he, having named her Undoing?

He had her brought to him but once a year, on the anniversary of his wife's death, that he might remind himself of her crime. That it was also the anniversary of Allerleirauh's birth, he did not remark. She thought he remembered, but he did not.

So the girl grew unremarked and unloved, more at home in the crofter's cottage where she had been born. And remembering each time she sat there in the rain—learning the homey crafts from the crofter's stout wife— that first rain.

The king did not marry again, though his counselors advised it. Memory refines what is real. Gold smelted in the mind's cauldron is the purer. No woman could be as beautiful to him as the dead queen. He built monuments and statues, commissioned poems and songs. The palace walls were hung with portraits that resembled her, all in color—the skin white as snow, the lips red as blood, the hair black as raven's wings. He lived in a mausoleum and did not notice the live beauty for the dead one.

Years went by, and though each spring messengers went through the kingdom seeking a maiden "white and black and red," the king's own specifications, they came home each summer's end to stare disconsolately at the dead queen's portraits.

"Not one?" the king would ask.

"Not one," the messengers replied. For the kingdom's maidens had been blonde or brown or redheaded. They had been pale or rosy or tan. And even those sent abroad found not a maid who looked like the statues or spoke like the poems or resembled in the slightest what they had all come to believe the late queen had been.

So the king went through spring and summer and into snow, still unmarried and without a male heir.

In desperation, his advisers planned a great three-day ball, hoping that—dressed in finery—one of the rejected maidens of the kingdom might take on a queenly air. Notice was sent that all were to wear black the first night, red the second, and white the third.

Allerleirauh was invited, too, though not by the king's own wishes. She was told of the ball by her nurse.

"I will make you three dresses," the old woman said. "The first dress will be as gold as the sun, the second as silver as the moon, and the third one will shine like the stars." She hoped that in this way, the princess would stand out. She hoped in this way to ruin the king.

Now if this were truly a fairy tale (and what story today with a king and queen and crofter's cottage is not?) the princess would go outside to her mother's grave. And there, on her knees, she would learn a magic greater than any craft, a woman's magic compounded of moonlight, elopement, and deceit. The neighboring kingdom would harbor her, the neighboring prince would marry her, her father would be brought to his senses, and the moment of complete happiness would be the moment of story's end. Ever after is but a way of saying: "There is nothing more to tell." It is but a dissembling. There is always more to tell. There is no happy *ever* after. There is happy *on occasion* and happy *every once in a while*. There is happy *when the memories do not overcome the now*.

But this is not a fairy tale. The princess is married to her father and, always having wanted his love, does not question the manner of it. Except at night, late at night, when he is away from her bed and she is alone in the vastness of it.

The marriage is sanctioned and made pure by the priests, despite the grumblings of the nobles. One priest who dissents is murdered in his sleep. Another is burned at the stake. There is no third. The nobles who grumble lose their lands. Silence becomes the conspiracy; silence becomes the conspirators.

Like her mother, the princess is weak-wombed. She dies in childbirth surrounded by that silence, cocooned in it. The child she bears is a girl, as lovely as her mother. The king knows he will have to wait another thirteen years.

It is an old story.

Perhaps the oldest.

BEAUTY AND THE BEAST: AN ANNIVERSARY

It is winter now,
and the roses are blooming again,
their petals bright against the snow.
My father died last April;
my sisters no longer write,
except at the turnings of the year,
content with their fine houses
and their grandchildren.
Beast and I
putter in the gardens
and walk slowly on the forest paths.
He is graying
around the muzzle
and I have silver combs
to match my hair.
I have no regrets.
None.
Though sometimes I do wonder
what sounds children
might have made
running across the marble halls,
swinging from the birches
over the roses
in the snow.

Fantasy Novels: Truth in Disguise?
—The Footnotes (by Dr. Jane Yolen)

Editor's note: The paper, "Fantasy Novels: Truth in Disguise?" was to have been published in Chimera: The Journal of the Society for Literary Invention. *When the manuscript was received in the mail, the envelope proved to contain only the footnotes for the paper.* Chimera's *editors declined to publish the one without the other, and could not locate the obviously pseudonymous "Dr. Yolen" to remedy the omission. We at* The Medusa *are not so nice in our notions.*

1. On the other hand, C. S. Lewis was quoted as saying that fantasy was "breathing a lie through silver," one of those gnomic utterances that sounds wonderful upon first hearing and becomes more puzzling as it is parsed: why *silver* and not *gold?* How does one breathe *through* silver? How does one *breathe a lie?*

2. Tolkien's words about the "secondary world where things happen with arresting strangeness" become so garbled by students that it is almost impossible to hope they will be remembered properly. For example, a Smith College senior, on a final exam, explained that fantasy "is a world of seconds where things happen with a resting stranger."

3. Of course Le Guin is a fanatic about such things. Consider her background.

4. This Scottish connection has been much noted. McKillip, McIntyre, McCaffrey, McKinley, McKee Charnas, and MacAvoy, to name six of the top women writers of fantasy, have even been called "Sisters of the Plaid."

5. Originally from the Zanzibar Swahili, the entire quote is "If the story was beautiful, the beauty belongs to us all; if it was bad, the fault is mine only, who told it." Joseph Campbell cites this in his introduction to a Grimm collection, but it is used here as commentary on Samuel (Chip) Delany's more abstract meanderings on behalf of deconstructionism.

6. In fact, fantasy writers are always garbling on about truth. "I am not paid to tell you the truth," proclaims Yolen's eponymous storyteller in her poem. Le Guin states, "Facts are about the outside. Truth is about the inside." And Kipling, that "Fiction is Truth's elder sister." But science fiction authors would rather natter on about other things, believing—with Soviet author/eductator Andrei Sinyavsky—that "The poet is a failed magician...who has substituted metaphor for metamorphosis."

7. Wouldn't Gene Wolfe, that consummate prose stylist, agree?

8. Just because he is so strong in his condemnation of such amateurism, doesn't make him right. See also Dylan Thomas's lines in "Over Sir John's Hill" that we are all "young Aesops fabling to the near night."

9. But then Grahame, in an introduction to *A Hundred Fables of Aesop,* reminds us that "...whatever its components, mere truth is not necessarily one of them. A dragon, for instance, is a more enduring animal than a pterodactyl. I have never yet met anyone who really believed in pterodactyls, but every honest person believes in dragons—down in the back-kitchen of his consciousness."

10. Not to mention Alice's meal with the Red Queen in which she is introduced to the mutton and pudding, Diana Wynne Jones's butter pies, and all those candies in Willie Wonka's factory.

11. That certainly reminds one of the German word *Ehrfurcht,* which means "a reverence for what one cannot understand."

12. Patricia Wrightson as well.

13. However, Chesterton is also right when he posits that one idea runs from end to end in fairy tales: the idea that "peace and happiness can only exist on some condition. This idea, which is the core of ethics, is the core of the nursery tale."

14. It can also be asserted, with Lloyd Alexander, that "Realism walks where fantasy dances."

15. Cf ff. 6. Still, if the ancient poets are to be cited, one must never forget the chief poets of Ireland who had to have:

Purity of Hand: Bright without wounding.
Purity of Mouth: Without poisonous satire.
Purity of Learning: Without reproach.

Such poets were second only to the king in rank as well as being his equal in authority, and had to be able to recite on demand 250 prime tales and 100 subsidiary ones.

16. But Daudet also wrote *Je rêve d'un aigle, j'accouche d'un colobri.*

17. When Melville changed the Galapagos into the fictional Encantados, was he not doing just that?

18. In philosophy, of course, *isomorphism* is a term that means a map or a picture or a description or a symbol that corresponds point to point with the thing it symbolizes. One has to wonder then, at her use of the word *isomorphic* when describing fantasy.

19. If this is so, then we should all have to agree with Dorothy Parker who, when reviewing *The House at Pooh Corner* in her "Constant Reader" column commented tersely, "Tonstant Weader Fwowed up."

20. He meant, of course, the medium Backhouse in David Lindsay's *A Voyage to Arcturus.* Backhouse also says, "I dream with open eyes and others see my dreams. That is all." It is, perhaps, the perfect description of a fantasy writer.

Become a Warrior

Both the hunted and the hunter pray to God.

The moon hung like a bloody red ball over the silent battlefield. Only the shadows seemed to move. The men on the ground would never move again. And their women, sick with weeping, did not dare the field in the dark. It would be morning before they would come like crows to count their losses.

But on the edge of the field there was a sudden tiny movement, and it was no shadow. Something small was creeping to the muddy hem of the battleground. Something knelt there, face shining with grief. A child, a girl, the youngest daughter of the king who had died that evening surrounded by all his sons.

The girl looked across the dark field and, like her mother, like her sisters, like her aunts, did not dare put foot onto the bloody ground. But then she looked up at the moon and thought she saw her father's face there. Not the father who lay with his innards spilled out into contorted hands. Not the one who had braided firesticks in his beard and charged into battle screaming. She thought she saw the father who had always sung her to sleep against the night terrors. The one who sat up with her when Great Graxyx haunted her dreams.

"I will do for you, Father, as you did for me," she whispered to the moon. She prayed to the goddess for the strength to accomplish what she had just promised.

Then foot by slow foot, she crept onto the field, searching in the red moon's light for the father who had fallen. She made slits of her eyes so she would not see the full horror around her. She breathed through her mouth so that she would not smell all the deaths. She never once thought of the Great Graxyx who lived—so she truly believed—in the black cave of her dressing room. Or any of the hundred and six gibbering children Graxyx had sired. She crept across the landscape made into a horror by the enemy hordes. All the dead men looked alike. She found her father by his boots.

She made her way up from the boots, past the gaping wound that had taken him from her, to his face which looked peaceful and familiar enough, except for the staring eyes. He had never stared like that. Rather his eyes had always been slotted, against the hot sun of the gods, against the lies of men. She closed his lids with trembling fingers and put her head down on his chest, where the stillness of the heart told her what she already knew.

And then she began to sing to him.

She sang of life, not death, and the small gods of new things. Of bees in the hive and birds on the summer wind. She sang of foxes denning and bears shrugging off winter. She sang of fish in the sparkling rivers and the first green uncurlings of fern in spring. She did not mention dying, blood, or wounds, or the awful stench of death. Her father already knew this well and did not need to be recalled to it.

And when she was done with her song, it was as if his corpse gave a great sigh, one last breath, though of course he was dead already half the night and made no sound at all. But she heard what she needed to hear.

By then it was morning and the crows came. The human crows as well as the black birds, poking and prying and feeding on the dead.

So she turned and went home and everyone wondered why she did not weep. But she had left her tears out on the battlefield.

She was seven years old.

Dogs bark, but the caravan goes on.

Before the men who had killed her father and who had killed her brothers could come to take all the women away to serve them, she had her maid cut her black hair as short as a boy's. The maid was a trembling sort, and the hair cut was ragged. But it would do.

She waited until the maid had turned around and leaned down to put away the shears. Then she put her arm around the woman and with a quick knife's cut across her throat killed her, before the woman could tell on her. It was a mercy, really, for she was old and ugly and would be used brutally by the soldiers before being slaughtered, probably in a slow and terrible manner. So her father had warned before he left for battle.

Then she went into the room of her youngest brother, dead in the field and lying by her father's right hand. In his great wooden chest she found a pair of trews that had probably been too small for him, but were nonetheless too long for her. With the still-bloody knife she sheared the legs of the trews a hand's width, rolled and sewed them with a quick seam. The women of her house could sew well, even when it had to be done quickly. Even when it had to be done through half-closed eyes. Even when the hem was wet with blood. Even then.

When she put on the trews, they fit, though she had to pull the draw-string around the waist quite tight and tie the ribbands twice around her. She shrugged into one of her brother's shirts as well, tucking it down into the waistband. Then she slipped her bloody knife into the shirt sleeve. She wore her own riding boots, which could not be told from a boy's, for her brother's boots were many times too big for her.

Then she went out through the window her brother always used when he set out to court one of the young and pretty maids. She had watched him often enough though he had never known she was there, hiding be-side the bed, a dark little figure as still as the night.

Climbing down the vine, hand over hand, was no great trouble either. She had done it before, following after him. Really, what a man and a maid did together was most interesting, if a bit odd. And certainly noisier than it needed to be.

She reached the ground in moments, crossed the garden, climbed over the outside wall by using a twisted tree as her ladder. When she dropped to the ground, she twisted her ankle a bit, but she made not the slightest whimper. She was a boy now. And she knew they did not cry.

In the west a cone of dark dust was rising up and advancing on the fortress, blotting out the sky. She knew it for the storm that many hooves make as horses race across the plains. The earth trembled beneath her feet. Behind her, in their rooms, the women had begun to wail. The sound was thin, like a gold filament thrust into her breast. She plugged her ears that their cries could not recall her to her old life, for such was not her plan.

Circling around the stone skirting of the fortress, in the shadow so no one could see her, she started around toward the east. It was not a direction she knew. All she knew was that it was away from the horses of the enemy.

Once she glanced back at the fortress that had been the only home she had ever known. Her mother, her sisters, the other women stood on the battlements looking toward the west and the storm of riders. She could hear their wailing, could see the movement of their arms as they beat upon their breasts. She did not know if that were a plea or an invitation.

She did not turn to look again.

To become a warrior, forget the past.

Three years she worked as a serving lad in a fortress not unlike her own but many days' travel away. She learned to clean and to carry, she learned to work after a night of little sleep. Her arms and legs grew strong. Three years she worked as the cook's boy. She learned to prepare geese and rabbit and bear for the pot, and learned which parts were salty, which sweet. She could tell good mushrooms from bad and which greens might make the toughest meat palatable.

And then she knew she could no longer disguise the fact that she was a girl for her body had begun to change in ways that would give her away. So she left the fortress, starting east once more, taking only her knife and a long loop of rope which she wound around her waist seven times.

She was many days hungry, many days cold, but she did not turn back. Fear is a great incentive.

She taught herself to throw the knife and hit what she aimed at. Hunger is a great teacher.

She climbed trees when she found them in order to sleep safe at night. The rope made such passages easier.

She was so long by herself, she almost forgot how to speak. But she never forgot how to sing. In her dreams she sang to her father on the battlefield. Her songs made him live again. Awake she knew the truth was otherwise. He was dead. The worms had taken him. His spirit was with the goddess, drinking milk from her great pap, milk that tasted like honey wine.

She did not dream of her mother or of her sisters or of any of the women in her father's fortress. If they died, it had been with little honor. If they still lived, it was with less.

So she came at last to a huge forest with oaks thick as a goddess's waist. Over all was a green canopy of leaves that scarcely let in the sun. Here were many streams, rivulets that ran cold and clear, torrents that crashed against rocks, and pools that were full of silver trout whose meat was sweet. She taught herself to fish and to swim, and it would be hard to say which gave her the greater pleasure. Here, too, were nests of birds, and that meant eggs. Ferns curled and then opened, and she knew how to steam them, using a basket made of willow strips and a fire from rubbing sticks against one another. She followed bees to their hives, squirrels to their hidden nuts, ducks to their watered beds.

She grew strong, and brown, and—though she did not know it—very beautiful.

Beauty is a danger, to women as well as to men. To warriors, most of all. It steers them away from the path of killing. It softens the soul.

When you are in a tree, be a tree.

She was three years alone in the forest and grew to trust the sky, the earth, the river, the trees, the way she trusted her knife. They did not lie to her.

They did not kill wantonly. They gave her shelter, food, courage. She did not remember her father except as some sort of warrior god, with staring eyes, looking as she had seen him last. She did not remember her mother or sisters or aunts at all.

It had been so long since she had spoken to anyone, it was as if she could not speak at all. She knew words, they were in her head, but not in her mouth, on her tongue, in her throat. Instead she made the sounds she heard every day—the grunt of boar, the whistle of duck, the trilling of thrush, the settled cooing of the wood pigeon on its nest.

If anyone had asked her if she was content, she would have nodded. Content.

Not happy. Not satisfied. Not done with her life's work. Content.

And then one early evening a new sound entered her domain. A drumming on the ground, from many miles away. A strange halloing, thin, insistent, whining. The voices of some new animal, packed like wolves, singing out together.

She trembled. She did not know why. She did not remember why. But to be safe from the thing that made her tremble, she climbed a tree, the great oak that was in the very center of her world.

She used the rope ladder she had made, and pulled the ladder up after. Then she shrank back against the trunk of the tree to wait. She tried to be the brown of the bark, the green of the leaves, and in this she almost succeeded.

It was in the first soft moments of dark, with the woods outlined in muzzy black, that the pack ran yapping, howling, belling into the clearing around the oak.

In that instant she remembered dogs.

There were twenty of them, some large, lanky grays; some stumpy browns with long muzzles; some stiff-legged spotted with pushed-in noses; some thick-coated; some smooth. Her father, the god of war, had had such a motley pack. He had hunted boar and stag and hare with such. They had found him bear and fox and wolf with ease.

Still, she did not know why the dog pack was here, circling her tree. Their jaws were raised so that she could see their iron teeth, could hear the tolling of her death with their long tongues.

She used the single word she could remember. She said it with great authority, with trembling.

"Avaunt!"

At the sound of her voice, the animals all sat down on their haunches to stare up at her, their own tongues silenced. Except for one, a rat terrier, small and springy and unable to be still. He raced back up the path toward the west like some small spy going to report to his master.

Love comes like a thief, stealing the heart's gold away.

It was in the deeper dark that the dogs' master came, with his men behind him, their horses' hooves thrumming the forest paths. They trampled the grass, the foxglove's pink bells and the purple florets of self-heal, the wine-colored burdock flowers and the sprays of yellow goldenrod equally under the horses' heavy feet. The woods were wounded by their passage. The grass did not spring back nor the flowers raise up again.

She heard them and began trembling anew as they thrashed their way across her green haven and into the very heart of the wood.

Ahead of them raced the little terrier, his tail flagging them on, till he led them right to the circle of dogs waiting patiently beneath her tree.

"Look, my lord, they have found something," said one man.

"Odd they should be so quiet," said another.

But the one they called lord dismounted, waded through the sea of dogs, and stood at the very foot of the oak, his feet crunching on the fallen acorns. He stared up, and up, and up through the green leaves and at first saw nothing but brown and green.

One of the large gray dogs stood, walked over to his side, raised its great muzzle to the tree, and howled.

The sound made her shiver anew.

"See, my lord, see—high up. There is a trembling in the foliage," one of the men cried.

"You fool," the lord cried, "that is no trembling of leaves. It is a girl. She is dressed all in brown and green. See how she makes the very tree shimmer." Though how he could see her so well in the dark, she was never to understand.

"Come down, child, we will not harm you."

She did not come down. Not then. Not until the morning fully revealed her. And then, if she was to eat, if she was to relieve herself, she had to come down. So she did, dropping the rope ladder, and skinning down it quickly. She kept her knife tucked up in her waist, out where they could see it and be afraid.

They did not touch her but watched her every movement, like a pack of dogs. When she went to the river to drink, they watched. When she ate the bit of journeycake the lord offered her, they watched. And even when she relieved herself, the lord watched. He would let no one else look then, which she knew honored her, though she did not care.

And when after several days he thought he had tamed her, the lord took her on his horse before him and rode with her back to the far west where he lived. By then he loved her, and knew that she loved him in return, though she had yet to speak a word to him.

"But then, what have words to do with love," he whispered to her as they rode.

He guessed by her carriage, by the way her eyes met his, that she was a princess of some sort, only badly used. He loved her for the past which she could not speak of, for her courage which showed in her face, and for her beauty. He would have loved her for much less, having found her in the tree, for she was something out of a story, out of a prophecy, out of a dream.

"I loved you at once," he whispered. "When I knew you from the tree."

She did not answer. Love was not yet in her vocabulary. But she did not say the one word she could speak: *avaunt*. She did not want him to go.

When the cat wants to eat her kittens, she says they look like mice.

His father was not so quick to love her.

His mother, thankfully, was long dead.

She knew his father at once, by the way his eyes were slotted against the hot sun of the gods, against the lies of men. She knew him to be a king if only by that.

And when she recognized her mother and her sisters in his retinue, she knew who it was she faced. They did not know her, of course. She was no longer seven but nearly seventeen. Her life had browned her, bronzed her, made her into such steel as they had never known. She could have told them but she had only contempt for their lives. As they had contempt now for her, thinking her some drudge run off to the forest, some sinister throwling from a forgotten clan.

When the king gave his grudging permission for their marriage, when the prince's advisers set down in long scrolls what she should and should not have, she only smiled at them. It was a tree's smile, giving away not a bit of the bark.

She waited until the night of her wedding to the prince when they were couched together, the servants a-giggle outside their door. She waited until he had covered her face with kisses, when he had touched her in secret places that made her tremble, when he had brought blood between her legs. She waited until he had done all the things she had once watched her brother do to the maids, and she cried out with pleasure as she had heard them do. She waited until he laid asleep, smiling happily in his dreams, because she did love him in her warrior way.

Then she took her knife and slit his throat, efficiently and without cruelty, as she would a deer for her dinner.

"Your father killed my father," she whispered, soft as a love token in his ear as the knife carved a smile on his neck.

She stripped the bed of its bloody offering and handed it to the servants who thought it the effusions of the night. Then she walked down the hall to her father-in-law's room.

He was bedded with her mother, riding her like one old wave atop another.

"Here!" he cried as he realized someone was in the room. "You!" he said when he realized who it was.

Her mother looked at her with half opened eyes and, for the first time, saw who she really was, for she had her father's face, fierce and determined.

"No!" her mother cried. "Avaunt!" But it was a cry that was ten years late.

She killed the king with as much ease as she had killed his son, but she let the knife linger longer to give him a great deal of pain. Then she sliced off one of his ears and put it gently in her mother's hand.

In all this she had said not one word. But wearing the blood of the king on her gown, she walked out of the palace and back to the woods, though she was many days getting there.

No one tried to stop her, for no one saw her. She was a flower in the meadow, a rock by the roadside, a reed by the river, a tree in the forest.

And a warrior's mother by the spring of the year.

Fat Is Not a Fairy Tale

I am thinking of a fairy tale,
Cinder Elephant,
Sleeping Tubby,
Snow Weight,
where the princess is not
anorexic, wasp-waisted,
flinging herself down the stairs.

I am thinking of a fairy tale,
Hansel and Great,
Repoundsel,
Bounty and the Beast,
where the beauty
has a pillowed breast,
and fingers plump as sausage.

I am thinking of a fairy tale
that is not yet written,
for a teller not yet born,
for a listener not yet conceived,
for a world not yet won,
where everything round is good:
the sun, wheels, cookies, and the princess.

THE WOMAN WHO LOVED A BEAR

It was early in the autumn, the leaves turning over yellow in the puzzling wind, that a woman of the Cheyennes and her father went to collect meat he had killed. They each rode a horse and led a pack horse behind, for the father had killed two fine antelopes and had left them, skinned and cut up and covered well with hide.

They didn't know that a party of Crows had found the cache and knew it for a Cheyenne kill by the hide covering it.

"We will wait for the hunter to come and collect his meat," they said. "We will get both a Cheyenne *and* his meat." It made them laugh at the thought.

And so it happened. The Cheyenne man and his daughter came innocently to the meat and the Crows charged down on them. The man was killed and his daughter was taken away as a prisoner, well to the north, to a village on the Sheep River which is now called the Big Horn.

> Is that the end of the story, grandfather?
> It is only the beginning. This is called The Woman Who
> Loved the Bear. I have not even come to the bear yet.

The man who carried the pipe of the Crow war party was named Fifth Man Over and he had two wives. But when he looked at the Cheyenne girl he thought that she was very fine looking and wanted her for his wife. Of course his two wives were both Crow women, which means they were ugly and hard. They were not pleased about the Cheyenne woman becoming his third wife. When they asked her name, she told them she was called "Walks with the Sun," so they called her "Flat Foot Walker." But they could call her what they wanted, it did not change the fact that she was beautiful and they were not.

So whenever Fifth Man Over was away from the lodge, they abused the Cheyenne girl. They hit her with quirts and sticks and stones till her arms and legs were bruised. But they were careful not to hit her in the face, where even Fifth Man Over would see and ask questions.

The days and weeks went by and the beautiful Cheyenne wife had to do all the hard work. She had to pack the wood and dress the hides; she had to make moccasins, not only for her Crow husband, but for his ugly wives as well.

> Grandfather, I have heard this story before. I have seen
> a movie of it. It is called "Cinderella."
> Is there a bear in "Cinderella"?
> No, of course not.
> Then you do not know this story. This is a true story,
> from the time when children played games suited to their
> years and spoke with respect to their grandfathers. You
> will listen carefully so that you may tell the story just as
> I tell it to you.

Now in Fifth Man Over's lodge there also lived a young man, about a year older than the Cheyenne woman, who was an Arapahoe and had been taken as a slave in a raid when he was a small child. He had the keeping and herding of Fifth Man Over's horses. He was not straight and tall like a Cheyenne, but limped because his left foot had been burned in the raid that made him a slave. But he had a strong nose and straight black hair and he spoke softly to the Cheyenne woman.

"These women abuse you," he said. "You must not let them do so."

"I cannot do otherwise," Walks with the Sun answered. "They are my husband's elder wives." It was the proper answer, but she was a Cheyenne woman and they were only Crows, and so she said it through set teeth.

"Make many moccasins," the Arapahoe told her. "Many more than are needed. Hide some away for yourself."

"Why should I do this?" she asked.

"Because you will need them on the trail back to your people."

She looked straight in his face and saw that there was no deceit there. She did not look at his crooked leg.

"You will wear out many moccasins on the trail," he said.

> When does the bear come in, grandfather?
> Soon.
> How soon?
> Soon enough. It is not time to cut this story off. Listen.
> You will have to tell it back to me, you know.

Walks with the Sun made many moccasins and for every three she made, she hid one away. This took her through winter and into the spring when the snow melted and the first flowers appeared down by the river bank.

"We will go in the morning for the buffalo," said Fifth Man Over to his wives. By this he meant he would ride a horse and they would come behind with the pack horse pulling the travois sled.

"She should not come with us," said his first wife, pointing to Walks with the Sun. "She is a Cheyenne and has no stamina and will not be able to keep up and will want more than her share of the meat."

"And she is ugly," said the second wife, but she did not say it very loud.

"I will stay, my husband," said Walks with the Sun, "and make the lodge ready for your return."

"And you will not break any of the pots we have worked so hard on," said the first wife.

"And you will not eat anything till we come back," said the second wife.

With all this Walks with the Sun agreed, though she would have loved to see the buffalo in their great herds and the men on their horses charging down on the bulls, even though they were Crow and not Cheyenne. She had heard that the sound of the buffalo running was like thunder on the great open plain, that it was a music that made the grasses dance. But she kept her head bent and her eyes modestly down.

So Fifth Man Over and his two wives and most of the other hunters and their wives left to go after the buffalo. And the Arapahoe went, too, for he was to take care of the horses along the way.

> Grandfather, a buffalo is not a bear, and you promised.
> There will be a bear.
> Buffalo do not eat beat. Bear eat buffalo. I prefer the bear.
> There will be a bear.
> There had better be.

But the young man returned the long way around, leaving his own horse in the timber outside of the camp. He came limping into the Crow village and the old people said to him, "Why are you here? What has happened to the people?" By this they meant the Crows.

"Nothing has happened to the people. They are following the buffalo. But my horse threw me and ran away and I have come back for another." He went to Fifth Man Over's lodge and saddled another horse and put two fine blankets on it, but not the best, because he was a slave after all. But before he mounted up, he went into the lodge and said to Walks with the Sun, "Now is your time. I have hidden my own horse in the timber down by the creek. You must take a large pot and go down as if for water and you will find it there. Put your extra moccasins in the pot, for should you lose the horse, you will surely need them."

"What of you?" asked Walks with the Sun. "Surely you want to leave here."

"I have no other home," he answered.

"Then you shall come home with me," she said.

"I am poor and I have a bad leg and I am not a Cheyenne," he said. "But I will watch out for you, never fear."

He rode away, but in a different direction from the creek, so that no one would suspect that the two of them had spoken. And Walks with the Sun did as he instructed. Taking a large pot, she put the moccasins in. Then she went to the creek. There she found the horse, saddled, with two blankets. Swinging herself up into the saddle, she began to ride south, towards her home.

> I am still waiting, grandfather.
> Patience is a good thing in the young.
> I am *not* patient. I am impatient.
> I did not notice. The bear, though, is coming. In fact, grandson, the bear is here.
> Here? Where?
> In the story. But you cannot see it unless you listen.
> I see with my eyes. I hear with my ears, grandfather.
> You must do both, child. You must do both.

Walks with the Sun rode many miles until both she and the horse were tired. So she got off, unsaddled it, and let the horse feed on the new spring grass. Then she re-saddled the horse and rode another long time past the Pumpkin Buttes. There she made camp, but without a fire in case anyone should be looking for her.

In the middle of the night she awoke because of a huffing and snuffling sound and the horse got frightened and screamed like a white woman in labor, and broke its rope. It ran off not to be found again.

And there, near here, with the moonlight on its back, was...

> The bear, grandfather.
> The bear, grandson.

Walks with the Sun spoke softly to the bear, not out of honor but out of fear. "Oh, Bear," she said, "take pity on me. I am only a poor Cheyenne woman and I am trying to get back to my own people." And then, quietly, carefully, she pulled on a pair of moccasins and stood. Carrying several more pairs in each hand, she backed away from the bear. When she could no longer see the great beast, she turned around and ran.

She ran until she was exhausted and then she turned and looked behind her. There was the bear, just a little way behind. So, taking a deep breath, she ran again until she could barely put one foot in front of the other. When she turned to look again, the bear was still there.

At last she was so tired that she knew she must rest, even if the bear was to kill her. She sat down on a hollow log, and fell asleep sitting up, heedless of the bear.

While she slept, she heard the bear speak to her. His voice was like the rocks in a river, with the water rushing over. He said: "Get up and go to your people. I am watching to protect you. I am stepping in your tracks so that the Crows cannot trail you, so that Fifth Man Over and his ugly wives cannot find you."

When Walks with the Sun awoke, it was still dark. The bear was squatting on its haunches not far from her, its head crowned with the stars. Awake, she did not think he could have spoken, so she was still afraid of him.

She rose carefully, put on new moccasins, and began her journey again, but this time she did not run. She walked on until she could walk no longer. Then she lay down under a tree and slept.

> You said he spoke in a dream; grandfather.
> I said he spoke while she slept, grandson.
> Is that the same as *really* speaking?
> You are sitting with me on the buffalo-calf robe. Do
> you need to ask such questions?

In the morning Walks with the Sun awoke and saw the bear a little ways off on top of a small butte. It did not seem to be looking at her but when she started to walk, it followed again in her tracks.

So it went all the day, till she reached the Platte River. Since this was early spring, the waters were full from bank to bank. Walks with the Sun had no idea how she could get across.

She sighed out loud but said nothing else. At the sound, the bear came over to her, looked in her face and his breath was hot and foul-smelling. Then he turned his back to her and stuck his great rear in her face. By this she knew that he wanted her to get on his back.

"Bear," she said, "if you are willing to take me across the river, I am willing to ride." And she crawled on his back and put her arms around his neck, just in front of his mighty shoulders. With a snort, he plunged into the water.

The water was cold. She could feel it through her leggings. And the river tumbled strongly over its rocky bed. But stronger still was the bear and he swam across with ease.

When they got to the other side, the bear waited while she dismounted, then he shook himself all over, scattering water on every leaf and stone. Then he rolled on the ground.

While he was rolling, Walks with the Sun started on. When she looked back, the bear was following her just as he had before.

So it went for many days, the Cheyenne woman walking, the bear coming along behind. When she was hungry, he caught a young buffalo calf and killed it. She skinned it, cut it into pieces, took her flint, made a fire, then cooked the meat. Some of it she ate, and some she gave to the bear. The rest she rolled in the skin, making a pack she carried on her back.

> Did she feed him by hand, grandfather?
>
> By hand?
>
> Did she hold out pieces for him to eat?
>
> That would be foolish, indeed, grandson. He could have taken her hand off at the wrist and not even noticed. Where do you young people come up with such foolish ideas, heh?
>
> Then how did she feed the bear?
>
> She put it down on the ground a little way from her and the bear walked up and ate it.
>
> Oh.

They came at last to the Laramie River and below was a big village, with so many lodges they covered the entire bank.

"I do not know if those are my people or not," Walks with the Sun said. "Can you go and find out for me?"

The bear went up close to the outermost lodge, but someone saw him and shouted and someone else, an old man whose hand was not so steady, shot an arrow at him. The arrow pierced his left hind foot and he ran back to Walks with the Sun, limping.

"Oh, Bear," she cried, "you are hurt and it is all my fault." She knelt down and pulled the arrow from his foot and stopped the bleeding with the heel of her hand.

When the people tracked the blood trail to them, she was still sitting there, holding the bear in her arms, Only he was no longer a bear, but a young man with a strong nose and straight black hair and a left foot that was not quite straight.

The bear turned into the Arapahoe slave, grandfather?
That is not what I said, grandson.
But I thought you said...
Listen, grandson, listen.

Walks with the Sun took the buffalo hide, shook it out, and turned it so the hair side was outward. Then she wrapped the Arapahoe in it to show he was a medicine man, Her people put great strings of beads around his neck and gave him feathers to honor him, Then they lifted him onto a travois sled and, pulling it themselves, brought him into the village,

He never walked as a bear again, except twice, when the people were threatened by Crows. Walks with the Sun became his wife and they had many children and many grandchildren, of which I am one, and you are another. The buffalo hide we are sitting on today is the very one of which I have spoken.

Is that a true story, grandfather?
It is a true story, grandson.
But how can it be true, grandfather? People can't turn into bears. Bears can't turn into people.
Heh, They do not do so today. But we are speaking of the time when the Cheyenne were a great nation and still in the north, when the land was covered with buffalo, and we passed the medicine arrows and buffalo hat from keeper to keeper.
And the buffalo hide, grandfather?
And the buffalo hide, grandson. This ties it off.
What does that mean?
That storytelling is over for the night. That it is time for children to ask no more questions but to sleep, For old men to dream by the fire.
This ties it off, grandfather.

AUTHOR'S NOTE:
This story is based loosely on the Cheyenne Mystery Story "The Bear Helper," as retold by George Bird Grinnell in *By Cheyenne Campfires* (University of Nebraska Press, 1971).

THE STORYTELLER

He unpacks his bag of tales
with fingers quick
as a weaver's
picking the weft threads,
threading the warp.
Watch his fingers.
Watch his lips
speaking the old, familiar words:

> "Once there was
> and there was not,
> oh, best beloved,
> when the world was filled with wishes
> the way the sea is filled with fishes..."

All those threads
pulling us back
to another world, another time
when goosegirls married well
and frogs could rhyme,
when maids spoke syllables of pearl
and stepmothers came to grief.

Belief is the warp
and the sharp-picked pattern
of motif
reminds us that Araby
is not so far;
that the pleasure dome
of a Baghdad caliph
sits side by side
with the rush-roofed home
of a Tattercoat or an animal bride.

Cinderella wears a shoe
first fitted in the East
where her prince—
no more a beast
than the usual run of royal son—
measures her nobility
by the lotus foot,
so many inches to the reign.
Then the slipper made glass
by a slip of ear and tongue.
All tales are mistakes
made true by the telling.

The watching eye takes in the hue,
the listening ear the word,
but all they comprehend is Art.
A story must be worn again
before the magic garment
fits the ready heart.

The storyteller is done.
He packs his bag.
But watch his fingers
and his lips.
It is the oldest feat
of prestidigitation.
What you saw,
what you heard,
was equal to a new Creation.

The colors blur,
time is now.
He speaks his final piece
before his final bow:

> *"It is all true,*
> *it is not true.*
> *The more I tell you,*
> *The more I shall lie.*
> *What is story*
> *but jesting Pilate's cry.*
> *I am not paid to tell you the truth."*

Ten Things You
May Not Know About Me
And Only Three of Them Are Lies

I lost my fencing foil in Grand Central Station while
waiting for a date, the crowds so sparse, I could stare at
each person passing by, but no one met my eyes.

I was a virgin till I was twenty-nine, and I wasn't kidding
about the foil, which I often set down on the bed between
me and a date, having read too much medieval lit.

My brother and I got free double bubble chewing gum
for posing with balloons in our mouths, the biggest damn
bubbles I ever blew. Never smoked, though.

I fell off a Colorado River raft, came up with my sunglasses
perched on my nose, my Aussie hat on my head, like an
Australian mermaid, though I could have used the gills.

My mother beat me with a belt, the buckle of which was
a gift from Gene Autry; I wore the imprint of his name,
like a getalong-little-dogie, for six days on my butt.

My father tried to fly a midget on a kite in Central Park, but was stopped by a big Irish cop. The midget was relieved. So was I.

I danced in ballet class till the blood filled my toe shoes; top heavy, bottom heavy, my feet too large for my height; still I wanted to dance for Mr. B.

I went mushing in Alaska behind a team of ten dogs who could run on three legs, lift the fourth and pee without stopping, a useful trait on the trail.

I found a West Virginia toad, kissed it, and it turned into a prince. You read poetry and you don't believe in metaphor?

I have written over two hundred books and half of them are poems, but wrote nothing of worth today.

The New England
Science Fiction Association (NESFA)
and NESFA Press

Selected books from NESFA Press:

The New England Science Fiction Association:

NESFA is an all-volunteer, non-profit organization of science fiction and
fantasy fans. Besides publishing, our activities include running Boskone
(New England's oldest SF convention) in February each year, producing
a semi-monthly newsletter, holding discussion groups relating to the field,
and hosting a variety of social events. If you are interested in learning
more about us, we'd like to hear from you. Write to our address above!

ACKNOWLEDGMENTS

NESFA Press books can't get done without loads of people earning their official work credits by helping out. Here they are.

Scanning: Lis Carey, Rick Katze, Mark Olson

Proofing: Dave Anderson, Ann Crimmins, Gay Ellen Dennett, Pam Fremon, David Grubbs, Suford Lewis, Tony Lewis, Mark Olson, Sheila Perry, Kelly Persons, Geri Sullivan

Expert suggestions on book design: Geri Sullivan

Help with musical notation (and for his magical eyes): Dave Grubbs

Research and procurement: Gay Ellen Dennett

Cover design (for chocolate): Alice Lewis

All-round help, support, contract (etc.) writing, technical expertise, and frequent sanity checks: Mark Olson

Dedicated to George Flynn—*requiescat in pacem.*

—Priscilla Olson
May, 2005